Religious Expression in the Workplace and the Contested Role of Law

The workplace is a key area where the issue of religion and its position in the public sphere is under debate. Desires to observe and express religious beliefs in the workplace can introduce conflict between employees and employers. This book addresses the role the law plays in the resolution of these potential conflicts.

The book considers the definition and underlying motives of religious expression, and explores the different ways it may impact the workplace. Andrew Hambler identifies principled responses to workplace religious expression within a liberal state and compares this with the state of the law in England and Wales at a court and tribunal level. The book determines the extent to which freedom of religious expression for the individual enjoys legal protection in the workplace in England and Wales, and asks whether there is a case for changing the law to strengthen that protection.

The book will be of great use and interest to scholars and students of religion and the law, employment law and religion and human rights.

"This is an important, incisive and detailed account of the difficulties that religious minorities have in securing their Article 9 rights with respect to employment in the courts."

Professor Anthony Bradney AcSS, FRSA

"This book makes a significant contribution to the current debate on the position of the religious employee in the secular workplace. Its focus on the 'internal viewpoint' of the religious employee is innovative. It will be a valuable resource for those interested in the legal protection of religious expression at work."

Professor Lucy Vickers, Professor of Law, Oxford Brookes University

Andrew Hambler is Senior Lecturer for Human Resources and Employment Law at the University of Wolverhampton Business School, UK.

Law and Religion

The practice of religion by individuals and groups, the rise of religious diversity and the fear of religious extremism raise profound questions for the interaction between law and religion in society. The regulatory systems involved, the religion laws of secular government (national and international) and the religious laws of faith communities are valuable tools for our understanding of the dynamics of mutual accommodation and the analysis and resolution of issues in such areas as: religious freedom; discrimination; the autonomy of religious organisations; doctrine, worship and religious symbols; the property and finances of religion; religion, education and public institutions; and religion, marriage and children. In this series, scholars at the forefront of law and religion contribute to the debates in this area. The books in the series are analytical with a key target audience of scholars and practitioners, including lawyers, religious leaders, and others with an interest in this rapidly developing discipline.

Series Editor: Professor Norman Doe, Director of the Centre for Law and Religion, Cardiff University, UK

Series Board:
Carmen Asiaín, Professor, University of Montevideo
Paul Babie, Associate Professor and Associate Dean, Adelaide Law School
Pieter Coertzen, Chairperson, Unit for the Study of Law and Religion, University of Stellenbosch
Alison Mawhinney, Reader, Bangor University
Michael John Perry, Senior Fellow, Center for the Study of Law and Religion, Emory University

Titles in this series include:

Religious Expression in the Workplace and the Contested Role of Law

Andrew Hambler

Routledge
Taylor & Francis Group

LONDON AND NEW YORK

First published 2015
by Routledge
2 Park Square, Milton Park, Abingdon, Oxfordshire OX14 4RN

and by Routledge
711 Third Avenue, New York, NY 10017

First issued in paperback 2016

Routledge is an imprint of the Taylor & Francis Group, an informa business

British Library Cataloguing in Publication Data
A catalogue record for this book is available from the British Library

Library of Congress Cataloging-in-Publication Data
Hambler, Andrew, author.
Religious expression in the workplace and the contested role of law /
Andrew Hambler.
pages cm — (Law and religion)
Includes bibliographical references and index.
ISBN 978-0-415-74662-5 (hardback) — ISBN 978-1-315-78064-1 (ebk)
1. Religion in the workplace—Law and legislation—Great Britain. 2.
Discrimination in employment—Law and legislation—Great Britain.
3. Freedom of religion—Great Britain. 4. Labor laws and legislation—
Great Britain. I. Title.
KD4100.H36 2014
342.4208'52—dc23
2014019862

ISBN 13: 978-1-138-24323-1 (pbk)
ISBN 13: 978-0-415-74662-5 (hbk)

Typeset in Baskerville
by FiSH Books Ltd, London

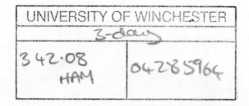

For my wife, Katharine

Contents

Table of cases

Acknowledgements

This book is based on a PhD thesis submitted in 2013 to the Law School at Durham University and written under the guidance of Professor Ian Leigh. I am very grateful to Ian for his wisdom, advice, guidance and, not least, patience both as primary supervisor during the PhD phase and subsequently as a critical reviewer of the early drafts of this book. Any errors or inelegances in what follows are of course my responsibility alone.

My thanks also to Tufyal Choudhury as second supervisor for his helpful comments on the original PhD thesis; to Professor Peter Edge and Dr Deidre McCann who examined the thesis and whose comments helped to refine it further; to the four anonymous reviewers of the book proposal whose comments, *inter alia*, have provided a useful framework for translating the thesis into a book format; to my colleagues at the University of Wolverhampton who have advised me in different ways during the course of writing and, in particular, Professor Steve Griffin, for his advice on an earlier version of Chapter 6, and Professors Roger Seifert and Mike Haynes, for their helpful comments on the book proposal; and to the excellent editorial and production teams at Routledge and FiSH Books, who have given me considerable support in the months leading up to publication.

I have drawn freely on material previously published in the form of journal articles. I am grateful to Oxford University Press (*Oxford Journal of Law and Religion*), the Ecclesiastical Law Society (*Ecclesiastical Law Journal*) and Brill (*Religion and Human Rights: An International Journal*) for their kind permission to do so. All Bible quotations are taken from the New King James Version.

Sincere thanks are due also to my parents, Geoff and Helen Hambler, who painstakingly proofread the original PhD manuscript and the subsequent updates and, most of all, to my wife, Katharine, who co-wrote the index and who has fully supported me throughout the long period during which this book (and particularly its antecedent) has slowly, and sometimes painfully, taken shape! This book is dedicated to her.

Andrew Hambler

Foreword

It is a particular pleasure to write this the foreword for the first book in the new Routledge Research in Law and Religion Series. All those associated with the Series are deeply indebted to Andrew Hambler for having produced a most scholarly study to inaugurate a Series one key function of which is to stimulate debate around the triad of religion, law and society. Andrew Hambler succeeds in this volume on three notable fronts integral to the spirit of the Series. His study is topical. Issues about religious expression in the workplace today attract headline attention in the media almost on a day-to-day basis. The study is a model in its potential for impact. The book will be of enormous utility to both employees and employers who have to function within a rapidly changing normative world in which pressures are brought to bear on this relationship from the State, international law and the expectations of society itself. His study is challenging. It exposes, with painstaking attention to detail, the arguments for and against law reform in this field. Whilst proposing practical solutions, the study is also rooted in a solid theoretical framework. It offers a major contribution to our understanding of the role of deep-seated motives behind religious expression, in so many of its forms, and does so within the context of a range of theoretical positions. The study is an inspiration to early career researchers. It grew from a doctoral study and is clear testament to the potential of early career researchers to challenge and test the fundamentals of law and religion today. Importantly, the book is accessible, clear, and lucid, engaging the subject at descriptive, explanatory and evaluative levels. It is a rare scholar indeed who is able to guide theorists and practitioners through the complexities of a legal discipline, not lose sight of the larger issues involved, and stimulate real reflection on the condition and limits of the law. Andrew Hambler is to be congratulated on an excellent volume which is the product of such hard work, meticulous observation, and thorough intellectual effort. He has certainly set the bar high.

Norman Doe
Series Editor of 'Law and Religion' series, and Professor and Director
for the Centre for Law and Religion, Cardiff

1 Introduction

The issue

In March 2010, six bishops and former bishops of the Church of England wrote to the *Sunday Telegraph* as follows:

> We are deeply concerned at the apparent discrimination shown against Christians … In a number of cases, Christian beliefs on marriage, conscience and worship are simply not being upheld. There have been numerous dismissals of practising Christians from employment for reasons that are unacceptable in a civilised country.[1]

These comments are reflective of a growing perception that the expression of Christian beliefs, in the workplace and elsewhere, is becoming increasingly difficult, owing to the hostility of others.[2] An interim report from the longitudinal survey of religious discrimination in Britain 2000–10 also tentatively concluded that discrimination (or at least perceptions of discrimination) against Christians had increased over the period.[3] A Parliamentary report in 2012 found evidence that 'Christians in the UK face problems in living out their faith and these problems have been mostly caused and exacerbated by social, cultural and legal changes over the past decade'.[4] There is also evidence that some Christians generally agree with

1   Letter to the Editor, *Sunday Telegraph* (London, 28 Mar 2010) 1; signed by: Most Revd Lord Carey of Clifton, Former Archbishop of Canterbury; Rt Revd Michael Scott-Joynt, Bishop of Winchester; Rt Revd Michael Nazir-Ali, Former Bishop of Rochester; Rt Revd Peter Forster, Bishop of Chester; Rt Revd Anthony Priddis, Bishop of Hereford; Rt Revd Nicholas Reade, Bishop of Blackburn.
2   This is also the view taken by the Archbishop of York; see J Sentamu, 'The Intolerance Towards Christians in the Public Sector is an Affront' *Daily Mail* (London, 13 February 2009), 17.
3   P Weller, *Religious Discrimination in Britain: A Review of Research Evidence, 2000–10*, EHRC Research Report 73, (Manchester: Equality and Human Rights Commission, 2011), 32–36.
4   Christians in Parliament, *Clearing the Ground Inquiry: Preliminary Report into the Freedom of Christians in the UK* (February 2012), 5.

this perception. For example, in a ComRes survey, conducted in May 2009 for the *Sunday Telegraph*, 19 per cent of 496 Christian respondents agreed with the statement 'I have faced opposition at work because I am a Christian'; five per cent agreed with the statement 'I have missed out on promotion at work because I am a Christian'; and six per cent agreed with the statement 'I have been reprimanded or cautioned at work for sharing my faith'.[5]

There is also evidence that members of other religions also face hostility when expressing their religious convictions at work. A report for the All Parliamentary Committee Group on Race and Community (2012–13), for example, considered evidence from Muslim women that the wearing of the headscarf negatively affected their prospects of securing a job at interview and that some felt pressured into removing it entirely.[6] As another example, in a survey of 662 Sikhs living in Britain, 36 per cent of all respondents reported experiencing discrimination at work.[7]

The perception of Christians and some other faith groups, however, that they face hostility in the workplace is not met with universal sympathy. For example, Terry Sanderson, President of the National Secular Society, adopts a rather different perspective, identifying religious expression, rather than discrimination against the religious, as the core problem:

> The never-ending religious demands are now beginning to permeate the workplace. … When the religious agitators realise that they have a new legal weapon at their disposal [discrimination law] … [t]hen will come the demand for prayer rooms and the conflict that they bring in their wake, then special holidays and after that uniform exemptions to be followed by dietary restrictions that will have to be imposed on everyone else. The work place should be a secular space. People should leave their religion at the door because once it's over the threshold, it will cause mayhem as it does everywhere else.[8]

5   Sunday Telegraph poll prepared by ComRes. Fieldwork conducted online between 22 April and 1 May 2009. Available online at www.comres.co.uk/poll/70/the-sunday-telegraph-cpanel-poll-june-2009.htm (accessed 4 June 2014).

6   All Party Parliamentary Group on Race and Community, *Ethnic Minority Female Unemployment: Black, Pakistani and Bangladeshi Heritage Women: first Report of Session 2012–2013* (London: Runnymede Trust, November 2012), 13.

7   *British Sikh Report: An Insight into the British Sikh Community* (2013) 37 Available online at www.britishsikhreport.org/wp-content/uploads/2013/06/BSR_2013_FINAL.pdf (accessed 4 June 2014). The report does not specify to what extent this discrimination related to religious expression rather than racial or religious identity.

8   *Religion In The Workplace Becomes An Issue* (National Secular Society, 23 February 2007). Available online at www.secularism.org.uk/religioninthe workplacebecomesani.html (accessed 4 June 2014).

It is therefore clear that there are different perceptions of freedom of religious expression in the employment sphere. There is the view that Christians, and perhaps members of other religions, face an increasingly hostile climate in the workplace, some of which has been caused by political and legislative change. There is a second view that, facing hostility or not, it is the religious employees who are the primary problem, with their disruptive and divisive desire to express their religious convictions in the workplace – a secular forum in which religion has no place.

There is thus a significant public debate concerning freedom of religious expression in the workplace: some advocate that this should be further constrained by law for the sake of organisational harmony; others advocate that it should be supported to a greater extent than it currently is, given the fundamental importance of religion for many.

Purpose and overview

The purpose of this book is to contribute to this debate with a particular focus on the individual employee. It presents an overall theoretical framework for understanding the issue. This framework is in two parts. The first involves conceptualising religion in terms of how it is held by individuals at work through inner belief, identity, association with others and, most significantly, outward manifestation or expression. It is noted that some forms of expression are likely to be uncontroversial, because they have no real impact on others; others will be potentially controversial because they may have an effect on other actors in the workplace, such as the employer, co-workers or customers. Forms of expression which are potentially controversial or contentious are of most interest in this book as they are most likely to engage the law. They are identified and classified, for analytical purposes, into the following three categories, depending on the effect on the workplace:[9]

- negative manifestation – the desire to 'opt-out' of either particular aspects of a job role for reasons of religious conscience (for example, a Muslim shop assistant who requests to be excused from handling alcohol) or more generally to be absent from working on particular days or at particular times because of religious obligations (such as attendance at a church service on Sunday);
- passive manifestation – the desire to display religious convictions visually through dress or personal grooming (such as the wearing of an Islamic headscarf, Christian cross or Sikh turban); and

---

9 The preferred term in European human rights jurisprudence is 'manifestation', although this term is more narrowly defined than expression (see Chapter 4). In practice, in this book, the two terms will be used interchangeably to a certain degree, although the term 'expression', because of its greater breadth of meaning, is generally preferred.

- active manifestation – the desire to articulate religious convictions to make an impact on others; for example, to seek to make converts to a particular religious faith or to rebuke the perceived 'sinful' activities of co-workers (such as involvement in same-sex or extra-marital relationships).

The second part of the overall theoretical framework seeks to identify different principled responses within a liberal society to these forms of religious expression and considers and critiques the possible rationale underlying each. Using academic literature drawn primarily from the disciplines of political philosophy and law, it is proposed that there are six possible models:

(I)   the *exclusion* model, which offers no support for individual religious expression and instead, to the extent that a liberal political model allows, acts to suppress religious expression;

(II)   support for *a preferred historic ('majority') religion* only where religious expression is actively valued for its cultural value in supporting a national culture or, less actively, supported by a legacy of lawmaking from an earlier age in which the majority religion was awarded legal privileges (not all of which have been repealed);

(III) *laissez-faire*, where the decision is taken to leave the issue of religious expression as entirely a contractual matter to be negotiated between employer and employee (and not one of sufficient import that a specific legal framework is warranted);

(IV) protection for religious expression, but only within *'islands of exclusivity'* – organisations with a religious character, possibly with a religious purpose, where people with religious convictions can work together and freely express their beliefs without this impacting on those with either no such religious convictions or other convictions;

(V) *protection*, under which religious expression is afforded a high value for its benefits either to individuals themselves or society in general; it is thus actively supported in the workplace with laws aimed at promoting religious expression and protecting religious employees from negative treatment by employers or others; and

(VI) *protection for minority religions* only, as religious expression is seen as an important element of cultural identity which needs to be supported and encouraged so that individuals from minority ethnic groups can fully participate in the workplace without compromising their group characteristics.

These models are then used as reference points in discussing the law applying in the legal jurisdiction of England and Wales and its interpretation. Features of most of the models can be discerned. For example, special 'occupational requirement' exemptions from the Equality Act allow religious organisations a measure of freedom to 'discriminate' in favour of recruiting staff from specific religious backgrounds to create (modified) 'islands of exclusivity'. As another example, employers still enjoy a degree of *laissez-faire* freedom of action (for example, as a justification for indirect discrimination, in determining what is a 'legitimate aim') when deciding how to respond to religious expression at work.

The picture that emerges most strongly, however, is a rather contradictory one, in which the dominant models prove to be at once protection and exclusion, although these imperatives can be discerned in different ways in the legal framework. For example, at a legislative level, the very fact that discrimination law was extended in 2003 to cover religion and belief claims is indicative of the 'protection' imperative; yet, at the same time, the way in which aspects of the relevant law are drafted reflects, intentionally or otherwise, an 'exclusionary' imperative (this is particularly true of the definition of harassment, under which initiating a religious conversation might create an 'offensive environment' and therefore 'harass' others).[10] As another example, at a judicial level, some (but by no means all) tribunals have interpreted discrimination law to prevent employers from penalising employees from 'negatively manifesting' by refusing to work on Sundays when there are viable alternatives available (see for example, *Williams-Drabble* v. *Pathway Care Solutions Ltd and anor*);[11] yet, the courts have entirely failed to offer any protection for employees (in non-medical fields) who wish to 'negatively manifest' because of conscientious objection to aspects of their jobs, even where the negative manifestation could be easily accommodated at a practical level. For example in *Ladele* v. *Islington Borough Council*,[12] a very significant case which will be considered in some detail at intervals in this book, a registrar of marriages was found not to have suffered discrimination when her employer refused to exempt her from civil partnerships work on the grounds of religious conscience, even though in practical terms all parties agreed that her request could have been easily accommodated. The court determined that the employer could justify a policy of insisting that all staff fully supported its equality and diversity goals, including non-discrimination on the grounds of sexual orientation, regardless of any other considerations such as the claims of religious conscience.

It is suggested that the underlying reason for the apparent contradictions is, to a large extent, rooted in the lack of consensus about the nature of religious expression and its importance to religious employees, such that it can be understood in very different ways. For instance, some see religious expression as essentially a private activity which should not be manifested in the workplace; others do not accept that religion can be so easily compartmentalised as it affects all aspects of life. Equally, some see certain

10   See discussion in Chapter 5.
11   (2005) ET Case No. 2601718/04. See discussion in Chapter 6.
12   EWCA Civ. 1357 (CA) [2009]; IRLR 211 [2010].

religious activities as 'core', such as the desire to worship with others, but other forms of expression as 'non-core' and less needing of protection. Similarly, some consider religious expression as a matter of free choice voluntarily assumed; others see it as a weighty obligation assumed under spiritual compulsion.

In this book, it is argued that conceptualising religious expression as a matter of free choice and as an essentially private, non-core, activity is inaccurate and serves to trivialise the situation of the religious claimant from the outset. Instead, it is suggested that religious expression is of primary significance to many individuals. To fail to fully recognise this undermines the dignity and potentially the autonomy of religious people (values which are fundamental to a liberal society). Equality is also undermined if other characteristics, such as sex or sexual orientation, are axiomatically afforded greater consideration. Thus, religious claims are weighty claims worthy of being taken very seriously, based on liberal values, such that infringements by employers require a high standard of justification. To move towards this view would require something of a shift in perspective on behalf of both the courts and many employers, and there may be a role for public bodies, such as the Equalities and Human Rights Commission, to help to achieve this through programmes of awareness raising.

If a high view of the importance of religious expression were to be adopted at a public policy level, then it follows that both the law and its interpretation should move further (and in a more principled and consistent way) in the direction of the protection model.

Materials and approach

This book is confined in scope to a discussion of religious expression in the workplace in England and Wales. It therefore draws most heavily on domestic law and, in particular, employment discrimination law: most significantly, the Equality Act 2010 and the Employment Equality (Religion and Belief) Regulations 2003,[13] and the way in which this legislation is interpreted in courts and tribunals. Where first-instance employment tribunal decisions are considered in this book, these are based on case reports which have been made public by one of the parties; these have been largely sourced through links from summary case notes prepared for the Equal Opportunities Review.[14]

The legal materials used are not limited, however, to employment discrimination law. Article 9 of the European Convention on Human Rights and Fundamental Freedoms, concerning freedom of religion and belief, is also considered in some depth, in particular its application to the workplace by the European Court of Human Rights and, indeed, by British

---

13   SI No.1660.
14   See www.eordirect.co.uk.

courts. The relevant cases, some of which go beyond the employment situation, are discussed. On occasion, this book also draws on case law relating to religious expression in some foreign jurisdictions. The purpose of referring to such case law is not to attempt a systematic comparative analysis; rather, it is largely restricted to identifying how another jurisdiction has treated a problem relevant to the discussion but which may not have been fully considered by an employment tribunal or court in England and Wales.

This book also draws on a wide range of academic writing from various disciplines, principally law, political philosophy, ethics and sociology, in support of the theoretical constructs which will be presented in Chapters 2 and 3. Some of these constructs are informed by a well-established literature, particularly on the role of religion in public life and the nature of equality, dignity and autonomy.[15]

In the later chapters, particular use is made of a more recent and expanding literature which expressly engages with religious freedom and the law, and often includes analysis of particular cases. This literature is sourced from published books and monographs and from specialist religion and law journals, such as the *Oxford Journal of Law and Religion*,[16] the *Ecclesiastical Law Journal*[17] and *Religion and Human Rights*.[18] Much of the literature is directly related to the question of the interplay between religious liberty (in its widest sense) and the legal systems of contemporary secular liberal societies, with a particular focus on the European Convention on Human Rights and how clashes of rights are resolved at that level.[19] Some of the literature is more specific to a particular manifestation of religion, usually the Islamic headscarf and often in an educational context.[20] Other literature is more localised, focusing on the interaction of religion and law in the United Kingdom.[21]

---

15 See, among many examples: J Rawls, *Political Liberalism* (New York: Columbia University Press, 1993); R Audi and N Wolterstorff, *Religion in the Public Square: The Place of Religious Convictions in Political Debate* (Lanham, MD: Rowman and Littlefield, 1997); and W Galston, *Liberal Purposes* (Cambridge: Cambridge University Press, 1991).

16 Published by Oxford Journals.

17 Published by Cambridge Law Journals.

18 Published by Martinus Nijhoff.

19 See, among many examples: the relevant chapters of R Ahdar and I Leigh, *Religious Freedom in the Liberal State*, 2nd ed. (Oxford: Oxford University Press, 2013) and C Evans, *Freedom of Religion under the European Convention on Human Rights* (Oxford: Oxford University Press, 2000).

20 For example, D McGoldrick, *Human Rights and Religion: The Islamic Headscarf Debate in Europe* (Cambridge: Hart, 2006) and E Howard, *Law and the Wearing of Religious Symbols* (Abingdon: Routledge, 2012).

21 For example, A Bradney, *Law and Faith in a Sceptical Age* (Abingdon: Routledge Cavendish, 2009); and M Hill, R Sandberg and N Doe, *Religion and Law in the United Kingdom* (The Hague: Wolters-Kluwer, 2011); and other articles by these authors.

Academic publications dealing with religious freedom specifically in the workplace are relatively uncommon. The most notable exceptions include a series of journal articles by Lucy Vickers and articles or book chapters by Gwyneth Pitt and Aileen McColgan. The most comprehensive published study of religious freedom in the workplace to date is the book by Vickers, *Religious Freedom, Religious Discrimination and the Workplace.*[22] It deals with the interaction of discrimination law and human rights law to create a framework for freedom of religion and it identifies a number of issues which, at the date of publication, had yet to be fully addressed, including approaches to resolving various conflicts between the rights of 'religious' employees and organisations and the rights of other actors such as employers, non-religious employees and employees protected under other strands of discrimination law.

This book is concerned with the same questions of religious freedom in the workplace but at an individual level – the rights of religious organisations, for example, are not a primary concern. It takes a specific interest in the situation of the religious employee in the secular workplace; it seeks, as far as possible, to enter into the world view of the religious employee in order to sympathetically understand and account for the different ways in which religion is expressed, the importance of this to the religious employee, and the implications of this when tribunals and courts balance it against other imperatives in situations where rights apparently conflict.

This approach also differs markedly with that of McColgan, for example, who conceptualises religious expression as an external expression of (collective) culture rather than something unique and important to the religious individual.[23] However, it finds a degree of support from McCrudden (writing from a wider discrimination law perspective) who argues that it is a problem when religious expression is viewed from an 'external viewpoint rather than a cognitively internal viewpoint'.[24] He applies his critique primarily to judges in cases involving freedom of religion but the point could equally be made in relation to a number of commentators, including McColgan and Pitt.[25] The analysis in this book adopts a different stance. Whilst not seeking to neglect or downplay other interests (including those of employers and co-workers), it is the particular focus on the 'internal viewpoint' of the religious employee which makes this book distinctive.

---

22 Lucy Vickers, *Religious Freedom, Religious Discrimination and the Workplace* (Oxford: Hart, 2008).

23 A McColgan, 'Class Wars? Religion and (In)equality in the Workplace' (2009) 38 *Industrial Law Journal* 1.

24 C McCrudden, 'Religion, Human Rights, Equality and the Public Sphere' (2011) 13 *Ecclesiastical Law Journal* 26, 32.

25 Pitt in large measure agrees with McColgan: see G Pitt, 'Religion or Belief: Aiming at the Right Target?' in H. Meenan (ed), *Equality Law in an Enlarged European Union* (Cambridge: Cambridge University Press, 2007).

Outline structure

The purpose of Chapter 2 is to arrive at a principled understanding of what constitutes legitimate 'religious expression' in the workplace. Three key areas are explored: the meaning of religion; categorising religious expression; and determining the underlying authenticity of individual claims.

Chapter 3 considers how a liberal state might respond to the challenge of religious expression by employees. It sets out six models representing approaches which might be taken, ranging from exclusion to full protection in law and the justification for these approaches. These models, and their attendant implications, are in turn subjected to critique.

The purpose of Chapters 4 to 8 is to consider the application of the theoretical frameworks set out in Chapters 2 and 3 to relevant legislation and case law. Chapter 4 focuses on the role of European Convention on Human Rights, in particular Article 9, whilst Chapter 5 considers the broader legislative and policy landscape of England and Wales. The chapters which follow examine the way in which employment tribunals and courts have responded when faced with claims involving religious expression. Such claims are examined with reference to a categorisation of religious expression set out in Chapter 2. Chapter 6 is concerned with an examination of tribunal responses to a claimant's desire to absent herself from work either at certain times (for reasons of religious devotion) or to avoid certain tasks because they clash with her religious-based conscience. In Chapter 7, the legal issues surrounding employees' desire to adopt particular styles of dress, jewellery or personal grooming are considered. In Chapter 8, an assessment is made of the freedom of the individual at work to 'witness' to (or proselytise) others and to object to, or challenge, the behaviour of colleagues.

In Chapter 9, overall conclusions are developed and a final assessment of the role of law as a support for, or a constraint on, religious expression in the workplace is made, followed by recommendations as to how, and in what ways, the law could better protect religious expression.

2   Conceptualising 'religious expression' in the workplace

Introduction

Religious expression differs from self-expression. The former commands stronger loyalties and deeper feelings, perhaps the deepest feelings of all; at best, it is less a matter of an individual choice than an inevitable and unavoidable response to divine obligation. Thus, the individual with strong religious beliefs will have an overriding interest in expressing these beliefs in some way. This is as likely to apply to the workplace as to other fora.

In expressing their religious beliefs, workers are responding to what they view as a divine imperative which, if it conflicts with the interests of other actors, such as an employer or a co-employee, is likely to be afforded greater weight by the religious employee. Self-expression, on the other hand, although an important human freedom, cannot make claims of this nature – it cannot invoke divine command to support the choices it has elected and thus is more easily circumscribed with reference to the requirements of others. Some indeed have argued that self-expression is not a human right in the fullest sense as the nature of self-expression varies according to societal and other contextual factors.[1] Religion, however, is different and, thus, in an important sense, 'special'.[2] It is also, potentially and most immediately for the employer, a 'problem'.[3] Two examples may help to illustrate this latter point. Firstly, a retail employer may engage in Sunday trading and may require that all employees are available to work, by rotation, that day. A Christian objects on the basis that Sunday is a day set apart and by divine command she cannot work on Sundays. Secondly, a supermarket chain requires that checkout staff process all customer

1   See, for example, L Alexander, *Is There a Right of Freedom of Expression?* (Cambridge: Cambridge University Press, 2005).
2   A term helpfully explained in S Bedi, 'Debate: What is so Special About Religion? The Dilemma of the Religious Exemption' (2007) 15 *Journal of Political Philosophy* 235. How special is a matter of debate which will be considered in the next chapter.
3   D Hicks, *Religion and the Workplace: Pluralism, spirituality, leadership* (Cambridge: Cambridge University Press, 2003), 71.

purchases. A Muslim store assistant objects that this will mean she must handle alcohol, which she believes is contrary to Islamic teaching. How should the employer respond to such instances as these where its own (or other) interests conflict with the fundamental beliefs of his religious employees? This important dilemma, amongst others, will be debated in Chapter 3. What this chapter is concerned with, however, is a necessary precursor to that question: how can this special, but potentially problematic, religious expression be recognised?

It is submitted that recognition is required on two levels. At the first level, there is a 'positive' recognition of forms of expression which stake a claim to be considered religious and therefore potentially fall into the 'special' category. Within this level, it will be possible to categorise such expression in various ways and, in so doing, to identify those which are also, potentially, a 'problem' to employers. For these types of expression, in particular, it may be thought desirable to consider a second level of recognition, which would consist of an attempt to determine the legitimacy of that form of expression on the assumption that not all claims to religious expression have a right necessarily to be recognised as such. This could be characterised as a form of 'negative' recognition as it is designed to limit the number of claims to be admitted into the 'special' category.

This chapter is thus divided into two parts: the first is concerned with an attempt to identify and classify 'religious expression' in its broadest terms; the second is concerned with the identification of principled approaches to distinguish between what might be regarded as 'legitimate' forms of religious expression and what might not be.

Identifying religious expression: a typology

The purpose of this section is to attempt to provide a broad classification of what is could be considered *prima facie* as 'religious expression'. As an initial reference point, the term will be used in its widest sense to encompass the ways in which an employee might wish to bring his or her religious beliefs into the workplace. From the religious employee's perspective, this may be very wide indeed, encompassing all forms of human activity (internal and external). As Ahdar and Leigh perceptively note:

> The most mundane of human behaviours can be 'spiritualised' and take on a religious connotation. One is practising one's religion when one eats, drinks, works, plays and gardens, as much as when one reads scripture, prays or meditates. ... On this view there is no activity which is not generated by one's obedience (or disobedience) to God.[4]

---

4   R Ahdar and I Leigh, *Religious Freedom in the Liberal State*, 2nd ed. (Oxford: Oxford University Press, 2013), 157.

If all human activity is inherently religious, it would then follow that forms of classification are unlikely to be significantly meaningful to the religious employee. Nevertheless, from the perspective of an employer, forms of classification are likely to be very useful, not least to identify and cluster thematically examples of religious expression which are, respectively, least and most likely to pose a 'problem' to others. For this reason, the mapping out of a typology of religious expression will be attempted here.

The European Court of Human Rights (ECtHR) has developed the notion of two fora in which religion and belief may be expressed – respectively, the *forum internum*[5] and the *forum externum*.[6] The *forum internum*, by strict definition, refers to that which is internal to the individual – a sphere of activity which is private in nature. Holding a religious belief is a function of this *forum internum*; it is entirely internal to the believer and therefore no one else need be aware of his religious convictions.[7] The *forum externum*, by contrast, involves those forms of religious expression that are overt and sometimes highly visible. This division is potentially helpful, as it allows courts to distinguish between the two categories, potentially giving an absolute guarantee of freedom to the former and a more qualified approach to the latter.[8] The problem with the *forum internum/externum* dichotomy[9] does become apparent, however, when considering the concept of belief in slightly wider terms. If an individual has publicly identified himself as holding religious beliefs, for example by attending church or placing a religious symbol on his car which he uses to travel to work, then, strictly speaking, he has stepped outside of the *forum internum* as he has acted on his beliefs.[10] However, because this activity has taken place, in private (i.e. in this case, outside of work),[11] including it as part of the *forum externum* would seem to so stretch that term as to render it less helpful analytically, particularly if the term is also used to describe

---

5   First used in ECHR jurisprudence by the Commission in *C* v. *United Kingdom* (1983) 37 DR 142.

6   See also discussion of these two terms in C Evans, *Freedom of Religion under the European Convention* (Oxford: Oxford University Press, 2000), 72–3.

7   As Trigg puts it, 'How does one know what someone believes if it is never manifested?', R Trigg, *Equality, Freedom and Religion* (Oxford: Oxford University Press, 2012), 99.

8   See also discussion of this distinction within the text of Article 9 ECHR in Chapter 4.

9   Or using different terminology, the belief/action distinction; see G Moens, 'The Action–Belief dichotomy and freedom of religion' (1989) 12 *Sydney Law Review* 195.

10   See the discussion in M Evans, *Religious Liberty and International Law in Europe*, (Cambridge: Cambridge University Press, 1997). In Chapter 1, he shows how the European Court of Human Rights has developed a broader view of the *forum internum* (which enjoys absolute protection), whilst leaving room for ambiguity at the margins.

11   But see discussion later in this chapter.

much stronger forms of overt religious expression such as proselytism of co-workers.

An alternative form of classification, therefore, may be a simple private/public divide where 'religious activities' in private are potentially viewed differently from religious activities in public. However, identifying where to draw the line between the two may also be problematic. Assuming that the terms are employed in the popular sense of distinguishing between a 'private life' and a 'public life', then private religious activities are likely to be inclusive of attending, for example, a mosque or synagogue. However, what exactly constitutes 'public' may be less straightforward. The workplace, for example, may be generally described as a public space but it does not necessarily follow that all activities which take place in it can be labelled 'public'.

Both the *forum internum/externum* and the public/private distinctions are arguably of limited analytical use, owing to the limitations imposed by a simple bifurcation on what is actually rather more nuanced an issue and a more sophisticated framework would be advantageous. Such a framework is provided by Edge, who proposes a fourfold typology of individual religious rights.[12] These are the right to hold a religious belief, the right to a religious identity, the right to be a member of a religious community and the right to act on such belief, identity or membership of a community. Edge's framework was not specifically designed for application to the workplace; however, it will be employed here to categorise the different means by which individuals may wish to bring their religious beliefs into the workplace but in a slightly adapted form.

Belief

Employees who hold religious convictions will, by definition, bring these into the workplace at the most fundamental level of holding a belief. If this is a form of expression, it is entirely an internal one and thus corresponds to a narrow definition of the *forum internum*. In its own terms, it has no impact on others and so cannot be a problem. Belief, or internal religious expression, is the most basic and least intrusive form of religious expression, occupying the bottom rung on any hierarchy of expression.

Although such an internal form of expression cannot pose a problem to others, it nevertheless remains 'special' and it is possible that its exercise could be subjected to interference by an employer. This scenario might arise if an employer sought to foster a particular set of organisational values which might run counter to the religious beliefs of some employees, and did so, for example, through intensive briefing and training, perhaps reinforced through the appraisal system or through other organisational policies and practices. If such values were promulgated with sufficient

---

12 P Edge, 'Religious rights and choice under the European Convention on Human Rights' (2000) 3 *Web Journal of Current Legal Issues*.

force, then this might put irresistible pressure on the integrity of the inner religious belief.[13] Within a modern workplace context, values associated with 'diversity' might, in some circumstances, fulfil these criteria.[14]

Employing a slightly wider understanding of the *forum internum*, there may be further instances where pressure might be placed on internal beliefs through the imposition of oaths of office for certain public sector roles and in certain professions. Whereas it is possible that such oaths might have a religious content or a holy book might be the vehicle by which such oaths were authenticated (and thus highly problematic to those of a different, or without, religious faith),[15] it is equally possible that an oath or a proxy for an oath, such as a signed commitment to certain professional standards of an entirely secular nature, might have the effect of requiring public commitment to values which would not be in keeping with an individual's inner beliefs. Although some individuals may be willing to accommodate the resulting tension, others might be extremely uncomfortable about such a compromise. An example might be a Christian school teacher who, as a requirement of registering with the appropriate professional body, is forced to accept a code of conduct requiring her to 'promote equality and value diversity in all [her] professional relationships and interactions'; allowing 'equality' and 'diversity' to be defined by the employer and potentially in a way which might force her to promote homosexual lifestyles in the classroom.[16]

13   There is a parallel here under ECHR jurisprudence where indoctrination of school pupils (through, for example, compulsory sex education) has been regarded in the past as potentially an interference with religious belief; see, for example, *Kjeldsen, Busk Madsen and Pedersen* v. *Denmark* (1979) 1 EHRR 71; and discussion in S Langlaude, 'Indoctrination, secularism, religious liberty and the ECHR' (2006) 55 *International and Comparative Law Quarterly* 929. (It should, however, be noted that, in other more recent cases, the court appears to have been less persuaded of the potential for interference: see, for example, *Alonso and Merino* v. *Spain* Appl No. 51188/99 (25 May 2000)).

14   See, for example, the concerns expressed by Lord Waddington and David Taylor MP about 'Police officers, pressurised by diversity training' in a letter to the *Times* during a debate on the incitement to homophobic hatred provisions of the Coroners and Justice Bill 2009; see 'Letters', *Times*, 9 November 2009.

15   As in *Buscarini* v. *San Marino* (2000) 30 EHRR 208 and also in *Alexandridis* v. *Greece* Appl No. 19516/06 (21 February 2008), where the ECHR found that a lawyer, in violation of Article 9 ECHR, was obliged to reveal that he was not an Orthodox Christian and, as a result, to partially reveal his religious beliefs so as to make a solemn declaration in lieu of a religious oath.

16   The wording of the controversial draft Code of Conduct produced by the General Teaching Council in the UK in 2008 and amended after religious objections were raised; see P Curtis, 'Teachers' anti-discrimination code reworded after faith groups object' *Guardian* (London, 2 July 2009). Available online at www.guardian.co.uk/education/2009/jul/02/teachers-discrimination-diversity-code-reworded-gtce (accessed 4 June 2014); and, for a critique of the code by the Christian Institute, see 'Draft Code of Conduct May Make Teachers "Hide Faith"'. Available online at www.christian.org.uk/news/ 20090625/draft-code-of-conduct-may-make-teachers-hide-faith (accessed 4 June 2014).

Identity

Edge's second category is that of religious identity. An individual may be known to identify with a particular religion through observable external evidence; for example, church attendance or subscription to a religious interest journal. It is submitted that this is unlikely to cause any form of workplace conflict and, in general, the 'special' status will be of limited importance. There are perhaps two exceptions. Firstly, some religious beliefs may be considered so offensive to others that merely to identify with them (particularly if there is some kind of formal or official connection) might be sufficient to cause conflict in the workplace. As an indirect example, involving political rather than religious identity, the offence given by membership of the British National Party alone in the UK has been sufficient to lead the Home Office to ban police officers from joining up.[17] Secondly, some organisations, either religious in character or with quasi-religious overtones, may fall under suspicion due to secrecy rules and solemn oaths of fraternity, and the resulting concerns that members may have divided loyalties which might compromise their operational roles. A good example in the UK is public concern (including two parliamentary enquiries) about police officers and members of the judiciary who are also members of secret societies, and who are sometimes suspected of feeling that they owe a greater loyalty to their fellows than to the general public.[18]

Membership of a religious community

As with religious identity, it seems unlikely that mere membership of a religious community, such as a church, would create a workplace 'problem' unless, as before, it was the particular religious community or the activities of some members of that community, that are considered offensive to others or dangerous in some other way. For example, some individuals may be excluded by the state from some areas of employment, not on the basis of overt expression of religious beliefs but by association with other individuals or groups suspected of subversive activity that may be motivated by their religious convictions. Such individuals are likely to be identified through some form of security vetting process either before or during employment.[19]

---

17 See 'ACPO bans police from joining BNP' *BBC News* (27 July 2004). Available online at http://news.bbc.co.uk/1/hi/uk/3930175.stm (accessed 4 June 2014).
18 See the Parliamentary report from the Home Affairs Committee, *Freemasonry in Public Life* (HC, 1998–99, 467), which recommended the creation of a voluntary register for freemasons working in legal services in the UK.
19 See, for a discussion of security vetting in employment, L Lustgarten and I Leigh, *In From the Cold: National Security and Parliamentary Democracy* (Oxford: Clarendon Press, 1994), 127–63.

Acting on belief, identity or community

When an individual chooses to act on (or 'manifest' or 'practise')[20] her beliefs or identity alone or in the community of others outside the workplace, there might reasonably be a general assumption that this is unlikely to pose 'a problem' to employers. This is based on the view that an individual should be free to express herself as she sees fit outside the workplace (including participation in any religious activities) and that freedom should not generally be fettered by the employer. Nevertheless, there may be exceptions to this general rule for specific reasons. A senior civil servant, for example, might be required to avoid political activity to preserve the perceived political impartiality of the role.[21] Where the employer does seek either to prevent employees from particular activities outside the workplace or to discipline them for non-work behaviour, this is most likely to be considered fair in circumstances when the nature of such expression can be shown to potentially compromise an employer or otherwise to bring the employer into disrepute. Employers may consider themselves potentially compromised if employees are seen to act, albeit outside the workplace, in ways that are contrary to the core values of that organisation or the role that they occupy.[22] Although not strictly a workplace example, it is nevertheless instructive to note that this was the argument voiced by members of the European Parliament in 2004 when they rejected the appointment of Rocco Buttiglione as European Commissioner for justice and security, a portfolio carrying responsibility for the implementation of European Union antidiscrimination and human rights law.[23] Buttiglione was a committed Roman Catholic who had, in the past, publicly endorsed official Roman Catholic teaching that homosexuality is a sin and expressed traditional views on gender roles and the family.[24] Members of the European Parliament argued that his expressed views made him unsuitable for the portfolio he was to receive and could not accept Buttiglione's own argument that he would separate his own private convictions from his public actions.

Equally, a religious organisation, espousing, for example, Christian values, might decide to dismiss an employee known to have engaged in

---

20   The preferred ECHR terminology; see discussion in Chapter 4.
21   See *Civil Service Management Code* (June 2011), s 4.4 (Annex A). Available online at www.civilservice.gov.uk/about/resources/civil-service-management-code (accessed 14 June 2014).
22   In some occupations there may be clear guidance on what constitutes conduct incompatible with the ethos of the employer; in the UK, for example, this is spelt out for school teachers in the School Standards and Frameworks Act 1998, s 60(5)(b).
23   D Gow, 'MEPs reject anti-gay commission candidate' *Guardian* (London, 12 October 2004) 15.
24   'EU panel opposes justice nominee' *BBC News* (London, 11 October 2004). Available online at http://news.bbc.co.uk/1/hi/world/europe/3734572.stm (accessed 4 June 2014).

extramarital sex and who thus compromised the aims and religious integrity of the organisation.[25] Employers may also take the view that their businesses have been brought into disrepute by employees who have committed a criminal act; or who have publicly criticised their employer online; or who have worn the company uniform (in full or in part) whilst engaging publicly in behaviour which might offend others; or who have caused (potentially) great offence to other employees or clients by their published opinions. An example of the latter, concerning offence on religious lines, involved the senior press officer of the British Council who was exposed as the author of a series of articles in the *Daily Telegraph* attacking 'the black heart of Islam'.[26] An investigation was carried out and the British Council dismissed him for writing articles 'offensive to Islam' and, presumably, thereby bringing the British Council itself into disrepute.[27]

Discipline, and particularly dismissal, for conduct outside of the workplace is highly contested and rights arguments are advanced to limit as far as possible employers' freedom of action in this regard. Mantouvalou observes that employer action in respect of conduct outside of work is usually justified on the basis of the public nature of that conduct (what she terms *spatial* criteria).[28] Most human rights instruments (including Article 8 of the European Convention on Human Rights and Fundamental Freedoms, which she quotes) are concerned with the right to a *private* life. Thus rights arguments can be circumvented by courts in dealing with behaviour, including of course religious expression, outside the domestic sphere.[29] In seeking to overcome this, Mantouvalou argues that a spatial understanding of the private/public dichotomy is inadequate and prefers to view privacy as 'contextually-dependent'. This involves, *inter alia*, the extension of privacy to encompass activities which might otherwise be regarded as taking place in public but outside work.

When applied to freedom of religious expression outside of the workplace, Mantouvalou's conclusions do not provide the basis of any more concrete protections for religious employees. However, the analysis does imply the possibility of a greater extension of the right to privacy. Quite

25 Per the facts of *O'Neill* v. *Governors of St Thomas More RCVA Upper School* [1996] IRLR 372.
26 For example, W Cummins, 'The Tories must confront Islam instead of kowtowing to it' *Daily Telegraph* (London, 18 July 2004) 21.
27 H Muir, 'British Council official sacked over anti-Islam articles' *Guardian* (London, 2 September 2004) 1.
28 V Mantouvalou, 'Human Rights and Unfair Dismissal: Private Acts in Public Spaces' (2008) 71 71 *Modern Law Review* 912.
29 Although in *Niemietz* v. *Germany* (1992) 16 EHRR 97, the ECtHR noted that a simple binary divide between work and (private) non-work life may not always be necessary or desirable when it observed that 'it is not always possible to distinguish clearly which of an individual's activities form part of his professional or business life and which do not' [29].

how far this might extend is open to question. Should, for example, a non-work conversation about religion between two work colleagues, where one is offended by what she hears, be regarded as a purely private matter or public and of interest to the employer?[30]

Acting on belief within the workplace

Thus far, religious belief, identity and expression outside of the workplace have been considered and the relatively rare, and often hypothetical, examples of occasions when that expression might pose a 'problem' to employers (and thus require a response) have been explored. The discussion will now turn to forms of religious expression which occur within the workplace and initially the first of Edge's categories – acting on belief.

Actions of course cannot remain private – but the source, in terms of the underlying motivations, of those actions might remain unknown to others. One of the areas in which examples are most likely to be found is in relation to workplace ethics. Amongst the effects of Christian belief, for instance, might be fidelity to an employer, maintaining the 'highest moral and ethical standards of behaviour and attitudes'[31] and a concern for the health and wellbeing of co-workers. These are legitimate expressions of the Christian belief in the workplace and yet do not require any overt public identification with Christianity – Jesus Christ need not be mentioned by an employee who helps his co-worker – or who adheres strictly to the time limits during 'breaks'. For Muslims, similarly, a strong workplace ethic is a requirement of Islam. This need not require the invocation of religious beliefs but simply that 'the good Muslim businessman should be guided by his conscience – and by God's written instructions – to do the right thing by other people'.[32]

Another important example of acting on religious belief lies in commitment to career and workplace. Within Christianity, for example, work in all its forms is highly esteemed. Martin Luther regarded human work as a direct extension of God's continuing creative work on Earth and made the colourful claim that God even milks the cows through those he calls to work.[33] This view of work charges it with spiritual significance – by working, men and women fulfil a specific calling to be 'cultivators and stewards of all the good gifts of his creation' in whatever work role or position they hold.[34]

---

30   See discussion in Chapter 8.
31   W Backus, 'How to be a Christian in the Workplace' *Decision Magazine* (July 1998).
32   M Tayeb, 'Islamic revival in Asia and human resource management' (1997) 19 *Employee Relations* 352, 356.
33   L Hardy, *The Fabric of This World* (Grand Rapids, IL: William B Eeardmans, 1990), 48.
34   Ibid. It should be noted that Luther did exclude certain occupations as unsuitable for Christians (those of monk, prostitute and usurer).

Calvin added to this sense of work, however humble, as divine vocation, a particular stress on its role in allowing the Christian to serve others and society.[35] This high view of work, essentially as a divine calling, should translate in practical terms in the workplace to a discerning choice of job role and then a strong commitment to that job role, the worker diligently seeking to carry out its demands to the best of his ability, to serve others and, in so doing, to serve and please God.[36]

As these examples in the realm of ethics and workplace commitment are normally aligned to organisational interests, they also lie within a wider category of religious responses in society identified by Robert Audi as 'secularly-aligned religious obligations'.[37] In other words, the religious beliefs produce actions and attitudes which would gain approval by the non-religious, regardless of the initial motivation which may therefore remain undisclosed.[38] In terms of the original proposition, such religious expression will not normally be expected to constitute a 'problem'.

There are, however, two qualifications to add to this analysis. Firstly, it assumes that the organisation is itself practising organisational virtue (akin to civic virtue in Audi's wider application to society). If this is not the case, then a dilemma may arise for those acting on religious belief. A good illustration of this is the position of the 'whistle-blower' who may feel obliged to act on his beliefs and report abuse of power, corruption or unlawful activities within the workplace. Secondly, it assumes that organisational virtue will generally travel in the same direction as religious virtue such that, at this level, there is unlikely to be a conflict. However, it remains possible that such a conflict may arise if the organisation conceptualises virtue in a very different way to the religious individual. The virtues of 'respect' and 'tolerance', which might form part of a dignity at work policy or a wider 'diversity' approach, have potential to create conflict for some religious employees who may be discouraged under this policy from speaking openly with others about their Christian faith or offering advice on lifestyle issues. This conflict is, however, most likely to emerge at a more overt level of religious expression, of the kind to be discussed in the next section. At the level discussed here it is difficult to envisage a conflict.

Thus religious expression can be uncontroversial, where it is aligned with organisational virtues and where the specifically religious motivation remains internalised. Controversy is only likely to arise if the behaviour of managers or colleagues is contrary to the principles of organisational virtue

---

35   Ibid. 58–9.
36   This is set out in some detail in ibid., 79–122.
37   R Audi, *Religious Commitment and Secular Reason* (Cambridge: Cambridge University Press, 2000), 118.
38   The potential synergies between corporate and religious values is discussed in M Bandsuch and G Cavanagh, 'Integrating Spirituality into the Workplace: Theory and Practice' (2005) 2 *Journal of Management, Spirituality and Religion* 221.

– the resulting conflict is unlikely to be perceived as a specifically religious problem, however.[39] Religious expression is most likely to be potentially 'a problem' when it is both externalised and is identifiably religious in character.[40] Inevitably, given its potentially controversial nature, it is this aspect of religious expression which is of most interest in this chapter.

Acting on religious identity within the workplace

Actions within the workplace which are identifiably and overtly religious in character are potentially many and varied. Such actions or forms of expression will differ in the level of challenge that they pose to the employer but all are potentially problematic. One way of categorising these overt forms of religious expression is in terms of their effect on aspects of the employment contract.[41] Thus, religious expression can be identified in terms of: requests for time off for religious devotions; implications for the company dress code; the effect of conscience in terms of a desire not to engage in a particular aspect of the job or workplace regime because it is considered distasteful or even sinful; and the desire to 'witness' to, or seek to convert co-workers, or to challenge their behaviour. An alternative approach to categorisation is to focus on the character of the form of expression. Thus, identifiably 'religious' expression is manifest either 'passively', 'negatively' or 'actively', with the latter representing potentially the greatest challenge to the organisation.[42] Examples of 'passive' manifestation include the wearing of an Islamic headscarf or a Christian cross or the decoration of workstations to form 'employee-created sacred space'.[43] 'Negative' manifestation involves either seeking to be absent from work at specified times (such as Sundays for mainstream Christian groups and Saturdays for Jews and Seventh-day Adventists) to enable them to engage in collective religious devotion outside the workplace, or seeking exemption from some aspects of a work role because of a conflict with religiously inspired

---

39   See, for example, *Moore* v. *Hartlepool Borough Council* (2009) ET Case No. 2501537/09, where a tribunal found that 'honesty' had an 'ethical' rather than a specifically religious foundation in an unsuccessful claim by a Christian employee who argued that he had suffered religious discrimination because he had been asked to behave in a manner which he considered to be dishonest.

40   Vickers identifies examples of explicitly religious expression which, because they are internalised do not cause any conflict; see Vickers, *Religious Freedom, Religious Discrimination and the Workplace* (Oxford: Hart Publishing, 2008) 98. Praying for co-workers (without their knowledge) would fall into this category.

41   For example, Vickers, ibid.

42   A Hambler, 'A Private Matter? Evolving Approaches to the Freedom to Manifest Religious Convictions in the Workplace' (2008) 3 *Religion and Human Rights* 111.

43   J Montgomery, 'A most delicate matter: religious issues and conflict in the US library workplace' (2003) 23 *Library Management* 442, 427.

conscience. An example of 'active' manifestation would be proselytism, with a view to gaining converts, in the workplace. An adapted version of this method of categorisation will be used in the analysis presented in the later chapters of this book.

Acting on religious community within the workplace

The final element of Edge's typology to be applied to the workplace is the desire to act on membership of a religious community. This could manifest itself in terms of a wish for people with the same religious convictions to meet together on the workplace premises, perhaps at lunchtimes or after work, to engage in collective religious devotion or prayer, or to meet for mutual encouragement or outreach to others. In the United Kingdom, there is an organisation known as 'Christians at Work', which exists to support individuals and 'Christian fellowships' meeting in the UK workplaces. According to its website, 'there are over 100 workplace Christian Fellowship groups affiliated to [Christians at Work]'.[44] On the basis that there are other non-affiliated groups, then it may be assumed that a number of Christians, at least, actively engage in a form of collective religious expression in the workplace. Similarly, Muslims, who are required individually by Islam to engage in short periods of daily prayer, may wish to do so 'in congregation'.[45] In these cases, there may be a consequent desire for the employer to provide some appropriate facilities to enable the collective religious activities to take place.[46]

Religious expression: a test of legitimacy

Thus far, an initial attempt to categorise, in various ways, expression which might stake a claim to be considered 'religious' has been made. It is now necessary to consider the extent to which such claims should be accepted. The reason why this is necessary is because, as argued earlier, religious expression is both 'special', and therefore likely to claim privileges for itself, and potentially, at least in some forms, a problem (for employers). As a result, there is a strong case for seeking to draw the boundary lines as narrowly as possible as to what actually represents religious expression without becoming overly exclusionary. This is clearly a delicate balance to be achieved and requires some tests to be formulated and applied to each instance of putative religious expression (and this will be particularly important for those forms of expression which are most likely to be controversial or problematic). The most significant of these tests is the widest of

44   See www.caw.uk.net/index.php (accessed 4 June 2014).
45   Muslim Council of Britain, *Muslims in the Workplace: A Good Practice Guide for Employers and Employees* (MCB/DTI 2005), 15.
46   Ibid.

all – legitimacy. Legitimacy can of course be defined in various ways, but how it is formulated here is in terms of conveying a sense of validity. Can a particular form of expression make a valid claim to be considered 'religious expression'? To make an assessment of validity, there is likely to be a requirement that there is some external standard for measurement.

The next stage of this analysis is thus devoted to exploring the legitimacy (with reference to external standards) with which an employee can in fact stake a claim that his particular form of expression is indeed 'religious' in nature.

'Legitimate' religion

A potential starting point is to consider the legitimacy of the particular religion itself which is being invoked as the basis of an act of expression. For example, the wearing of a headscarf-*hijab*[47] is a potential act of religious expression which invokes Islam. The initial question in determining legitimacy might therefore be to examine first the question, is Islam, upon which this act of putative religious expression relies, a legitimate religion? Here legitimacy is most likely to be defined in terms of 'recognised' or 'worthy of recognition' (by society). Having determined on this basis that, yes, Islam is in fact a legitimate religion, it would then be possible to progress to consider the particular form of religious expression which is associated by the employee with Islam to judge whether this form is indeed a valid (or legitimate) expression of Islam. In essence, this approach involves a two-stage test.[48] Most commentators do not follow a two-stage approach and go directly to the particular religious belief being expressed as their initial reference point.[49] This religious belief is then scrutinised in various ways to determine its legitimacy. This may indeed be the preferred approach in many legal jurisdictions. Nevertheless, it remains at least theoretically possible to seek an initial definition of religion as a first hurdle to be overcome before addressing the substantive issue of the particular way in which a consequent belief is being made manifest.

To identify whether this first hurdle has been crossed requires therefore a consideration of how to recognise a legitimate religion. The attempt to define the essence of 'religion' has preoccupied academics from various fields and constructs have appeared from within a number of disciplines

---

47   Terminology used by McGoldrick, *Human Rights and Religion: The Islamic Headscarf Debate in Europe* (Cambridge: Hart Publishing, 2006).

48   See, for example, G Van Der Schyff, 'The Legal Definition of Religion and Its Application' (2002) 119 *South African Law Journal* 228. The author envisages a two stage approach, in which establishing the presence of a religion is the first.

49   See, for example, Ahdar and Leigh, *Religious Freedom in the Liberal State*, 139–52.

such as theology, philosophy, sociology, socio-economics and psychology.[50] Conceptualising religion itself, therefore, would be a complex and controversial enterprise. Fortunately, it is unnecessary for the purposes of the law and this chapter. The need is not to define religion with a view to explaining it as a phenomenon but rather to define it descriptively for the purposes of being able to recognise it when it is engaged. This is potentially a more manageable exercise, though not without its difficulties.

For the purposes of seeking this kind of definition, it is submitted that there is, theoretically, an identifiable continuum. At one end, anything which a person sincerely believes and values and claims this belief as a religion on whatever basis could be regarded as such by society and, as a result, by the law.[51] This would be the most open and all-embracing definition. At the other end of the continuum, religion could be extremely tightly defined such that only certain (probably ancient) religions are recognised as legitimate (and in their orthodox forms).[52] Both of these approaches are problematic. The major problem with the latter is its inflexibility. Inflexible fixed categories deny any protection to new (authentic) religions or, potentially, to new movements within religions. The major problem with the former is that it risks becoming so all inclusive that the term loses its significance. Clarke and Byrne highlight this with their modern American examples of devotion to baseball or playing the stock market.[53] If these are regarded as 'religious' then not only is the term trivialised but there can be no meaningful protections when all can claim religious rights on each and every pretext. An allied problem with the former is the possibility which is opened up for protection to be claimed for highly individualised forms of 'spirituality' (sometimes vaguely defined), again hugely widening the scope of protection.[54] A third problem is the difficulty which arises in attempting to gauge levels of sincerity.[55] Whilst this problem could arise in any event, it is particularly significant where sincerity is the only real test to be

---

50 There is a chapter devoted to each of these disciplines in P Clarke and P Byrne, *Religion Defined and Explained* (London: Macmillan, 1993).

51 For example, in *United States* v. *Kuch* 288 F Supp 439 (1968) an attempt was made to claim recognition for 'the Neo-American Church' (whose key 'sacramental' practice involved the collective partaking of marijuana and LSD).

52 This possibility is recognised by Ahdar and Leigh, *Religious Freedom in the Liberal State*, 141–2.

53 Clarke and Byrne, *Religion Defined and Explained*, 8.

54 'Spirituality' is an elastic concept which can encompass traditional religion (see the literature review in J Coyle, 'Spirituality and health: towards a framework for exploring the relationship between spirituality and health' (2002) 37 *Journal of Advanced Nursing* 589); but it can significantly depart from this as, for a 'spiritual' individual, 'the God in whom his life revolves may be his work, physical activity or even himself': see R Stroll, 'Guidelines for Spiritual Assessment', (1979) 79 *American Journal of Nursing* 1574.

55 Van Der Schyff, 'The Legal Definition of Religion and It's Application', 292.

employed. Sincerity is an extremely important requirement and it will be considered in some detail later in this chapter.

Returning to the notional continuum between the two polar opposites outlined above, there are a variety of ways of defining religion for descriptive purposes which seek in some way to limit the reach of the term whilst remaining generally inclusive. Clarke and Byrne provide a useful classification of the possible approaches to providing what they describe as an 'operational' definition of religion.[56] Firstly, they identify 'experiential' definitions which seek to identify some general type of experience which could be described as religious in nature, such as 'a disposition which enables men to apprehend the infinite under different names and disguises'.[57] The experiential definition is perhaps worryingly close to the subjective approach already considered (as it relies to a large extent on individual perception) and, as such, is likely to be similarly flawed. Secondly, there is a substantive or content-based definition which considers the substance of the beliefs associated with a religion. Vickers considers that Tillich's famous definition of faith as 'ultimate concern' falls into this category,[58] although other content-based definitions are more explicit in making reference to man's awareness of a deity.[59] There is a third approach, which looks at the function that 'religion' plays in people's lives. Deep social or individual needs are identified and religion is the institutional medium by which these needs are met. Yinger amplifies this 'functional' definition:

> Religion then can be defined as a system of beliefs and practices by means of which a group of people struggle with these ultimate problems of human life. It expresses their refusal to capitulate to death, to give up in the face of frustration, to allow hostility to tear apart their human aspirations.[60]

---

56   Clarke and Byrne, *Religion Defined and Explained*, 3–27.
57   F Mulleur, *Introduction to the Science of Religion* (London: Longman, 1893), 13, as quoted by Clarke and Byrne, ibid., 5.
58   P Tillich, *The Dynamics of Faith* (New York: Harper and Row, 1957), 1; see also Vickers, *Religious Freedom, Religious Discrimination and the Workplace*, 16–22.
59   Clarke and Byrne, *Religion Defined and Explained*, 6.
60   J Yinger, *The Scientific Study of Religion* (New York: Macmillan, 1970), 7. The United Kingdom Supreme Court appears to have recently found a functional approach helpful (when debating the religious status of Scientology) describing a religion as 'a spiritual or non-secular belief system, held by a group of adherents, which claims to explain mankind's place in the universe and relationship with the infinite, and to teach its adherents how they are to live their lives in conformity with the spiritual understanding associated with the belief system', in *R (Hodkin & Anor)* v. *Registrar General of Births, Deaths and Marriages* [2013] UKSC 77 [57] (Lord Toulson).

Another definition is based around Wittgenstein's concept of 'family resemblance', which he famously applied in a discussion of 'games'. Wittgenstein observed that it may not be possible to identify a feature or characteristic that is common to all games. Instead, he proposed that such games are connected instead by a series of observable similarities.[61] A number of writers have sought to apply this notion in the search for a definition of religion.[62] The starting point is usually to create a list of typical features of generally recognised religions against which the features of a putative religion can be compared. Audi appears to adopt such an approach in suggesting nine features which might assist in determining whether or not a religion is present: (1) belief in supernatural beings; (2) a distinction between sacred and profane objects; (3) ritual acts focused on those objects; (4) a moral code believed to be sanctioned by the god(s); (5) religious feelings of awe; (6) direct communication with the god(s), such as prayer: (7) a world view concerning the role of the individual in the universe; (8) a comprehensive approach to life based on the worldview; and (9) a collective organisation bound up with the latter.[63] Greenawalt adopts a similar set of criteria, explicitly based on observable commonalities between those religions which 'virtually everyone' would accept are religions (without the need to explain why).[64] Both Audi and Greenawalt stress that not all the features need to be present to establish that a legitimate religion is being described. This is, of course, crucial to the approach. It is how closely the features of a putative religion resemble at least some of these criteria that matters.

Notwithstanding the claims of the family resemblance approach, one of the most controversial issues, historically, in the search for a definition of religion is whether in fact theistic beliefs must be present for a religion to be so classified. Durkheim influentially thought not, given his observation that Buddhism, Taoism and Jainism, whilst in other ways performing the function of a religion and generally acknowledged as such, are non-theistic in character.[65] Other writers argue that if reference to the divine is not a necessary requirement for a religion then the term becomes vague and it becomes difficult in consequence to draw any meaningful distinctions

61 L Wittgenstein, *Philosophical Investigations* (Oxford: Blackwell, 1953).

62 One of the first was W Alston, 'Religion' in P Edwards (ed.) *The Encyclopedia of Philosophy* (New York: Macmillan, 1967), vol. 7, 140–5.

63 R Audi, 'Liberal Democracy and the Place of Religion in Politics' in R Audi and N Wolterstorff, *Religion in the Public Square: The Place of Religious Convictions in Political Debate* (Lanham, MD: Rowman and Littlefield, 1997), 5. Audi acknowledges that his list of categories builds on that presented in W Alston, *Philosophy of Language* (Englewood Cliffs, NJ: Prentice-Hall, 1964), 88.

64 K Greenawalt, 'Religion as a Concept in Constitutional Law' (1984) 72 *California Law Review* 753, 767–8.

65 E Durkheim, *The Elementary Forms of the Religious Life*, trans. J Ward Swain (London: Allen and Unwin, 1976), 29–36.

between a system of beliefs and a religion.[66] For advocates of a functional-ist approach this is not a difficulty – if a non-theistic belief system performs the social or individual role of a religion then it is better to classify it as such.[67] Only in this way could religion be seen to be a universal phenome-non.[68] This in turn elevates the importance of religion because '[s]omething fundamental to human life in society is being tackled by the theory of religion and not merely an institution important in some locali-ties and epochs'.[69] It should be noted, however, that such a conclusion could only be possible from an entirely external perspective. Amongst those who accept the truth claims of a particular religion, many are likely to reject this purely functionalist premise as *per se* human-centred. Religion, for Christians, Jews and Muslims, for example, could be characterised rather as humankind's obligation towards or response to the divine and, as such, it is God-centred in the sense that God and not humankind is the initial reference point.

Thus, in addition to the extremes of exclusivity and inclusivity of defini-tion initially outlined, law makers and judges have a range of intermediate approaches to draw on when seeking to identify whether or not a legitimate religion is being invoked. They can draw on experiential, substantive, func-tionalist or family resemblance definitions, or some combination of these. The issue of whether or not a religion requires reference to a divine pres-ence need only be of significance if, in a legal system, religion is privileged above some form of coherent philosophical framework for understanding life. Many legal jurisdictions may prefer to bracket the two together to create a joint classification of 'religion and belief'.[70] This, *inter alia*, would sidestep the debate over, for example, the precise status of Buddhism – whether it is a religion or a similar philosophical belief becomes unimpor-tant if it is to receive the same legal privileges in either case.[71]

Legitimate religious expression

If the two-stage test is adopted and the legitimacy of a religion is accepted, the second stage of the test will then take effect. This will involve an assess-ment of the legitimacy of the particular form of expression seeking to invoke the legitimate religion. Alternatively, if the two-stage test is rejected,

66   M Spiro, 'Religion: Problems of Definition and Explanation' in M Banton (ed.), *Anthropological Approaches to the Study of Religion* (London: Tavistock, 1966), 85–126.

67   A point also made by Lord Toulson who opined that a religion 'may or may not involve belief in a supreme being'; see *R (Hodkin & Anor)* [57].

68   See discussion in Clarke and Byrne, *Religion Defined and Explained*, 8–9.

69   Ibid. 9.

70   For example, in the UK, under the Equality Act 2010 and, in Europe, Article 9 ECHR.

71   See Vickers, *Freedom, Religious Discrimination and the Workplace*, 22.

this is the initial point of inquiry. The question, in either case, can be stated thus, is the form of religious expression to be invoked 'legitimate' or not? It should be recalled that, in practice, this question is only likely to arise in relation to potentially contentious forms of religious expression.

Addressing this initial question involves encountering the same problem already considered when seeking to identify legitimate religion. Once again, there is a continuum which, at one end, would allow individuals to express their religion in any way they wish, without any other form of legitimatisation, and, at the other end, would strictly recognise only certain forms of religious expression based on either an independent observation of how adherents of the major recognised religions choose to express their religious faith or an interrogation of the sources of authority within each religion to determine what the religion requires (or desires) of its adherents. Between these two points, there may be some intermediary positions which seek, in different ways, to maintain a balance between the twin dangers of 'under-inclusiveness' and 'over-inclusiveness', with a recognition of the former as the worst evil.[72]

Individual interpretation

The problem with regarding as legitimate unrestrained individual expression 'hooked on' to a recognised religion is perhaps obvious. In a trenchant comment on the judgment in the Canadian case of *Syndicat Northcrest* v. *Amselem*,[73] Ogilvy notes the application in a property dispute of what she regards as just this approach – the only requirement the court imposed before recognising the legitimacy of the chosen 'religious' expression of a group of Orthodox Jews was sincerity of belief or what she styles 'a subjective sincerity in any self-concocted beliefs whatever'.[74] This decision avoided what the court thought undesirable – that it should be involved in any way in seeking to determine whether or not religious doctrine could be invoked in any particular case. Indeed, this may be the advantage of allowing individuals (as long as they are sincere) to be the sole arbiters of the justice of their own forms of religious expression. Unfortunately, there is a considerable disadvantage, as observed in an Australian case: '[t]he mantle of immunity would soon be in tatters if it were wrapped around beliefs, practices and observances of any kind whenever a group of adherents chose to call them a religion'.[75] In other words,

---

72 Ahdar and Leigh, *Religious Freedom in the Liberal State*, 143.
73 [2004] 2 SCR 551.
74 M Ogilvy, 'And Then There Was One: Freedom of Religion in Canada – the Incredible Shrinking Concept' (2008) 10 *Ecclesiastical Law Journal* 197, 200.
75 *Church of the New Faith* v. *Commissioner for Pay Roll Tax* (Vic) (1983) 154 CLR 120 (Judges Mason and Brennan).

the broader the view that is taken of what constitutes religious expression, the weaker the protection (or 'immunity') is likely, of necessity, to be.

External observation

Another way of seeking to identify legitimate religious expression is through the study of adherents of recognised religions in order to identify types of religious expression which are common amongst adherents of those religions. This approach has been explicitly endorsed by Australian judges of the High Court:

> There is no single characteristic which can be laid down as constituting a formalized legal criterion [for the recognition of religious practices] … The most that can be done is to formulate the more important of the indicia or guidelines by reference to which that question falls to be answered. These indicia must, in the view we take, be derived from empirical observation of accepted religions.[76]

Some academic treatments of 'religion in the workplace' adopt a similar approach.[77]

Whereas this overall 'external' approach is useful, not least because it allows ready linkages to be made between religious and workplace practices, there are attendant disadvantages. Durkheim identifies the major problems with

> observing the complex religions which appear in the course of history. Every one of these is made up of such a variety of elements that it is very difficult to distinguish what is secondary from what is principal, the essential from the accessory.[78]

In other words, there are two disadvantages to the observation-driven approach. Firstly, it fails to fully capture the complexity of different forms of religious expression and is therefore, at best, a rough and ready gauge, potentially unsuitable for application in complex cases in the courtroom or tribunal chamber. Secondly, it fails (or may fail) to distinguish between forms of expression that are primary to a religion and forms of expression that are secondary or perhaps entirely unnecessary. Such information might be useful in an initial assessment of the cost to the religious employee of being prevented by an employer from engaging a particular form of religious expression in the workplace; being denied the right to

---

76 Ibid. 173 (Judges Wilson and Deane).
77 For example, Hicks, *Religion and the Workplace.*
78 Durkheim, *The Elementary Forms of the Religious Life,* 5.

wear a turban might, for the sake of argument, be more costly to a Sikh man than being denied the right to wear a headscarf might be to a Muslim woman – the observation approach would not assist in making that judgment.

Religion-led approach

A very different approach would involve a consideration of legitimate religious expression based on the requirements of the particular tenets or belief systems of the respective religion invoked. The great advantage of this approach is that it allows not only the identification of legitimate practices but permits more nuanced distinctions to be explored. For example, Ahdar and Leigh identify three types of 'conduct' or expression – those that are respectively permitted, required or prohibited by a given religion.[79] Absolute requirements or prohibitions may be considered, from an external perspective, more fundamental to a religious adherent than that which is simply permitted (in the sense of practices or conduct encouraged by a given religion, i.e. supererogation). It is surely only possible to make these kinds of distinctions satisfactorily with the aid of some form of analysis of belief systems themselves.

When such an analysis is applied, however, it would appear to yield some interesting results and, indeed, might call into question even the most seemingly well-established examples of religious expression. The debate on whether or not the wearing by Muslim women of a headscarf is mandated by Islam is well known – with a number of scholars denying that it is a tenet of the faith at all but, rather, a voluntarily assumed practice.[80] Roman Catholic Christians claiming a religious obligation to wear a crucifix will find this deeply contested within the Christian tradition – some Protestants regard the display of a crucifix (a visual image of God the Son) as breaking the second of the Ten Commandments and thus a grave sin.[81] Even the wearing of a turban by Sikh men has been contested as a religious obligation. This is on the basis that the actual requirement in Sikhism under the *Khalsa* (a ritual instituted by the last of the ten gurus of Sikhism) is for hair to remain uncut, not to be covered by a turban.[82] The turban, in fact, started life as simply the most practical way of achieving this.[83]

79   See Ahdar and Leigh, *Religious Freedom in the Liberal State*, 158–63.
80   See S Benhabib, *The Claims of Culture: Equality and Diversity in the Global Era* (Princeton, NJ: Princeton University Press 2002), 94–100.
81   This is an application of the Reformed (Calvinist) interpretation of Deuteronomy 5: 8 ('You shall not make you any graven image, or any likeness of anything that is in heaven above, or that is in the earth beneath, or that is in the waters beneath the earth').
82   Bedi, 'Debate: What is so Special About Religion?' 239.
83   W McLeod, 'The Turban: Symbol of Sikh Identity', in P. Singh and N Barrier (eds), *Sikh Identity: Continuity and Change* (New Delhi: Manohar, 1999), 61.

Thus it might appear that, under a religion-led approach to identifying legitimate forms of religious expression, there is danger of finding limited support for a number of forms of apparently religious expression in which a large number of followers of particular religions engage. However, this need not be the case. This problem only arises if the bases of religious belief are approached narrowly or selectively and a broader approach should provide a surer foundation for identifying legitimate forms of religious expression. Religious belief systems are in fact derived from a range of religious authorities. Audi is helpful in identifying such a range within the Judeo-Christian tradition, although also claims an application (in varying degrees) to other religious traditions. He identifies five sources:

> (1) scripture; (2) non-scriptural religious authority, especially that of the clergy, but including the authority of the relevant community, such as the religion's theological community if there is one; (3) tradition, which may be quite authoritative, including as it does presumptions regarding one's religions obligations and also habits that, whether or not they have a scriptural or theological endorsement, can have strong momentum in a community; (4) religious experience; and (5) natural theology.[84]

Some of these categories may be problematic – above all 'religious experience' which, unless 'triangulated' by another source of authority, runs the risk of creating precisely the kind of individualised religious expression already considered. This form of authority aside, Audi's inclusion of recognised 'secondary' forms of authority (akin to the writings of the Church Fathers, for example) and of well-established and widely shared (though not necessarily universal) religious tradition, is extremely helpful. Edge considers that English courts historically have shown a preference for drawing on well-established textual authority (which he calls 'the wisdom of the dead') and, in more recent times, an increasing reliance on the contemporary practices of religious communities themselves.[85] Allowing additional sources of authority such as these would legitimise the Islamic headscarf, as representing a well-established religious tradition. The turban would be legitimised on the same basis, given that over time it has developed a deep symbolic importance crucial to the way in which many Sikhs understand their religious identity.[86] The wearing of a crucifix could perhaps also represent a well-established, if controversial, religious tradition and might also derive authority from a secondary source; as Addison notes, the Seventh Ecumenical Council of 787AD set out a Christian duty to venerate and

---

84   Audi, *Religious Commitment and Secular Reason*, 117.
85   P Edge, 'Determining Religion in English Courts' (2012) 1 *Oxford Journal of Law and Religion* 402, 409–11.
86   McLeod, 'The Turban', 58–60.

display certain objects such as icons, statues and crosses.[87] What the religion-led approach might also do is indicate the contexts in which forms of religious expression might be regarded as legitimate. It is one thing to wear a crucifix on good authority and another to feel *obliged* to do this in the workplace – the religion-led approach would yield information as to why and when certain forms of religious expression are required by religious adherents.

Despite the merits of this approach, particularly in its broadest terms, there remain problems. Those who view religious practices as 'frequently contested and subject to change'[88] are unlikely to support an approach (heavily weighted towards ancient sources and historical traditions) which would appear to be hostile to recognising the legitimacy of innovation in religious practice. Secondly, and perhaps most significantly, a religion-led approach may require courts to involve themselves in some way in determining the requirements of religious doctrine. For many commentators this represents an unacceptable intrusion by the courts into an area beyond its legitimate scope.[89] Others, however, appear to be more sanguine, pointing to the likely reliance on expert witnesses from within a particular religious tradition who would be (presumably) steeped in the knowledge and experience of the religious practices in question.[90]

The importance of sincerity

Thus far, a range of possible approaches towards recognising 'legitimate' religious beliefs and practices has been considered. Whatever the approach taken there is a hugely significant question which must also be addressed – is the individual sincere in the religious beliefs she holds? This question is clearly absolutely central if no other test of legitimacy is applied. However, it is also important in cases where religious beliefs and forms of expression are accepted as legitimate for doctrinal or historical reasons. It is one thing to invoke a belief, particularly if there is a perceived benefit in so doing; it is another to actually hold that belief with integrity. An investigation of sincerity should therefore greatly assist in separating 'sham' claims and claims based on genuine belief and practice. It is to this issue of sincerity – how to conceptualise and measure it – that this discussion will now turn.[91]

---

87 N Addison, *Religious Discrimination and Hatred Law* (Abingdon: Routledge Cavendish, 2006), 72.
88 B Parekh, *Rethinking Multiculturalism: Cultural Diversity and Political Theory*, 2nd ed. (London: Macmillan, 2000), 148. Parekh sees religion as a manifestation of culture (see discussion in Chapter 3).
89 See, for example, Ahdar and Leigh, *Religious Freedom in the Liberal State*, 156.
90 See, for example, Ogilvy, 'And Then There Was One'.
91 For a more detailed analysis, see A Hambler, 'Establishing sincerity in religion and belief claims: a question of consistency' (2011) 13 *Ecclesiastical Law Journal* 146. The discussion in this section also draws heavily on that article.

A helpful definition of 'sincerity' from a court's perspective is that provided in *Syndicat Northcrest* v. *Amselem* as 'imply[ing] an honesty of belief and the court's role is to ensure a presently asserted belief is in good faith, neither fictitious nor capricious and that it is not an artifice'.[92] An individual's 'sincerity' is generally framed as a question of fact for the court to determine.[93] As the court is therefore required to engage in some form of legal inquiry, it seems not inappropriate to refer to this as a 'test'.

A test of sincerity can be criticised on an operational level as at best somewhat elusive in spite of judicial efforts to define it more clearly.[94] Indeed, it may be so elusive that courts in the West have tended, as Ahdar and Leigh note, to accept all but the most 'palpably phoney' claims.[95] This being the case, and given its key role in differentiating between worthy and unworthy claims, there is surely merit in subjecting the issue of individual sincerity to greater levels of scrutiny with a view to developing a more consistent and robust approach which might be useful to both courts and, in modified terms, to those such as employers who might sometimes be required to take a view on whether or not a professed religious faith is genuine.

Sadurski, whilst rather sanguine about the need to do so, explores this issue from a judicial perspective and identifies three elements for measuring the sincerity of a claim for religious exemption:

i.   the conformity of this claim with the written or empirically verifiable traditions and proscriptions of the religion or the cult;
ii. congruence between the professed religious tenets and one's actions; and
iii. the willingness to undertake alternative duties and burdens, equally onerous but neutral from the point of view of that religion's proscriptions, etc.[96]

Unless applied at a very basic level indeed, the first element does look rather like a test of doctrine (in its loosest sense), which is surely, in reality, quite different from a sincerity test. The second and third elements are, however, more compelling. With regard to the third, certainly in the

---

92   *Amselem* [52].
93   *R (on the application of Williamson and others)* v. *Secretary of State for Education and Employment and Others* [2005] UKHL 15 [22].
94   Noonan points out some of the ambiguities between truth and sincerity in religious experience. For example, a religious truth can be believed to be literally true or metaphorically true – do both positions equate to 'sincere' belief? See J Noonan, 'How Sincere Do You Have to Be to Be Religious?' (1988) *University of Illinois Law Review* 713.
95   Ahdar and Leigh, *Religious Freedom in the Liberal State*, 142.
96   W Sadurski, *Moral Pluralism and Legal Neutrality* (Kluwer 1990), 174 (enumeration, mine).

workplace, requiring that a religious employee makes some form of reciprocal 'sacrifice' in exchange for being excused from a particular task on religious grounds, might quickly reveal how far there is a genuinely held desire to abstain from that task. For example, a Muslim factory worker might authenticate the genuineness of a request for time off for prayers on Friday afternoons by accepting a potentially unattractive Saturday evening shift as an alternative. However, not all occupations and not all religious beliefs lend themselves to such an easy trade-off. The case of *Ahmad* v. *Inner London Education Authority*,[97] for example, illustrates the difficulty of finding an appropriate time trade-off in a profession with fixed hours such as that of a school teacher. In this case, Ahmad, a Muslim, wished to absent himself from the classroom on Friday afternoons for prayer. The only trade-off which could be contemplated was the financially disadvantageous one of a reduction in wages to reflect the reduction in hours worked – and this was not acceptable to him. It is more problematic still to see how the principle of reciprocal sacrifice might work in cases where the right to wear a particular form of religious dress or adornment is the key claim.[98] The immediate difficulty would involve quantifying the 'loss' to another party (such as an employer) and the second very practical difficulty would lie in quantifying an appropriate means by which 'compensation' might be made for this loss.

Sadurski's second element, however, appears to be potentially more all-embracing of the various ways in which individuals might manifest their religious beliefs. This element is very close, if applied systematically, to what might be termed 'a consistency test'. In brief, this could be defined as a measure of how far the individual's actions are in conformity with the religious belief or beliefs on which he is relying. This is potentially a very useful means of measuring sincerity as it relies on the congruence between belief and action,[99] and is worthy of fuller development.

It would seem that something very like a consistency 'test' was considered by the ECtHR in *Kosteki v. the Former Yugoslav Republic*.[100] Kosteki (on two separate occasions) took a day's unauthorised absence at the expense of his employer, the Electric Company of Macedonia, during Muslim festivals. On both occasions, he was fined by his employer as a disciplinary sanction. In a subsequent court case, the Bitola Municipal Court found that

---

97 [1976] ICR 461.
98 Unless of course the sacrifice was of the job itself through resignation or willingness to accept dismissal – although this is more likely to be a final resort than a first option. See more generally on this issue, P Jones, 'Bearing the Consequences of Belief' in R Goodwin and P Pettit (eds), *Contemporary Political Philosophy, An Anthology*, 2nd ed. (Oxford: Blackwell, 2006).
99 This is by no means a new concept; see James 2: 14, 'What does it profit, my brethren, if someone says he has faith but does not have works? Can faith save him?'.
100 [2006] ECHR 403.

Kosteki had not provided evidence that he was a Muslim. His previous conduct weighed heavily with the court which noted that: he had never been absent from work during a Muslim holiday before a particular date; instead, he had celebrated Christian holidays; his way of life suggested that he was a Christian and both this parents were Christians. The approach by the Court was challenged by Kosteki under Article 9. The ECtHR dismissed the case and judged that a requirement to show evidence of allegiance to a particular faith was 'not unreasonable or disproportionate' and that it was within the scope of the margin of appreciation for member states to require this.

It should perhaps be noted at this point that there may be occasions where an individual appears to have acted inconsistently but where this may not necessarily be indicative of insincerity. Inconsistency may sometimes result from fear or other pressures;[101] an unconscious double standard rooted in an individual interpretation (or, to others, misinterpretation) of religious doctrine;[102] or may be the natural effect of a very recent religious conversion or decision to take one's religion more seriously.[103] Thus, the test should be approached with caution and contextual factors fully explored. With appropriate provisos, however, it is submitted that a consistency test is nevertheless an extremely useful aid for determining sincerity in religion and belief claims.

The nature of the workplace

The term 'workplace' has been used in this chapter (and will be elsewhere in this book) in broad terms, to be inclusive of a variety of fora (in the private, public, quasi-public and voluntary sectors) where people work under various different contractual arrangements, such as employees (full time, part-time or fixed term), office-holders, self-employed contractors, casual workers and agency workers).

Although in UK law there is a distinction made between the broad categories of 'employees' and 'workers' (employees work under 'a contract of service' and workers do not necessarily do so),[104] in practice this distinction

---

101   See *McClintock* v. *Department for Constitutional Affairs* [2007] UKEAT 0223/07/3110; [2008] IRLR 29, where a Christian magistrate did not initially admit the religious basis for his objections to making same-sex adoption orders.

102   As Lord Nicholls put it in *Williamson*, '[e]ach individual is at liberty to hold his own religious beliefs, however irrational or inconsistent they may seem to some.' [22].

103   For a more general analysis of the shifting priorities which may be accorded to religious beliefs by individuals, see S Leader, 'Freedom and Futures: Personal Priorities, Institutional Demands and Freedom of Religion (2007) *Modern Law Review* 713.

104   Employment Rights Act 1996, s 230.

is of limited consequence when discussing religion and belief in the workplace, as the protections under discrimination law apply equally to workers and employees.[105] The only substantial area where the distinction is significant is in the discussion of the protections of unfair dismissal law – these apply only to the narrow category of employees.

There is a perhaps a more significant distinction to be drawn, which is relevant to the analysis in this book, between public and private sector workers. It can be argued that public sector workers, perhaps particularly office holders, because they carry out the functions of the government (for example, as judges, magistrates, registrars, tax officials) could be said to 'represent' the state in ways that private sector workers clearly do not. If they represent the state then, under one argument, they should be more constrained in their religious expression, particularly if that form of religious expression might be perceived to have negative implications for particular communities, such as people of other religious faiths or gay and lesbian people, otherwise the impression may be given that the state is supportive of discriminatory conduct against particular social groups and the perceived neutrality of the services provided by government would therefore be compromised. Such arguments will be considered in more detail when applied to the office of Registrar of Marriages in Chapter 6.[106]

In addition to legal obligations or protections under UK employment law, workers in the UK are likely to be bound also by organisational internal policies and procedures, although these are often most detailed for employees (and may sometimes form part of the employment contract). Some public office holders will be bound by additional regulations of various kinds, such as a professional oath of office (for example in the case of judges or legislators). Members of professions will also be regulated by professional bodies, some of which have had authority conveyed upon them, by statutory instrument, to issue codes of conduct and other binding regulations on their members, and with the power to police these – an important example of this is the General Medical Council in the United Kingdom. This means that some groups of employees will be bound by two sets of 'regulations': those applying to them by virtue of their specific professions and those applying to them more generally in their capacity as employees of particular organisations.

---

105 Equality Act 2010, ss 39–52.
106 A second distinction can be made between the two workplaces, given that the state is the ultimate employer in the public sector and so cannot absolve itself of responsibility for determining the questions of freedom of religious expression in the public sector workplace in the way in which it theoretically can in relation to the private sector (see the discussion of the 'laissez-faire' model in Chapter 3).

Conclusion

Two central concerns have occupied this chapter. The first has been to seek to map out the various ways in which an individual might express his religious convictions and to consider the consequent effects, if any, on the workplace and, in particular, other actors therein. It has been suggested that certain forms of religious expression, those which are overtly religious in nature, have the strongest potential to pose a 'problem', whilst not discounting the possibility that expression which is less overt and even identity and belief itself may, in some instances, lead to conflicts of some kind – although instances are likely to be rare. With this in mind, the focus of the next chapter will be concerned primarily with outward forms of manifestation of religion and the potential legal interest in regulating any resultant conflicts within the workplace.

In recognising the potential for conflict, the second part of this chapter was premised on the resulting desirability of seeking to limit any recognition of the right to expression of religious belief to situations where such belief can be considered 'legitimate'. Whilst a measure of agreement can be found that only sincerely held beliefs should be recognised (and it has been argued here that the consistency of individual conduct, with appropriate provisos, should be the key test to determine this), opinions differ on any further filters which should be applied. Those commentators supportive of religious rights are divided on this issue. Nevertheless, it is perhaps possible to identify two emergent positions. Those who adopt a relativist approach to religion, for whom there is a blurring of boundaries between religion, belief and free expression (all of which are regarded as fluid), are most likely to be supportive of a form of 'individual' subjective understanding of legitimate religious expression. Those who adopt a more traditional approach to understanding religions as clear, bounded and (to some extent) complete systems governing the central questions of human life, may be attracted to the less individualised approaches, perhaps particularly the religion-led approach outlined here. For those with such a traditional interpretation of religion and its role, the individual-subjective approach is potentially dangerously reductionist; as Ogilvy warns, in a modern secularist state, 'religious belief will be reduced to whimsy' if the only legal test of legitimacy applied is that of personal sincerity.[107]

It may be that a religion-led approach to identifying legitimate forms of religious expression (such as that outlined earlier) is to be preferred. Taking into account a range of recognised sources of religious beliefs, practices and traditions (such as those proposed by Audi) would help to prevent courts from taking an unduly narrow approach to identifying legitimate religious practices (which might follow, for example, from reliance on one source alone such as a sacred text). At the same time, limiting the range of

107 Ogilvy, 'And Then There Was One', 204.

reference points (albeit in a nuanced and generous way) would help to guard against an unattractive and ultimately unmanageable 'free-for-all' as individuals adopt the language of religion to refer to quite individualised 'spiritual' practices of various kinds. As has been seen, an indulgent over-inclusiveness risks widening any available legal protection unsustainably. More concerning, as Ogilvy recognises, is that it risks trivialising religious expression in a way which might provide useful ammunition to those generally hostile to it. Why such hostility might arise will be considered in the next chapter when the discussion will turn from the nature and legitimacy of religious expression to the position taken in response to incidence of religious expression in the workplace by the other actors referred to by Ogilvy and, in particular, the state.

3 Restricting or guaranteeing religious freedom in the workplace: legal models

Introduction

The purpose of this chapter is to consider the possible legal and policy approaches which might be taken within a modern liberal state towards the restriction or guarantee of religious freedom of expression in the workplace, ranging from a deliberate strategy of suppression to the provision of an absolute guarantee. Each model, taken individually, would represent respectively a surprisingly homogenous approach towards state intervention in respect of religious freedom in the workplace. In reality, it is likely that a given state may, over time, rely on aspects drawn from several of these models and so a complex patchwork of approaches, some of which may be at points mutually contradictory, is likely to emerge. Nevertheless, there is value for analytical purposes in examining and critiquing each model individually.

In this chapter, six models of state approaches are first presented and briefly described. Following this, each model is considered individually in more detail, to explore the respective underlying rationale and implications and to offer a critique.

The six models

I Exclusion

Under the first model, the law acts specifically to exclude religious expression from the workplace. Within this overall approach, characterised by a desire to suppress, there are degrees of exclusion. Entirely exclusionary approaches, such as the imposition of a religious test to deny absolutely workers who identify themselves as holding religious beliefs from entry into the workplace, would usually be characterised as illiberal and are therefore likely to lie outside the parameters of this study.

In a liberal society, it is surely more likely as a general but not an absolute rule, that the focus would be less on workers' actual (or suspected) beliefs and more on the ways in which those beliefs find expression in the workplace (as discussed in the previous chapter). Here, there might be possible justifications for imposing restrictions, for example, on particular forms of dress, or the right to follow conscience, or on workers to trying to influence others from a religious perspective.

II Support for a preferred historic religion

Under the second model, the law supports the expression of a preferred religion or religious denomination in the workplace. This religion may be the established religion or, historically, the majority religion in a particular state. For example, certain government offices or posts might be reserved for adherents of a particular religious faith. In seventeenth-century England, this was achieved through the Tests Acts of 1672 and 1678, which required that all public officeholders should take the oaths of allegiance to the Crown and acknowledge royal supremacy over the Church, denounce transubstantiation and receive the sacrament of Holy Communion according to the rites of the Church of England. Thus, non-Anglicans were disbarred from all public office.[1] In a modern liberal state, preference for an historic religion is unlikely to involve such blatant discrimination against others. However, if examples of mild preferential treatment for a preferred historic religion continue to exist, this may result from a lingering desire to preserve its cultural value (or contribution to the national 'heritage').

III Laissez-faire

Under the third model, the state does not consider it has a sufficiently strong interest in supporting or restricting workplace religious expression. It allows employers to determine how much freedom to offer employees and employees, in turn, can accept or reject those terms. This model is clearly applicable to private enterprises but its application to government workers is more problematic, given that the model gives discretion to employers to determine the level and forms of religious expression to be tolerated – the state as employer (rather than as legislator) would need to determine this for its own workers.

IV 'Islands of exclusivity'

There is a tradition within Christianity of separation between 'sacred' work and 'secular' work.[2] This tradition was based on an understanding of the binary division that the monastic movement developed in the fourth and

---

1 Until the passage of the Sacramental Test Act 1828 and the Roman Catholic Relief Act 1829.
2 See I Benson, 'Notes Towards a (Re)Definition of the "Secular"' (2000) 33 *University of British Columbia Law Review* 519, for a discussion of both the origins of this distinction and the modern misuse of the same terminology.

fifth centuries, creating small communities of individuals, living, working and worshipping together, having voluntarily accepted considerable restrictions on their liberty, including famously the vows of poverty, chastity and obedience.[3]

A modern state, preferring a secularised workplace, may wish to draw inspiration from this to legislate to provide 'safe havens' (or 'islands of exclusivity')[4] where groups of people with particular strong religious convictions could work together, with their right to associate in this way protected by law, although how far this might extend is likely to be more controversial.

V Protection for religion

Under this model, there is legal recognition for a right of religious expression in the workplace and a degree of corresponding protection, either through negative or positive means. Negative means might involve the employment of a basic form of anti-discrimination law preventing direct discrimination and possibly indirect discrimination.[5] Positive means might involve the creation of statutory rights which protect religious expression or the use of a more advanced form of anti-discrimination law preventing harassment and/or requiring the promotion of equality for religious employees in the workplace.[6] A variant of this model involves the widening of 'religion' to include 'belief' and thus offer equivalent protections to non-theistic belief systems in the same way as to theistic religions.

VI Protection for minority religions

This model is a variant of the fifth model. Under this model, however, the focus is on protection for religious minorities and assumes that they are disadvantaged groups. Specifically protecting the religious traditions of these minority groups, in a variety of contexts, is considered desirable until such time as these groups are no longer perceived (by themselves or others) as suffering disadvantage. If and when such a point is reached, then any 'special' protections may be lifted.

---

3   For a short account of the rise of the movement, see M Dunn, *The Emergence of Monasticism: From the Desert Fathers to the Early Middle Ages* (Oxford: Blackwell, 2003).

4   A Esau, '"Islands of Exclusivity": Religious Organizations and Employment Discrimination' (1999) 33 *University of British Columbia Law Review* 720.

5   So-called 'second generation discrimination law'; see B Hepple, M Coussey and T Choudhury, *Equality: A New Framework. Report of the Independent Review of the Enforcement of UK Anti-Discrimination Legislation* (Oxford: Hart, 2000).

6   So-called 'fourth generation discrimination law', ibid.

Summary

Each of the six models presented here rests upon the adoption of a number of assumptions and values within a modern state, although each can be traced to a particular principle. For the first, the principle is to ascribe most value to secularism. For the second, the principle is to value a particular religion either for its own sake or for its role in the national heritage. For the third, the principle is the primacy in the workplace of freedom of contract. For the fourth, the principle is to make special accommodations for those out of step with the social and economic 'mainstream'. For the fifth, the principle is to ascribe (some form) of value to religious expression within the social and economic mainstream. For the sixth, a guarantee of freedom of religious expression is one means of correcting group disadvantage for members of minority groups. All of these principles require explanation and justification and are open to critique. This is the purpose of the rest of this chapter. The overall headings used when setting out the models will be employed a second time for ease.

Exclusion

As a general rule, it is religious expression rather than belief which is likely to be the target of any state interest in exclusion and this will be the primary area for discussion in this section. Nevertheless, the possibility was raised earlier that there is at least one example in a liberal society where exclusion of individuals from certain employment positions might be justified on the basis of belief rather than expression. This is on the grounds of national security where the religious belief in question is either considered subversive in its own right or a number of adherents of that religion are thought to be (or likely to be) engaged in activities which in some way are subversive of state interests. This possibility is considered briefly now, as a preface to the more substantive issue of religious expression.

Religious belief

The notion that individuals might be excluded from employment because of belief is most likely to be justified as a result of the perceived threat to the state that they pose. Thus, it is likely that the roles in question will be few in number and in areas where there is potential to do grave damage to the interests of the state. Such roles are therefore likely to encompass a restricted number of public appointments (such as officers of the security services, officials in the foreign office, the police and members of the armed forces) and an even smaller number of private sector roles (such as employees of government defence contractors or private security services commissioned by the government).

Prospective and current occupants of such roles might go through a 'vetting procedure' of some kind. The purpose of this vetting procedure will be to identify the potential threat (if any) that they pose. Such vetting in a modern liberal state will aim to 'exclude the disloyal or those considered prone to disloyalty' as opposed to 'those who appear to lack the necessary impartial public stance'.[7] Nevertheless, it may be a difficult distinction, in practice, to identify.

It is unlikely that a vetting process would be aimed at the exclusion of employees with religious convictions *per se*. Nevertheless, this may be an indirect result of the process. Writing in 1994, Lustgarten and Leigh insightfully predicted that the list of those attitudes to be excluded with potential for subversion 'could be extended in future (say) to views such as radical Muslim fundamentalism'.[8] Thus, the link is established between religiously motivated ideas which could be characterised as political and which have the potential to subvert the state. The logical conclusion therefore is that individuals with particular religious beliefs might qualify for exclusion through a vetting process.

Many people would consider that a strong case might exist for such exclusion where the national interest is threatened in some way, particularly if a terrorist threat is suspected. Nevertheless, it is perhaps worth considering in more detail exactly the basis on which an 'exclusionary' decision might be made following vetting. Lustgarten and Leigh provide the following examples of factors considered in the British so-called 'enhanced positive vetting' process of the early 1990s. Not only did the process involve inquiries into the personal history of the individual but also details of relatives, contacts with individuals in 'suspect' countries (then the communist and former communist nations of the east), and 'all visits abroad since the age of 14'.[9]

Within such a regime, it is not difficult to see that the clear possibility might exist that an individual, entirely innocent of holding subversive beliefs, might be excluded from certain employment roles by virtue of an unfortunate, even unintended, association with someone less innocent. In *Home Office v. Tariq*,[10] for example, the Home Office successfully appealed a Court of Appeal judgment in favour of a Muslim immigration officer who had his security clearance withdrawn on the grounds of national security when the Home Office learned that his brother and cousin were being investigated for alleged Islamic terrorist offences. The Home Office justified its stance on the basis that his 'close association with individuals suspected of involvement in plans to mount terrorist attacks' made Tariq

---

7   L Lustgarten and I Leigh, *In From the Cold: National Security and Parliamentary Democracy* (Oxford: Clarendon Press, 1994), 128.
8   Ibid., 136.
9   Ibid., 137.
10   [2011] UKSC 35.

'vulnerable to attempts to exert undue influence on [him] to abuse his position'.[11] In another example, a Muslim police officer who applied to join a protection unit for senior politicians was reportedly excluded from such employment because the imam at the mosque that his family attended was suspected of links with a terrorist organisation.[12] The possibility of an 'unfair' outcome from such a vetting procedure, at times indirectly restrictive of those with a particular religious identity, will be magnified in proportion to the extent to which 'subjective assessments of character, attitude and risk' are intrinsic to the vetting procedure employed.[13]

It should be noted from the argument presented thus far that outright exclusion of people with religious beliefs, however problematic in practice, can be justified in a liberal democracy only on the basis of genuine concerns for the security of the state or its citizens. There is, however, the further possibility, considered in Chapter 2, that public distaste, either real or imagined, for a particular religious worldview to lead to the exclusion from certain workplace roles of adherents of that religion. Reconciling this within a liberal polity is likely, however, to be much more problematic.

Religious expression: rationale and implications

The discussion now turns from the relatively rare overt examples of exclusion because of religious belief from certain employment roles to the more contested area of exclusion on the basis of religious expression.[14]

The notion that the expression of religion or religious beliefs, verbally, through dress and grooming or through conscientious objection (as discussed in Chapter 2), might be excluded from the workplace at first glance appears somewhat illiberal and therefore requires early justification. In order to seek such justification, it is necessary to first consider a significant debate about the role of religion in public life. The essential question on which the debate rests is how far is it permissible for a person 'A' to offer reasons for courses of action which will restrict the liberty of another person 'B' that are based on the religious beliefs of A (which B does not share)? The reason the question is pressing is the desire to avoid the strife which might be caused within a pluralistic, liberal society based on conflicting religious and non-religious beliefs.

---

11   Ibid. [5].
12   See 'Muslim PC taken off Blair guard duties claims discrimination' *London Evening Standard* (London, 7 November 2006), 5.
13   Lustgarten and Leigh, *In From the Cold*, 137.
14   Some of the material in this section was first published in an abridged form in A Hambler, 'A No-Win Situation for Public Officials with Faith Convictions' (2010) 12 *Ecclesiastical Law Journal* 3.

In response to this question, Rawls developed an influential theory (which will be referred to here as 'the 'public reason' requirement),[15] a theory subsequently adopted, with significant variations in terminology and application, by a number of liberal political philosophers such as Audi,[16] Greenawalt,[17] Lamore,[18] Nagel[19] and Habermas.[20] In brief, Rawls believes that it is necessary, when engaging in debate on what he terms 'constitutional essentials', to refrain from presenting arguments based on what he calls 'comprehensive views', a term embracing both religious and other worldviews and defined helpfully by Greenawalt as 'overall perspectives that provide a (relatively) full account of moral responsibilities and fulfilling human lives'.[21] Constitutional essentials include not only the fundamental principles on which a particular political democracy rests but also 'equal basic rights and liberties of citizenship ... such as the right to vote and to participate in politics, liberty of conscience, freedom of thought and of association, as well as the protections of the rule of law'.[22]

Rawls believes that on these issues (particularly if they involve the possibility of the coercion of others),[23] legislators and public office holders, as well as citizens who wish to exhibit 'civic virtue', have a duty of civility to employ arguments which rest on foundations accepted as legitimate by all 'reasonable' citizens. These foundations are rooted in a so-called 'overlapping consensus' of opinion between holders of various different comprehensive views, with a consensus emerging from a disciplined effort to identify those 'values that the others can reasonably be expected to endorse'[24] within the area of overlap – public discussion based on anything else is *ultra vires* as it fails the test of 'public reason'.

Rawls later added a 'proviso' to his theory, in which he accepted the legitimacy of 'introducing at any time our comprehensive doctrine ...

---

15   Rawls argument is first articulated in his book, *Political Liberalism* (New York: Columbia University Press, 1993), 227–54; and then, with some revisions, in J Rawls, 'The Idea of Public Reason Revisited' (1997) 64 *University of Chicago Law Review* 765.

16   R Audi, *Religious Commitment and Secular Reason* (Cambridge: Cambridge University Press, 2000).

17   K Greenawalt, *Private Consciences and Public Reasons* (New York: Oxford University Press, 1995).

18   C Lamore, *Patterns of Moral Complexity* (Cambridge: Cambridge University Press, 1987).

19   T Nagel, *Equality and Partiality* (New York: Oxford University Press, 1991).

20   For his current position, see J Habermas, 'Religion in the Public Sphere' (2006) 14 *European Journal of Philosophy* 1.

21   Greenawalt, *Private Consciences and Public Reasons*, 5.

22   Rawls, *Political Liberalism*, 227.

23   Audi points out that 'most laws and public policies do restrict human conduct to some extent and the more restrictive the laws or policies in question, the stronger the relevant obligation', Audi, *Religious Commitment and Secular Reason*, 87–8.

24   Rawls, *Political Liberalism*, 226.

provided that in due course we give properly public reasons to support the principles and policies our comprehensive doctrine is said to support'.[25] In other words, a religious individual may introduce arguments based on religious beliefs but is required to justify them absolutely according to the demands of public reason. The duty of civility is therefore breached if an individual introduces religious arguments which cannot be justified by another (very different) route. Audi goes further by introducing another precondition, his 'principle of secular motivation', which requires that not only must one offer adequate secular reasons but one must also be motivated by those reasons to the extent that one would still advocate a particular course of action even if one's additional religious reasons were removed.[26]

Having set out the essence of the 'public reason' theory, the discussion now turns to an application to workers. Rawls' theory is explicitly applied to public officials (above all judges) who must be guided in their decision making and public pronouncements by the dictates of public reason. As regards public sector workers more generally, it is logical to conclude, with Pava, that those in positions of authority of various kinds in the public sector are also bound by the requirements of public reason in the execution of their duties.[27] It is possible to see an application of the public reason requirement to workers in the private sector also, although this requires a slightly greater stretching of the theory. As Pava notes, although Rawls does identify social institutions within which actors are exempt from the requirements of public reason; the business organisation is not amongst these but neither is the business organisation specifically cited as a public institution where a public reason requirement might be inferred.[28]

A relevant argument has already been presented in support of the notion that the workplace is (to a certain extent) part of the public square, at least from the perspective of the religious employee.[29] From a secular perspective, such a conclusion may also be reached. Pava, although he allows the business organisation only 'quasi-public' status, notes that two key variables in a theory of liberalism are membership and power and that these concepts can also be applied to the workplace: '[m]ore often than not one is a member, in a broad sense of a corporation whether he likes it or not, and one is subject to corporate power, even if it is against one's will'.[30]

Thus, if Pava's argument is accepted, then it is possible to extend the theory so that workers in the private sector (or at least private corporations

25 Rawls, 'Public Reason Revisited', 776.
26 Audi, *Religious Commitment and Secular Reason*, 96.
27 M Pava, 'Religious Business Ethics and Political Liberalism: An Integrative Approach' (1998) 17 *Journal of Business Ethics* 1633.
28 Ibid.
29 See discussion in this chapter (above).
30 Pava, 'Religious Business Ethics and Political Liberalism', 1637.

exhibiting some or all of the features considered above) are also covered by the requirements of public reason in the exercise of any authority they may have over others, because such 'corporate' power can be coercive of others in the same way as power exercised at a political level. This conclusion is apparently shared by Greenawalt, in respect of chief executive officers of organisations, although, frustratingly, he does not elaborate.[31]

Thus far, it has been noted that, according to Rawls and others, public reasons must be offered in support of any actions which might lead to the coercion of others – for Audi, it is necessary to go further and have a personal commitment to these reasons as well – and that the theory can be applied to public office, the public sector and the private workplace. However, to infer from this a case for legal suppression of religious expression in any or all of those three domains requires two further steps.

The first step is to deal with an obvious objection to this inference which is that Rawls in particular is explicitly clear that his public reason requirement is intended to impose 'a duty of civility' and not a legal obligation. However, the difficulty of relying merely on moral suasion is apparent if it is assumed that the problem to which Rawls proposes a solution (that of discord based on conflicting religious and non-religious world views in a pluralistic society or organisation) is so pressing as to require a greater imposition than mere reliance on the attractions of (what is held out to be) virtuous behaviour alone.[32] If a state was persuaded to such a view, it might indeed seek to impose public reason, in some form, through legal as well as moral means.[33] Finding an overt legal mechanism to achieve this is likely to be very difficult, even impossible, without recourse to non-liberal means. This is not to say that the state might not be able to achieve this in more covert ways. The US Supreme Court has identified a concept in freedom of expression cases known as the 'chilling effect'. At its most general, this concept refers to the recognition of 'the potential deterrent effect [on freedom of expression] of a vague, or more commonly, an overbroad statute'.[34] By way of example, in *Dombrowski* v. *Pfister*,[35] the US Supreme Court identified that federal laws (against subversion activities) had been used to harass members of a civil rights organisation (through means including search

---

31   Greenawalt, *Private Consciences and Public Reasons*, 163.
32   In dissenting from this view, Wolterstorff points to the far greater incidence of conflict in the twentieth century arising from secular reasons or ideology, see N Wolterstorff, 'Why We Should Reject What Liberalism Tells Us' in P Weithman (ed.), *Religion and Contemporary Liberalism* (Notre Dame, IN: University of Notre Dame Press, 1997), 167.
33   The danger of the forcible imposition by the state of the 'liberal' ideal is identified in M McConnell, 'Why is Religious Liberty the "First Freedom"?' (2000) 21 *Cardozo Law Review* 1243, 1259.
34   F Schauer, 'Fear, Risk and the First Amendment: Unravelling the "Chilling Effect"' (1978) 58 *Boston University Law Review* 685, 685.
35   (1965) 380 U.S. 479.

and seizure and arrest without intention to prosecute); the operation of the anti-subversion statutes had in fact created a 'chilling effect' on the first amendment right of members of the organisation to freedom of expression. It should be noted that the chilling effect does not presuppose malign intent on behalf of lawmakers but rather it results from the inevitable imperfections in the legal system (and indeed may be an unforeseen consequence).[36] Nevertheless, it remains possible that a state (or some of the actors within a state) might actively seek to manufacture such a 'chilling effect', as a conscious and deliberate strategy, by framing or implementing law in such a way as to allow it to be used to suppress conduct incompatible with public reason.

The second difficulty is reconciling a state-imposed public reason requirement with the notion that this would lead to the suppression of religious expression *per se*. Public reason applies to the words or actions of those exercising power or seeking to exercise power, over others. It would therefore most obviously affect at least some forms of verbal religious expression, particularly the justification of decision making on the basis of religious reasons or the imposition of religious practices or opinions on others (particularly subordinates) in the workplace. However, there are some forms of verbal expression of religion where a public reason argument would be more difficult to mount; in such cases, it would be rather more difficult (though not impossible) to convincingly demonstrate that an employee was seeking to 'exercise power' over or otherwise constrain others. Examples in this category might include a member of staff who wishes to invoke God's blessing when talking to clients or colleagues[37] or a nurse who offers to pray for an elderly patient.[38]

Moreover, public reason would not appear, at least at face value, to have anything to say about non-verbal religious expression such as dress, grooming or personal adornment (such as a member of staff at an airline wearing a small cross),[39] nor about negative manifestation of religious convictions through conscientious objection (such as a Muslim checkout assistant refusing to handle alcohol)[40] or for attendance at church services or religious festivals. This is, in fact, a likely conclusion for many as to the limits

---

36   Schauer, 'Fear, Risk and the First Amendment', 688.

37   Reportedly forbidden for employees of Wandsworth Council; see the facts of *Amachree* v. *Wandsworth BC* (2009) ET Case No. 2328606/2009 (discussed in Chapter 8).

38   Caroline Petrie, an NHS bank nurse, was suspended for offering to pray for a patient; see C Gammell, '"Thousands are at risk" in NHS after nurse in prayer row is suspended' *Daily Telegraph* (London, 4 February 2009), 9; see discussion in Chapter 8.

39   Per the facts of *Eweida* v. *British Airways* [2010] EWCA Civ. 80; [2010] IRLR 322, discussed in Chapter 7.

40   See D Foggo and C Thompson, 'Muslim checkout staff get an alcohol opt-out clause', *Sunday Times* (London, 30 September 2007), 3.

of the reach of a public reason requirement. However, there are strong arguments that the analysis need not be restricted to verbal expression: non-verbal religious expression is also considered by some to be capable of exercising power over others.[41] The most obvious example of this is the Islamic headscarf-*hijab* or a more conservative variant of it such as the *burka*, the wearing of which is sometimes perceived as capable of pressuris-ing, even intimidating, other women of the same faith to conform to conservative Islamic values.[42] As such (under a public reason analysis), it is as potentially capable as verbal forms of religious expression, such as pros-elytism, of creating disharmony and discord in the workplace (as elsewhere).

Thus, the imposition of a public reason requirement could be a power-ful stepping stone towards the suppression of many forms of religious expression, not merely verbal expression. Certainly, a number of secularists might seek to pursue, as a logical extension of the suppression of religion-based verbal expression in the workplace, the suppression of other forms of religious expression in pursuit of the (apparent) overall aim of harmony within a religiously plural society and organisation.

Critique

There are significant objections to this position. The extension of the public reason requirement from a matter of voluntary restraint based on civility to a matter of legal enforcement would amount to an illiberal restraint on liberty and is firmly ruled out by Rawls.[43] Nevertheless, given the potential for reaching an illiberal position from the public reason approach (through overt or, perhaps more likely, covert means), it is neces-sary to consider a critique of the pillars on which the notion of a public reason requirement rests. Objections to the public reason requirement tend to cluster around three important points: firstly, the notion that there can be a 'consensus' around what is 'reasonable' is disputed; secondly, the potential incompatibility of the restraint imposed by public reason and the idea of liberal democracy is highlighted; and thirdly, the issue of personal integrity is raised.

One of the most searing critiques of Rawls' theory is to be found in an essay by Paul Campos.[44] Campos is particularly effective in illuminating the apparent lack of a clear explanation as to what 'reasonable' means. Given

---

41   See A Renteln, 'Visual Religious Symbols and the Law' (2004) 47 *American Behavioral Scientist* 1590. The author argues that a Western viewpoint often underplays the powerful significance of religious symbolism particularly to members of minority faiths.
42   See discussion in Chapter 7.
43   Rawls, 'Public Reason Revisited', 769.
44   P Campos, 'Secular Fundamentalism' (1994) 94 *Columbia Law Review* 1814.

that the theory of public reason requires a consensus about what can and what cannot be *reasonably* assumed to be a shared value, then this is a significant gap. Campos thus opens up the fact that what is 'reasonable' may not necessarily be reached through the 'consensus' of 'reasonable people' with the apparent ease that Rawls, and others, seem to assume. Even if it were possible to identify such a 'reasonable consensus', it would not follow that religiously minded people would necessarily be persuaded by the consequent duty of civility (an obligation to fellow humans) to adhere to it. Religious people feel they have a higher calling (an obligation to God) which, if it were to conflict with a liberal duty of civility, may well be the overriding motivation. After all, as Wolgast puts it, '[c]itizens have to live with their God and their consciences as well as the requirements of citizenship, and must harmonize the various moral demands as best they can'.[45]

Moreover, as Dworkin (in his later writings) observes, the objection may run deeper still. If people with religious convictions believe that non-believers are wilfully and stubbornly refusing to accept a revealed divine truth, then they may well ask the question, 'Why should they abandon the profound ambitions of their faith simply to satisfy those who persist in their stubbornness?'.[46] To succumb would be less a duty of civility then an act of surrender to hostile pressure and is likely to be deeply unattractive.

Secondly, as Wolterstorff points out, there is an inherent tension in the idea that people whose primary motivations are drawn from deep religious conviction, should be constrained epistemologically from drawing on those motivations in public expression (particularly if the result of their argument would effectively be the same as that reached through a secular route, although Wolterstorff's overall argument does not rest on this point). To impose such a restraint on the religious person would, in a sense, violate a core principle of liberal democracy (at least as an 'idea') which 'implies the absence of any such restraint'.[47] As Trigg points out, '[a] restriction on the idea of public reason, confining it to what is generally acceptable, prejudges democratic debate before it has even begun. We cannot be told what cannot be discussed'.[48]

Eberle argues that each citizen should seek, diligently, to provide secular reasons when seeking to coerce others but, if he or she cannot provide

---

45   E Wolgast, 'The Demands of Public Reason' (1994) 94 *Columbia Law Review* 1936, 1942.

46   R Dworkin, *Is Democracy Possible Here?* (Princeton, NJ: Princeton University Press, 2006), 65.

47   Wolterstorff, 'The Role of Religion in Decision and Discussion of Political Issues' in Audi, Robert and Nicholas Wolterstorff, *Religion in the Public Square: The Place of Religious Convictions in Political Debate* (Lanham MD: Rowman and Littlefield, 1997), 77.

48   R Trigg, *Religion in Public Life: Must Faith Be Privatised?* (Oxford: Oxford University Press, 2007), 207.

these, there is no impediment within a liberal society to placing reliance on a religious reason.[49] Habermas argues that religious citizens should try to consider their faith 'reflexively from the outside and to relate it to secular views' (what he calls the 'institutional translation proviso').[50] However, if they cannot find a secular 'translation' for their views, he agrees with Eberle that they should be allowed to express themselves using religious language (at least in 'the informal flows of public communication').[51] Indeed, if this were not permissible, a number of people who wish to make public statements drawn from their religious convictions but are unable to arrive, via a secular rationale, to the same statement would be disenfranchised as they would be unable to comply with the demands of public reason and so would lose their voice on an important issue.

It should be noted, however, that Habermas does not extend his concession into the 'political public sphere and the formal proceedings within political bodies', for which 'translation' into non-religious terms is first required before arguments can be advanced.[52] For public officials then (and citizens who may wish to conform to the strict Rawlsian version of public reason), there must exist the constant requirement to maintain a dichotomy between their 'secular' public and 'religious' private selves[53] – it is not hard to speculate on the possible psychological effects of trying to sustain long term such tension.

Thirdly, the requirements of public reason (per Rawls' version) have been criticised on the basis that, to accommodate views motivated by religious convictions (or those based on other comprehensive views), a degree of deception is required to the extent that an individual is required to put forward these views resting on principles drawn from the overlapping consensus. The individual is not necessarily likely to be particularly committed to (or even personally persuaded by) these principles. Not only is this disingenuous, forcing religiously motivated people to carry 'hidden agendas' but it actually distorts the views being articulated as, arguably, '[o]ne's reasons for holding a position are integral to the position itself'.[54]

In summary, there are sufficient objections to the notion of public reason to suggest that arguments drawn from these principles should not be used to seek to suppress religious expression in the workplace; to do so would actually represent a challenge to the very liberalism which the public reason

---

49   C Eberle, *Religious Convictions in Liberal Politics* (Cambridge: Cambridge University Press, 2002).

50   Habermas, 'Religion in the Public Sphere', 10.

51   Ibid.

52   Ibid.

53   SL Carter, *The Culture of Disbelief: How American Law and Politics Trivialize Religious Devotion* (New York: Basic Books, 1993).

54   Wolgast, 'The Demands of Public Reason', 1943. It should be noted that Audi's principle of secular motivation (see above) resolves this issue of integrity but at a cost of further limiting the free speech of the religious individual.

requirement is said to support. However, there may be a qualification to this argument in respect of legislators and other public officials (both of whom are *inter alia* 'workers'). Even those writers who are opposed in principle to a public reason requirement sometimes concede that it should apply in certain circumstances. For Chaplin, focusing on legislators, this occurs after deliberation has concluded (at which stage there should be no bar to religious argument) and at the point where decisions are taken and publicly justified.[55] Wolterstorff, focusing on the position of public officials, argues (indirectly) that it applies to the way they carry out their duties:

> Accordingly, when people are functioning in the role of executive or judge, the question of whether they personally approve the laws and provisions never arises ... The role of the executive is only to administer and enforce, of judge, to adjudicate. If anyone in the role has moral or religious scruples against doing so, then, depending on how serious the scruples, he or she must get out of the role.[56]

Under this view, the public official is merely charged with implementation not moral reflection on the fundamentals of the policies he or she is required to implement. There is therefore no space for the voicing of objections. This is not to say that Wolterstorff does not accept and welcome the influence (which may be openly expressed) of religious 'comprehensive views' in areas where there may be discretion given to the public official. There is a critical literature on this subject in respect of North American judges and all current writers are broadly agreed that judicial opinion must at times find a basis outside of the boundaries of the usual legal materials and arguments.[57] Writers then differ as to what is acceptable as that basis and whether religious insights should be largely excluded.[58] This is not, of course, the real issue here, where the issue of conscience is (almost axiomatically) outside the range of personal discretion. Within this context, Wolterstorff's conclusion does seem bleak, at least in so far as the words 'he or she must get out of the role' are taken to mean permanent self-exclusion. An alternative approach might be temporary self-exclusion, through principled conscientious objection on religious grounds.

55   J Chaplin, 'Law, Religion and Public Reasoning' (2012) 1 *Oxford Journal of Law and Religion* 319, 336. This is in contrast to Habermas, who would exclude religious argument even from the deliberative stage.
56   Wolterstorff, 'The Role of Religion in Decision and Discussion of Political Issues', 117.
57   See, for example, R Dworkin, *Taking Rights Seriously* (London: Duckworth, 1977), 68–71.
58   Perhaps the most representative writers on the two sides of this particular debate are Greenwalt; see Greenwalt, *Private Consciences and Public Reasons* (New York: Oxford University Press, 1995); and Carter; see for example, S Carter, 'The Religiously Devout Judge', (1989) 64 *Notre Dame Law Review* 932.

Support for a preferred (historic) religion

Rationale and implications

The notion that the expression of one particular religion should be supported whilst others are not rests on the view that religious homogeneity is in the best interests of social stability. Where a measure of tolerance for people of different religious beliefs is permitted, it is likely that this would not extend to influential positions and public offices in society. This has certainly been the active view, with varying degrees of rigour in application, for the best part of the history of Western civilisation since the fall of the Roman Empire.[59] It is beyond the scope of this book to provide an in-depth treatment of different theological approaches historically to the right to religious freedom.[60] Suffice to say that among all the major Christian groupings, with the exception of the anabaptists[61] and some of the later non-conformists, there has existed an intolerant attitude towards people holding other religious beliefs based on assorted scriptural texts, with particular emphasis on the parable of the wheat and the tares[62] and the great banquet.[63] Biblical arguments are also supported by a profound conviction historically that the fabric of society would be undermined by religious pluralism.[64]

Critique

In modern liberal states, the rationale supporting this position is no longer considered credible, given that '[a] distinctive, indeed for some the

59   See for example, R Evans, *A Brief History of Heresy* (Oxford: Blackwell, 2003) and, in particular, Chapter 5.

60   For a detailed overview see R Ahdar and I Leigh, *Religious Freedom in the Liberal State*, 2nd ed. (Oxford: Oxford University Press, 2013), 23–50.

61   The first well-considered theological arguments in favour of non-compulsion in religion (even for atheists) were penned by the Anabaptist, Balthasar Hubmaier in 1524 in his remarkable treatise, 'Of Heretics and those who Burn them'. By cruel irony, Hubmaier was himself burnt as a heretic on 10 March 1528. See W Estep, *The Anabaptist Story: An Introduction to Sixteenth Century Anabaptism*, 3rd ed. (Grand Rapids, IL: William B Eerdmans, 1996).

62   Matthew 13: 24–30. This parable refers to 'tares' growing up amongst the wheat – the sower is advised not to uproot the tares lest he uproot some wheat at the same time. It is for the owner to perform this division at harvest time. Remarkably, a passage identified by Hubmaier and others as a proof text for religious tolerance was read by Augustine and Aquinas as a justification for persecution if the tares are sufficiently distinct from the wheat, see P Zagorin, *How the Idea of Religious Toleration Came to the West* (Princeton, NJ: Princeton University Press, 2003).

63   Luke 14: 21–23, where the host instructs that people should be 'compelled' to come into the banquet (a metaphor for heaven).

64   C Cookson, *Regulating Religion: The Courts and the Free Exercise Clause* (Oxford: Oxford University Press, 2001).

defining, feature of liberalism is its commitment to neutrality or impartiality between competing conceptions of what constitutes a good or worthwhile life'.[65] Arriving at this point in the Christian West has involved a gradual development with significant change arriving only with the advent of the Enlightenment and the work of John Locke, amongst others.[66]

Nevertheless, all versions of liberalism in practice are imperfect.[67] Many societies, given their respective historical contexts, may come to a liberal position on the basis of a gradual evolution from something more restrictive of freedom and this may leave a cultural or institutional legacy. This legacy need not be a matter of regret; there may be, for example, positive benefits for the health of Western society which still arise from the impact of its specifically Christian heritage.[68] Some states may indeed retain an 'established' form of Christianity which enjoys some kind of preferential legal treatment over other religions, however trivial.[69] In these circumstances, it is possible that, in consequence of state actions, past or present, some or other form of preference, directly or indirectly, for particular religious beliefs may be institutionalised within certain workplaces or within the wider socioeconomic sphere. The structuring of work in Western states around the Christian calendar, with a rest day on a Sunday and a 'shutdown' period over Christmas, might be examples. Bradney, writing about the UK, surely describes these institutionalised arrangements accurately as '[v]estigal remnants of a largely Christian, Anglican past'.[70] 'Vestigal remnants' are likely to be 'religiously benign' at best and so widely accepted by people with little religious affiliation as to represent national traditions rather than religious 'norms' – as such they are historical features of society rather than modern evidence of the imposition of a particular religious approach. Such a view is open to challenge, however.[71]

65   Ahdar and Leigh, *Religious Freedom in the Liberal State*, 56.
66   In particular an essay in 1689; see J Locke, 'A Letter Concerning Toleration', *The Works of John Locke*, vol. 6 (Aalen: Scienta Verlag Aalen, 1963). There was some significant theological work in this area prior to the enlightenment, chiefly by Sebastian Castellio (1515–1563); see Zagorin, *How the Idea of Religious Toleration Came to the West*, who devotes a whole chapter to the writings of Castellio, 93–144.
67   Wolterstorff, 'The Role of Religion in Decision and Discussion of Political Issues'.
68   See, for example, D Holloway, *Church and State in the New Millenium* (London: Harper Collins, 2000).
69   See Ahdar and Leigh, *Religious Freedom in the Liberal State* (100–9), for a discussion of 'Establishment' and some arguments in favour of retaining this arrangement where it exists.
70   A Bradney, *Law and Faith in a Sceptical Age* (Abingdon: Routledge Cavendish, 2009), 1.
71   See discussion later in this chapter.

Laissez-faire

Rationale and implications

Whilst the state may choose to operate state-run enterprises at arm's length using artificially created market mechanisms, in reality, a large part of the public sector is likely to operate as an administrative arm of the state. Thus, this model is likely to apply almost exclusively to the private sector. The model represents an outworking of a classical *laissez-faire* approach to managing the economy. Professor Richard Epstein is a helpful exponent of this view.[72] He argues that statutory interference in the labour market (and particularly regulation to outlaw discrimination) imposes indefensible costs on others and is thus an infringement of 'ordinary liberties'.[73]

Epstein argues that laws preventing discrimination should be swept away, leaving the common law to provide what little regulation is needed in the labour market, which is chiefly around the enforcement of private contractual terms. He argues that the ability of the individual worker to resign and seek work elsewhere is the most powerful protection against the employer. Epstein acknowledges that a *laissez-faire* approach will allow employers to decide with whom to associate. There is therefore a risk of discrimination against certain groups occurring. For Epstein, however, this is not a problem. A decision to discriminate against certain groups may be rational (as in the case of age discrimination to which he devotes a full chapter in both of his books). Where it is irrational, Epstein follows Becker in suggesting that the market will eventually drive the discriminator out of business. In Becker's view, discrimination is a 'taste' for which employers decide they are prepared to pay.[74] This will impose additional costs, as irrational discrimination will lead to a less productive workforce than would a 'merit-based' non-discriminatory approach. In the world of competition, the employer with a taste for discrimination, given the additional costs involved, will eventually be put out of business. That said, in organisations less constrained by market realities, Epstein for one is relaxed about allowing any kind of discrimination, including voluntary 'reverse discrimination', as a lesser evil than forced association.

If the absence of any kind of anti-discrimination law broadly favours employer discretion, albeit tempered by the threat of resignation by the unhappy employee, there is one way in which the argument is construed to benefit employees. Posner contends that the existence of discrimination law can militate against the hiring of members of a protected group

---

72   R Esptein, *Forbidden Grounds: The Case Against Employment Discrimination Laws* (Cambridge, MA: Harvard University Press, 1992). He extends his analysis to UK discrimination law in R Epstein, *Equal Opportunity or More Opportunity? The Good Thing about Discrimination* (London: Civitas, 2002).
73   R Epstein, *Equal Opportunity or More Opportunity?* 4.
74   G Becker, *The Economics of Discrimination* (Chicago, IL: Chicago University Press, 1957).

because of the difficulties involved in later dismissing them or because of other costs associated with employing them.[75] Thus, anti-discrimination law incentivises employers to find covert means of directly discriminating against members of protected groups. Interestingly this argument may be less universally relevant to discrimination on the grounds of religion as religious affiliation, like sexual orientation, may not be immediately obvious to an interviewer, unlike, say, sex, race or age.[76]

Critique

There is a welter of objections to the thesis of Epstein and other neo-classical economists, with probing questions about the reality of rational behaviour by both employers and consumers and the effect of imperfections in the market.[77] The strongest objection, however, must be where Epstein's thesis is surely weakest and this is in its confidence in the employee's right to resign as a bulwark against the misuse of employer power. A number of commentators, writing in the industrial relations tradition, have provided strong arguments to illustrate that an imbalance of power exists between the individual employee and the employer, and this imbalance is very much in favour of the employer.[78] No less a figure than the father of classical economics, Adam Smith, appears to concur: 'it is not difficult ... to see which of the two parties must, upon all occasions, have the advantage in the dispute and force the other into compliance with his terms'.[79] As Deakin points out (in reply to Epstein), 'jobs are not always interchangeable, and searching for an alternative can be costly. Labour and skills cannot be stored, so that few employees can afford to be without employment for long'.[80]

This criticism is strongly relevant to the subject at hand. Other theorists who would not travel far with Epstein nevertheless find this measure of agreement with him that a person's freedom of religious expression is protected by the fact that he is free to resign if his work and religion

75   R Posner, *Economic Analysis of Law*, 8th ed. (New York: Aspen Publishers, 2011).
76   P Elias, 'Religious and related discrimination' (2008) 175 *Equal Opportunities Review* 16.
77   See A Davies, *Perspectives on Labour Law*, 2nd ed. (Cambridge: Cambridge University Press, 2004) 118–23, for a summary of these.
78   For a summary, see J Gennard and G Judge, *Managing Employment Relations*, 5th ed. (London: Chartered Institute of Personnel and Development, 2010) Chapter 2.
79   A Smith, *An Inquiry into the Nature and Causes of the Wealth of Nations*, Book II (London: Nelson, 1886), 26.
80   S Deakin, 'Equality, Non-discrimination, and the Labour Market: a Commentary on Richard Epstein's critique of Anti-discrimination laws', in R Epstein *Equal Opportunity or More Opportunity? The Good Thing about Discrimination* (London: Civitas, 2002), 49.

become incompatible and that this protection is sufficient.[81] This is a controversial view, for essentially the same reasons advanced by Deakin, and has been subject to considered critique.[82]

'Islands of exclusivity'

Rationale and implications

This model is based on the perceived desirability of permitting people with particular religious convictions to associate together to form workplace 'communities' to the exclusion of those with different convictions or no convictions. This might be seen as an attractive means of satisfying those who might feel that their own freedom of religious expression could only be fully realised within the company of the like-minded and, at the same time, by removing such people from mainstream employment, finding a solution to the 'problematic' effects (if so perceived) of religious expression for other actors in the workplace. As a general principle, there are significant objections to this approach, particularly if it is seen as the only approach to accommodating religious expression. These are considered shortly. Prior to this discussion, however, there are also some further issues to consider as to the circumstances in which these exclusive workplace communities might be permitted to exist and how this might be achieved.

It is submitted that it is possible to subcategorise the principle governing the operation of these religious communities in three main ways. Firstly, such 'islands of exclusivity' might be occupied solely by groups of individuals engaging in specifically religious work, intimately connected with the forms and worship or promotion of a respective religion – modern monasteries, a cathedral, a theological seminary or an organisation whose sole function is to distribute sacred texts – might be appropriate examples. This would be the closest match to the mediaeval Christian notion of a functioning religious community – the main purpose of all activity is spiritual, albeit that practical work might be encouraged as a means of fostering spiritual disciplines or achieving other religious goals.

Secondly, the occupants of such 'islands' might also be engaged in work specifically inspired by their religious beliefs (and privately funded), such as a Hindu charity working towards poverty relief, or a pressure group whose purpose is to promote Christian values, or a private Islamic secondary school. Here, the nature of the work is slightly different from the first

---

81   See A Bradney, *Religions, Rights and Laws* (Leicester: Leicester University Press, 1993). Vickers regards the right to resign positively as an important 'residual right'; L Vickers, *Religious Freedom, Religious Discrimination and the Workplace* (Oxford: Hart Publishing, 2008), 52–3.

82   For example, G Morris, 'Fundamental Rights: Exclusion by Agreement?' (2001) 30 *Industrial Law Journal* 49.

model, in the sense that it is religiously motivated work as opposed to religious work *per se.*

Thirdly, the 'islands' might be populated by groups of workers with strong religious convictions who work together in organisational groups either to provide a 'secular' service, such as a Christian medical practice, a Roman Catholic adoption agency (both of which might draw on state funds) or a Church of England state-funded secondary school, or to provide goods and services to others (not necessarily of the same religion) for a profit, such as a Christian motor dealer or a Jewish law practice. Here, the work (in terms of a constituent bundle of tasks) is neither religious in character nor directly religiously motivated; rather, it is the employees who are motivated by their religious convictions and who believe that by choosing to infuse the way they approach their secular work with shared religious values, the work itself will be more successful and possibly more pleasing to God than it would be in the absence of those shared values.

In practical terms, for such 'islands' to function, they would need to be endowed with protections against the reach of some aspects of anti-discrimination law on the grounds of religion or other grounds (such as sex and sexual orientation). This could be achieved in one of two ways. Firstly, these organisations could be given specific exemptions in discrimination law for their employment policies on the basis that a particular religious belief is an 'occupational requirement' for each employment position. In practice, this would provide some useful protection but it may be problematic in that it would require the employer to establish a specific justification in respect of each employment position. For example, a Catholic school might be able to mount a strong claim for an occupational requirement that its religious education teacher should be a practising Roman Catholic (otherwise the religious ethos of the school would be undermined) but it may find difficulty in justifying as an occupational requirement that its laboratory technician should also be a practising Roman Catholic, however desirable this might seem to be. As a second and alternative approach the state could provide an 'associational group rights exemption',[83] which would allow the religious employer on whom this was bestowed a general legal immunity from any discriminatory consequences of operating a religious test for employment or within employment. Under this regime, the example Roman Catholic school would be able to invoke an exemption to allow it to impose a religious test on applicants for all its posts, including both the religious education teacher and the laboratory technician.

Critique

There are a number of potential objections to the 'islands of exclusivity' approach, both general and specific. In general terms, Esau notes the likely

---

83   Esau, '"Islands of Exclusivity"'.

root of liberal objections to legal protections for religious groups who wish to remain exclusive:

> The normative claim of the religious group that some characteristic or behaviour of a person should lead to their exclusion from the group, directly clashes with the normative claim of liberal society that such characteristics or behaviour should be treated as irrelevant.[84]

Esau's point is that the liberal state tends towards inclusivity[85] and so has an innate discomfort with the idea of granting rights which embody the opposite principle. With this in mind, it might be assumed that a liberal state, whilst grudgingly recognising that there may be occasions where 'islands of exclusivity' may be justified, might seek to take a narrow rather than a broad construction of entitlement to inhabit such islands. Thus, an 'occupational requirement' as opposed to a general exemption approach is likely to be preferred and, in terms of the taxonomy of religious groups presented earlier, the first category is likely to be the least objectionable to liberal sensibilities. Here, workers are all fully involved in explicitly religious activity and non-religious workers are unlikely to be able to fulfil the actual duties. The third category, on the other hand, is likely to be most objectionable, given that, as observed earlier, the respective bundles of tasks which form the actual work roles will be primarily non-religious in character. By that logic, secular work should not be withheld from potential workers on the basis of their religious beliefs (or sexual preferences) and an occupational requirement defence might be hard to mount.

Esau counters this view by suggesting that it assumes an '*instrumental* view of employment [where] a person is given a defined task to do and the duty of the employee is to do that task and no more'.[86] For Esau, an '*organic*' view of employment is more characteristic of religious organisations; under this model, 'the employee is expected to participate in the mission of the organisation as a whole, and is expected to join the whole community, the whole body, in a way that transcends any narrowly defined job description'.[87] Esau's point is a powerful one, as it provides a stronger justification for a broad approach to island dwelling. His organic approach to employment, as representing commitment beyond merely the wage–effort bargain, finds considerable support amongst those modern management theorists with a concern for the so-called 'psychological contract' that is said to apply in a range of employment contexts, not simply religious

---

84   Ibid., 736.
85   Some writers in the liberal tradition, however, would restrict this inclusivity to those who share 'liberal beliefs'; see discussion later in this chapter.
86   Esau, '"Islands of Exclusivity"', 734.
87   Ibid.

ones.[88] The psychological contract is a metaphor for the various expectations of employer and employee about their mutual commitment, which overlays the instrumental requirements of the strictly legal contract, and is of greater overall significance for both parties.[89]

There are two further objections to the 'islands of exclusivity' approach from a very different perspective. The model as described here could serve either as the only platform for workers to express their religious beliefs in the workplace (where there is no protection or even state hostility to protection in mainstream employment) or as one part of a broader approach to offering protections to religious workers. If it were the former, then religious workers would suffer both marginalisation into their own work 'ghettos' and total exclusion from a range of occupations (including the entire range of public sector job roles). Moreover, those religious workers who perceive the secular workplace as a 'mission field'[90] would object, on religious grounds, to being denied access to it.

The second objection is that special protection by the state might in some way compromise the integrity of the religious workers themselves and their organisations, who might become in a sense dependent on secular patronage and so lose their 'prophetic' edge in the public square.[91]

In summary, the 'islands of exclusivity' approach is controversial. It may well convey benefits but only (to avoid the creation of religious ghettos) if pursued alongside other approaches within mainstream employment.

Protection for religion

Rationale

The notion that religious expression in the workplace is worthy of protection is entirely dependent on the value ascribed within a particular society to that right. The various arguments in support of a right of religious expression in the workplace therefore require elucidation here to provide a rationale. The nature and extent of these protections is a consequent 'implication' that is considered separately, before a critique is considered. Prior to this, it is perhaps helpful to emphasise that the protection envisaged in this section is for the manifestation and expression of religious beliefs and identity. The protection attaches to the individual rather than the beliefs that he is seeking to articulate or act on. Thus, the kind of protection under discussion is not for 'religious feeling' (that an

---

88   D Rousseau, *Psychological Contract in Organizations: Understanding Written and Unwritten Agreements* (Newbury Park, CA: Sage, 1996).

89   J Bratton and J Gold, *Human Resource Management Theory and Practice*, 3rd ed. (London: Palgrave-Macmillan, 2003), 13.

90   Ahdar and Leigh, *Religious Freedom in the Liberal State*, 348.

91   Esau, '"Islands of Exclusivity"', 825.

individual's beliefs should be immune from criticism or even mockery)[92] but for religious expression.[93]

The idea that any human characteristic or activity should be valued by others must have an underlying basis. There is, however, a critical question as to whether it is possible to identify this ultimate rationale. For people with religious convictions, there is no difficulty. The Judeo-Christian view of human worth, for example, is based on the notion that men and women are made in the image of God[94] (often referred to as the *imago dei*).[95] As a consequence, they are also essentially equal in their humanity.[96] In Islam, as another example, there similarly exists an elevated concept of human worth, owing to the belief that there rests a divine spark (sometimes known as the *taqwa* or *hidaya*) within each human which supplies the ultimate source of moral guidance (or conscience).[97]

Others search for an underlying foundation without reference to a divine creator but rather on the basis that human beings are afforded a high level of importance by virtue of their humanity itself. For some, this can find adequate foundation on the Kantian notion that human beings are special on the basis of their capacity for rational thought and as such should be treated individually as an 'end' rather than a 'means'.[98] Others choose not to probe too deeply, for fear that this would reveal the lack of an ultimately satisfying rationale.[99] Yet others are more sanguine; for them, the attempt to find the ultimate foundation is either futile or unnecessary and so they do not attempt it.[100]

---

92   Albeit that there may be a degree of such protection within the workplace if 'harassment' law is drafted in a way to be inclusive of offence on the grounds of religion – see Chapter 5.

93   For the case against extending protection to religious feelings (except in extreme cases), see R Ahdar, 'The Right to Protection of Religious Feelings' (2009) 11 *Otago Law Review* 629.

94   See Genesis 1: 27: 'So God created man in His own image; in the image of God He created him; male and female He created them.'

95   See N Wolterstorff, *Justice: Rights and Wrongs* (Princeton, NJ: Princeton University Press, 2008) 342–73, for an extended and nuanced treatment of the *Imago Dei* concept.

96   A key biblical text is Galatians 3: 28, 'There is neither Jew nor Greek, there is neither slave nor free, there is neither male nor female; for you are all one in Christ Jesus.'

97   I Oh, *The Rights of God: Islam, Human Rights, and Comparative Ethics* (Washington DC: Georgetown University Press, 2007), 28.

98   See D Meyerson, *Rights Limited* (Cape Town: Rustica, 1997), 12–13.

99   J Waldron, *God, Locke and Equality: The Christian Foundations in Locke's Political Thought* (Cambridge: Cambridge University Press, 2002). Waldron notes that some secularists outside of the modernist tradition, such as 'various Nietzscheans or radical Freudians' pose that exact challenge, 239. See also the discussion on the effects of post-modernism in Trigg, *Religion in Public Life*, 193–208.

100   See, for example, B Barry, *Culture and Equality: An Egalitarian Critique of Multiculturalism* (Cambridge: Polity, 2001), 126.

Essentially, whether or not an ultimate rationale is established, human worth translates into three concepts on which rights theories are usually based: equality, dignity and autonomy. These three concepts are to a large extent interlocked[101] and the boundaries between them may not always be apparent. 'Equality' is the oldest concept, with its foundation in the Aristotelian ideal of treating likes alike and which has subsequently broadened to encompass also the notions of equal opportunity and substantive equality.[102] 'Dignity' as a concept has developed subsequently and some theorists make a direct *a fortiori* link from equality. Dworkin, for example, writes that there is 'a natural right of all men and women to equality of concern and respect, a right they possess … simply as human beings with the capacity to make plans and give justice'.[103]

It is, of course, possible to reverse the direction of travel and see dignity as the foundational concept. One consequence of human dignity would be of course the need for equality of treatment and, indeed, dignity may have a softening effect on the manifestation of equality (compared with the conception of equality which might result from rationality, the alternative foundation).[104] For example, the introduction of dignity into the equality equation might require a 'levelling up' in situations of inequality rather than a 'levelling down' which might equally result from equality as rationality.[105]

'Dignity' however, is a complex concept. Although it may mark a recognition of the need to 'protect the special status and integrity of the species',[106] the substantial content of 'dignity' beyond this recognition may be hard to capture precisely.[107] One helpful approach is provided by Feldman, who presents human dignity as a multilayered concept with an application at a 'species' level, at a group level and at an individual level.[108] When considered at an individual level, Feldman draws a dichotomy

---

101 Vickers, *Religious Freedom, Religious Discrimination and the Workplace.*
102 S Fredman, *Discrimination Law,* 2nd ed. (Oxford: Oxford University Press, 2011), 4–32.
103 Dworkin, *Taking Rights Seriously,* 182.
104 Fredman, *Discrimination Law.*
105 Ibid., 21.
106 D Feldman, 'Human dignity as a legal value: Part 1' (1999) Winter *Public Law* 682, 684. See also McCrudden, who, in a discussion of the uses of the dignity concept in human rights legal discourse, argues that there is an acceptance that human beings have some intrinsic worth, that this is worthy of respect by others, and that the state should exist for the benefit of the individual; beyond this 'minimum core' definition, however, there is no consensus: C McCrudden, 'Human Dignity and Judicial Interpretation of Human Rights' (2008) 19 *European Journal of International Law* 655.
107 D Reaume, 'Discrimination and Dignity (2002–2003) 63 *Louisiana Law Review* 645, 646.
108 Feldman, 'Human dignity as a legal value', 684.

between 'objective' and 'subjective' dignity. Objective dignity derives from characteristics that are unrelated to personal effort or endeavour – they are in a sense the immutable characteristics of humanity (although Feldman does not use this terminology). Drawing on Feldman's overall analysis, religious expression can find a basis for protection at both a group and at an individual level. At a group level, such a conception of dignity would allow religious groups 'to assert a right to respect for their existence and at least some of their traditions which is at least equal to that of other groups'.[109] At an individual level, dignity requires that people 'be treated in particular ways which advance or do not unduly interfere with the acquisition or maintenance of … physical or moral integrity'.[110] The notion that 'moral integrity' is protected by 'dignity' provides a powerful platform for respecting the individual's right to religious expression in many fora, including, potentially, the workplace.

The notion of autonomy in liberal political thought recognises the right of individuals to make choices and to develop and pursue their own version of the good life.[111] Clearly, there is a large area of overlap with the notion of dignity but the emphasis here is on valuing and protecting the decisions and choices made by individuals. To be worthy of protection, such decisions and choices need concern matters of fundamental importance to an individual's view of the world and version of the good.[112] Expressions of religious faith would, however, undoubtedly qualify.

It should perhaps be noted at this point that it is possible to advance the case for protecting religious expression based on principles unrelated to equality, dignity or autonomy. Vickers, for example, argues that protection may also be extended to promote 'social [and presumably organisational] cohesion', 'conflict resolution and social inclusion' and in response to the 'aesthetic' value of religious expression.[113] Ahdar and Leigh note that a case could be mounted for protecting religious expression on the basis that religious people are likely to display personally and perhaps help to advance generally 'civic virtue' (which could also be translated into organisational virtue).[114] It is accepted that these might provide useful secondary arguments in favour of supporting religious expression in the workplace. The argument based on the value of social cohesion might in particular be a powerful one in certain social contexts, where religious identity is a particular and enduring source of antagonism, such as Northern Ireland. However, it is hard to see how this and other arguments can compete at a principled level with arguments based on the powerful concepts discussed earlier and which form the focus for the discussion below.

109 Ibid.
110 Ibid., 686.
111 Ahdar and Leigh, *Religious Freedom in the Liberal State*, 76.
112 Vickers, *Religious Freedom, Religious Discrimination and the Workplace*.
113 Ibid., 33–6.
114 Ahdar and Leigh, *Religious Freedom in the Liberal State*, 74–6.

Implications

If religious expression is given high status for its role in promoting the dignity, equality and autonomy of individuals, then there is a compelling case for the right to religious expression to be protected in a variety of fora and this is very likely to include the workplace.

As noted earlier, such protection could take two forms – either creating positive 'rights' for religious expression or creating 'negative' protections against discrimination. A combination of these two approaches is possible. Within either approach it is likely that there will be some mechanism required to deal with any clashes with other claimants to rights in the workplace. One such clash may be between sexual orientation rights and religious rights.[115] Employers may also have contractual rights which may conflict with religious expression. A mechanism for addressing these issues might create a clear hierarchy of rights, where one right is clearly identified as subordinate to another; or it might involve the emergence of a judicial formula or approach involving the balancing of one set of rights against another to determine which has the strongest claim in any given circumstances.

Critique

A number of critics question the importance of religious expression on the basis that religious identity is a mutable characteristic. People can opt to change religion and in this sense it is a matter of personal choice (autonomy) and levels of commitment can be 'flexed' accordingly. This reduces its status as an inalienable right deserving of a full measure of dignity which most properly belongs to immutable characteristics, such as race and sex.[116] Under this analysis, religious expression may be accorded some value but it is subordinate to a range of other rights which are deserving of 'objective' dignity.

The counter argument is in four parts. Firstly, it is possible to deconstruct the concept of immutability. For example, whereas 'race' might appear an obvious contender for the status of an immutable characteristic, it has been argued that racial characteristics owe more to social context than physiology and so cannot really be described as immutable.[117] Unfortunately, as the same reasoning cannot realistically be applied to

---

115 See I Leigh, 'Hatred, Sexual Orientation, Free Speech and Religious Liberty' (2009) 10 *Ecclesiastical Law Journal* 337; and I Leigh, 'Homophobic Speech, Equality Denial, and Religious Expression' in I Hare and J Weinstein (eds), *Extreme Speech and Democracy* (Oxford: Oxford University Press, 2009).

116 Vickers sets out the basic principles of this argument; see Vickers, *Religious Freedom, Religious Discrimination and the Workplace*, 30–1.

117 See Fredman, *Discrimination Law* 50–1.

sex,[118] age and disability, this argument may serve more to cast doubt on the place of race in a potential hierarchy of rights than to fully undermine the concept of immutability itself.

Secondly, the apparent mutability of religious belief may be questioned on observational grounds, given that a very large proportion of people with religious affiliations do not in fact change those affiliations over their lifetime.[119] However, the fact that there plainly are conversions from one religion to another (however exceptional) does somewhat undermine this argument. Moreover, some argue that individuals do exercise choice in the degree of dedication with which they pursue their religious convictions and this in turn may change over time.[120]

Thirdly, the notion that religious identity is mutable can also be challenged by those who believe these 'choices' are predetermined and thus choice in any meaningful sense is excluded. There are those who argue this case from a religious perspective on the basis that they have been compelled to faith by God and not by their own free will.[121] This is, for example, the position held by Christians in the Calvinist tradition. Some argue this case using secular reasoning from a biological–environmental perspective.[122] Others point to the importance of socialisation and culture in forming religious beliefs.[123]

The fourth and surely strongest counter argument is to question the importance of mutability *per se*. As discussed earlier, autonomy is considered to be a significant value, informing an individual's identity and self-respect, and this is given effect through choice over the fundamentals of life.[124] From the religious adherent's point of view, this ultimate choice is about something more significant still, beyond the normative values of self-respect and identity, as it involves a decision relating to both an objective reality of universal significance (God and his claims on humankind)[125] and

---

118 Ibid., 131–2. Fredman does argue that transsexualism points to the essential mutability of sex as a characteristic.

119 Vickers, *Religious Freedom, Religious Discrimination and the Workplace.*

120 S Leader, 'Freedom and Futures: Personal Priorities, Institutional Demands and Freedom of Religion (2007) *Modern Law Review* 713.

121 K Greenawalt, 'The Significance of Conscience' (2010) 47 *San Diego Law Review* 901, 916.

122 See, for a discussion on this point, P Edge, 'Religious rights and choice under the European Convention on Human Rights' (2000) 3 *Web Journal of Current Legal Issues.*

123 This view can also be held in a moderate form, see P Jones, 'Bearing the Consequences of Belief' in R Goodwin and P Pettit, *Contemporary Political Philosophy, An Anthology*, 2nd ed. (Oxford: Blackwell, 2006), 610. Jones points to the complications in establishing the link between socialisation and belief – as he notes, the degree of 'choice' involved may depend upon circumstances, individuals and the belief system itself.

124 Vickers, *Religious Freedom, Religious Discrimination and the Workplace.*

125 Trigg, *Free to Believe?* 203.

a personal and urgent concern for 'the state of one's soul'.[126] In a sense, there is less of a choice than an acceptance of an individual's obligation or duty towards God under conviction of conscience.[127] Many secular liberals have great difficulty in acknowledging that religious beliefs have this level of 'transcendent importance'[128] and prefer to value them as equivalent to 'other and deep genuine commitments'.[129] Although this may be held to reflect a limited willingness to imaginatively enter into the worldview of someone with deep religious convictions, for the purposes of this particular argument, both the religious adherent and the secular liberal may be able to arrive at a similar conclusion (albeit perhaps the one more enthusiastically than the other); that is, that there is no obvious reason why the result of a fundamental 'choice' should be regarded as less worthy of protection than an immutable characteristic. If this point is accepted then the very question of the significance of mutability fades from the stage.

The final objection to be considered here is that religious expression undermines other rights cherished in a liberal state, particularly those related to sex and sexual orientation. Some feminist scholars, for example, deplore forced marriage, polygamy and the veiling of women that are often associated with the cultural subordination of women based on religious beliefs.[130] Equally, many liberals are critical of the religious condemnation of homosexual acts as sinful.[131] If religious employees are seen to be insufficiently tolerant of other 'rights' then this in turn serves to undermine the claim of religion itself as a right to be respected.[132]

In recent years the bar of tolerance has been raised by a number of liberal scholars who argue that it is no longer sufficient merely to 'bear with' others and their practices, per the historical understanding of the meaning of tolerance (i.e. to make a 'deliberate choice not to interfere with the conduct of which one disapproves').[133] More is required. This is

---

126 P Diamond, 'Religion or belief: the right to be wrong' (2009) 187 *Equal Opportunities Review* 14.

127 See Ahdar and Leigh, *Religious Freedom in the Liberal State*, 46–8.

128 Dworkin, *Is Democracy Possible Here?* 68.

129 D Meyerson, 'Why Religion Belongs in the Private Sphere not the Public Square' in P Cane, C Evans and Z Robinson (eds), *Law and Religion in Theoretical and Historical Context* (Cambridge: Cambridge University Press, 2008), 54–5.

130 See, for example, SM Okin, *Is Multiculturalism Bad for Women?* (Princeton, NJ: Princeton University Press, 1999).

131 For example, R Rorty, 'Religion in the Public Square: A Reconsideration' (2003) 31 *Journal of Religious Ethics* 141.

132 Barry adopts this view, whilst again employing the language of culture: 'Equal respect for people cannot therefore entail respect for their cultures when these cultures systematically give priority to, say, the interests of men over women', in Barry, *Culture and Equality*, 127.

133 J Horton, 'Liberalism, Multiculturalism, and Toleration' in J Horton (ed.), *Liberalism, Multiculturalism, and Toleration* (Basingstoke: Palgrave Macmillan, 1993), 3.

based on the assumption that toleration is extended by the 'majority' to 'minority groups' the members of which feel, by reason of their minority status *per se*, unable to fully express their respective identities and, in this sense, are 'invisible', e.g. gay and lesbian people.[134] To tolerate members of minority groups and their practices merely in a non-interfering way will do nothing to demonstrate 'public respect' and encourage the building up of 'adequate self-esteem'.[135] Thus, to be fully 'tolerant' now requires more – that members of minorities should be 'affirmed' or 'embraced' for their personal characteristics and in terms of their lifestyle choices so they can achieve the 'full citizenship' which would otherwise be denied them.[136] For some religious people, able to conform to the older definition of tolerance, the new, proactive requirements of tolerance may be far more problematic in certain cases. Taking the example of rights connected to sexual orientation, a Roman Catholic Christian, with traditional beliefs, is likely to be perfectly able to, courteously and respectfully, 'bear with' a gay colleague; however, she is unlikely to be able to positively 'affirm' the worth of that sexual lifestyle as to do so would, in her eyes, amount to encouraging an individual to remain under God's displeasure, in a state of sin, and thus, spiritually, to do grave harm to her gay colleague.

In a workplace context, there may be pressure to restrict religious expression should it either conflict with other aspects of equality or be seen in some way to be less than affirming of the perceived rights or choices of co-workers. In such cases, religious expression may indeed be regarded by some as 'harmful' to the dignity of others and thus worthy of censure and possibly prohibition.[137] Critics of this perspective draw attention to the fact that, in effect, it creates a situation where certain other rights are routinely allowed to 'trump' religious rights.[138] For a state to explicitly sanction such practices would also mean that in a sense it 'takes sides' against religious rights and many liberals, not to mention religious employees, would find this unsatisfactory as a general principle.[139]

There is a deeper problem here. In a society which cherishes a number of fundamental rights, there is likely to be inherent competition and conflict at some stage. As Galston notes, 'in the very act of sustaining diversity, liberal unity circumscribes diversity. It could not be otherwise. No form of social life can be perfectly or equally hospitable to every human orientation'.[140] This is likely to be as true of the workplace, where 'diversity' as a

---

134 See A Galeotti, *Toleration as Recognition* (Cambridge: Cambridge University Press, 2002), 10–14.
135 Ibid., 12.
136 Ibid., 10–14.
137 See discussion in Meyerson, *Rights Limited*, 5–6.
138 See Trigg, *Free to Believe?*
139 R Dworkin, 'Liberal Adoption' (2007) March *Prospect* 16.
140 W Galston, *Liberal Purposes* (Cambridge: Cambridge University Press, 1991), 4.

value may itself be promoted, as it is of other public fora of human activity. How to reconcile differences is 'not a simple question'[141] and, at some stage, one right will be preferred over another in any given instance. To make an absolute decision that it should be the religious right that gives way is, for some, peremptory and unjustified.[142] An alternative is to treat each clash individually and seek to develop some principles which 'directly address and fully analyze … competing interests' in each case to determine finally which right must give way.[143]

A variant of the model: protection for religion and belief

As noted in Chapter 2, there may be sound practical reasons for extending the definition of that which is to be protected in the workplace from 'religion' to 'religion and similar philosophical beliefs'. This extension helps to overcome the problem, for example, of how to classify non-theistic belief systems such as Buddhism, which may fall outside many definitions of religion but which many people would regard as worthy of protection on the basis that they function as religions in the life of some people and (often) their communities.

There are, however, reasons of principle that may be invoked to support protection for beliefs which may not necessarily be as closely aligned, from a functional perspective, to religion. Many of these reasons may be derived from the arguments presented in this section concerning the importance of recognising the significance of choice and self-expression in support of the important liberal value of individual autonomy. This may be bolstered by an empirical recognition that increasing numbers of people are rejecting mainstream religions and pursing highly individualised forms of spirituality. Many would contend that people deserve protection for these beliefs too. A difficulty which is then encountered is how to conceptualise what it meant by 'belief'. As Vickers notes, there are two possibilities, either the meaning of 'belief' is construed narrowly to refer to an overall system of belief or philosophical outlook analogous to a religion; or it might be expanded to refer to a single issue (such as a belief in man-made climate change or pacifism). Vickers favours protecting the former rather than the latter, lest the net of protection be cast too wide.[144] Indeed, this is the major problem with widening the scope of protection to include belief – the inevitable consequence of protecting more people is that the nature of that protection is likely to become weaker:

---

141 Trigg, *Free to Believe?* 12.
142 For example, Trigg: ibid., 36.
143 D Kaminer, 'When Religious Expression Creates a Hostile Work Environment' (2000) 81 *New York University Journal of Legislation and Public Policy* 139.
144 Vickers, *Religious Freedom, Religious Expression and the Workplace*, 22–4.

The word [belief], however, introduces a further vagueness into the definition which courts have to wrestle with. The problem is that the more the category covers, the more limitations will be found legally necessary. ... The more outlandish the beliefs tolerated, the more a society will have to be careful about how they are expressed.[145]

Furthermore, the very act of widening the definition to encompass belief weakens any argument that religion is 'special' – inevitably, when equated with 'belief' it becomes a subset of the latter and loses any *sui generis* claims.[146] As Sadurski notes: '[t]here is no basis, in an ideology of a liberal and secular state, to draw the line between the religiously-motivated and other deep moral beliefs'.[147] In other words, religious beliefs will be viewed in exactly the same way as deep moral beliefs.[148] This is in keeping with liberal ideals (of neutrality) and will thus be the inevitable result of equating religion and belief in terms of the distribution of protection.

Protection for minority religions

Rationale and implications

The rationale for providing specific protection for minority religions, as opposed to religion in general, is premised on the notion that religion is one means by which groups in society that depart from the 'norm' identify themselves.[149] The major determinant of group membership is ethnicity and ethnicity can be strongly linked to religion.[150] Members of such 'ethnic-and-religious' minority groups are disadvantaged in the West, owing to institutional factors such as the structuring of the working calendar around a Christian norm and the conventional expectations of the majority culture about dress, food and drink.[151] Special protection should therefore be offered to guarantee minority religious expression to counter the inherent disadvantage of operating within a majority culture with its institutional legacy (in the West) of Christian practices in many workplaces. Such protection might permit practices (such as allowing Sikhs to carry a *kirpan*,

---

145 Trigg, *Free to Believe*, 46.
146 Trigg makes a similar point; see Trigg, *Free to Believe*, 45.
147 W Sadurski, *Moral Pluralism and Legal Neutrality* (The Hague: Kluwer, 1990) 190.
148 Bradney, *Law and Faith in a Sceptical Age*, 32.
149 Pitt is a proponent of this model: see G Pitt, 'Religion or Belief: Aiming at the Right Target?' in H. Meenan (ed), *Equality Law in an Enlarged European Union* (CUP 2007).
150 Fredman, *Discrimination Law*, 73–5. In the earlier edition of her book, Fredman made this point more strongly.
151 A McColgan, 'Class Wars? Religion and (In)equality in the Workplace' (2009) 38 *Industrial Law Journal* 1.

a small dagger) which would not be permitted to non-members of minority religious groups.[152] As such, this approach might be characterised as a mild form of 'affirmative action' or 'positive discrimination' entailing a degree of preferential treatment.[153]

Indeed this may be an element of a more radical strategy of positive discrimination which would aim to increase the workplace participation (at various levels) of members of ethnic and religious minority groups in pursuit of 'substantive equality'.[154] Substantive equality takes the final outcome for members of different groups (a relevant example here might be the relative proportions of members of different ethnic groups in a management cadre) as its starting point, as opposed to equality of opportunity, which emphasises a level playing field for all individuals at the point of entry (recruitment or promotion). The substantive equality approach, at an organisational level, is essentially a 'redistributive' strategy which seeks to directly intervene in decision making on personnel matters to the benefit of members of disadvantaged groups.[155]

A society pursuing such a strategy might either permit or impose a 'quota' system (or otherwise set targets) requiring organisations to recruit a certain percentage of employees, managers, directors, etc., from minority religious groups. Clearly, in reserving posts for members of religious minorities, it would be a necessary corollary that forms of religious expression be protected so that members of religious minorities would be willing to take up the available positions.

In summary, under this analysis, the focus of protecting religion and religious expression is on removing disadvantage experienced because of membership of a minority religious group. Once disadvantage is alleviated, the justification for protection for minority religion disappears and should be removed.[156] Thus, under this model, there also exists an expectation that, in parallel with legal protection for minority religions at an individual level, legal and policy efforts are also made as a matter of urgency to tackle sources of disadvantage at an institutional level. For some commentators, such as McColgan, this also involves removing any lingering workplace features of the historical majority religion (such as the institutional legacy of Christianity considered earlier).[157]

152 See B Parekh, *Rethinking Multiculturalism: Cultural Diversity and Political Theory*, 2nd ed. (London: Macmillan, 2000), 248.
153 See discussion in Fredman, *Discrimination Law*, 232–78.
154 Ibid., 25–33.
155 C McCrudden, *Buying Social Justice* (Oxford: Oxford University Press, 2007), 70.
156 Barry, *Culture and Equality*, 13.
157 McColgan, 'Class Wars?' 14.

Critique

This model is most vulnerable to critique in that it is not based on any over-all acceptance that religion is important and deserving *per se*. Instead, the governing principle is that religion is a proxy for race or ethnicity. Inevitably, this leads to a view of religious expression as one form of 'cultural expression' and the terms of the debate change.[158] It would, of course, be naive to deny or underplay the links between religion and culture but, if the language of culture only is adopted, religion becomes a secondary characteristic of something apparently more important – collective identity. Religious practices are assumed by people as expressions of identity with a particular culture and not as ends in themselves. In a related point, as Jones notes, 'a person's culture may be invoked as a *causal* explanation of his beliefs but it cannot be offered by the believer himself as a *reason* for believing what he does'.[159] This model makes no assumption that there is any kind of serious thought about the truth or merit of a religion's claims on behalf of its adherents – religion becomes instead 'a mere quirk of culture'[160] and is worthy only for its role in shoring up that culture or even for sentimental reasons connected to the value of heritage. This, of course, serves to strongly undermine any special *sui generis* claims for religion that might otherwise be advanced. This point is clearly recognised by a proponent of this model, McColgan, who, in support of her own argument, is keen to underline it: '[t]he identification of ... practices as "religious" as distinct from "cultural" is strongly contested, and privileging those accepted as "religious" from merely "cultural" increases the incentive to categorise them as "religious" and thereby helps to perpetuate them'.[161]

A second line of critique stems from the fact that this model encourages the dismantling of the legacy of Christianity in the workplace (and elsewhere) in pursuit of the reduction of disadvantage. There are objections to this at a practical as well as a theoretical level. Galeotti, whilst keen to promote the questioning of 'traditions and conventions', acknowledges the 'difficulty for society as a whole of finding a new network of conventions that suits everyone from every group'.[162] Taking the example of the 'Christian' tradition of structuring of the working week to allow Sunday as a holiday, an attempt to change this, whilst for Galeotti, potentially desirable at one level, 'would create enormous practical problems in all sectors of social life, from business to school ...' and is thus impractical as

---

158 Both Barry and Parekh are leading thinkers who tend to merge the boundaries between religion and culture; see Barry, *Culture and Equality* and Parekh, *Rethinking Multiculturalism*.

159 Jones, 'Bearing the Consequences of Belief', 610.

160 Ibid.

161 McColgan, 'Class Wars?' 12.

162 Galeotti, *Toleration as Recognition*, 92–3.

a solution.[163] Indeed, as Jones observes, it appears hard to escape the conclusion that seeking to remodel institutionalised features of life such as the working week to make them 'religiously neutral' would in actual fact risk creating a situation which was 'equally inconvenient for all religions' thus 'making some people worse off whilst making no one better off'.[164]

As Parekh notes, removing the cultural legacy of Christianity in the UK might also create potentially a new source of disadvantage to religious and ethnic minority groups in terms of incurring the resentment of members of the majority population and any ensuing effects of this.[165] For Parekh, however, it is not even a case that the cure is worse that the cause. He also argues positively that the central proposition is wrong: the continued existence of the Christian legacy need not in itself result in disadvantage to minority groups:

> Besides, once the religious beliefs of all citizens are equally respected, no apparent injustice is done to minorities if the religion of the overwhelming majority is given some precedence over theirs, especially when it is a long-established part of the structure of the state and doing so has no adverse effects on their rights and interests.[166]

A third and potentially most significant criticism is that this model is potentially implicitly hostile to the expression of a major religion, Christianity, which, as 'mainstream', is seen as a major contributor to the 'disadvantage' that requires removal. Thus, Christians would not be 'protected' in law whilst members of other religions would be – creating a major inequality. Arguably, this might not matter if, as is assumed under this model, Christian self-expression is mainstream and is not subject to serious challenge.[167] The problem is that, although perhaps even a majority of the Western population self-identifies in some vague way as Christian,[168] they do so, as Bradney observes, without necessarily knowing what being Christian actually means;[169] moreover '[f]or such people their religion neither tells them what they should do nor does it prevent them from pursuing anything that they see to be in their interest. It is neither a guide nor a limitation to their behaviour on a day-to-day basis'.[170]

163 Ibid., 201–2.
164 Jones, 'Bearing the Consequences of Belief', 617.
165 Parekh, *Rethinking Multiculturalism*, 259.
166 Ibid.
167 Vickers appears to take this view; see Vickers, *Religious Freedom, Religious Discrimination and the Workplace*, 92.
168 See G Davie, *Religion in Britain Since 1945: Believing Without Belonging* (Oxford: Blackwell, 1994).
169 Bradney, *Law and Faith in a Sceptical Age*, 8.
170 Ibid., 9.

Others, whilst taking their Christianity slightly more seriously, perhaps through Church attendance, may fall within a different grouping – those who exhibit 'religiosity' as opposed to a genuine commitment to the doctrines of the Christian faith.[171] Neither of these groups is likely to challenge the dominance of secular thinking and mores which are surely the more defining characteristic of Western European states. Thus, it might be suggested that this model rests on a false premise – Christianity (in any meaningful sense) as representative of the 'mainstream' in Western society. It may be suggested rather that this honour falls to secularism. If this is the case, then it follows that practising Christians are a minority group and are just as likely to face hostility as any other religious grouping.[172] Thus, Christians need as much legal protection as people of other religious faiths and, under this model, they fail to receive it.

Conclusion

Six overarching models of legal approaches towards religious expression by employees in the workplace have been presented and the implications discussed and critiqued. As stated at the outset, it is unlikely that a liberal society would adopt any one of these models as a single strategy. The models all rest on particular assumptions, economic and sociopolitical in nature, which are likely to be a subject of debate within a liberal society. Approaches may alter over time, depending on the point at which the debate rests and, as a result, legal responses to religious expression may be, at times, ad hoc and even inconsistent.

The models presented here are used again in the next chapter to consider how far law in England and Wales, at a legislative level, can be seen to embody aspects thereof. What is of value in the concluding part of this chapter is to identify any cross-cutting themes and key questions which might have a strong influence on overall state approaches at different times, depending upon the nature of the political and social context and other factors.

One of the key questions is how religion is perceived in terms of its effect on society. One underlying view would be to see religion essentially as divisive and a barrier to 'socially progressive' ideas, such as gay rights and equality for women. Another view would be to see religion in much more positive terms for its positive moral and other individual and social effects. If the initial perception is negative, a degree of hostility, implicit or explicit, is likely to characterise attitudes towards religious expression in whatever

171   Such a group is likely to be shrinking as 'obligation' declines as a motive for church attendance; see G Davie, 'From Obligation to Consumption: A Framework For Reflection in Northern Europe' (2005) 6 *Political Theology* 281.
172   See Christians in Parliament, *Clearing the Ground Inquiry: Preliminary Report into the Freedom of Christians in the UK* (February 2012).

forum. A second important question (which to some extent follows from the first) is how far religious convictions, where not shared by others, should be kept private – the expression of religious convictions excluded from the public square (including the workplace) either by voluntary restraint or through some form of imposition (whether directly by law or indirectly through a 'chilling effect').

If the answers to these initial questions are positive from a religious employee's perspective, then a third and vital question arises. If society perceives some value in religious expression then how great is this value? This hinges to a large extent on whether religion is seen as either one of many important choices which give expression to an individual's personal autonomy or as an expression of culture and identification with members of an ethnic grouping or whether it is seen as a response to an obligation to the divine – where 'choice' as normally understood is not a factor. If it is the latter, then religious expression is likely to be seen as worthy of a greater level of protection certainly than the first and possibly than the second category. This leads on to a further question, which is how to treat religious expression in the face of competing rights in the workplace (such as employers' rights or rights connected to sex or sexual orientation) – what should its place be in any hierarchy of rights? At what point is it appropriate to subdivide religious expression into different forms, some being more 'offensive' than others? Those who see religion as obligation as opposed to choice are likely to have a much stronger case to argue for a high place for religious expression in its various forms in the hierarchy. Those who see religion as a manifestation of culture only risk trivialising religion by seeking to subordinate to another category (race) which may be thought to have a higher standing in the hierarchy of rights. This also has the effect of forcing the disaggregation of the term 'religion' in practice as different religious groups will be afforded different protections according to how far they can show an obvious link between the way they manifest their religion and to 'ethnic' culture.

There is, finally, a significant question as to whether or not the state has a legitimate role at all in seeking to intervene in the employment relationship to protect or proscribe forms of religious expression. Some would argue that such matters should be resolved through the normal process of negotiation between employer and employee. Those employees unhappy with the arrangement reached could work instead for other organisations (perhaps organisations with a religiously exclusive employment policy) which are more accommodating. Others would argue that religious expression is sufficiently important to require protection even in the workplace, particularly in a context where other characteristics or choices are similarly protected and where the bargaining power of employers far outweighs that of employees.

4 The effect of the European Convention on Human Rights and its application

Introduction

The purpose of this chapter and the next is to explore the legal authorities relevant to freedom of religious expression in the UK workplace, both European and domestic; the two most significant areas of law concerned being human rights law and employment law. The law and, in very broad terms, the way in which it has been interpreted (including at a policy level) are examined with reference to the European Convention on Human Rights and Fundamental Freedoms and also to domestic law in England and Wales, most of it employment law (which, in turn, is largely derived from European Union directives). As each area of legal jurisdiction is examined, its congruence with the models set out in Chapter 3 is considered.

There are two overarching areas of European legal authority that are fundamental. Although they represent two very different legal jurisdictions, there are significant overlaps in the way they take effect, and domestic courts in the UK are obliged to take account of both. The first, under the authority of the Council of Europe, is the European Convention on Human Rights (ECHR). The second, under the authority of the European Union, entails those clauses of the European Commission General Framework Directive,[1] which deal with religion and belief, as mediated into domestic law originally through the Employment Equality (Religion and Belief) Regulations and, since 2011 (when it came into force), the Equality Act 2010.

The subject of this chapter is the effect of the ECHR and the way in which it has been interpreted to apply to the workplace. The discussion begins by considering those articles of the Convention relevant to freedom of religion, of which Article 9 is the most significant. The way in which religious 'manifestation' is understood and separated from 'belief' in the interpretation of Article 9 are considered before the debate turns to the application of Article 9 to the workplace and, in particular, the two mechanisms by which applications have been traditionally filtered out before

1   2000/78/EC.

reaching a full hearing (the 'necessity test' and the 'specific situation rule', respectively). However, it will be noted that these filters are now largely historic. The way in which the European Court of Human Rights (ECtHR) deals with Article 9 claims in the workplace was radically altered by the decision in January 2013 in *Eweida and Ors* v. *United Kingdom.*[2] This case is discussed in some detail in the later part of this chapter and the admissibility decisions with reference to Article 9 and their implications explored. The judgment in *Eweida and Ors* is also considered for how, in the absence of clear precedent, the ECtHR chose to deal with the need to balance religious and other rights in reaching its decisions, and the likely implications of this for future Article 9 decisions.

Convention rights and freedom of religion

There are two articles of particular relevance to religious freedom of (adult) individuals in the Convention – Articles 9 and 14, respectively – although other articles could also be construed as offering protections for religious freedom, particularly Article 10, which guarantees freedom of expression.[3] Article 9 states that:

1. Everyone has the right to freedom of thought, conscience and religion; this right includes freedom to change his religion or belief, and freedom, either alone or in community with others and in public or private, to manifest his religion or belief in worship, teaching, practice or observance.
2. Freedom to manifest one's religion or beliefs shall be subject only to such limitations as are prescribed by law and are necessary in a democratic society in the interests of public safety, for the protection of public order, health or morals, or for the protection of the rights and freedoms of others.

Article 10 reads:

1. Everyone has the right to freedom of expression. This right shall include freedom to hold opinions and to receive and impart information and ideas without interference by public authority and regardless of frontiers. This article shall not prevent States from requiring the licensing of broadcasting, television or cinema enterprises.
2. The exercise of these freedoms, since it carries with it duties and responsibilities, may be subject to such formalities, conditions, restrictions or penalties as are prescribed by law and are necessary in a

---

2   Appl Nos. 48420/10, 59842/10, 51671/10 and 36516/10 (15 January 2013).
3   See the discussion in M Evans, 'The Freedom of Religion or Belief and the Freedom of Expression' (2009) 4 *Religion and Human Rights* 197.

democratic society, in the interests of national security, territorial integrity or public safety, for the prevention of disorder or crime, for the protection of health or morals, for the protection of the reputation or rights of others, for preventing the disclosure of information received in confidence, or for maintaining the authority and impartiality of the judiciary.

Article 14 reads:

The enjoyment of the rights and freedoms set out in this Convention shall be secured without discrimination on any grounds such as sex, race, colour, language, religion, political or other opinion, national or social origin, association with a minority, property, birth, or social status.

Of these articles, the meaning and implications of Article 9 is of most concern here. Article 14, however, offers, at face value, significant protection for, *inter alia*, adherents of religious faiths, setting out clearly the principle of non-discrimination against them in the enjoyment of their Convention rights (although it is only exercisable 'within the ambit' of other Convention rights).[4] In the jurisprudence of the ECtHR, however, Article 14 has been significant in only a handful of judgments in respect of religion and belief.

In *Thlimmenos* v. *Greece*,[5] for example, an applicant had been refused work in his chosen profession because of a criminal conviction which had resulted from his religiously motivated refusal to perform conscripted military service in Greece. His Article 14 application (in conjunction with Article 9) was successful because the treatment was discriminatory on the grounds of religion and belief. In this case, an Article 9 claim alone might have failed on the basis that there is no Convention right to a job.

Article 14 was also invoked in respect of one of the applications (Ladele) in *Eweida and Ors*. However, on this occasion, the Court did not engage in a structured approach to weighing up the claim under Article 14 but instead carried out what was in essence an Article 9(2) analysis only.[6] This is arguably rather more typical of the Court's approach when considering Article 14 claims in conjunction with Article 9; the focus of the substantive legal analysis is under Article 9.

---

4   *Rasmussen* v. *Denmark* (1985) 7 EHRR 371.
5   (2000) 31 EHRR 15.
6   See I Leigh and A Hambler, 'Religious Symbols, Conscience and the Rights of Others' (2014) 3 *Oxford Journal of Law and Religion* 2. The discussion in this chapter draws, at intervals, on that article. For another useful commentary on *Eweida and Ors*, see M Hill, 'Religious Symbolism and Conscientious Objection in the Workplace' (2013) 15 *Ecclesiastical Law Journal* 191.

In terms of the models presented in Chapter 3, it is clear that Article 9(1) creates putative rights protective of religion and religious expression. These positive rights explicitly extend beyond the right to hold a religious belief in private and encompass the right to 'manifest' religion in various ways (including in 'practice') and to do this in 'public'. In its interpretation of the ECHR, the ECtHR takes a high view (in theory at least) of the importance of Article 9 rights, basing these rights on the importance of religious expression as a function of individual autonomy and dignity. As it famously said in *Kokkinakis* v. *Greece*:

> As enshrined in Article 9, freedom of thought, conscience and religion is one of the foundations of a "democratic society" within the meaning of the Convention. It is, in its religious dimension, one of the most vital elements that go to make up the identity of believers and their conception of life, but it is also a precious asset for atheists, agnostics, sceptics and the unconcerned. The pluralism indissociable from a democratic society, which has been dearly won over the centuries, depends upon it.[7]

Although a very positive statement of the importance of religious belief and expression, overall and in context it is clear that the Convention does not, in fact, place particular and unique value on religion itself. This is apparent in two ways. The first arises from the juxtaposition of the terms 'religion' and 'belief' in the overall definition under Article 9. The two are seen as inextricably linked. Evans argues that it is not in fact necessary

> to distinguish those patterns of thought and conscience which are religious in nature from patterns of belief which are not since all those systems of thought and conscience which fall within the scope of the article are to be equated with 'beliefs', the manifestation of which is to be protected.[8]

Evans' analysis of Article 9 thus reduces religion to a function of 'belief' which is arguably more representative of ECHR jurisprudence – there is no sense in which religion itself carries *sui generis* claims to special protection, despite the warm words in *Kokkinakis*. The second arises from the scope of Article 10. Although Article 10 arguably increases or at least reinforces protection for religious expression, it also provides a separate avenue to protect many different types and forms of individual expression.[9] As the ECHR does not

7   (1993) 17 EHRR 397 [31].
8   Evans, 'The Freedom of Religion or Belief and the Freedom of Expression', 205.
9   Ibid.

distinguish between the rights it conveys in terms of a hierarchy of importance, Article 10 potentially serves, *inter alia*, to widen and thereby potentially reduce protection for religion (and analogous beliefs) by creating a further category which provides equivalent protection for forms of individual expression which fall short of admission into the Article 9 category.

Another problem is how 'manifestation' of religion has been interpreted historically under Article 9 (although this has recently changed radically). In its well-known ruling in *Arrowsmith* v. *UK,* an application brought by a campaigner convicted under the Incitement to Disaffection Act 1934 for distributing pacifist literature outside army bases (encouraging soldiers, *inter alia*, to desert the army), the European Commission of Human Rights (ECommHR) originally adopted a restrictive interpretation, arguing that 'Article 9(1) does not cover each act which is motivated or influenced by a religion or belief'.[10] Whilst the Commission accepted pacifism as a belief, it went on to reject the Article 9 application on the basis that the act of distributing pamphlets was motivated by Arrowsmith's pacifism but was not in fact a manifestation of that pacifism. Thus, the Commission set out a 'manifestation/motivation requirement',[11] which focused on the nature of the manifestation itself and whether it is truly and fully related to the religion or belief espoused, rather than the motivation of the individual which underpins it.[12] Looked at from the perspective of the claimant, this meant that an individual needed to show that the particular practice, for which he wished to obtain protection as a 'manifestation' of religion or belief, was necessary to, or mandated by, the religion or belief system he espoused.[13] This has been referred to as a 'necessity test'.[14] Such a test was applied by the High Court in the high-profile case of *Playfoot* v. *Governing Body of Millais School*[15] to reject an Article 9 claim by a schoolgirl forbidden to wear a silver ring that was said to symbolise her Christian commitment to sexual abstinence before marriage but which the court found not to be necessary to that belief.[16]

---

10   (1978) 3 EHRR 218 [15].
11   M Hill, R Sandberg and N Doe, *Religion and Law in the United Kingdom* (The Hague: Wolters-Kluwer, 2011), 51.
12   See P Cumper, 'The Public Manifestation of Religion' in R O'Adair and A Lewis (eds), *Law and Religion* (Oxford: Oxford University Press, 2001), 320.
13   See also *Valsamis* v. *Greece* (1997) 24 EHRR 294.
14   Cumper, 'The Public Manifestation of Religion', 323. Cumper draws a distinction, however, between the 'manifestation/motivation requirement' and the 'necessity test'.
15   [2007] ELR 484.
16   In a similar claim under race discrimination, a Sikh schoolgirl challenged a decision made in 2007 by her school, which prevented her from wearing a *Kara* bracelet; see *Sarika Watkins-Singh* v. *Aberdare Girls' High School* [2008] EWHC 1865 (Admin). The claimant was successful, the Court determining that if the *Kara* bracelet was not strictly necessary to Sikhism it fulfilled a closely related test, that of 'exceptional importance' to the claimant's religion [56B] (Silber J).

It is strongly arguable that the necessity test was always unhelpful and the use of it difficult to defend;[17] therefore, perhaps inevitably, inconsistencies emerged over time in the way in which the ECtHR and other courts applied it. For instance, in its decision in *Jakowbski* v. *Poland*,[18] the ECtHR found that the refusal of a Buddhist prisoner's request for vegetarian food engaged Article 9 (even though vegetarianism is not a requirement of the Buddhist religion). In *Bayatyan* v. *Armenia*,[19] the same court accepted that, when opposition to military service is motivated (rather than required) by sincerely held religious beliefs, then it falls within the protection of Article 9. In *R (Imran Bashir)* v. *The Independent Adjudicator and Anor*,[20] the High Court of England and Wales accepted that a prisoner's decision to fast before a court appearance was motivated by his religious beliefs and, as a result, consideration should have been given to his Article 9 rights. This was in spite of the fact that his decision to fast was a personal one rather than a requirement of his Islamic faith.

In its important ruling in *Eweida and Ors* v. *UK*, the Court at length confronted the inconsistencies in its own jurisprudence. This judgment addressed four applications (*Ewedia, Chaplin, Ladele* and *McFarlane*) by individuals who argued that their Convention rights had not been protected by the domestic courts in unsuccessful claims for religious discrimination brought against their employers.[21] It was argued by the UK Government, in its respondent's observations, that 'behaviour or expression that is *motivated* or *inspired* by religion or belief, but which is not an act of *practice* of religion in a *generally recognised form* is not protected by Article 9'.[22] The ECtHR begged to differ. Admitting all four claims, the Court explicitly rejected the necessity test, stating 'there is no requirement on the applicant to establish that he or she acted in fulfilment of a duty mandated by the religion in question'.[23] Instead, it established that 'a sufficiently close and direct nexus between the act and the underlying belief',[24] assuming that belief is also judged to be both cogent and important, is sufficient to establish that the Article 9 claim is a *bona fide* one.[25] By admitting all four claims

17 See discussion in Chapter 2.
18 (2010) 30 BHRC 417.
19 Appl. No 23459/03 (7 July 2011).
20 [2011] EWHC 1108 (Admin).
21 The respective domestic cases (including a detailed summary of the facts of each case) are discussed in Chapter 6 (*Ladele* and *McFarlane*) and Chapter 7 (*Eweida and Chaplin*); the ECtHR ruling is further considered below.
22 Foreign and Commonwealth Office, *Respondent's Observations in the Cases of Ewedia and Chaplin* v. *United Kingdom* 14 October 2011 [6].
23 *Eweida and Ors* [82].
24 Ibid. [82].
25 Interestingly, the importance of considering individual sincerity before admitting a claim is not emphasised in this judgment, although the jurisprudence of the Canadian Supreme Court, which attaches some significance to it, is quoted as a reference point, ibid. [49].

in *Eweida and Ors*, the Court made it clear that the 'close and direct nexus' is to be interpreted broadly, albeit that the outer limits of that breadth may require testing in the future.

Application to the workplace

The Convention itself is binding upon the United Kingdom[26] and any breaches at a national level can be appealed directly to the ECtHR. In addition, the Convention has been applied in domestic law in the form of the Human Rights Act 1998. This Act provides an avenue of redress for individuals where public authorities have breached their Convention rights.[27] Within the context of the workplace, this means that public sector workers can, in theory, make a claim directly against their employer, as can anyone working for a privately owned enterprise that performs a public function (e.g. a former public utility company).[28] On the face of it, this might imply that public sector workers have potentially more 'rights' than those in the private sector.[29] However, the Human Rights Act expressly states that employment tribunals and courts are themselves public bodies,[30] to which the ECHR therefore applies. The Act also states that '[s]o far as it is possible to do so, primary legislation and subordinate legislation must be read and given effect in a way which is compatible with the Convention rights'.[31] Thus, Convention rights must also be taken into account by the courts as part of the interpretation of statute, including employment statutes – to what extent there is an implied obligation to interpret common law in this way is less certain.[32]

Convention rights extend to apply to public bodies and, to a certain degree, private employers. However, this has not necessarily provided additional legal rights for workers as, prior to the decision in *Eweida and Ors*, Convention rights (and particularly those arising under Article 9) have traditionally been construed to apply to individuals but not necessarily in all contexts – the employment sphere being one of those contexts where applications have often been ruled to be inadmissible.[33] This approach has

---

26   The UK signed up to the Convention in 1950; this was ratified by Parliament in 1951.

27   Human Rights Act 1998, s 6.

28   L Vickers, *Religious Freedom, Religious Discrimination and the Workplace* (Oxford: Hart Publishing, 2008), 85.

29   See L Vickers, *Freedom of Expression and Employment* (Oxford: Oxford University Press, 2002), 74–6.

30   Human Rights Act 1998, s 6(3).

31   s 3(1).

32   See I Leigh and R Masterman, *Making Rights Real – The Human Rights Act in its First Decade* (Oxford: Hart, 2008) 238–42.

33   Originally, by the European Commission of Human Rights, which determined admissibility; see C Evans, *Freedom of Religion under the European Convention on Human Rights* (Oxford: Oxford University Press, 2000), 8.

been referred to by some commentators as 'the specific situation rule' as it has served to limit the exercise of Article 9 rights in 'specific situations',[34] perhaps the most important of which would appear to be the workplace, although it has also been applied in the context of education.[35] The justification for this has relied on the premise that a worker 'voluntarily surrenders' his rights when accepting employment and has the right to resign if he wishes to reclaim them.

An early example of this principle at work in Convention case law is the judgment in *Ahmad* v. *UK*.[36] In this case, a Muslim schoolteacher claimed that his Article 9 rights had been violated when his employer refused to allow him a 45-minute absence from his school on Fridays to attend a mosque without reducing his paid working week from five to four and a half days.[37] The ECommHR, in refusing to admit his claim, concluded that refusal to provide time off did not amount to an interference with Ahmad's Article 9(1) rights. Ahmad had accepted the contract 'of his own free will', thereby voluntarily surrendering the claims on his time of religious duties and what remained of his Article 9 rights were guaranteed by the fact that he was free to resign. The same principle was at work in *Konttinen* v. *Finland*[38] where a Seventh-day Adventist, dismissed for repeatedly leaving work before sundown on Fridays, complained that his Article 9(1) rights had been interfered with – the ECommHR disagreed because he retained the 'ultimate guarantee' of his religious freedom (the right to resign).[39]

In *Stedman* v. *UK*,[40] this principle was applied in different circumstances, when the applicant was dismissed for refusing to sign a new contract with her employer that included Sunday working. The Commission found that she had been dismissed for a failure to agree to adopt a particular work pattern rather than for her religious beliefs. In this case, the Commission was unable to argue that the employee had voluntarily forgone any rights upon entering the employment relationship as it was for refusing to surrender such rights (upon variation of her contract) that she was dismissed.

---

34   *Kalac* v. *Turkey* (1997) 27 EHRR 552 [27]. See also discussion in Hill, Sandberg and Doe, *Religion and Law in the United Kingdom*, 53.

35   For example, in the context of a university student, see *Karaduman* v. *Turkey* (1993) 74 DR 93.

36   (1982) 4 EHRR 126.

37   His claim for constructive unfair dismissal against his employer had been rejected by the Court of Appeal; see *Ahmad* v. *Inner London Education Authority* [1978] 1 QB 36.

38   Appl No. 24949/94 (3 December 1996).

39   See also *Pichon and Sajous* v. *France* Appl No. 49853/99 (2 October 2001), where an Article 9 claim by two French pharmacists who had been penalised for refusing to prescribe contraceptive pills was ruled inadmissible by the ECtHR because the applicants were free to manifest their beliefs outside the work sphere.

40   (1997) 23 EHRR CD (Commission).

Thus, it relied entirely on the argument that the ability to leave employment was sufficient to guarantee her religious freedom.

In a case before the Court of Appeal of England and Wales, *Copsey* v. *Devon Clays Limited*,[41] in which an employer had sought to vary an employee's working hours to require Sunday working despite his long-standing objection, Lord Justice Mummery, in rejecting an Article 9 application, endorsed the specific situation rule:

> There is, however, a clear line of decisions by the Commission to the effect that Article 9 is not engaged where an employee asserts Article 9 rights against his employer in relation to his hours of working. The reason given is that if the employer's working practices and the employee's religious convictions are incompatible, the employee is free to resign in order to manifest his religious beliefs.[42]

In *R (Shabina Begum)* v. *Headteacher and Governor of Denbigh High School*,[43] a case involving a schoolgirl forbidden to wear the *jilbab* at the secondary school she attended, the same approach was applied in an educational context because 'there was nothing to stop her [the claimant] from going to a school where her religion did not require a jilbab or where she was allowed to wear one'.[44] The rule was stated more generally that 'Article 9 does not require that one should be allowed to manifest one's religion at any time and place of one's choosing'.[45] This reasoning was swiftly followed by Lord Justice Silber in *X* v. *Headteacher of Y School*[46] and became a problematic precedent in education as well as employment cases.[47]

In a partially dissenting opinion in *Copsey*, Lord Justice Rix took a more sceptical view of the European precedents, arguing that the circumstances of *Ahmad* and *Konttinen* did not in fact apply to those of *Copsey*. This was because, in these two cases, it was the employee and not the employer who was seeking to change the terms of the contract. The facts of *Stedman* alone were materially similar because the employer had attempted to vary the terms of employment. However, in this case, Rix argued that the Commission had acted 'without attempt at explanation'.[48] Thus, the court

41 [2005] EWCA Civ. 932.
42 Ibid. [31].
43 [2007] 1 AC 100; [2006] UKHL 15.
44 Ibid. [50] (Lord Hoffman). Hill and Sandberg point out that it is difficult to see how the rule could apply in full as a school pupil has not voluntarily chosen to accept a role which might limit his Article 9 rights; see M Hill and R Sandberg, 'Is nothing sacred? Clashing symbols in a secular world' (2007) *Public Law* 488–506.
45 [50] (Lord Hoffman).
46 [2007] EWHC 298.
47 See Hill and Sandberg, 'Is nothing sacred?'
48 *Copsey* v. *Devon Clays Ltd* [2005] EWCA Civ. 932 [65].

was under no obligation to apply the decision in *Stedman*, nor any of the other decisions, as this line of apparent authority failed to meet the test of 'clear and constant jurisprudence'.[49]

It is not difficult to find evidence to support Lord Justice Rix's critique. Although, as has been seen, the voluntary surrender of rights and the right to resign arguments have been employed to deny opportunities to exercise Article 9 rights in the workplace, such exclusion is not derived from a plain reading of the ECHR itself; moreover, the ECtHR has not been consistent in applying these exclusionary principles to other convention rights. Although there have been some instances in largely older case law of other convention rights being declared non-admissible in employment,[50] there are numerous examples to the contrary. In *Halford* v. *UK*,[51] for instance, the Court determined that a senior police officer's right to privacy was infringed when her telephone calls from work were intercepted without her permission. Similarly, in *Niemietz* v. *Germany*,[52] the Court determined that the right to privacy was violated by the search of an employee's work-place office. In *Sidabras* v. *Lithuania*,[53] the 'exclusionary approach' was rejected in circumstances where a former KGB officer was dismissed from a public appointment under legislation restricting the employment of former KGB officers. The ECtHR judged this dismissal a violation of the right to a private life, as more than just work life is affected by the denial of employment opportunities (and earning potential). In *Sorensen and Rasmussen* v. *Denmark*,[54] the ECtHR explicitly rejected an argument that employees who were forced to join a trade union against their wishes to secure employment were free to take up alternative employment and so there could be no infringement of their Article 11 rights.[55] In so doing, it commented on the labour market realities which constrain employees' freedom of action when applying for jobs.

The reasoning in these rulings under Articles 8 and 11 runs directly counter to the equivalent Article 9 jurisprudence in failing to impose a 'specific situation rule' to filter out the claim. However, there has also been a degree of historic inconsistency in applying the specific situation rule to Article 9 itself. In an educational context, the ECtHR did not invoke the

---

49 Ibid. [66].
50 For example, *Kosiek* v. *Germany* (1986) 9 EHRR; *Glasenapp* v. *Germany* (1986) 9 EHRR 25; and *Bozhilov* v. *Bulgaria* Appl No. 41978/98 (22 November 2001).
51 Appl No. 20605/92 (25 June 1997).
52 16 EHRR 97.
53 Appl Nos. 55480/00 and 59330/00 (27 July 2004).
54 Appl Nos. 52562/99 and 52620/99 (11 January 2006).
55 See also *Young, James and Webster* v. *UK* [1981] IRLR 408, where a closed-shop arrangement was considered to interfere with an individual's Article 11 rights; and *Sibson* v. *UK* (1994) 17 EHRR 462, where a closed shop was not an interference but only because the applicant had no objection to union membership.

specific situation rule as a filter in either *Leyla Sahin* v. *Turkey*,[56] nor in *Dahlab* v. *Switzerland*[57] (although in neither case was it asked to do so). In applications concerning other employment situations, there have also been departures from the rule. For example, in *Pitkevich* v. *Russia*,[58] the ECtHR found that Article 9 was *prima facie* engaged in respect of a judge dismissed for expressing her religion (by praying audibly in the court room and promising favourable outcomes to parties willing to join her church). Similarly, in *Siebenhaar* v. *Germany*,[59] where an applicant had been dismissed from employment as a daycare worker by a church, having been found to be a member of a religious group whose views were incompatible with those of her employer, the ECtHR did not apply the specific situation rule but instead focused its enquiries on whether the national courts had sufficiently balanced the interests concerned.

Thus far, it has been seen that the application of the specific situation rule to Article 9 claims in the workplace context has been both inconsistent (and increasingly so) and, partly as a result of this, difficult to justify in principle. The situation was clearly ripe for change and the four joined applications in *Eweida and Ors*[60] were therefore timely, representing as they did a significant challenge, *inter alia*, to the specific situation rule – a challenge it was unable to survive. Significantly, in this case, the ECtHR declared:

> Given the importance in a democratic society of freedom of religion, the Court considers that, where an individual complains of a restriction on freedom of religion in the workplace, rather than holding that the possibility of changing job would negate any interference with the right, the better approach would be to weigh that possibility in the overall balance when considering whether or not the restriction was proportionate.[61]

This statement is very important, as it represents the removal of a real barrier to those seeking redress under Article 9. As such, it is clearly a step in the direction of greater protection for religion in the workplace; applications are now unlikely to be rejected merely because they relate to manifestations within the workplace itself. It should be noted, however, that

56   Appl No. 44774/98 (SC) (29 June 2004).
57   Appl No. 42393/98 (15 Feb 2001).
58   Appl No. 47936/99 (8 February 2001).
59   Appl No. 18136/02 (3 February 2011).
60   Albeit that this was not a foregone conclusion – the UK Government's submission in *Eweida and Ors* continued to rely on the doctrine to argue that the claims were inadmissible; see Foreign and Commonwealth Office, *Respondent's Observations* [35].
61   *Eweida and Ors* [83].

the Court has not entirely abandoned the 'specific situation rule' but, rather, it appears to have repositioned it, in a way that it notably has not done with the now defunct necessity test, as a reference point in weighting the claim under Article 9(2).[62] This is surely to be welcomed, at least in the way in which it was applied in the instant cases. The fact that one of the applicants, McFarlane, had sought a role (in sex therapy) that would conflict with his religious beliefs (insofar as he might reasonably be expected to realise that this would occur) rightly weighs against him to a certain extent.[63] Equally, in a full reversal of the application in *Stedman*, it was surely right that, since the employer had unilaterally varied her contract of employment to put her in a position where she would be forced to act against religious conscience (by registering same-sex civil partnerships), this was to be weighed in favour of another applicant, Ladele.[64] However, it is notable that, in both cases, the situational context was lightly weighted compared with other relevant factors. Why this should be so was not clearly articulated by the Court.

Nevertheless, albeit that it can now be expected that Article 9 applications in workplace cases will be accepted *prima facie*, there is another potential impediment to the full flourishing of protection for religious expression. This is evident from Article 9(2), which sets out the limitations on the freedom to 'manifest' religion or belief that a Convention signatory state may impose. No such limitations are placed on the freedom to hold a religion or belief itself.[65] Of the range of rationales for limitations on the manifestation of religion (listed in Article 9(2)), 'the protection of the rights and freedoms of others' must surely be the most wide-ranging in potential scope, particularly in a workplace context. As with other freedoms, the ECtHR allows signatory states a 'margin of appreciation', albeit under European oversight,[66] to determine for themselves the circumstances in which Article 9(2) may be invoked (and enshrined in national law).[67] In exercising its margin of appreciation, a member state is nevertheless expected to show evidence that its courts have considered the extent to which any restrictions on ECHR rights are 'proportionate' and in the process that they have sought to balance the interests involved.[68]

As a result of its admissibility decision in *Eweida and Ors*, the ECtHR was forced to engage in a considered proportionality balancing exercise. For

---

62   Ibid. [83].
63   Ibid. [109].
64   Ibid. [106].
65   See discussion in Chapter 2 on the distinction between the *forum internum* and *forum externum*.
66   See Leigh and Masterman, *Making Rights Real*, 53–6.
67   See *Handyside* v. *United Kingdom* (1979) 1 EHRR 737 [22].
68   For an insightful discussion of proportionality in this context, see A Baker, 'Proportionality and Employment Discrimination in the UK' (2008) 37 *Industrial Law Journal* 305.

the reasons noted earlier, this represents something of an innovation in workplace cases and the decisions and the accompanying reasoning set an important (but not altogether satisfactory) precedent. For this reason, the judgment will now be discussed in some detail.

Balancing rights: *Eweida* and *Ors*

In this section, the way in which the ECtHR addressed the issue of proportionality for each of the four applications in *Eweida and Ors* is considered and critiqued.

With regard to the first application brought by Nadia Eweida, a British Airways employee refused permission to wear a visible Christian cross in a customer-facing role, the Court determined that the UK courts had failed to strike the right balance by affording too much weight to British Airways' imperative to display a consistent corporate image, as balanced against Eweida's right to manifest her religion and her natural desire 'to communicate [her] belief to others' (something which should be encouraged in a healthy democratic society).[69] The factors it considered relevant were: the 'discreet' size of Eweida's cross;[70] that there appeared to be no adverse impact on British Airways of the wearing of 'permitted' religious dress such as *hijabs* or turbans; and that the company had encountered no difficulties when it reversed its original policy. The Court found in Eweida's favour, as there had been no evidence of any 'real encroachment' on the rights of others arising as a result of her stance.[71]

In response to the second application, brought by Shirley Chaplin, a nurse refused permission to wear a cross over her uniform, the Court reached a rather different conclusion. Noting from evidence submitted to the employment tribunal that Chaplin's managers feared that her cross on its chain might be seized by a disturbed patient or come into contact with an open wound, it observed that 'the protection of health and safety on a hospital ward was inherently of a greater magnitude than that which

69   Ibid. [94].
70   'Discreet religious symbols' have, in the past, attracted a more favourable reaction from the ECtHR than 'powerful external symbols' such as the Islamic headscarf; see *Dahlab* v. *Switzerland* 7.
71   *Eweida and Ors* [95]. Two judges (Bratza and Bjorgvinsson) disagreed. In their view, the domestic Court of Appeal had taken a broad but not incorrect approach to balancing the interests involved in deciding in favour of British Airways. These were: that Eweida herself had observed the company dress code for two years without objection and, having changed her position, had been unwilling to wait for the outcome of her internal grievance before wearing her cross visibly; British Airway's 'conscientious' approach in dealing with the grievance, including the offer of temporary back-office work for Eweida whilst the uniform policy was reviewed; and, finally, the relaxation of the policy to accommodate Eweida in her original job role (Partially Dissenting Opinion of Judges Bratza and Bjorgvinsson [7]).

applied in respect of Ms Eweida'.[72] It considered that health and safety was a field where a wide margin of appreciation should be afforded to domestic authorities and considerable weight should be given to the decisions of hospital managers. On that basis, any interference with Chaplin's Article 9 rights was justified as necessary in a democratic society.

It is interesting to note how the Court chose to constrain its own discretion by affording overwhelming weight to the employer's assessment of the health and safety concerns associated with Chaplin's religious expression. Such an approach, taken to its logical conclusion, risks giving a *carte blanche* to employers to invoke 'health and safety' to choke off religious manifestation without proper scrutiny by national courts. In other jurisdictions, courts have shown more willingness to examine health and safety arguments more closely (and, on occasion, to prefer religious manifestation when balancing the two imperatives).[73] Whereas there is obvious wisdom in giving due weight to the decisions of domestic authorities, there is no reason why the Court should give such a wide margin of appreciation in the field of health and safety and, to some extent, this is a new (and regrettable) development. In the UK, some curious decisions have been handed down in the past, the courts giving priority to health and safety over religious obligations, and it would be disappointing if an avenue for legitimate challenge before the ECtHR were to be curtailed.[74] In earlier decisions, the Court and the former Commission felt able to form their own assessment of national practices as either necessary[75] or 'not unreasonable'[76] in protection of health and safety and it is strongly arguable that this approach is to be preferred.

In its disposal of the application by the relationships therapist, Gary McFarlane, the Court accepted that an objection by the applicant to providing psychosexual counselling to same-sex couples was motivated by his

---

72   *Eweida and Ors* [99].

73   See especially the Supreme Court of Canada, *Multani* v. *Commission Scolaire Marguerite-Bourgeoys* [2006] 1 SCR 256, [59]–[67], emphasising the lack of violent incidents in Canadian schools arising from pupils' wearing the *kirpan* (the Sikh ceremonial dagger) and the failure of the authorities to justify the need for an absolute prohibition.

74   For example, the indirect race discrimination decisions in *Singh* v. *Rowntree Mackintosh* [1979] IRLR 199 (EAT Sc) and *Panesar* v. *Nestlé* [1980] ICR 60, (EAT); 64 (CA), in which Sikh job applicants were turned down on 'hygiene' grounds after indicating their refusal to remove facial hair for religious reasons (although alternative forms of facial covering might have been safely utilised). These decisions are discussed in Chapter 7.

75   *X* v. *United Kingdom* Appl No.7992/77 (Commission Decision of 12 July 1978), 235 (rejecting a Sikh's application concerning the compulsory wearing of motorcycle crash helmets).

76   *Dogru* v. *France* Appl No. 27058/05 (4 December 2008), [73] (declaring inadmissible an application by a Muslim schoolgirl required to remove her headscarf during physical education classes).

orthodox Christian beliefs and, thus, the state had a positive obligation to secure his Article 9 rights. Whilst it did not address the question of a legitimate aim specifically, it did go on to consider the extent to which different interests had been balanced, noting *inter alia* that McFarlane had voluntarily sought to engage in the role which subsequently led to the objection and that the employer's policy was one aimed at 'providing a service without discrimination'.[77] In the light of the margin of appreciation to be afforded in such cases, the Court determined that there had been no violation of Article 9, alone or alongside Article 14.

In response to a further application brought by the marriages registrar, Lilian Ladele, the Court noted that the applicant held the 'orthodox Christian view' of exclusively heterosexual marriage and that she believed it would be wrong for her to participate in the creation of a same-sex union equivalent to marriage.[78] It agreed that both ECHR Articles 9 and 14 were engaged, as Ladele's stance was 'directly motivated by her religious beliefs'.[79] She had been designated a 'civil partnerships registrar' against her wishes and it was her refusal to accept this which had directly led to her losing her job.

In considering whether or not Ladele's employer, Islington Borough Council, had a legitimate aim, the Court noted that the Court of Appeal had accepted that the aim was not simply the provision of an effective civil partnerships service (which it could provide without Ladele's involvement)[80] but, rather, a wider aim of requiring all employees to 'act in a way which does not discriminate against others', in accordance with its own equal opportunities policy, to which it was 'wholly committed'.[81] These two ways of constructing what would amount to a legitimate aim in the context of indirect discrimination were at the root of some significant legal argument before the domestic courts.[82] In finding this wider aim to be legitimate, the Court declared that its Article 14 jurisprudence had established that 'differences in treatment based on sexual orientation require particularly serious reasons by way of justification'.[83] It also noted that same-sex couples were in a 'relevantly similar situation' to heterosexual couples in terms of requiring legal recognition, although, because this situation was evolving amongst contracting states, a wide margin of appreciation was to

77   Ibid. [109].
78   *Eweida and Ors* [102].
79   Ibid. [103].
80   Indeed, it was accepted by the Court of Appeal that the employer was able to offer an 'effective' civil partnerships service without Ladele's contribution; see *Ladele* v. *Islington Borough Council* [2009] EWCA Civ. 1357 (CA); [2010] IRLR 211 [44].
81   *Eweida and Ors* [105].
82   *Ladele* v. *Islington Borough Council* (CA) [43–53].
83   *Eweida and Ors* [105], citing *Karner* v. *Austria* Appl No. 40016/98 (24 July 2004), *Smith and Grady* v. *United Kingdom* Appl No. 20605/92 (25 June 1997) and *Schalk and Kopf* v. *Austria* Appl No. 30141/04 (24 June 2010).

be afforded to domestic authorities.[84] Whilst neither observation appears to address clearly the issue at stake, the Court nevertheless concluded that, given the 'background' that it had outlined, the wider aim of the local authority could be said to be legitimate.

Moving on to assess the proportionality of the means used to fulfil this legitimate aim in respect of Ladele, the Court observed that Ladele had not voluntarily put herself in a position in which she would be required to perform civil partnerships and this apparently weighed in her favour; nevertheless, as the local authority's policy aimed 'to secure the rights of others who are protected under the Convention', and as both it and the domestic authorities enjoyed a wide margin of appreciation, then, on balance, there was no violation of Article 14 or Article 9.[85]

The cursory nature of this reasoning is disappointing and sets a weak precedent for future applications. The decision was not unanimous and a dissenting opinion (by Judges Vucinic and De Gaetano) provides an alternative and in some ways more convincing analysis, conceptualising Ladele's claim not simply as one of religion and belief but as one primarily of moral conscience. The consequences of their insight are potentially significant. The judges note that conscience is referred to for protection under Article 9(1) but is 'conspicuously absent' from the qualifications available to member states in Article 9(2).[86] They conclude therefore that conscience, once a certain threshold is reached, is an absolute right (akin, it may be said, to the *forum internum*) which cannot be qualified (*inter alia*, with respect to the rights of others) in the way that religious manifestation more generally might be.[87]

In adopting the language of conscience and affording such a high view of this as an absolute right, the judges consider that there was consequently no requirement to engage in any kind of balancing exercise in consideration of sexual orientation rights – the majority had misdirected themselves in this respect. This is because the fundamental human right to exercise moral conscience cannot give way to an 'abstract' right. They treated sexual orientation rights as 'abstract' because there had been no actual complaint relating to specific discrimination by a service user seeking a same-sex civil partnership.[88]

Perhaps the most significant insight in this dissenting judgment is the recognition that in weighing up different rights and interests, in this case

---

84   *Eweida and Ors* [105].
85   Ibid. [106].
86   Partially Dissenting Opinion of Judges Vucinic and De Gaetano [2].
87   An alternative reading is that there is no convention right to 'manifest' conscience at all: see Evans, *Freedom of Religion under the European Convention on Human Rights*, 52–3.
88   The conceptualisation of Ladele as a 'conscientious objector' is considered in some detail in Chapter 6.

between religion and sexual orientation, 'concrete' rights should carry more weight than the right to be free from offence. This issue is explored in some depth in Chapter 6 in terms of the domestic decision in *Ladele* and it is suggested that there are serious deficiencies in the reasoning underlying that judgment. Rather than accepting the decision of the domestic authorities so uncritically, it would surely have been preferable for the Court to have engaged in a more structured balancing exercise invoking some of the principles from its own jurisprudence (for instance that there is no Convention right not to be offended).[89] Leigh and Hambler propose a 'reversibility test' in such cases in which:

> [T]he Court should ask itself whether if the state were to give priority to the less favoured right (here the Article 14 in conjunction with Article 9 right) would another disappointed person have an admissible Convention claim? Put another way, can we identify the 'others' whose rights and freedoms are being protected by the state at the cost of applicants like Ladele? Had the UK courts upheld her case under domestic discrimination law could another claimant have stepped forward with a claim that either their right to respect for their private life (Article 8), their right to marry (Article 12) or non-discrimination (Article 14) had been violated?[90]

The authors conclude that the answer is 'no'. Thus, a better judgment, certainly in respect of *Ladele*, would have been to uphold the claim. Ladele's was the only real Convention right which had been infringed; other claims fell short of Convention right status and so the state did not have the same obligation to protect them in the way that it should have protected Ladele.

Ultimately, in *Eweida and Ors*, the Court failed to conduct a full and adequate proportionality balancing exercise under either Article 9 or Article 14, to the detriment of the religious claimants concerned and to the effective operation of the Convention as a whole.

Conclusion

ECHR jurisprudence under Article 9(2) is at a very early stage, owing to the fact that most applications under Article 9 have been hitherto filtered out when considered under Article 9(1). This is clearly set to change. However, on the basis of its disposal of *Eweida and Ors*, the omens do not look promising, as the Court would appear to be prepared to accept, with little in the way of sophisticated legal analysis, national decisions on legitimacy of aim and

---

89   *Otto-Preminger Institute* v. *Austria* (1995) 19 EHRR 34 [47].
90   Leigh and Hambler, 'Religious Symbols, Conscience and the Rights of Others', 2.

proportionality, at least where a *prima facie* 'weighty' reason as justification is advanced, such as 'health and safety' or sexual orientation rights. However, if the Court were prepared to delve deeper, it may be that these reasons are not nearly as compelling as they first appear. It is likely that, in the future, the Court will be called on to fundamentally reconsider its reasoning in *Eweida and Ors* as Article 9(2) jurisprudence develops, as it now surely will.

The discussion turns in closing to an application of the models presented in Chapter 3 to the legal issues considered in this chapter. As noted earlier, Article 9 ECHR (potentially alongside other articles) is a guarantee of religious rights which *prima facie* is in step with 'protection'. The value of this in the workplace has, however, unfortunately been negligible, as claims have been filtered using the devices of the necessity test (under which manifestations have been interpreted narrowly) and the specific situation rule (which allowed for resignation to guarantee Article 9 rights); acting together, these filters have represented a near-insuperable barrier to applications for violations of the right to religious expression. Thus, a better construction of the role of Article 9 ECHR in support of the 'models' has been, at best, that it is in step with *laissez-faire*, given that the Court has refused to recognise rights in the workplace forum and has left it to other authorities to adjudicate; at worst, it has been in step with the 'exclusion' model, as it has provided domestic 'authorities' (courts and employers) with weapons against the recognition of religious expression in the form of the filters to workplace claims which are transferable to other contexts, particularly the domestic courts but also, most obviously in the case of the necessity test, to policy making at an organisation level.[91]

The Court's departure from its approach of filtering the claims at Article 9(1) stage towards an apparently much broader approach of acceptance is suggestive of a movement away from *laissez-faire* or 'exclusion' in the direction of 'protection'. However, if the Court does now act to protect religious expression in the workplace, the extent of this protection should not be exaggerated. The *laissez-faire* imperative is still strong in terms of the Court's willingness to defer to national authorities, with minimal scrutiny where 'weighty' reasons (connected with other rights) are apparently invoked, when those authorities exercise their margin of appreciation, even where those national authorities, as in *Chaplin* and *Ladele* (and to some extent in *McFarlane*), appear to be acting to exclude religious expression for reasons that are highly contentious and, it may be argued, flawed. Nevertheless, as the decision in *Eweida* shows, there is now the possibility of some more effective protection for religious expression, if only in limited circumstances such as where other rights are not seen as sufficiently weighty (e.g. the whims of a commercial employer's uniform policy).

---

91   See the discussion in Chapter 7 for the conscious application of the necessity test, by both employer and employment tribunal, in relation to *Chaplin*.

5   The legislative and policy landscape in England and Wales

Introduction

This chapter continues the discussion of legal authorities relevant to freedom of religious expression in the workplace which began in the previous chapter. The focus of this chapter is on law specifically designed for the workplace in England and Wales. The chapter is structured to reflect the importance of the extension of the coverage of discrimination law to religion and belief in 2003, such that the legal landscape prior to 2003 is examined first (in particular those aspects still in force), followed by a more lengthy discussion of the law post-2003. The following section of the chapter considers public policy and its importance in relation to the expression of religion and belief at work. The concluding section summarises all aspects of law and policy considered in this chapter and suggests appropriate linkages, for the purposes of an overall assessment of the role of the law, to the models presented in Chapter 3.

England and Wales (before 2003)

The purpose of this section is to present a brief survey of domestic legislation and its context which directly or indirectly addresses religious expression in the workplace (or some aspect of it) prior to the major legislative innovation in 2003.

Vestigial remains of historic legislation

Public appointments

Some of the legislation which has applied historically was surveyed earlier in Chapter 3 in considering the approach of providing exclusive protection for Christianity as the national religion. Historically and directly, this took the form of legal measures which had the effect of excluding Roman Catholics and Dissenters from public office and the professions. Most of these 'disabilities' were removed in 1829,[1] although a few remained. For

1   Under the terms of the Roman Catholic Relief Act 1829.

example, until as late as 1974, the position of Lord Chancellor could not be occupied by a Roman Catholic on the basis that he was 'keeper of the Queen's conscience' and had a ceremonial role in appointing bishops.[2] It is for a similar reason (i.e. the office-holder's role in appointing Church of England bishops) that the convention exists that neither a Roman Catholic nor a Jew should occupy the office of Prime Minister. Cumper and Edge point out that although there is no absolute legal bar to a Roman Catholic taking up the appointment, in practice, there are significant legal constraints, not least amongst these being that a Roman Catholic (or Jewish) Prime Minister may not advise on clerical appointments on pain of criminal prosecution and loss of office,[3] but no provision is made for this power to be delegated to another officeholder.[4] The continued influence of this convention can be seen in the decision by the former Prime Minister, Tony Blair, to delay his public conversion to the Roman Catholic Church until after his tenure in that office had come to an end.[5] Nevertheless, the significance of this convention should not be overstated. The convention merely refers to allegiance to the Church of England. It does not require the incumbent Prime Minister to act in conformity with Anglican teachings, either in private or public.[6]

There is, however, one remaining office, excepting those specific to the Church of England, for which there remains a legal requirement that the incumbent is a Protestant Christian – this is the office of monarch.[7] The monarch must attest to this by means of a coronation oath[8] and must join the Church of England to perform the functions of Supreme Governor.[9]

2   The Lord Chancellor (Tenure of Office and Discharge of Ecclesiastical Functions) Act 1974 permits the office to be held by a Roman Catholic, albeit that some of the ceremonial functions must then pass to another office-holder; see R Ahdar and I Leigh, *Religious Freedom in the Liberal State*, 2nd ed. (Oxford: Oxford University Press, 2013), 105, ft 102.
3   Roman Catholic Relief Act 1829, s 18; Jews Relief Act 1858, s 4.
4   P Cumper and P Edge, 'First Among Equals: The English State and the Anglican Church in the 21st Century' (2005–2006) 83 *University of Detroit Mercy Law Review* 601, 605–6. The authors do concede, however, that the office of Prime Minister 'is a creature of convention and so can be changed informally' (606).
5   S Bates, 'After 30 years as a closet Catholic, Blair finally puts faith before politics' *Guardian* (London, 22 June 2007) 3.
6   Thus, the Prime Minister, David Cameron, was entirely at liberty, in 2012, to initiate a legislative process intended to legalise same-sex marriage, despite the fact that this conflicts with official Church of England teaching.
7   Under the terms of the Act of Settlement 1701.
8   Coronation Oath Act 1688, s 3.
9   Act of Supremacy 1558.

Working patterns

With the exception of the unique public office of monarch, which to a limited extent reflects the a model II imperative ('religion as heritage'), the only other institutional arrangements which serve to support Christianity uniquely in the workplace concern the structuring of the working calendar. In terms of their entrenchment in legislation, there are now few examples.

Dealing first with the working year, it is notable that four of the eight officially recognised public holidays in England and Wales are timed to coincide with the two major Christian festivals of Christmas and Easter. Significantly, a fifth public holiday, the Christian festival of Whitsun, a holiday which used to fall on a date between 11 May and 14 June, was secularised in 1971 as the second May public holiday (observed on the last Monday of that month) and has so lost its Christian associations.[10] Although these holidays are officially recognised, the Working Time Regulations 2008[11] do not entitle employees to these specific days as holiday.[12] The tradition is quite entrenched, however, such that the Trade Union Congress estimates that only one-third of all workers work on at least one public holiday in the year.[13]

In terms of the working week, there is an established convention that Sunday is the day when most workers expect to take a holiday. This convention is firmly rooted in notions of the Christian 'Sabbath' as falling on a Sunday; the Sabbath being a day which, by divine command, is kept separate from work as a day of rest.[14] As late as 1950, this principle continued to form the basis of actual lawmaking in England and Wales. Part IV of the Shops Act of that year regulates Sunday trading, with restricted exceptions, starting from the principle that '[e]very shop shall, save as otherwise provided by this Part of this Act, be closed for the serving of customers on Sunday'.[15] It is clear that the rationale behind this general prohibition of Sunday trading was at least in part religious, from the fact that some of the exceptions were specifically and uniquely available to 'person[s] of the Jewish religion'[16] who would not be celebrating the Sabbath on a Sunday

10   See Schedule 1 of the Banking and Financial Dealings Act 1971, which sets out the statutory bank holidays in England and Wales, Scotland and Northern Ireland. In addition, there are common law public holidays such as Good Friday in England and Wales.
11   SI 1998 No. 1833.
12   s 15.
13   Trade Union Congress, *TUC Launches Search for New Bank Holiday* [press release]. Available online at www.tuc.org.uk/workplace-issues/chemicals-and-dust/welfare-and-benefits/campaigns/tuc-launches-search-new-bank (accessed 6 June 2014).
14   One of the Ten Commandments: see Exodus 20: 8–11; Deuteronomy 5: 12–15.
15   Shops Act 1950 s 47 as originally enacted; repealed by the Sunday Trading Act 1994 s 1(2).
16   s 53(1). A legacy of these provisions also appears in reduced form in the Sunday Trading Act 1994, Sch 2, part II.

but rather the day before. It is also of note that this Act did not repeal but, rather, modified more explicitly 'Christian' restrictive legislation in the forms of, for example, the Sunday Fairs Act 1448 and the Sunday Observance Act 1677.[17] This position changed with the passage of the Sunday Trading Act 1994, which relaxed, to a considerable extent, Sunday trading restrictions. Indeed, any meaningful restrictions apply only to 'large shops' (those where the floor space exceeds 280 square metres)[18] and again with some exceptions.[19] Those falling within the restrictions may only open for a maximum of six consecutive hours on a Sunday, between 10am and 6pm; and they may not open on Easter Sunday or on Christmas Day when it falls on a Sunday.[20]

Where workers themselves are concerned, there are some exemptions in the retail and betting trades (such that employers cannot force employees, who started work before a certain date, to work on Sundays)[21] but the general principle from the perspective of the state is that of *laissez-faire*, such that workers are expected to work as their contracts require. Sunday is not even mentioned in the Working Time Regulations 2008, although there is (consciously or perhaps unconsciously) a recognition of a Christian pattern of weekly rest by the requirement that, with very limited exceptions, workers must be given a minimum rest period of an uninterrupted 24 hours in every seven-day cycle.[22]

It should be noted that Knights sees the existence of the protections from Sunday working for shopworkers as an example of a favouring the established religion and, for that reason, should be 'subject to challenge'.[23] Assuming that her analysis is to be accepted (although no actual reference is made in the legislation to religion and thus all eligible employees can benefit from the option of refusing to work on Sunday, irrespective of religious convictions), Knights arguably underplays the context in which the exemptions came into force – they are, of course, concessions in the face of a loss of much greater freedoms (since 1994) to observe Sundays as a day for worship and rest for the Christians, rather than positive rights created specifically to favour the established religion.

17 See s 59(2).
18 Sunday Trading Act 1994, Sch 1, s 1.
19 Sch 1, s 3.
20 A temporary relaxation of these restrictions occurred during the period surrounding the London Olympics in the summer of 2012, opening up the controversial possibility that a more permanent relaxation might follow; see A McSmith, 'A Sunday trading trade-off too far?' *Independent* (London, 22 August 2012) 22.
21 Employment Rights Act 1996 s 36. The dates are: 26 August 1994 (for a shop worker); and 3 January 1995 (for a betting worker).
22 Working Time Regulations 1998, SI 1998 No. 1833, reg 11.
23 S Knights, *Freedom of Religion, Minorities and the Law* (Oxford: Oxford University Press, 2007), 149.

This example notwithstanding, it is submitted that there is little at a statutory level that amounts to evidence of exclusive ongoing support in 'a workplace context' for the historical religion of England and Wales. In fact, there remain two examples. In terms of public office, the role of the monarch continues to require a religious test of commitment to Anglican Protestant Christianity and this is largely for reasons connected to the constitutional position of the Church of England and the role of the monarch as supreme governor. In terms of the working calendar, there now remains only Easter Sunday where large shops must be closed; otherwise, there are few restrictions on Sunday trading. However, although there is little in the way of statutory restriction, the convention of treating Sunday as a weekly day of rest remains strong such that on that day 'many social activities (such as education and government) are suspended'.[24]

Race discrimination protection

It will be argued that anti-discrimination law provides the most obvious vehicle for the protection of religious expression in the workplace. Although specific protection for religion and belief has only been available since 2003, there is some older anti-discrimination law in the form of the Race Relations Act 1976, which has been interpreted to offer protection to workers who are members of certain religious groups on the basis that these also represent defined 'racial groups'.[25] The Race Relations Act, in its amended version, outlaws discrimination on 'racial grounds' or against 'racial groups' where the latter term means 'a group of persons defined by reference to colour, race, nationality or ethnic or national origins'.[26]

This principle that this definition might encompass groups more usually identified as religious was first established at the Employment Appeals Tribunal, with reference to a Jewish man. Although without employing any significant legal reasoning, except that it reflected a

---

24   R Gavison and N Perez, 'Days of rest in multicultural societies: private, public separate' in P Cane, C Evans and Z Robinson (eds), *Law and Religion in Theoretical and Historical Context* (Cambridge: Cambridge University Press, 2008), 189.

25   There is also a potential (but rather less obvious) avenue of redress for women who are denied the opportunity to manifest their religion originally under the Sex Discrimination Act (now under the sex discrimination provisions of the Equality Act). For example, Hepple and Choudhury note the unreported tribunal case of *Sardar* v. *McDonalds* (1998), where the claimant, a Muslim woman, was successful in a sex discrimination claim, having been denied the right to wear a headscarf at work; B Hepple and T Choudhury, *Tackling Religious Discrimination: Practical Implications for Policy-Makers and Legislators*, Home Office Research Study 221 (London: Home Office Research, Development and Statistics Directorate, 2001), 5.

26   Race Relations Act 1976, s 3(1).

common understanding between the parties, the Tribunal determined that he could be considered to be a member of an ethnic or racial group for the purposes of the Race Relations Act.[27]

The same principle was recognised in respect of Sikhs, and with much more sophistication, in the House of Lords judgment in *Mandla* v. *Dowell Lee*.[28] This case was brought under the wide reach of the Race Relations Act by the father of an orthodox Sikh, who was a prospective pupil at a private school. The headmaster, who, in the cause of racial harmony, wanted to minimise religious and social distinctions in the school, refused to admit the boy unless he removed his turban and cut his hair. Mandla and his father held that this represented indirect discrimination which could not be justified, as the rationale rested on the headmaster's subjective opinion and was therefore unlawful. The case rested on whether or not the Sikh identity was purely a function of religion or also a function of ethnic origin. The House of Lords determined that unlawful indirect discrimination had occurred under the Race Relations Act. In determining that Sikhs are in fact members of an ethnic group, the following 'content-based' rationale was offered:

> The conditions which appear to me to be essential are these: (1) a long shared history, of which the group is conscious as distinguishing it from other groups, and the memory of which it keeps alive (2) a cultural tradition of its own. ... In addition to those two essential characteristics the following characteristics are, in my opinion, relevant: (3) either a common geographical origin, or descent from a small number of common ancestors (4) a common language, not necessarily peculiar to the group (5) a common literature peculiar to the group (6) a common religion different from that of neighbouring groups or from the general community surrounding it (7) being a minority or being an oppressed or a dominant group within a larger community ... A group defined by reference to enough of these characteristics would be capable of including converts, for example, persons who marry into the group, and of excluding apostates. Provided a person who joins the group feels himself or herself to be a member of it, and is accepted by other members, then he is, for the purpose of the 1976 Act, a member.[29]

These criteria have been used in subsequent cases to determine that Rastafarians are not an ethnic group because they cannot show a separate identity either from other Jamaicans or indeed from the rest of the Afro-Caribbean community.[30] Muslims have been unable similarly to establish

27   *Seide* v. *Gillette Industries Ltd* [1980] IRLR 427.
28   [1983] 2AC 548 (HL).
29   Ibid., 4 (Lord Fraser of Tullybelton).
30   *Dawkins* v. *Department of the Environment* [1993] IRLR 284 (CA).

protection on the grounds of race because they are geographically widely dispersed and so cannot point towards a common ethnic origin.[31] Jehovah's Witnesses have also failed to establish that they are a distinct ethnic or racial group.[32]

As noted by Hepple and Choudhury, the concept of indirect discrimination (discussed below) has also been invoked under the Race Relations Act to seek redress for detriments suffered on religious grounds.[33] In *JH Walker* v. *Hussain*, for example, a blanket rule by an employer preventing employees taking leave during a busy period of time (which happened to be a Muslim holiday) was challenged by 17 employees under the Race Relations Act. Their case relied on the fact that all 17 claimants originated from the Indian subcontinent and could thus claim a common ethnic origin. Both the first instance tribunal and the Employment Appeals Tribunal found that the respondent had indirectly discriminated against the claimants; the only group affected (negatively) by the application of the blanket rule were 'Asian Muslims' and the respondent was unable to offer a satisfactory justification. Although, in this case, the claimants were successful, when the same reasoning under the Race Relations Act was applied in different circumstances, the limitations of this avenue of redress for 'religious' claimants is clear. For example in *Safouane & Bouterfas* v. *Joseph Ltd and Hannah*[34] two Muslim employees had been summarily dismissed for, *inter alia*, taking time for prayers during the lunch period. An industrial tribunal concluded that this did not amount to indirect racial discrimination by the employer, because both the claimants and the respondents belonged to the same North African ethnic Arab minority – the former were Muslim, the latter respectively Jewish and Christian Coptic.

'Conscience clauses'

Outside discrimination law, there are a small number of specific exemptions from certain workplace activities enshrined in particular statutes.[35] Probably the most well-known and longstanding example is the clause in the Abortion Act 1967, which allows medical staff to refuse to participate in abortion procedures if they have a 'conscientious objection'.[36] This right of

31 *JH Walker Ltd* v. *Hussain* [1996] IRLR 11 (EAT).
32 *Lovell-Badge* v. *Norwich City College of Further and Higher Education* (1999) ET Case No. 1502237/97.
33 Hepple and Choudhury, *Tackling Religious Discrimination*, 4–5.
34 (1996) ET Case No. 12506/95 and ET Case No. 12568/95, cited by Hepple and Choudhury, *Tackling Religious Discrimination*, 5.
35 This section draws on A Hambler, 'Recognising a right to "conscientiously object" for registrars whose religious beliefs are incompatible with their duty to conduct same-sex civil partnerships' (2012) 7 *Religion and Human Rights* 157.
36 Abortion Act 1967, s 4(1).

refusal was extended to embryo research in 1990[37] and would have been extended to apply to 'assisted dying' under a private members Bill introduced to Parliament in 2004.[38] Where abortion is concerned, conscientious objection is not referenced to a religious or other form of belief. In fact, no grounds for this objection are specifically required, albeit that the burden of proof that a genuine objection exists rests with the medical practitioner.[39] It is perhaps safe to assume that a large number of practicing members of religious faiths will be amongst those medical practitioners who avail themselves of this clause[40] but it is significant that it is the objection, not the motivation for the objection, which triggers the available protection.

There are limits on the exercise of the conscience clause under the Abortion Act. For example, those medical professionals who oppose abortion in all circumstances absolutely are required, conscientious objections notwithstanding, to participate in abortions if this is required to save the life or prevent serious and permanent physical or mental injury to a pregnant woman.[41] This is likely to affect only a small group of particularly stringent conscientious objectors. However, many more are likely to be affected by a more significant limitation on the exercise of conscientious objection – that it has been held to apply to medical treatment only. Thus, in *R* v. *Salford AHA ex parte Janaway*,[42] a doctor's secretary, who was Roman Catholic, was unsuccessful in arguing that she was entitled to use the exemptions under Section 4(1) of the Abortion Act to justify her refusal to type a letter of referral for a patient seeking an abortion. The exemption was held to apply only to actual participation in the hospital *treatment* leading to abortion. Similarly, in a Scottish case under the same legislation, *Doogan & Anor, Re Judicial Review*,[43] the exemptions for conscience were held not to apply to two midwifery sisters (both Roman Catholic) who opposed being required to 'delegate, supervise and support staff in the treatment of patients undergoing termination of pregnancy'.[44] These activities were held not to constitute direct involvement in abortion because

---

37   Human Fertilisation and Embryology Act 1990, s 38.
38   Assisted Dying for the Terminally Ill Bill [HL] 2004, s 7; interestingly, however, such a clause was not included in the End of Life Assistance (Scotland) Bill 2010.
39   Abortion Act 1967, s 4(1). In Scotland, this can be discharged simply by 'making a statement on oath by any person to the effect that he has a conscientious objection' (s 4 (3)).
40   It is known, for example, that members of the Christian Medical Fellowship have been amongst those who have used the conscience clauses; see P Saunders, 'Abortion and Conscientious Objection' (1999) Spring *Nucleus*, 4.
41   Abortion Act 1967, s 4(2).
42   [1988] 3 All ER 1079.
43   [2012] ScotCS CSOH_32 (29 February 2012).
44   Ibid. [10].

'[n]othing [the applicants] have to do as part of their duties terminates a woman's pregnancy'.[45]

These judgments strongly suggest that any *indirect* participation in abortion does not fall within the available protections for conscientious objection. Thus, participation in pre- and post-operative care would be excluded, including potentially the referral by GPs to an abortion clinic.[46] There is, however, a second conscience clause, which permits GPs to refuse to make such referrals where they have a conscientious objection to abortion but which requires them to make 'prompt referral to another provider of primary medical services who does not have such conscientious objections'.[47] What this means is that the GP must indirectly assist the patient to be referred to an abortion clinic via another GP who is not opposed to terminating a pregnancy. This represents a serious limitation on the exercise of conscience. *Inter alia*, it excludes from protection those GPs who struggle to see a moral difference between referring a patient to an abortion clinic and referring a patient to another GP for inevitable onward referral to an abortion clinic.[48] In other words (to adopt the language of moral philosophy), it accommodates only those who adopt a rigidly deontogical view of the moral rightness of their own actions and not those who take a broader consequentialist view of the likely ultimate effect of those same actions.[49]

Equally, for those to whom it does apply, the mechanism for conscientious objection may also be flawed so as to make it difficult, in the face of various pressures, to exercise it without cost.[50] This point was made clearly in the Parliamentary debate on the issue of abortion during the passage of the Human Fertilisation and Embryology Bill in 1989:

> Unfortunately, however, there are many different ways in which the present conscience clause of the Abortion Act does not work effectively. Management can indicate that promotion prospects will be

45   Ibid. [80].
46   D Hill, 'Abortion and Conscientious Objection' (2010) 16 *Journal of Evaluation in Clinical Practice* 344.
47   The National Health Service (General Medical Services Contracts) Regulations 2004, s 3(e).
48   See J Jackson, *Ethics in Medicine* (Cambridge: Polity, 2006).
49   For a discussion of these concepts, see T Beauchamp, *Philosophical Ethics: An Introduction to Moral Philosophy*, 2nd ed. (London: McGraw Hill, 1991).
50   There is some evidence of an increasing intolerance in practice of doctors who object to abortion. For example, a survey of Christian doctors by the Christian Medical Fellowship revealed a perception, by a sizeable minority of respondents, of 'discrimination' against them because of their views on abortion, including some instances of being refused jobs; see E Burton and A Fergusson, *Members' Attitudes to Abortion: A Survey of Reported Views and Practice* (London: Christian Medical Fellowship, 1996).

damaged if medical personnel do not take part in abortions. Candidates for interview for medical appointments will not be success-ful in some cases unless they agree in advance that they will take part in abortions. Peer group pressure – the burden falling upon other overworked medical personnel – can persuade individuals to become involved in abortions about which they are unhappy.[51]

These criticisms of an 'opting out' arrangement may well find an echo in other examples where conscientious objection is a legitimate option but is not viewed with a friendly eye by managers to whom it may create a meas-ure of administrative or operational inconvenience.

Another example of an apparently religiously neutral conscience clause, which was noted earlier, is that available to retail and betting workers.[52] Here, the mechanism is very different to that employed in the Abortion Act – rather than requiring the conscientious objector to 'opt-out' or otherwise be assumed to have consented to involvement, the retail or betting worker is assumed *not* to be a Sunday worker, unless she chooses to 'opt in' (a simi-lar arrangement to that in force for those who wish to waive their rights to work only a 48-hour week).[53] Thus, any need to establish the basis of any conscientious objection is entirely obviated.

A rather different conscience clause is that available to Sikh construction workers. They are excused from wearing a hard hat in place of a turban on construction sites by virtue of the Employment Act 1989.[54] This represents a rare example of a specific statutory exemption relating to employment (in this case from health and safety legislation) on the apparent grounds of 'religion'.[55] There are some extenuating circumstances which help to explain why, uniquely, health and safety legislation has been subordinated to the rival claims of Sikh religious obligations. This is a function of the universal requirement that construction workers should wear hard hats (this is distinct from other occupations where Sikhs might be accommo-dated by being assigned to other duties not requiring the wearing of a hard hat) – thus, without an exemption, Sikhs would be entirely excluded from construction work, thought (at the time) to be an important source of paid

51   HC Deb 27 July 1989, vol 157, col 1371–72, Mr Kenneth Hargreaves MP.
52   Employment Rights Act 1996 Part IV.
53   Working Time Regulations 1998, reg 5.
54   Ibid., s 11.
55   Another example existed from 1971–92. Prior to the ending of the 'closed shop' under the Trade Union and Labour Relations (Consolidation) Act 1992 s 137 and, where this practice existed, a 'genuine religious objection' was one of the few reasons accepted, without loss of position, for refusal to join a trade union; see R Benedictus, 'Closed Shop Exemptions and their Wording' (1979) 8 *Industrial Law Journal* 160.

occupation for Sikhs in the UK.[56] In another example with implications beyond employment, Sikhs enjoy an exemption from the otherwise universal obligation to wear a motorcycle helmet; *inter alia*, this prevents their exclusion from courier and delivery work.[57] Whether such provisions, considered in terms of the models in Chapter 3, actually represent significant concessions specifically for freedom of religious expression is cast into doubt by the curious position of the Sikh, for whom, as has been noted, the boundaries are blurred between religion, race and culture. This being the case, the exemptions for Sikhs, limited as they, may rather represent support for the model VI (protection for minority religions only), where religion is a proxy for the apparently more important 'rights' connected to race under its widest meaning.

There is a further source of conscientious objection provisions which may exist by virtue of professional codes of conduct. For example, empowered by the Pharmacy Order 2010,[58] the General Pharmaceutical Council has produced a binding code of conduct which includes, at face value, a potentially wide-ranging conscience clause; it requires pharmacists to 'make sure that if your religious or moral beliefs prevent you from providing a service, you tell the relevant people or authorities and refer patients and the public to other providers'.[59] As the services which pharmacists may refuse to provide are not specified,[60] nor the circumstances in which such refusals may be made, this represents a much more inclusive approach to conscientious objection than that contained, for example, within the Abortion Act.

---

56   See Barry, *Culture and Equality: An Egalitarian Critique of Multiculturalism* (Cambridge: Polity, 2001) 49. However, it should be noted that an amendment to the Employment Act s 11 has been proposed by the Health and Safety Executive which would widen the scope of the exemption potentially to all occupations, on the basis that most occupations are less dangerous than those involved in construction and there is currently a legislative 'anomaly' in offering exemptions only to construction workers; see Health and Safety Executive, *Consultation Letter – Proposal to Amend the Provisions of Section 11 of the Employment Act 1989 to Extend the Exemption Afforded to Turban Wearing Sikhs* (27 January 2014). Available online at www.hse.gov.uk/consult/condocs/sikh-letter.htm (accessed 6 June 2014).

57   See the Road Traffic Act 1988 s 16(2).

58   SI 231/2010.

59   General Pharmaceutical Council, *Standards of Conduct, Ethics and Performance* (London: General Pharmaceutical Council, July 2012) [3.4]. Available online at www.pharmacyregulation.org/standards/conduct-ethics-and-performance (accessed 6 June 2014).

60   It is likely that the morning-after pill will be amongst those services which some pharmacists will refuse to provide, on grounds of conscience (as it is seen as destroying post-conception human life); see E Fenton and L Lomasky, 'Dispensing with Liberty: Conscientious Refusal and the Morning-After-Pill' (2005) 30 *Journal of Medicine and Philosophy* 579 (the authors present a nuanced case in favour of a conditional right of conscientious objection for pharmacists).

There are thus a small number of statutory exemptions for workers on the basis of 'conscience'. Those that that are controversial relate to medical practice and are religion-neutral: objections do not need to be located with reference to a particular religious or philosophical world view. As has been seen, these exemptions are narrowly interpreted by the courts. They are fiercely opposed by some, particularly in respect of abortion.[61]

For conscience exemptions on other grounds that affect workers, there appears to be little appetite to legislate to accommodate these grounds. This is clearly evident from the failure to amend legislation to include 'opt-outs' for workers and officials required to implement legislation advancing same-sex rights, such as civil partnerships and gay adoption, and who might object on religious grounds. Such an amendment[62] was unsuccessfully moved in 2003 by Lady Blatch during a debate on the Local Government Bill of that year; had it been successful, it would have permitted a right to 'opt-out' for Christian social workers who did not want to participate in adoptions by homosexual couples.[63] A more recent amendment,[64] wider in potential scope, was moved by Lady O'Cathain in the House of Lords during a debate on the Equality Bill in 2005:[65]

(1A) For the avoidance of doubt the prohibition in subsection (1) shall include –

(a) requiring a registrar or any other person to arrange, officiate at or otherwise participate in the registration of a civil partnership under the Civil Partnership Act 2004 (c. 33),

(b) requiring a registrar or any other person to arrange, solemnise or otherwise participate in the registration of a marriage involving a person whose gender has become the acquired gender under the Gender Recognition Act 2004 (c. 7),

(c) requiring any person to participate in any placement under section 18 of the Adoption and Children Act 2002 (c. 38) (placement for

---

61 One argument against conscientious objection to abortion is to see the practice as a core part of the job of clinicians – those who oppose are quite simply entering the wrong profession; see J Savulescu, 'Conscientious objection in medicine' (2006) 332 *BMJ* 294. Another argument is that conscientious objection to abortion imposes unnecessary obstacles to a woman's 'rights' in this respect; see discussion in B Dickens and R Cook, 'The scope and limits of conscientious objection' (2000) 71 *International Journal of Gynecology and Obstetrics* 71. In response, it may be argued that the business of medicine is a 'moral enterprise' and doctors are bound by professional codes of ethics based on the ancient Hippocratic oath, where respect for life (including, for many, the life of the unborn child) is a core value, trumping other considerations; see M Wicclair, 'Conscientious Objection in Medicine' (2000) 14 *Bioethics* 205.

62 Amendment No. 217.

63 HL Deb 23 Jun 2003, vol 650, col 39GC.

64 Amendment No. 191A.

65 Enacted as the Equality Act 2006.

adoption by agencies), or any application under section 49 of that Act (application for adoption) where the placement is with, or the application is made by, a couple who are not a married couple, or one applicant is part of a couple within the meaning of section 144(4)(b) of the Adoption and Children Act 2002 (general interpretation etc.), where the person concerned has a conscientious objection on the basis of his religion or belief.[66]

Lady O'Cathain withdrew the amendment after the government refused to accept it. Baroness Scotland, on behalf of the government of the day, supported this decision with reference to the more general protections offered by the Employment Equality (Religion or Belief) Regulations 2003 – the inference being that these offer sufficient protection in such cases (although, with hindsight, this has proved to be somewhat misleading).[67]

The reliance on the Employment Equality (Religion or Belief) Regulations (and now the relevant provisions of the Equality Act 2010) in lieu of a specific conscience clause does, of course, create a much more qualified right to protection for conscience as opposed to the absolute right which would be conveyed through a specific opt-out clause.

What is not explained is why these regulations are considered to provide sufficient protection for those opposing, for example, civil partnerships and not those opposing abortion. Indeed, the passage of the Human Fertilisation and Embryology Act 2008 provided a clear and recent opportunity to withdraw the conscience clause on the basis that sufficient protection for conscientious objection lay elsewhere in domestic law. This did not occur. An explanation as to the differential treatment of these two types of conscience claim is mooted by Kenneth Norrie. He suggests that:

> health care professionals are not carrying out public duties in the way that registrars are; abortion is not an inherent and necessary part of health care, in the way that registration of civil partnership is within the registration system; and refusing to perform abortions does not constitute systemic discrimination against an equality-vulnerable class.[68]

Norrie's analysis implies, firstly, that there is a critical distinction of some kind between the conduct of a public duty, for which no opt-out can be countenanced, and the conduct of an activity which cannot be so classified; secondly, there is a distinction between activities which are core and non-core to the job role, and opting out of the former is less acceptable than

---

66   HL Deb 13 Jul 2005, vol 684, col 1147.
67   HL Deb 13 Jul 2005, vol 684, col 1154.
68   K Norrie, 'Conscience and Public Service' *Journal of the Law Society of Scotland* (14 April 2008). Available online at www.journalonline.co.uk/Magazine/53-4/1005151.aspx (accessed 6 June 2014).

opting out of the latter; thirdly, the characteristics of the group in some way potentially disadvantaged by the conscience clause should be taken into account – if this group is considered to be disadvantaged then this should be weighted against the conscientious objector (who is recast as a 'discriminator'). The problem with this analysis is that it considers the case from all perspectives save that of the conscientious objector. The demands of individual conscience presumably do not change in response to the public nature of the role or task in question, nor how core the task is thought to be, nor who might be in some way 'offended' by the objection. Nevertheless, from the perspective of the legislature, it would seem that it is a policy decision not to promote religious rights in these circumstances and to insist that public officials act against conscience or leave their role. This aspect of public policy is most congruent with model I (exclusion).

England and Wales (post-2003)

Based on Article 13 of the Treaty of Amsterdam, the European Union adopted the Framework Equality Directive in 2000.[69] The directive outlawed discrimination in employment and vocational training on the grounds of religion or belief, sexual orientation, disability and age. In transposing the Directive into law, the British Government introduced, *inter alia*, the Employment Equality (Religion or Belief) Regulations 2003, which came into force on 2 December 2003 and apply in England, Wales and Scotland.[70] These regulations were, in turn, replaced by the Equality Act 2010, where the drafting was broadly replicated with minor changes.

Definitions

How religion is defined is of some significance. The relevant EU directive provides little steer in terms of definition. 'Religion and belief' is one of the prohibited grounds for discrimination in employment but no further elucidation of the reach of these terms is offered.[71]

This was transposed into the original text of the 2003 Regulations in an expanded form as follows: 'In these Regulations, "religion or belief" means any religion, religious belief, or similar philosophical belief'.[72] Under the Equality Act,[73] the definition changed slightly, largely to incorporate protections for those without religion or belief:

69   EC Directive 2000/34 on equal treatment [2000] OJ L303/16.
70   Separate legislation applies in Northern Ireland (The Fair Employment and Treatment Order 1998).
71   See the preamble to EC Directive 2000/34.
72   Reg 2(1), Regulations as enacted.
73   s 10.

(1) Religion means any religion and a reference to religion includes a reference to a lack of religion.
(2) Belief means any religious or philosophical belief and a reference to belief includes a reference to a lack of belief.

In 2006, the Regulations had been amended to remove the word 'similar' from 'philosophical belief' and this revised formula was carried across into the Equality Act.[74] Ostensibly, this would appear to weaken the link between religion and belief suggesting that the bar was being in some way lowered to allow beliefs which are not sufficiently similar to a religion or a religious belief. Vickers suggests, however, that the change in wording was put into effect merely to placate some humanists and atheists who objected to the implication that their beliefs were similar to religious beliefs.[75] This issue was considered by the judge in *Grainger Plc & Others* v. *Nicholson*[76] who, examining the relevant debates in Hansard, agreed with Vickers and thus concluded that the amendment to the wording was not materially significant in terms of adding or subtracting from the original definition.

Nevertheless, *Grainger* was a highly significant ruling in terms of understanding the legal definition of belief. In brief, the case was concerned with whether or not a belief in man-made climate change was capable, if genuinely held, of being a philosophical belief for the purpose of the 2003 Religion and Belief Regulations. The judge in the case concurred with the employment tribunal (pre-hearing review) that it was. In doing so, he determined five criteria to apply in determining whether or not a given belief or set of beliefs fall under the scope of the 2003 Regulations:

(i)   The belief must be genuinely held.
(ii)   It must be a belief and not … an opinion or viewpoint based on the present state of information available.
(iii) It must be a belief as to a weighty and substantial aspect of human life and behaviour.
(iv)   It must attain a certain level of cogency, seriousness, cohesion and importance.
(v)   It must be worthy of respect in a democratic society, be not incompatible with human dignity and not conflict with the fundamental rights of others.[77]

In applying these criteria in the instant case, the judge found that a belief in man-made climate change was capable of being protected under the

---

74   Equality Act 2006, s 77(1).
75   L Vickers, *Religious Freedom, Religious Discrimination and the Workplace* (Oxford: Hart Publishing, 2008), 23.
76   (2009) UKEAT 0219/09/0311; [2010] IRLR 4 (EAT).
77   Ibid. [24] (Burton J).

Regulations, despite the fact that it may be 'a one-off belief' (as opposed to a comprehensive world view or, in the judge's words, an '-ism') and not necessarily shared by others.[78] This judgment would seem to suggest a broadening of protection for sincerely held beliefs, including beliefs based on science and political beliefs,[79] albeit that the judge clearly intended that boundaries should still apply – not all beliefs will qualify. Perhaps particularly interesting is the fifth criterion – compatibility with dignity and the fundamental rights of others – a criterion drawn from European Convention on Human Rights and Fundamental Freedoms (ECHR) jurisprudence and originally applied in considering the definition of 'belief' in *McClintock* v. *Department for Constitutional Affairs*.[80] Although perhaps a mechanism to continue to exclude racist beliefs from protection,[81] it nevertheless imposes a relative requirement that a belief should be generally considered acceptable 'in a democratic society'. Unless the meaning here is restricted to outlawing physical harm to others (akin to beliefs in human sacrifice, genital mutilation, etc.) and then extended to apply to religious beliefs, then a number of beliefs which might otherwise be worthy of protection could be called into question, including, for example, any religious beliefs which may appear to be incompatible with the dignity of women or gay and lesbian people, or which might involve a denial of vital medical treatment to minors.

Direct discrimination

The focus in this section is on how far the direct discrimination provisions of the Equality Act offer protection for forms of religious expression in the workplace.

The definition of direct discrimination is found under section 13 of the Equality Act: 'A person (A) discriminates against another (B) if, because of a protected characteristic, A treats B less favourably than A treats or would

---

78 Ibid. [27] (Burton J).
79 Ibid. [28–30]. See also subsequent cases, as a result of which the following have been accepted as protected beliefs: opposition to fox hunting and harecoursing (*Hashman* v. *Milton Park (Dorset) Limited t/a Orchard Park* (2011) ET Case No. 3105555/09); a belief in the 'higher purpose' of public service broadcasting (*Maistry* v. *BBC* (2011) ET Case No. 1313142/10); and a commitment to vegetarianism (*Alexander* v. *Farmtastic Valley Ltd and others* (2011) ET Case No. 2513832/10). A belief in wearing a poppy does not, however, qualify (*Lisk* v. *Shield Guardian Co and others* (2011) ET Case No. 3300873/11).
80 [2007] UKEAT 0223/07/3110; [2008] IRLR 29 [41] (Elias J).
81 BNP beliefs have been deemed beyond the scope of the regulations (*Baggs* v. *Fudge* (2005) ET Case No. 1400114/05) as have socialist beliefs (*Kelly and others* v. *Unison* (2010) ET Case No. 2203854-57/08). The failure in discrimination law to protect employees because of political beliefs is likely to fall foul of the ECHR as a result of the decision in *Redfearn* v. *United Kingdom* [2012] ECHR 1878 (although protection from unfair dismissal has been extended to cover political beliefs; see the Enterprise and Regulatory Reform Act 2013, s. 13).

treat others'.[82] Religion and belief is 'a protected characteristic', as are age, disability, gender reassignment, marriage and civil partnership, pregnancy and maternity, race, sex and sexual orientation.[83]

Fundamentally, the definition of direct discrimination is designed to identify and render unlawful any behaviour by an employer (or another actor in the workplace) that involves subjecting a worker to a 'detriment' because of their protected characteristic. For example, a failure to promote someone because she is a Hindu would amount to direct discrimination because of the protected characteristic of religion and belief.

Direct discrimination is potentially a powerful protection for employees for a number of reasons. Firstly, the normal obligation on the claimant to show an adequate degree of 'proof' before proceeding with a claim is reversed.[84] The claimant need only show a *prima facie* claim; the onus is then on the employer to satisfy a tribunal that it did not in fact engage in discrimination.[85] Secondly, aside from the occupational requirement provisions of the legislation, there is no defence against a direct discrimination claim on the basis of religion and belief (unlike indirect discrimination which can be defended as proportionate). As noted in *R (E)* v. *JFS Governing Body*,[86] this means that direct discrimination in favour of minority religious or racial groups cannot be justified, just as discrimination against such groups cannot. For some, this represents a regrettable 'defect' in the law;[87] certainly, it does not align with model VI (protection for minority religions).

For a direct discrimination claim to succeed, a 'comparison' is usually required.[88] In religion and belief cases, a tribunal will examine whether or not, for instance, a Buddhist was treated less favourably than a Hindu either was, or would have been, treated in the same circumstances. Thus, the comparison can be either real or hypothetical but the circumstances of the comparator and the claimant must be the same, with only the religion being different. Once less favourable treatment has been established, the question then arises, was religion the ground of the less favourable treatment or did the less favourable treatment have some other cause? The formula was set out by the House of Lords thus: would the claimant have been treated in the same way *but for* his (in this case) religion or belief?[89]

---

82   This wording essentially replicates the definition in the Employment Equality (Religion and Belief) Regulations 2003, at Reg 3(1).
83   Equality Act 2010, s 4.
84   Ibid., s 136.
85   *Igen* v. *Wong* [2005] EWCA Civ. 142; [2005] IRLR 258.
86   [2009] UKSC 15; [2010] 2 AC 728 [9] (Lord Phillips).
87   Ibid. See also, in a similar vein, Lady Hale's comments [69] and those of Lord Hope [184].
88   *Glasgow City Council* v. *Zafar* [1988] ICT 120 HL.
89   *James* v. *Eastleigh Borough Council* [1990] 2 AC 751 HL.

The pressing question for the subject at hand is how far the basis of direct discrimination, thus defined, actually protects religious 'expression' as opposed to 'belief' itself; in other words, how far might tribunals adopt the European Court of Human Rights (ECtHR) approach of distinguishing between a *forum internum* and a *forum externum* and protecting the latter not the former? If they do so, how might they draw the line between the two? For example, would a blanket requirement that all male staff be clean-shaven directly discriminate on the basis of belief (protected) or merely on the basis of conduct inspired by belief (unprotected)?[90] As a second example, might an employer be able to treat a grievance from a Christian member of staff less favourably than a grievance from a gay member of staff, if it could argue that the Christian's grievance was, or was related to, a manifestation of the belief rather than the belief itself? Could it thus admit that it subjected the Christian to a detriment but claim that this was on a basis unprotected by the Regulations, arguing that the circumstances were not the same?[91]

Indirect discrimination

Indirect discrimination is defined under section 19 of the Equality Act as occurring when:

(1) A person (A) discriminates against another (B) if A applies to B a provision, criterion or practice which is discriminatory in relation to a relevant protected characteristic of B's.

(2) For the purposes of subsection (1), a provision, criterion or practice is discriminatory in relation to a relevant protected characteristic of B's if –
   (a) A applies, or would apply, it to persons with whom B does not share the characteristic,
   (b) it puts, or would put, persons with whom B shares the characteristic at a particular disadvantage when compared with persons with whom B does not share it,
   (c) it puts, or would put, B at that disadvantage, and
   (d) A cannot show it to be a proportionate means of achieving a legitimate aim.[92]

90　Such an employer would be unlikely to avoid an indirect discrimination claim in these circumstances!

91　See the facts of *Ladele* v. *Islington Borough Council* [2009] EWCA Civ. 1357; [2010] IRLR 211.

92　This is essentially the same formula for defining indirect discrimination which appears at Reg 3(1) of the Employment Equality (Religion and Belief) Regulations 2003.

Indirect discrimination, because of the protected characteristic of religion and belief, extends protection to workers whose employer imposes an apparently neutral requirement which has a much more significant and detrimental effect on people (otherwise in the same circumstances as others to whom the requirement applies) who hold a particular religious belief. For example, if an employer imposed a uniform requirement which prevented staff wearing any form of head covering, then this would be a requirement which would be difficult for many Muslim women to meet on the basis of their faith-based conviction that they must wear a headscarf in the company of men.[93] This requirement would be therefore 'indirectly discriminatory'. As another example, if a pharmacy required that all staff issue contraceptives to customers this would indirectly discriminate against Roman Catholic Christians who have a faith-based objection to the practice of contraception and who would thus find it difficult to comply with the requirement.

To be successful in an indirect discrimination claim, the claimant must show that he has suffered (or would suffer) a 'particular disadvantage' as a Christian, Muslim, etc., as a result of a specific requirement in the workplace, a disadvantage from which others do not or would not suffer. Thus, at its most basic, the claimant would need to show that a specific requirement has disadvantaged or would disadvantage a religion to which he belongs or a belief arising from that religion which is shared by others. This test is more relaxed than its forerunner; the wording of the Sex Discrimination Act 1975, as originally enacted, required proof that the proportion of women who could comply with a work requirement was 'considerably smaller' than the proportion of men who could so comply.[94] As Fredman notes, quantifying what was meant by 'considerably smaller' gave rise to some considerable legal dispute.[95] The wording of the Equality Act (and before that the Religion and Belief Regulations), by avoiding the need to quantify the scope of the disadvantage, tends to obviate the first problem. The second problem may, however, remain to some extent. For example, is a 'particular disadvantage' suffered by a single Roman Catholic protected or is it necessary to identify a group or 'pool' of Roman Catholics who share the same disadvantage?[96] Tribunals may favour the need to identify a group disadvantage as this is more in the spirit of the origins of the

---

93   It is not necessary to show that it is impossible to meet the requirement; see *Price* v. *Civil Service Commission* [1978] ICR 27.

94   Sex Discrimination Act 1975, s 1(1)(b)(i), before amendments.

95   S Fredman, *Discrimination Law*, 2nd ed. (Oxford: Oxford University Press, 2011), 110–11.

96   This issue was tested in *Eweida* v. *British Airways* [2008] UKEAT 0123/08/11; [2009] IRLR 78 (see discussion in Chapter 6); see also on this point, G Pitt, 'Keeping the Faith: Trends and Tensions in Religion or Belief Discrimination' (2011) 40 *Industrial Law Journal* 384–404.

concept of indirect discrimination.[97] However, there is also a view that more individualised religious beliefs should be admitted into the scope of protection.[98] This argument has become all the more compelling since the admissibility decisions in *Eweida and Ors* v. *United Kingdom* marking the end of the necessity test, which, in some ways, acted in lieu of a group test.[99] As a result, more individualised claims are likely to be accepted by the ECHR and this may put some pressure on courts and tribunals to relax the plural test in indirect discrimination (in cases of religion and belief) so that it should be read compatibly, where possible, with Article 9 ECHR.[100]

If *prima facie* indirect discrimination can be demonstrated, the employer has an opportunity to present a justification defence in which it must show that a particular criterion, provision or practice, which has an adverse effect on a particular group, represents 'a proportionate means of achieving a legitimate aim'. For example, a chocolate factory might be able to justify as proportionate a policy of requiring all staff who are directly involved in the production process to be clean shaven for reasons relating to the legitimate aim of hygiene, even though this would represent *prima facie* indirect discrimination towards would-be Sikh employees.[101] It should be noted that the notion of a legitimate aim is not restricted to the economic interests of the employer and there is the clear possibility that employers may be able to offer justification arguments based on, for example, the interests of other staff members or the desire to project a secular image to the public.[102]

It is worth noting the difference in this wording from that used in the original directive which requires that the indirectly discriminatory provision, criterion or practice 'is objectively justified by a legitimate aim and the means of achieving that aim are appropriate and necessary'.[103] As Vickers observes, although tribunals are required to interpret discrimination law in

---

97 The concept was first articulated and applied in the US case of *Griggs* v. *Duke Power* 401 U.S. 424 (1971), and was based on the desire to tackle the 'group disadvantage' which might result from apparently neutral employment practices.

98 See, for example, L Vickers, 'Indirect discrimination and individual belief: *Eweida v British Airways plc*' (2009) 11 *Ecclesiastical Law Journal* 197.

99 Appl Nos. 48420/10, 59842/10, 51671/10 and 36516/10 (15 January 2013). A practice is only likely to be regarded as necessary to a religion if there is also strong support for it amongst adherents of that religion.

100 See, for a consideration of these issues, *Mba* v. *Merton Borough Council* [2013] EWCA Civ. 1562; [2013] WLR (D) 474 (CA) (discussed in Chapter 6).

101 See *Singh* v. *Rowntree Mackintosh* [1979] IRLR 199 (EAT Sc) and *Panesar* v. *Nestlé* [1980] ICR 60; (EAT), 64 (CA).

102 Vickers, *Religious Freedom, Religious Discrimination and the Workplace*, 132.

103 Directive 2000/78/EC, Art 2(2)(b)(i). This directive follows an earlier European Court of Justice ruling that indirect discrimination can only be justified when it corresponds to a real need of the employer's and is necessary (*Bilka-Kaufhaus Case* C-170/84 [1987] ICR 110).

the light of the original, the alternative wording of the regulations (and subsequently the Equality Act) appears to put less emphasis on the 'necessity' of any practice before an assessment of proportionality is carried out,[104] which would appear to be to the potential advantage of the employer. Baker locates the responsibility for the same problem with the judiciary, arguing that judges in the UK have deliberately avoided the 'necessity' requirement 'in order to avoid exposing employers to the harsh scrutiny represented by the European Court of Justice requirement that indirectly discriminatory rules be necessary to meet a real need for the business'.[105] Instead, he argues, the UK courts have applied a form of 'proportionality balancing' which allows an employer to offer apparently acceptable reasons to justify its indirectly discriminatory provision, criterion or practice but without needing to show a real need for that provision, criterion or practice. Thus, the employer's justification 'succeeds regardless of the availability of less discriminatory means'.[106]

Harassment

The general definition of 'harassment' is defined under section 26(1) of the Equality Act as follows:

> (1) A person (A) harasses another (B) if –
>> (a) A engages in unwanted conduct related to a relevant protected characteristic, and
>> (b) the conduct has the purpose or effect of –
>>> (i) violating B's dignity, or
>>> (ii) creating an intimidating, hostile, degrading, humiliating or offensive environment for B.[107]

Harassment is a legal concept which originally emerged from case law as a form of direct discrimination. A successful claim for harassment (under one of the protected grounds under discrimination law) therefore required the claimant to identify a comparator. As a result of the staged implementation of the 2002 European Union Equal Treatment Amendment Directive,[108] existing domestic law changed and new

---

104 Vickers, *Religious Freedom, Religious Discrimination and the Workplace*, 131.
105 A Baker, 'Proportionality and Employment Discrimination in the UK' (2008) 37 *Industrial Law Journal* 328.
106 Ibid. 312. The force of this point is particularly clear when considering the judgment in *Ladele* (see discussion at Chapter 6 below). It should be noted that Baker favours a more sophisticated form of proportionality balancing based on the approach taken by the ECtHR in Article 14 ECHR judgments.
107 This is essentially the same wording as that found at Reg 5 under the Religion and Belief Regulations 2003.
108 Directive 2002/73/EC.

discrimination legislation thereafter incorporated a free-standing definition of harassment. Harassment no longer requires a comparator to be identified; rather, the law now reflects an approach based on the concept of 'dignity'. If someone's dignity is (seriously) violated on the grounds of a protected characteristic, then it is likely to constitute an unlawful act of harassment. Since the implementation of the Equality Act 2010, it is not necessary for an individual actually to possess the relevant protected characteristic to make a claim of harassment.

The primary determinant of harassment is individual perception, above a certain threshold of 'reasonableness' to protect against claims by those who are (or choose to appear) very easily offended. A single act, if sufficiently serious, can be considered to constitute actionable harassment but, in most cases, more than a single act will be required. It is generally agreed that fairness requires that the would-be harasser ('Person A') should be aware that his actions are offensive to Person B on the grounds of the protected characteristic.[109] This will not necessarily be immediately obvious to Person A, not least if Person B's religious sensibilities are unknown. Nevertheless, the perception of B remains highly significant,[110] such that what might be inoffensive, even amusing to some, might be sufficiently offensive to another to trigger a harassment claim.

When an act of harassment takes place against one employee by another, it is primarily the employer who is considered liable for the consequences under the doctrine of vicarious liability which applies in discrimination law even if the employer does not know that a discriminatory act has taken place.[111] The employer can mitigate its liability by demonstrating that it took all reasonable steps to prevent discrimination or harassment taking place.[112] Having a policy that is communicated to staff is one way in which it can seek to do this.[113]

An illustrative example of harassment on the grounds of religion and belief is provided by the Muslim Council of Britain:

> Following a particular incident, Islam features largely in the media. Consequently, stereotypical and hurtful comments in the workplace are routinely made about Muslims, upsetting certain Muslim employees. Such behaviour may amount to harassment, even if not specifically

---

109 The law changed in respect of sex discrimination in 2007 so that unlawful harassment may be 'sex-related' rather than on the grounds of sex – the former reflecting more closely the wording of the original EU directive and widening the scope of protection.
110 This is made explicit at section 26(4) of the Equality Act 2010.
111 Equality Act s 109.
112 Equality Act s 109(4).
113 *Balgobin and Francis* v. *London Borough of Tower Hamlets* [1987] ICR 829.

directed at one or more individuals, but at Islam as a religion or Muslims as a group more generally.[114]

Equally, harassment might result from unwelcome remarks about a co-worker's chosen form of religious expression, such as the wearing of a headscarf or cross, or to beliefs that he or she is thought to hold.[115] To this extent, the harassment provisions of the Equality Act are likely to provide a degree of protection for employees who wish to express their religious identity or religious convictions without enduring various forms of hostility from co-workers or managers.

Far more problematic, for the purposes of this book, is the potential for the protection against religious harassment to be used as a means of *suppressing* religious expression in the workplace. Harassment on the grounds of religion could easily encompass giving offence to non-religious co-workers or co-workers of a different religious faith. The intention is not likely to be a deliberate attempt to cause offence – this is merely a potential byproduct of a more worthy aim. The religious employee may well rather have an urgent concern for the spiritual wellbeing of co-workers and strongly desire to see them converted to the same religious faith. This is quite distinct from a deliberate desire to offend, which may come from taunting religious colleagues because of their religious faith. The distinction between the two has led some American commentators to distinguish between 'animus-based' and 'non-animus-based' harassment.[116] However, although it is helpful to consider analytically the difference in motive, motive is in fact irrelevant in the UK; from a legal point of view, it is the 'offensive' result that is of significance.[117] There is a further possibility which exists by virtue of the harassment provisions of other aspects of discrimination law. For example, a religious employee may feel constrained to point out to a homosexual colleague that her lifestyle is 'sinful' and urge her to repent. This may constitute harassment because of the protected characteristic of sexual orientation, again despite the non-animus motive. However, there exists a further complication. To discipline a religious

---

114 Muslim Council of Britain, *Muslims in the Workplace: A Good Practice Guide for Employers and Employees* (MCB/DTI 2005), 7.

115 Interestingly, the possibility that a religious employee might be subjected to harassment because of a perceived negative attitude to homosexuality is noted by the British Humanist Association, *Guidance on Equality of 'Religion or Belief'* (undated), 9. Available online at https://humanism.org.uk/campaigns/equalities/equality-project-and-resources/guidance-document (accessed 6 June 2014).

116 See, for example, DN Kaminer, When religious expression creates a hostile work environment' (2000) 81 *New York University Journal of Legislation and Public Policy* 139.

117 Although intention may affect the remedies awarded; see B Hepple, *Equality: The New Legal Framework* (Oxford: Hart, 2011), 68.

employee for harassment when seeking to convert or morally guide a colleague is likely to infringe his rights if he sincerely believes that to seek to convert or to point out sin in others is a requirement of his religious faith. Thus, he himself may be subject to indirect discrimination and possibly harassment by his employer.[118]

With this in mind, the harassment provisions are potentially a double-edged sword, with one blade congruent with model V (protection) and one blade congruent with model I (exclusion).[119]

A duty to make reasonable adjustments

Under the provisions of the Equality Act an employer is under what is known as 'a duty to make reasonable adjustments' to the workplace or to work practices to accommodate the needs of disabled employees such that they are able to work in particular roles.[120] The duty may involve some additional costs to the employer and may also entail a modest element of 'positive discrimination' in favour of disabled employees.[121] Such a duty does not extend beyond the protected characteristic of disability. However, it has been mooted that a similar duty should be introduced in the UK in respect of religion and belief akin to that employed, for example, in the USA under Title VII of the Civil Rights Act 1974,[122] which establishes a duty to 'reasonably accommodate' the needs of religious employees.[123] Such a duty would require employers to alter workplace rules and practices in order to accommodate workers' religious beliefs where it is 'reasonable' to do so. For example, it may be that an employer would be required to alter a shift rota to accommodate the wish of a Christian employee not to work on a Sunday.

What is meant by 'reasonable' is perhaps the area which is likely to be most problematic. In the USA, for example, the duty of reasonable accommodation is circumscribed at the point that it creates 'undue hardship on

---

118 See also L Vickers, 'Is All Harassment Equal? The Case of Religious Harassment' (2006) 65 *Cambridge Law Journal* 579.
119 That harassment laws could negatively impact on religious expression, at least where broadly drawn, was also recognised (in the case of sexual orientation harassment in the provision of goods and services) in an *Application for Judicial Review by the Christian Institute & ORS* [2007] NIQB 66; [2008] IRLR 36. The application was successful and the harassment clauses of the Equality Act (Sexual Orientation) Regulations (Northern Ireland) 2006 were quashed.
120 Equality Act 2010, s 20.
121 *Archibald* v. *Fife Council* [2004] UKHL 32; [2004] IRLR 651 HL.
122 42 U. S. C. 2000e-2 (1994).
123 It was recommended, for example, that 'reasonable accommodation' be adopted in religion and belief claims in advance of the drafting of the Religion and Belief Regulations (2003): see Hepple and Choudhury, *Tackling Religious Discrimination*.

the conduct of the employer's business'.[124] Courts in the United States have interpreted this in favour of employers such that undue hardship is suffered if the costs of accommodation are more than 'de minimis' and complaints by other workers can be considered a 'cost'.[125] Although this formula, applied to the United Kingdom, is satisfactory to some commentators,[126] it is submitted that it is unlikely to provide a significant boost to the protection model.[127] However, there is no reason to adopt a 'de-minimis' threshold and the more stringent requirements of the duty to make reasonable adjustments for disabled employees might provide a more robust template for future innovations. Equally, as Gibson argues, a model based on the Canadian approach to reasonable accommodation, which requires rather weightier evidence of 'undue hardship' from the employer than that demanded in the United States, could be considered.[128]

Either proposal is likely to encounter some resistance, however, as they arguably create more protection for religion than is enjoyed in respect of other protected characteristics, thus potentially creating unequal treatment.[129] How far differential treatment for religion and belief vis-à-vis other protected characteristics can be justified will depend on the extent to which it is possible to argue that religion and belief by its very nature requires a different legal approach to that which is applied for example to sex or race. If so, it would not be unique amongst the protected characteristics; as has been seen, disability is also treated differently.

Occupational requirements

Given the presentation in Chapter 3 of model IV ('islands of exclusivity'), attention will now turn to those aspects of discrimination law that have a bearing on opportunities for people to work together within the environment of the religious beliefs they share – that is, within a religious organisation. One consequence of anti-discrimination legislation, in terms of general principles, is that it acts to prevent discrimination on the grounds of religion in any context unless by exception. Thus, organisations with a religious character would normally be prevented from failing to

---

124 Title VII Civil Rights Act 1964, s 701(j).
125 *Trans World Airlines* v. *Hardison* 432 U.S. 63 (1976).
126 See, for example, Vickers, *Religious Freedom, Religious Discrimination and the Workplace*, 223.
127 Gibson, an advocate of reasonable accommodation, is in agreement on this point; see M Gibson, 'The God "Dilution"? Religion, Discrimination and the Case for Reasonable Accommodation' (2013) 72 *Cambridge Law Journal* 578.
128 Ibid.
129 R Allen and G Moon, 'Substantive Rights and Equal Treatment in Respect of Religion and Belief: Towards a Better Understanding of the Rights and their Implications' (2000) *European Human Rights Law Review* 580, 601.

consider candidates for employment with a different or no religious affiliation. This effect led to some Christian groups opposing the original legislation on the basis that it would be potentially injurious to the religious identity of churches and religious organisations.[130] It will be recalled that there are two basic legal mechanisms to address this problem in order to protect organisations from the reach of particular aspects of discrimination law, in full or in part – through general exemption or through the mechanism of (in the UK) occupational requirement exceptions.

Under the Equality Act 2010,[131] occupational requirement exceptions are made in two circumstances for employers with a religious ethos. The first circumstance is to allow such employers to make it a requirement for a jobholder 'to be of a particular religion or belief' if they can show that, based on the 'nature or context of the work', it is an 'occupational requirement' to reserve a particular job for someone holding a particular set of religious beliefs and that it is 'a proportionate means to achieve a legitimate aim' to apply this requirement.[132] The Explanatory Notes to the Act illustrate how this occupational requirement exception is intended to apply:

> A religious organisation may wish to restrict applicants for the post of head of its organisation to those people that adhere to that faith. This is because to represent the views of that organisation accurately it is felt that the person in charge of that organisation must have an in-depth understanding of the religion's doctrines. This type of discrimination could be lawful. However, other posts that do not require this kind of in-depth understanding, such as administrative posts, should be open to all people regardless of their religion or belief.[133]

It may be objected, however, that this example takes an instrumental rather than an organic view of the nature of working for a religious organisation.[134] A religious organisation may well argue that a very large number of job roles, even those apparently lacking a particular 'religious' purpose, should be reserved for people with a shared religious commitment, given the context in which the religious organisation operates. This argument was

130 See, for example, Christian Institute, 'Government "Equality" Plans Will Kill Freedom of Religion' [press release] 30 June 2000. Available online at www.christian.org.uk/press-releases/government-equality-plans-will-kill-freedom-of-religion (accessed 6 June 2014).

131 As previously under the Religion and Belief Regulations 2003.

132 Equality Act 2010, Sch 9, s 3.

133 *Explanatory Notes to the Equality Act 2010* [796]. See also *St Matthias Church of England School* v. *Crizzle* [1993] IRLR 472, [1993] ICR 401 (EAT), a race discrimination case, where it was found to be justifiable for an Anglican school to appoint a communicant Christian as head teacher.

134 See discussion of 'islands of exclusivity' in Chapter 3.

successful in *Muhammed* v. *The Leprosy Mission International*,[135] where a tribunal accepted that it was a legitimate occupational requirement for a Christian ethos organisation to restrict the job of finance administrator to Christians because of the context in which the job role was carried out, in particular a core emphasis on the importance of Christian prayer across all of its activities. However, in two cases brought against *Prospects*, a Christian charity dedicated to helping adults with learning disabilities, a rather different conclusion was reached.[136] In these cases, Prospects' staffing policy, which required all staff except some administrators to be practising Christians, was found to be discriminatory: each post should have been considered separately to determine whether or not it could be reasonably covered by an occupational requirement exception.

On the face of it, therefore, the occupational requirement exceptions for religion under the Equality Act 2010 do permit employees sharing the same religion to work together where their organisation has a religious ethos and where it is considered 'proportionate' in the particular 'employment context' to be inclusive only of those of a particular religion.[137] These conditions do, however, represent two considerable caveats and how narrowly they will be applied by an employment tribunal is somewhat uncertain.

There is, however, a further issue to explore. This is the detailed interpretation of what constitutes a religious ethos. For example, if for these purposes an organisation is considered to have a 'Christian' ethos and is thus able, subject to the caveats highlighted, to employ only Christians, then there remains the question of what actually constitutes a Christian – is this for the organisation to decide? One possibility is to allow further subdivisions by Christian denomination or, perhaps more helpfully, by broad theological grouping, such that an organisation's evangelical Christian ethos or Anglo-Catholic Christian ethos might be recognised as distinctive – even then, owing to differences of emphasis within theological traditions,[138] it would perhaps be desirable that organisations define their own

---

135 (2009) ET Case No. 2303459/09.

136 *Sheridan* v. *Prospects* (2008) ET Case No. 2901366/06; and *Hender* v. *Prospects* (2008) ET Case No. 2902090/06.

137 There is a partial exemption from these requirements in the case of schools with a religious ethos. Under the School Standards and Framework Act 1998 (s 58), such schools may reserve up to one-fifth of their teaching posts for staff sharing the religious doctrines of the school. For a critical commentary, see L Vickers, 'Religion and Belief Discrimination and the Employment of Teachers in Faith Schools' (2009) 4 *Religion and Human Rights* 137.

138 See the reports of a split amongst evangelical Anglicans in a theological seminary and a consequent tribunal application alleging religious discrimination by 'conservative evangelicals' against 'open evangelicals' by Dr Elaine Storkey: B Bowder, 'Wycliffe Hall admits breach of law over sacked lecturer' *Church Times* (Issue 7556, 11 January 2008). Available online at www.churchtimes.co.uk/articles/2008/11-january/news/wycliffe-hall-admits-breach-of-law-over-sacked-lecturer (accessed 6 June 2014).

ethos, for example, by way of a 'statement of faith' to which would-be job applicants would be required to subscribe.

The second area of occupational requirement exceptions under the Equality Act apply in circumstances where a religious ethos organisation would be otherwise engaged in unlawful discrimination on the basis of other protected characteristics such as sex, sexual orientation and gender reassignment. It is strongly arguable that religious employees are not free to associate together within 'islands of exclusivity' if their respective religion's requirements for individual lifestyle are not enforceable. A Christian organisation may be able to justify a policy of reserving the job role of, for example, youth worker, for practising Christians but can it also insist that the youth worker conforms to Christian teaching on human sexuality and so agrees to abstain from same-sex activity? In employment such exemptions apply when 'the employment is for the purposes of an organised religion'[139] and the exemption is necessary to meet either of what are referred to as the 'compliance' and the 'non-conflict' principles.[140] The compliance principle is engaged if the exception is applied 'so as to comply with the doctrines of the religion'.[141] The non-conflict principle is engaged if the exception is applied 'so as to avoid conflicting with the strongly held religious convictions of a significant number of the religion's followers'.[142] In other words, people can be excluded from certain employment roles in religious organisations because the religion itself teaches that certain protected characteristics are incompatible (in certain employment roles) with that religious belief or because a significant number of adherents of that religion believe that there is an incompatibility (as examples, and on either basis, women can be lawfully excluded from the Roman Catholic priesthood[143] or the Church of England episcopacy).[144] The second principle is helpful, as it circumvents the need for a court to conduct a detailed inquiry into religious doctrine.

This second category of exceptions from the effects of discrimination because of religion and belief on the basis of other protected characteristics is more narrowly drawn than the first category of occupational requirement exceptions for religion and belief *per se*.[145] Critically, this

---

139 Equality Act 2010, Sch 9, s 2(1)(a).
140 Ibid., s 2(1)(b).
141 Ibid., s 2(5).
142 Ibid., s 2(6).
143 An example offered in the *Explanatory Notes to the Equality Act 2010* [793].
144 Although there were calls in parliament for this occupational requirement defence to be removed following the defeat of legislation in the Church of England General Synod to appoint women bishops in November 2012; see, for example, HC Deb, 12 Dec 2012, vol 555, col. 406–7, Ms Diana Johnson MP.
145 See also on this point, in reference to the previous legislation, R Sandberg and N Doe, 'Religious Exemptions in Discrimination Law' (2007) 66 *Cambridge Law Journal* 302, 308.

category applies only to 'organised religion' rather than religious ethos organisations. The significance of this was explored in *R (Amicus MSF Section)* v. *Secretary of State for Trade and Industry*,[146] a case in which aspects of discrimination law relating to religious exemptions on the basis of sexual orientation as it then stood were challenged as to their compatibility with the relevant parts of the original European Union Framework Directive 2000. Richards observed that the term 'organised religion' was narrower than 'religious organisation' and provided the rather significant example that the employment of a teacher in a faith school is likely to be 'for purposes of a religious organisation' rather than 'for purposes of an organised religion' and thus likely to be outside the scope of the exemption.[147] Vickers concludes, writing in 2003, that overall there is 'significant leeway to religious organisations to discriminate in favour of their own members but [it] stops short of allowing discrimination on other grounds in the name of religion'.[148] It would seem that this conclusion might, in certain circumstances at least, apply to 'organised religions' (applying the *Amicus* bifurcation) following the (first instance) decision in *Reaney* v. *Hereford Diocesan Board of Finance*,[149] where the refusal by a diocese (clearly conforming to the definition of organised religion) to employ a gay Christian youth worker was judged to constitute sexual orientation discrimination. This case was complicated by the fact that Reaney had undertaken, at interview, to remain celibate whilst employed in the role but the diocese seemingly had doubts about whether or not he would be able to meet that commitment. It was this issue, rather than the requirement for gay employees to be celibate *per se*, which resulted in the particular outcome of the case.[150]

Although the exemptions under discussion are narrowly drawn, it is significant that, during the passage of the then Equality Bill 2009, the government attempted to narrow them further: by recasting the exemptions as applying exclusively to roles wholly or mainly concerned with the 'liturgical or ritualistic practices of the religion' or 'promoting or explaining the doctrine of the religion';[151] and by requiring that this be applied only when it is 'proportionate' to do so.[152] It is clear that the job prospects of a prospective gay Christian youth worker (such as Reaney) were prominent in the minds of those involved in the drafting of the Bill, hence an

146 [2004] EWHC 860 (Admin); [2004] IRLR 430.

147 Ibid. [116].

148 L Vickers, 'Freedom of Religion and the Workplace: The Draft Employment Equality (Religion or Belief) Regulations 2003' (2003) 32 *Industrial Law Journal* 23, 36.

149 (2007) ET Case No. 1602844/06.

150 Interestingly, the *Explanatory Notes to the Equality Act 2010* suggest that a church youth worker who 'mainly teaches Bible classes' may be included within the scope of the exemption [793].

151 Equality Bill 2009, Schedule 9(2)(8).

152 Ibid., Sch 9(2).

explanatory note which stated: 'This exception is unlikely to permit a requirement that a church youth worker who primarily organises sporting activities is celibate if they are gay'.[153] Faced with strong opposition in the House of Lords over the possible consequences for religious freedom,[154] and with limited time before the 2010 general election, the government accepted an amendment[155] proposed by Lady O'Cathain and carried by the House, which had the effect that the legal position in respect of occupational requirements, enshrined in the Equality Act 2010, remains fundamentally that of 2003.[156]

A further issue is concerned with whether or not religious employees within the islands of exclusivity are actually able to conduct their work according to the religious principles that they espouse. Whereas it may be assumed that there is no reason why this should not generally be the case, it may be more difficult in certain circumstances which typically arise when the religious organisation is involved in providing an educational, commercial or a funded 'public service'. The most high-profile example of such a difficulty arose during the passage of the Equality Act (Sexual Orientation) Regulations 2007,[157] which outlawed discrimination on the grounds of sexual orientation in terms of the provision of goods and services, with only a narrow exemption for 'organisations relating to religion or belief' (with the same caveats which apply under the Equality Act 2010), *unless* they are educational establishments, mainly 'commercial' in character, or they provide services with and 'on behalf of a public authority under the terms of a contract' – in which cases there are no exemptions at all.[158] The plight of the Roman Catholic adoption agencies which faced either closure under the Regulations or the requirement to act against faith by asking their staff to facilitate adoptions by homosexual couples is illustrative of the difficulties which religious employees will encounter if the religious organisation to which they belong is required to act against the teaching or doctrines of that religion. For most religious organisations the resulting strains may well become intolerable forcing their closure[159] (or at best secularisation) and

---

153 Equality Bill 2009, *Explanatory Notes* [778].
154 HL Deb, 25 January 2010, vol 716, cols 1211–40.
155 Amendment 98.
156 See *Explanatory Notes to the Equality Act 2010* [796].
157 SI 2007 No. 1263.
158 Ibid., reg 17.
159 As was predicted to be the case for the Roman Catholic adoption agencies by Cardinal Cormac Murphy O'Connor, the head of the Roman Catholic Church in England and Wales; see discussion in Sandberg and Doe, 'Religious Exemptions in Discrimination Law', 308. One such adoption agency lost a subsequent attempt to secure exemption from the reach of the regulations (*Catholic Care (Diocese of Leeds)* v. *Charity Commission for England and Wales* [2012] UKUT 395 (TTC)).

thus, *inter alia*, leading to the abrupt exile from an island of exclusivity for religious employees who had hitherto found refuge there.

Public policy

Procurement and the equality duty

Daintith employs the classical term *imperium* to describe the state's power to identify and define rights and to enforce these rights through the imposition of sanctions.[160] However, he uses a second term, *dominium*, to describe the power the state exercises through its influence, particularly the influence based on its 'buying power'. As modern states have considerable procurement power and seek to engage the private sector in providing numerous services, it is argued that they have an immense power to influence organisations which seek lucrative contracts with the state government to provide such services. This power could be used in the equality field, for example to require organisations to behave in particular ways which might constrain their normal freedom of action and require them to promote objectives which they might not otherwise have pursued.[161]

In the United Kingdom, there is clear evidence that state buying power has been used in this way. For example, any organisation tendering to supply legal aid work is required by the Legal Services Commission (a non-departmental public body) to have an equality and diversity policy which 'sets out how you will promote equality and tackle discrimination in your organisation and meet the diverse needs of the clients you serve'.[162] Some quite detailed guidelines are provided on what should be included in the policy and how it should be monitored.

For many organisations, such requirements may not be unduly burdensome. However, for some religious ethos organisations, the effects may be, for them, malign. For example, in 2008, residents at a care home belonging to the Christian charity, Pilgrim Homes, refused to circulate a questionnaire four times a year to residents asking about their sexual orientation, in support of its 'fair access and diversity policy'; nor would it agree to use images of elderly gay, lesbian, bisexual and transgender people in its promotional literature, arguing that this would be disrespectful to the

---

160 T Daintith, 'The Techniques of Government' in J Jowell and D Oliver (eds), *The Changing Constitution*, 3rd ed. (Oxford: Oxford University Press, 1994).

161 See C McCrudden, *Buying Social Justice* (Oxford: Oxford University Press, 2007).

162 Legal Services Commission, *Equality and Diversity Guidance and Policy 2010* (London: Legal Services Commission, July 2010). Available online at www.justice.gov.uk/downloads/legal-aid/civil-contracts/LSC_Equality_and_Diversity_Policy_Guidance_for_Providers.pdf (accessed 6 June 2014).

beliefs and values of its Christian residents.[163] The local authority withdrew £13,000 of funding from the charity as a result, on the basis that 'there had been limited progress in making the home open to the gay and lesbian community'.[164] Although this decision was later overturned after Pilgrim Homes threatened legal action, it illustrates the difficulties that islands of exclusivity (and by extension those who work there) can have if they are found not to be sufficiently committed to promoting aspects of 'equality', such as sexual orientation equality, which are fundamentally at odds with their religious ethos. Where these organisations are reliant on funding from central or local government, withdrawal of funds may be a significant threat to their continued financial viability.

That public policy should be used to promote equality, including in procurement activities[165] has to a large extent become a legal obligation as a result of the Equality Act 2010. In the Act, there is a proactive 'equality duty', which applies to 'public authorities'.[166] This includes a general duty which requires public authorities, in the exercise of their functions, to have due regard for the need to:

(i) eliminate discrimination, harassment, victimisation and any other conduct that is prohibited by or under this Act;

(ii) advance equality of opportunity between persons who share a relevant protected characteristic and persons who do not share it; and

(iii) foster good relations between persons who share a relevant protected characteristic and persons who do not share it.[167]

Having due regard to the need to foster good relations between persons who share a relevant protected characteristic and persons who do not share it is further defined as involving duties to 'tackle prejudice' and 'promote understanding'.[168]

It has been suggested that one of two possible effects of such an objective on state approaches to religious ethos organisations is likely to follow over time. The first would be that public authorities increase their funding of

---

163 D Harrison, 'Christian Care Home Victorious in Gay Dispute' *Daily Telegraph* (London, 7 February 2009). Available online at www.telegraph.co.uk/health/healthnews/4548761/Christian-care-home-victorious-in-gay-dispute.html (accessed 6 June 2014).

164 Ibid.

165 That the reach of the equality duty includes procurement is implied by the general duty; the Act also gives government ministers the power to impose additional specific duties on public authorities, including those relating to their respective public procurement functions (Equality Act, s 155(3)).

166 Defined by Equality Act 2010, Sch 19.

167 Ibid., s 149(1).

168 Ibid., s 149(5).

religious ethos organisations to increase the reach of these organisations, on the assumption that they contribute to 'fostering good relations' and 'advancing equality' (a model V interpretation of the duty). The second would be that public authorities would reduce or even cease financial support for religious organisations, presumably on the basis that they are divisive and do not contribute to the relevant equality goals (a model I interpretation).[169]

Promoting religious equality?

As one of the protected characteristics that the equality duty commits public authorities to promote is religion and belief, it might be anticipated that efforts would be made in support of religious manifestation at an individual level. Although the duty dates back to the implementation of the Act in 2011, it is nevertheless telling to consider the efforts made by the government in support of religious equality before 2010. Two areas are examined: first, the role of the EqHRC and, second, government-sponsored guidance in the area of religion and belief.

The Equality and Human Rights Commission (EqHRC) was established under the Equality Act 2006 and became operational on 1 October 2007, at which point three earlier commissions became defunct – the Commission for Racial Equality, the Equal Opportunities Commission and the Disability Rights Commission.[170] The purpose of the EqHRC is to promote equality and diversity across all of the protected characteristics; to encourage good practice and to work towards eliminating unlawful discrimination and harassment.[171] This clearly includes the workplace. It is also required to promote understanding and good relations between members of different groups (defined as those who share a protected characteristic) and to work towards reducing hostility and prejudice.[172]

It is important therefore to highlight that the EqHRC is required to promote equality on the basis of religion and belief in the same way as for any other protected characteristic. Thus, on the face of it, the creation of the EqHRC is congruent with model V (protection for religious expression). However, at the time the EqHRC was set up, there began to be concerns that 'relatively powerful interest groups … would swamp other less powerful interests' and so the EqHRC might not be impartial and even-handed in upholding the interests of the various protected characteristics.[173] If this analysis is correct, there is other evidence which suggests that religion and belief (particularly with regard to religious

---

169 A Lester and P Uccellari, 'Extending the equality duty to religion, conscience and belief: Proceed with caution' (2008) *European Human Rights Law Review* 567.
170 Hepple, *Equality*, 145.
171 Equality Act 2006, s 8(1).
172 Ibid., s 10.
173 Hepple, *Equality*, 146.

expression) may be one of the characteristics which has been 'swamped'. Indeed, it is possible to go further and contend the EqHRC has at times displayed a degree of hostility towards religious expression, particularly the expression of Christianity in the workplace. When the then Chairman of the EqHRC, Trevor Phillips, was interviewed by the *Daily Telegraph* in 2011, he made the following rather telling observations about those seeking protection for their religious beliefs:

> I think for a lot of Christian activists, they want to have a fight and they choose sexual orientation as the ground to fight it on. I think that whole argument isn't about the rights of Christians. It's about politics.[174]

The comments would appear to imply a rather negative assumption about the motivation of evangelical Christians with which many may disagree; it also minimises the difficulties that they face in response to legislation which impinges on their freedom of conscience or freedom of religious expression, which is apparent in the workplace. Clearly these are only comments by an official of the EqHRC (albeit the most senior official). However, the actions of the EqHRC itself also appear to suggest, at times, a lack of sympathy towards Christian religious expression.[175] In *Bull & Bull* v. *Hall & Preddy*,[176] a case where the rights of Christians to run their bed and breakfast establishment in conformity with their religious beliefs clashed with the rights of a homosexual couple to share a double room, the EqHRC financially supported the sexual orientation rights against the religious rights, funding the legal expenses of the homosexual couple concerned.[177] Earlier, when the Christian bed and breakfast owners lost their case at first instance, it was the EqHRC who, apparently against the wishes of the gay couple involved, and thus unnecessarily, decided to cross-appeal for more damages (an appeal it later dropped on the basis that it had been an 'error of judgment').[178] This and other evidence suggests that the EqHRC may at

---

174 J Wynne-Jones, 'I'll Defend Faith, Says Equality Chief: Watchdog Can Help Lift "Siege" on Religious Believers, Trevor Phillips Tells Jonathan Wynne Jones Interview' *Sunday Telegraph* (London, 19 June 2011), 12.
175 A report commissioned by the EqHRC confirmed that this perception is widely held by Christians; see A Donald, *Religion or Belief, Equality and Human Rights in England and Wales* (Equality and Human Rights Commission Research Report no. 84, 2012), 124–30.
176 [2013] UKSC 73.
177 Lady Hale later suggested that 'a more neutral stance of the Commission might have been to seek to intervene in, rather than to prosecute, these proceedings', *Bull and Bull* [4].
178 'Dramatic U-turn as gay couple who won £3,600 from Christian B&B owners ditch taxpayer-funded fight for more cash' *Daily Mail* (London, 9 May 2011). Available online at www.dailymail.co.uk/news/article-1365168/Gay-couple-won-3k-Christian-B-B-owners-ditch-taxpayer-funded-fight.html#ixzz1sZoSqBzR (accessed 6 June 2014).

times display a degree of hostility to (Christian) religious expression (a model I approach).[179]

The discussion will now turn to government-funded sources of advice and their content, concerning how the law affects religious expression in the workplace. Perhaps the most significant of these is a guide prepared by the Advisory, Conciliation and Arbitration Service (ACAS), a non-departmental public body with a brief, *inter alia*, to provide legal and good practice guidance to employers and employees.[180] Written in 2005, the guide dwells largely on dress and grooming requirements and religious holidays. Supportive of religious expression in these domains, the ACAS guide tends to focus on accommodating the practices of minority religions in the workplace (in keeping with model VI).[181] No references are made to forms of active manifestation or conscientious objection to activities involving the promotion of sexual orientation rights, which have become closely associated with Christian forms of expression in the workplace, except a critical and rather unlikely example of active manifestation (which is clearly designed to discourage it as a form of harassment):

> A member of staff is devout in her belief. She continually refers to her colleagues as 'heathens' and warns them of the consequences they may suffer as a result of their lack of belief. Distressed by her intimidating behaviour, her colleagues complain to their manager that they are being harassed.[182]

Whereas the ACAS guide is the source of guidance most likely to be used in the workplace, other guidance is available that has been funded or part-funded by the UK government.[183] It is perhaps telling that the following organisations have been provided with government funding to provide quasi-official 'good practice' guidelines for employers on religion and

---

179 Another example was the reference in a legal submission for the EqHRC to Christian moral views as an 'infection' – for which the EqCHR was forced to issue an apology; see 'Johns V Derby City Council'. Available online at www.equalityhumanrights.com/legal-and-policy/legal-updates/johns-v-derby-city-council/ (accessed 6 June 2014).

180 ACAS, *Religion or Belief in the Workplace: A Guide for Employers and Employees* (March 2014). Available online at www.acas.org.uk/media/pdf/f/l/religion_1.pdf (accessed 6 June 2014).

181 Of the examples of religious expression given, only one refers directly or indirectly to specifically Christian religious expression; seven relate directly or indirectly to Muslim religious expression; three refer directly or indirectly to Hindu religious expression; three relate directly or indirectly to Sikh religious expression and three relate directly or indirectly to Jewish religious expression; three are generally applicable to religious expression (analysis, mine).

182 ACAS, *Religion or Belief in the Workplace*, 7.

183 Either by the Department of Trade and Industry (now Business Innovation and Skills) or the EqHRC.

belief in the workplace: the Muslim Council of Britain,[184] Stonewall[185] and the British Humanist Association.[186] That a Muslim organisation should be supported in providing advice to employers on religion in the workplace is unsurprising. Rightly, the Council's guidance focuses on issues specific to Muslims. It is surprising, however, that no guidance has been provided by other religious groups with support from a government department or other public authority.[187] What is more surprising still is that the government should be providing funding to organisations with interests which are frequently opposed to religious interests, to advise on religion in the workplace. Such guidelines are unlikely to be free from influence from the interests of Stonewall and the British Humanist Association. The latter, for example, suggests that '[a]ttempts by employees to convert people or to use the work environment to proselytise are highly likely to amount to harassment of their colleagues'.[188] This statement is controversial as it ignores the distinction between 'proper' and 'improper' proselytism[189] and seems likely to mislead employers as to the likely reach of the law, and may thus have a chilling effect on religious speech.[190] The net effect of all the guidance appears to be support for both model I (exclusion) and, not without contradiction, model IV (support for minority religions).

It should be noted at this point that there are also ethical codes of practice issued by professional bodies (often as a result of secondary legislation empowering them to do so) which may act to encourage or discourage religious expression. Such codes, for example, have been issued by the (now defunct) General Teaching Council for England (GTCE), the General Social Care Council, the General Pharmaceutical Council, the General Medical Council and the Nursing and Midwifery Council. Some of these codes (in fact those applying in the healthcare sector) make specific reference to a practitioner's own religious beliefs and provide guidelines as to

---

184 Muslim Council of Britain, *Muslims in the Workplace*.
185 R Hunt, *Religion and Sexual Orientation: How to Manage Relations in the Workplace* (London: Stonewall, 2009).
186 British Humanist Association, *Guidance on Equality of 'Religion or Belief'*.
187 An unofficial guide advising Christians of their rights in the workplace has been published by the Christian Institute; see M Jones, *Religious Liberty in the Workplace: A Guide for Christian Employees* (Newcastle upon Tyne: Christian Institute 2008).
188 British Humanist Association, *Guidance on Equality of 'Religion or Belief'*, 8.
189 As recognised by the ECtHR in *Kokkinakis v. Greece* (1993) 17 EHRR 397; see discussion in Chapter 8.
190 See comments to this effect in J Wynne-Jones, 'Christians Risk Rejection and Discrimination for Their Faith, a Study Claims', *Telegraph* (London, 30 May 2009). Available online at www.telegraph.co.uk/news/religion/5413311/Christians-risk-rejection-and-discrimination-for-their-faith-a-study-claims.html (accessed 6 June 2014). See also Chapter 8 for a more detailed discussion of proselytism and religious speech in the workplace.

how these may or may not influence their professional activities.[191] Other guidelines do not make specific reference to a practitioner's religious beliefs but provide general guidelines on upholding equality and diversity as values which have the potential to impact negatively on an individual's religious beliefs.[192]

The draft code of conduct for secondary school teachers, written by the GTCE in 2009, is illustrative of this problem. One of the underlying principles of the code ('principle 4') was that teachers should 'promote equality and value diversity' and this included the obligation to '[p]roactively challenge discrimination, stereotyping, and bullying, no matter who is the victim or the perpetrator'.[193] Concerns were raised about this draft principle by Christian groups, on the basis that the wording might require Christian teachers to act against their consciences to 'promote', for example, homosexual relationships or the teachings of another religion with which they disagreed.[194] In this case, the problem was obviated by the response of the GTCE, which changed the wording to remove the requirements to 'promote diversity' and to 'proactively challenge' discrimination.[195] However, not all professional bodies have been willing necessarily to accommodate such concerns and professional obligations with regard to valuing diversity may remain a stumbling block for religious expression.[196]

Conclusion

In this chapter, various legal and policy materials have been considered, all of which have a bearing, directly or indirectly, on freedom of religious expression in the UK workplace. In the process of examining these materials, consideration has been given, in each instance, to the congruence with the models presented in Chapter 3. The purpose of this concluding section is to provide a summary and an overall assessment.

Given the range of legal and policy materials and the overall time frame during which they have appeared, it is perhaps unsurprising that the

---

191 The guidelines for pharmacists were considered earlier in this respect and the GMC and NMC guidelines, respectively, are considered in Chapter 8.

192 It should be noted that the 'healthcare' professional codes also allude to equality and diversity more generally.

193 General Teaching Council for England, *Code of Conduct and Practice – Draft for Consultation* (November 2008), 14.

194 See, for example, the briefing document by the Christian Institute: 'Help Protect Christian Teachers From the New "Equality" Code', Christian Institute (12 February 2009). Available online at www.christian.org.uk/pdfpublications/gtccode_feb09.pdf (accessed 14 June 2014).

195 See Curtis, 'Teachers' anti-discrimination code reworded after faith groups object'. Since the abolition of the GTCE (on 31 March 2012) the Code ceased to be in force, and has been withdrawn from the internet.

196 The NMC code exemplifies this problem – see discussion in Chapter 8.

picture is complicated. *Prima facie*, it might appear that overall 'protection for religious expression' (model V) is the dominant model. After all, the ostensible purpose of much of the legislation is to support religion. This includes both the recognition of positive rights, principally through the incorporation of the ECHR into UK law (through the Human Rights Act 1998) and also the recognition of 'negative' rights (the right not to be discriminated against because of religion and belief) through the relevant provisions of the Equality Act 2010 (and earlier discrimination law). Under the provisions of UK discrimination law, religious belief and identity are protected, chiefly through direct discrimination provisions. However, in terms of religious expression, employers are able to provide a justification defence for 'indirectly' discriminating against people when they manifest their religious beliefs in the workplace. There are a few examples of opt-outs to particular laws which serve to protect some very specific examples of religious expression in particular contexts (e.g. in healthcare) but these are few, often historic, and narrow in scope. Attempts to extend opt-outs to other areas have been resisted by the UK government.

In respect of the other models, it is plain that the law itself provides virtually no 'special' support for Christianity, the historical religion of the United Kingdom (model II), albeit that the 'convention' that many economic and social activities cease on a Sunday, is still strong (although not in the retail sector). There is perhaps more evidence in support of model VI (protection for minority religions) at least in terms of the development of discrimination law. The Race Relations Act 1976 provides an ongoing basis for supporting Sikh and Jewish expressions of religion and it was partly in response to Muslim pressure that discrimination law was extended to cover religion and belief (a development opposed by some Christian groups), with the clear expectation that other minority religions, thus far unprotected, would benefit. It is may also be inferred from the ACAS guidance, published shortly after the introduction of the original Employment Equality (Religion and Belief) Regulations, that the needs of religious minorities were at the forefront of policy development at that time. The very specific regulations applying to Northern Ireland only are perhaps the clearest example of the law seeking to protect 'minority' religion (in this case Roman Catholicism).

The Equality Act 2010 does recognise 'religious ethos organisations' and 'organised religions' for the purposes of 'occupational requirement' exceptions to discrimination law. To this extent, at least, the concept of 'islands of exclusivity' and the rights of religious staff to populate them (model IV) are recognised. However, the freedom of such islands is significantly curtailed by the very limited extent of the exceptions on religious grounds (not least the apparent need to justify exceptions for each post rather than according to a more generally applicable principle) and the even greater limitations when other strands of equality are invoked, such as sexual orientation. No religious ethos organisations seem able to restrict employment according to religious teaching on sexual orientation and organised religions appear able to do this only in very restricted circumstances.

There is one form of 'prohibited conduct' which has significant potential to adversely affect workplace religious expression – this is 'harassment' on the basis of a protected characteristic. As the law is unconcerned with motive, both animus and non-animus harassment are prohibited. As a result, there is a significant question mark concerning how far employees are free to express their religious beliefs verbally, particularly if those beliefs have the capacity to offend others on the grounds of their religion (or non-religion), sexual orientation or gender. Employers concerned about their liability for religious harassment of employees may have an incentive to significantly restrict religious speech in the workplace. This aspect of the law is therefore congruent with model I (exclusion of religious expression). Religious expression for some employees may also be constrained by the provisions of codes of conduct issued by professional bodies (which are empowered to do this by secondary legislation).

Thus far, it is clear that elements of the various models (with the exception of model II) can be identified from the legislation and policy landscape presented in this chapter. What is also evident is that there has been a considerable expansion in the reach of the relevant legislation, particularly since 2003. This in turn has had a considerable impact in reducing employer discretion (model III, *laissez-faire*). As noted above, employers can still restrict forms of religious expression when they can provide a clear justification of the need to do so (i.e. where this represents a proportionate means of achieving a legitimate aim). However, in respect of any employer who consciously chooses to support religious expression, there are also some potential legal restrictions, particularly in terms of verbal expression. Policy initiatives too may affect an employer's approach towards religious expression by employees (it might for example ban proselytism in the workplace outright on the advice of the EqHRC-funded British Humanist Association guidance), this is particularly likely when acting on such policy advice might bring rewards (such as success in a bid for government funding).

6   Negative manifestation

Introduction

This chapter considers how tribunals have dealt with cases in which employees have objected to performing aspects of their contractual work for reasons connected to their religious beliefs. The objections fall into two broad categories. The first concerns objections to working at particular times or on particular days, owing to the desire or perceived obligations of (in the language of Article 9 ECHR) 'worship' and 'observance', 'either alone or in community with others'. For example, a Muslim employee might object to working during Friday lunchtime because he feels obliged to attend Friday prayers; equally, a Christian may object to working on a Sunday because she feels obliged to attend Church. The second category concerns objections for reasons intrinsic to the work itself, or an aspect of it, because it is objectionable on religious grounds.

Both categories are reactive to the demands of the workplace itself, rather than proactive – it is the employer who initiates or perpetuates the work or environment that gives rise to the objection. They can thus be characterised as forms of 'negative manifestation' of religion in the workplace and some of the consequent legal and policy issues raised will be the same, not least whether or not the employer is bound to rearrange contractual work to accommodate the religious employee and, if so, in what circumstances. However, objections to the nature of the work (or some aspects of it)[1] are rather different in a number of ways from objections to the structuring of that same work. The employee is, after all, saying that he disapproves of something the employer wants him to do – there is an

---

1   Generally, objections for religious conscience have been raised concerning particular tasks or duties of employment. There has been, however, at least one recent tribunal claim (for sexual harassment) involving an objection by a young Muslim woman to the wearing of uniform she considered to be immodest; see L Cockcroft, 'Muslim waitress told to wear sexy, low-cut dress wins payout' *Daily Telegraph* (London, 16 June 2009), 13. Cases such as this raise questions overlapping conscientious objection and symbolic expression (considered in Chapter 7).

implicit moral judgment which is absent from requests to rearrange the timing or structure of that something. The former arguably represents a different and more direct challenge to the employer, its discretion or its values, than the latter. From the point of view of the employee, this form of what may reasonably be termed 'conscientious objection' is also likely to be more personally challenging. It is arguably rather more difficult to say to an employer that one feels that something an employer wants one to do offends against conscience than to say that the timing is wrong. To make a stand in this way will thus require more courage. For both parties to the employment relationship, the stakes may thus be higher.

In this chapter both categories of negative manifestation are considered in turn before a general conclusion is drawn.

Negative manifestation during working time due to religious obligations

In the first part of this chapter, how far the desire (or obligation) felt by employees with religious convictions to engage in either worship or observance might relate to their employment obligations is considered. There is clearly potential for conflict if the employer requires the employee to be present in the workplace at a time when the employee has a religious obligation that he may well consider to be more important than the obligation owed to the employer. In such cases, the employee may wish to 'negatively manifest' his religious convictions by seeking to 'opt-out' of working at particular times to pursue worship or observance alone or in the company of others. Such activities are most likely to take place outside of the workplace, although in some instances the religious obligation might be discharged on the employer's premises (e.g. daily Islamic prayers in a dedicated prayer room).

In the following sections, the relevant case law is examined. Prior to this analysis, there is a brief discussion of the issues concerned from the perspective of the religious employee. As these issues are to some extent dependent on the nature of the religion itself, this discussion is structured with reference to different religious traditions.

Religious obligations requiring 'time off'; some examples by religion

Judaism

In Judaism there is a divinely ordained day of rest from work known as the Sabbath. This was first ordained in the creation narrative: having created the heavens and the earth in six days, God rested on the seventh and made this a holy day.[2] The obligation was made more specific in the form of the tenth commandment given to Moses:

2   Genesis 2: 3.

Remember the Sabbath day, to keep it holy. Six days you shall labour and do all your work, but the seventh day is the Sabbath of the Lord your God. In it you shall do no work: you, nor your son, nor your daughter, nor your male servant, nor your female servant, nor your cattle, nor the stranger who is within your gates. For in six days the Lord made the heavens and the earth, the sea, and all that is in them, and rested the seventh day. Therefore the Lord blessed the Sabbath day and hallowed it.[3]

The Jewish Sabbath begins at sunset on Friday night (a time which varies greatly depending on the seasons) and it ends at nightfall on Saturday.[4] Keeping the Sabbath remains mandatory for observant Jews. The rules of Sabbath observance are strict and most forms of working, both domestic and commercial, are forbidden.[5] In addition, Jews attend the synagogue for collective prayer on Friday nights and Saturday, and many also meet in the synagogue collectively on weekday evenings, when they may recite both obligatory afternoon and evening prayers at the same time.[6]

Christianity

After the death and resurrection of Jesus, the early Christians began to use the first day of the week as a day set aside for worship in community (sometimes known as 'the Lord's day') and that practice became established and continues to this day. How far the obligations imposed by the Jewish Sabbath apply to the Christian Sunday is a point of theological dispute. This has led to different positions emerging among Christians. One position is to view Sunday as the Christian Sabbath. Although this does not mean that all the obligations incumbent upon Jews on the Sabbath apply; the fundamental principle that the Sabbath must be strictly observed as a day of rest from secular labour (unless, by concession, this labour is required to provide emergency services)[7] still applies to Christians.[8] Another position is to take a more relaxed view of the Christian Sunday and to see it as a New Testament innovation and therefore fundamentally different from the Jewish Sabbath – in fact, more of an opportunity for rest and

---

3   Exodus 20: 8–11; see also Deuteronomy 5: 12–15.
4   Y Green, 'When Does the Day Begin?' (2008) 36 *Jewish Bible Quarterly* 81.
5   See, for a discussion of the restrictions on Sabbath activities for observant Jews, Gavison and Davison, 'Days of Rest in Multicultural Societies: Private, Public Separate' in Cane, Peter, Caroline Evans and Zoe Robinson (eds), *Law and Religion in Theoretical and Historical Context* (Cambridge: Cambridge University Press, 2008) 190–3.
6   G Robinson, *Essential Judaism* (New York: Pocket Books, 2000), 7–54.
7   Jesus healed on the Sabbath, and spoke of the lawfulness of 'saving life' and 'doing good' on that day (Mark 3: 4).
8   See, for a contemporary version of this argument, I Campell, *On the First Day of the Week: God, the Christian and the Sabbath* (Leominster: Day One Publications, 2005).

spiritual activity rather than a day to be observed in a traditional Sabbatarian manner.[9] This distinction is important, as it suggests that taking time off work on a Sunday is considered mandatory under the traditional Sabbatarian view but not mandatory under the more flexible 'New Testament' view. However, although there are differences amongst Christians in the view taken of obligations towards Sabbath observance, the majority of practising Christians share an imperative to attend worship in congregation with others – this almost invariably takes place on a Sunday.

Certain Christian sects take different positions. Seventh-day Adventists, for example, reject the decision by the Christian Church to celebrate Sunday as the Lord's day and retain Saturday as their Sabbath, which is to be 'observed' as 'the day of rest, worship and ministry' in accordance with 'God's unchangeable law' from Friday evening until Saturday evening.[10] Jehovah's Witnesses, on the other hand, reject the entire concept of the Lord's day, although they do tend to meet on a Sunday, as well as mid-week; attendance at weekend and mid-week meetings is considered equally obligatory.[11]

Islam

In Islam, the practice of the daily *Salah* of praying five short prayers (whilst kneeling towards Mecca) at different times of the day (of which, between two and four may take place during normal working hours) is considered mandatory by some Muslim groups.[12] This will have a clear impact on the workplace, as it will be necessary to briefly withdraw from workplace activities for the duration of the prayers. However, this requirement is not recognised as binding by all Muslims: some permit the afternoon and evening prayers to be said together at the same time;[13] whilst others omit to say the prayers at all.[14] Where these prayers are carried out, there is no obligation to do so in company with others, except on a Friday, where a congregational prayer, the *Jumu'ah*, is held on Friday lunchtimes (between 1 and 2 pm); for most Muslim groups it is mandatory to attend this at a

---

9   See for example, JM Boice, *Foundations of the Christian Faith* (Downers Grove IL: InterVarsity Press, 1986), 234.

10   Seventh-day Adventist Church, 'Beliefs'; see www.adventist.org/beliefs/ fundamental/index.html.

11   A Holden, *Jehovah's Witnesses: Portrait of a Contemporary Religious Movement* (Abingdon: Routledge, 2002).

12   B Zaheer, 'Accommodating Minority Religions Under Title VII: How Muslims Make the Case for a New Interpretation of Section 701(J)' (2007) *University of Illinois Law Review* 497, 502.

13   Muslim Council of Britain, *Muslims in the Workplace: A Good Practice Guide for Employers and Employees* (MCB/DTI 2005), 14.

14   W Shadid and P van Koningsveld, *Religious freedom and the position of Islam in Western Europe* (Kampen: Kok Pharos, 1995), 101.

mosque.[15] Indeed, there is a specific injunction in the Quran with particular application to refraining from work in order to attend Friday prayers:

> O you who believe, when the Salat is announced on Friday, you shall hasten to the commemoration of God, and drop all business. This is better for you, if you only knew. Once the prayer is completed, you may spread through the land to seek God's bounties, and continue to remember God frequently, that you may succeed.[16]

To facilitate the *Salah* prayers, there is an argument that an employer with sufficient resources (e.g. an appropriate room that is not used or is used infrequently) should provide some basic facilities. The Muslim Council of Britain guidance makes the following observation:

> Employers are not required to make costly adjustments for religious observance at work. However, employees may request access to a place to pray, and if it is possible to provide a room without an unacceptable adverse impact on business or other staff, then employers may be found to be indirectly discriminating if they refuse such a request.[17]

The guidance goes on to specify that the room should be quiet and unadorned with posters, pictures or photographs. It also makes recommendations about the supply of facilities for the *wudhu* ritual of feet washing that often precedes prayer – this could, for example, involve providing 'storage in the washroom areas for a plastic washing-up basin and a small jug'.[18]

There are some further requirements specifically affecting Muslims. It is, for example, suggested that Muslims may wish to take time off for lunch later than they might normally so do, in order to break their fast at the permitted time during the Ramadan period of fasting.[19] There are also certain religious holidays where many Muslims are likely to request leave, including the three most important: *Eid-ul-Fitr*, *Eid-ul-Adha* and *Yawm Al-Ashura*. These annual holidays occur at different times each year, according to the lunar calendar. Equally, Muslims are mandated to go on a pilgrimage to Mecca (the *Hajj*) at least once in their lifetime (and must accompany a widowed mother or sister).[20] This is estimated to require an extended period of leave of between two and three weeks in duration.[21] The period

15   Muslim Council of Britain, *Muslims in the Workplace*, 14.
16   *Quran* 62: 9–10.
17   Muslim Council of Britain, *Muslims in the Workplace*, 15.
18   Ibid., 16.
19   Ibid., 16.
20   Participation in pilgrimages is encouraged in other religious traditions (e.g. Roman Catholic and Orthodox Christianity and Hinduism).
21   Muslim Council of Britain, *Muslims in the Workplace*, 17.

where Muslims engage in the *Hajj* is fixed each year in accordance with the lunar calendar and so falls on different dates in the solar year.[22] It may be that particular circumstances arise when a Muslim employee has a pressing conviction that he should embark on the *Hajj* during work time; certainly, there may be a strong desire to do so, as Muslims are encouraged to perform the *Hajj* as soon as they have sufficient funds to do so.[23]

The case law

Thus far, the religious basis of the desire for time off for religious observance and worship has been considered. In Chapter 4, consideration was given to the European Convention on Human Rights and Fundamental Freedoms (ECHR) jurisprudence, which chiefly concerns the issue of conflict between religious obligations outside the workplace and work time. Attention now turns to the relevant domestic case law. What is helpful to the analysis is the thorough consideration given to the implications of Article 9 in *Copsey* v. *Devon Clays Limited*[24] and how this case may be contrasted with very similar cases under the Religion and Belief Regulations 2003, in particular the decision in *Mba* v. *Merton Borough Council.*[25]

In *Copsey*, the claimant had been employed by Devon Clays since 1988 as a team leader in the sand processing plant. A shift system was in operation from Monday to Friday with frequent weekend overtime, particularly on Saturdays.[26] In late 1999, Devon Clays Limited won a new contract, which substantially increased production in the sand processing plant. This led to a decision to extend the operating hours to seven-day working, 24 hours per day, with a new shift system for all staff covering the whole period.[27] Copsey (and three other staff) objected to working on a Sunday and a special provision was temporarily made for him not to work on that day, with a corresponding reduction in pay.[28] However, some two years later, another increase in production was necessary in response to a further new order. A meeting was held with Copsey and he was required either to join the Sunday shift system or to accept a redundancy package. At this point, he indicated that his opposition to Sunday working had a religious basis.[29] He was given the option, which he refused, of working in the resin coated sand plant where there would be a reduced requirement for Sunday shifts.

22   Zaheer, 'Accommodating Minority Religions Under Title VII', 504.
23   Ibid.
24   *Copsey* v. *Devon Clays Limited* [2005] EWCA Civ. 932.
25   [2013] EWCA Civ. 1562; [2013] WLR (D) 474 (CA).
26   *Copsey* [10].
27   Ibid. [11].
28   Ibid. [12].
29   Ibid. [14].

Following the failure of further negotiations, including the possibility of an alternative lower-paid laboratory job that he was unwilling to accept, Copsey was dismissed (without a redundancy payment) on 31 July 2002.[30] He then lodged his claim at an employment tribunal. Copsey argued that his employer had been under an obligation to accommodate his religious objections, which it had failed to do, and he had been unfairly dismissed.

The tribunal found that Devon Clays had made some efforts to accommodate Copsey, including the offer of alternative positions, and had approached his colleagues to discover how far they might be willing to take on disadvantageous additional Sunday shifts in the place of Copsey (but found that there was little support for his position). Equally, Copsey himself did not adopt an entirely inflexible stance. He had said he was willing to work on a Sunday in an 'emergency' although the judgment records that it was not possible to agree on what such an emergency might be.[31]

The tribunal determined that Copsey's dismissal was not connected to his religious beliefs but was the direct result of his refusal to conform to a seven-day shift pattern. It found this dismissal to be fair under the category of 'some other substantial reason'. Devon Clays had a sound business reason to require Copsey to work on Sundays, in response to 'significant increases in production requirements', which was more than a mere whim.[32] The Employment Appeals Tribunal rejected Copsey's appeal and, following this, he applied to the Court of Appeal.

The Court of Appeal gave a much more nuanced consideration of the possible impact of Article 9 ECHR on Copsey's unfair dismissal claim. Lord Justice Mummery observed that, in the absence of other authority, the 'link between [Copsey's] dismissal and his wish to manifest his religious beliefs [was] sufficiently material to bring the circumstances of the dismissal within the ambit of Article 9'.[33] Thus, the issue would become one of justification under Article 9 (2). However, he applied the EComHR rulings in *Ahmad*, *Konttinen* and *Stedman*,[34] to determine that, on the basis of this line of authority, in Copsey's 'specific situation'[35] (in the workplace) there was no interference with his Article 9 rights:

> so far as working hours are concerned, an employer is entitled to keep the workplace secular. In such cases an employee is not in general entitled to complain that there has been a material interference with his Article 9 rights.[36]

30   Ibid. [15].
31   Ibid. [16].
32   Ibid. [8(5)].
33   Ibid. [30].
34   *Ahmad* v. *UK* (1982) 4 EHRR 126; *Konttinen* v. *Finland* Appl No 24949/94 (3 December 1996); *Stedman* v. *United Kingdom* (1997) 23 EHRR CD (Commision).
35   *Copsey* [37].
36   Ibid. [38] (Mummery LJ).

As Article 9 did not therefore apply in this case, there was thus no need to consider justification arguments, although Mummery stated that, as Devon Clays had 'done everything that they could to accommodate Mr Copsey's wish not to work on Sundays' then, had there been any interference with Article 9, it would probably be justified.[37]

It will be recalled from the discussion in Chapter 4 that Lord Justice Rix, in a partially dissenting opinion, took a more sceptical view of the consistency and application of the ECHR case law; however, he agreed with Mummery that the employer had acted reasonably in its eventual decision to dismiss Copsey and had thus discharged its obligation to justify its interference with the claimant's Article 9 rights, if engaged.[38] In the process, however, Rix clearly articulated the need for an employer to demonstrate that it had sought to make reasonable accommodations to justify restrictions on the religious rights of its employees:

> It seems to me that it is possible and necessary to contemplate that an employer who seeks to change an employee's working hours so as to prevent that employee from practising his sincere adherence to the requirements of his religion in the way of Sabbath observance may be acting unfairly if he makes no attempt to accommodate his employee's needs.[39]

The exact nature of the anticipated accommodation is naturally not articulated in full. However, there is a general implication that the obligation belongs to the employer to initiate and a corresponding onus on the employee to respond constructively. However, in Lord Justice Neuberger's opinion, there is a suggestion that the onus may be on the religious employee, when asked by his employer to work on a Sunday, 'to identify another worker, with his particular skills, who would be prepared to work in his place on a Sunday'.[40] It is submitted that this is unsatisfactory. The burden should naturally be on the employer to seek alternative ways of meeting its objectives (as indeed occurred in *Copsey*), not the employee.

One of the first cases to test similar issues under the Religion and Belief Regulations was *Williams-Drabble* v. *Pathway Care Solutions Ltd and anor.*[41] The employment tribunal judgment in this case just predated the Court of

---

37   Ibid. [41].
38   Interestingly, Lord Justice Neuberger took the view that the test of reasonableness required by law to demonstrate that a dismissal is fair under the Employment Rights Act 1996 provided equivalent protection for employees such as Copsey to Article 9 if it could be applied to the workplace. As he put it: 'the provisions of the 1996 Act would have the same effect, in my view, with or without any impact from Article 9' (see *Copsey* [93]).
39   Ibid. [71] (Rix LJ).
40   Ibid. [88] (Neuberger LJ).
41   (2005) ET Case No. 2601718/04.

Appeal decision in *Copsey* and is therefore particularly ripe for comparison. Article 9 arguments were not raised in *Williams-Drabble* – thus similar issues were examined under entirely different legal provisions.

The facts of the case were as follows. Williams-Drabble was a practising Christian. She made this clear when she applied to work for Pathway Care Solutions Limited in 2003 and it was agreed at the subsequent interview that she would not be rostered to work shifts on Sundays that would prevent her from attending a church service which began at 5 pm. In 2004, Williams-Drabble was told that she would in fact be required to work a shift beginning at 3 pm on Sunday. Williams-Drabble refused. She was told that she had a choice: to work the Sunday shift, to ask another employee to exchange shifts with her or to hand in her notice. She chose to resign and lodged a claim at an employment tribunal for discrimination on the grounds of religion and belief.

The tribunal found that Williams-Drabble had indeed suffered indirect discrimination. Requiring her to work when she normally went to church on a Sunday imposed a provision, criterion or practice which had an adverse impact on Christians. The employer was unable to show that the changes to the work rosta were a proportionate means of achieving a legitimate aim.

There is an issue in *Williams-Drabble* which was not fully explored by the employment tribunal but which was considered in *Copsey*. This is the question of how far the employer's responsibility to accommodate the religious employee in these circumstances extends. In *Williams-Drabble*, it could be argued that the employer had made some *de-minimis* attempts to accommodate the claimant by allowing her the option of finding a substitute for the Sunday shift if she possibly could and this would appear to be in line with Neuberger's *obiter dicta* in *Copsey*, but somewhat out of step with the implications of Lord Justice Rix's comments about the obligations on the employer to make reasonable accommodation. It would have been helpful to hear an opinion in the context of a claim brought under discrimination law on whether or not putting the onus on the employee to accommodate herself could ever be sufficient to discharge an employer's justification defence for indirect discrimination.[42]

---

42   Indeed, as the statutory right for employees to request changes in their individual patterns of work to promote 'flexible working' was amended under the Children and Families Act 2014 to be inclusive of all requests made after 30 June 2014 (including presumably those made to accommodate religious obligations outside of work) then the case law may take a different turn in future, assuming that employees requesting regular time off for religious obligations do so using this mechanism. One of the reasons that employers may rely on to turn down a flexible working request is an 'inability to reorganise work among existing staff' (Employment Rights Act 1996, s 80G(1)(b)(iii)). This strongly suggests that the onus is on the employer to demonstrate that staffing rotas cannot be reorganised, not on the employee to demonstrate that they can.

The same rationale was applied, with the same result, in *Edge* v. *Visual Security Services Limited*.[43] In this case, the claimant had been employed as a security officer by Visual Security Services Limited. Edge was a committed Christian and did not wish to work on a Sunday. It had been agreed at interview that he would not normally do so. Despite this, he found he was increasingly rostered to work that day. At length, he informed his employer by letter that he was no longer willing to do so. He was dismissed as a result. The employment tribunal found that the employer did not need to roster Edge to work on a Sunday – there was evidence that the work could have been completed without his involvement that day. As the tribunal also found that Edge was disadvantaged on religious grounds by the requirement to work on a Sunday, he was successful in his claims for indirect discrimination and unfair dismissal. Interestingly, the tribunal made a rare reference to both underlying rationales for absence from work on a Sunday (observance and worship):

> Sunday working would put people of the same religion as the claimant (Christians) at a particular disadvantage when compared with other persons because they would not be able to attend Church Services on Sunday, quite apart from the narrower, but perhaps equally important requirement, to observe Sunday as a day of rest.[44]

There is a tribunal judgment concerning time off for the *Hajj, Khan* v. *G and J Spencer Group plc t/a NIC Hygiene Ltd.*[45] In this case, the claimant had received an unclear response to his request for extended leave (including an element of unpaid leave) to go on the pilgrimage. He had chosen to go anyway and on his return he was dismissed for having taken unauthorised absence. The reasoning in this case did not extend to a discussion of how far the *Hajj* was mandatory and the possible implications of a conclusion on that point; however, the case was decided in favour of the claimant, due in large part to the ambiguity of the employer's response to the holiday request and the fact that there was some evidence that it was practicable to accommodate it.[46]

Whereas these three early tribunal judgments are positive from the perspective of protecting this form of 'negative' religious expression, many subsequent decision have been more mixed (some of which are considered

---

43   (2006) ET Case No. 1301365/06.
44   Ibid. [25].
45   (2005) ET Case No. 1803250/04.
46   There has also been an interesting claim by a Roman Catholic employee who chose to take unauthorised time off for a pilgrimage and was, in consequence, dismissed; this was held to be fair at tribunal partly due to the fact that pilgrimages are not considered mandatory for Roman Catholics: see *Moise* v. *Strettons Limited* (2011) ET Case No. 3203326/09.

below, including the Court of Appeal's judgment in *Mba* v. *Merton Borough Council*).

In *Patrick* v. *IH Sterile Services Ltd*,[47] the claimant, a Jehovah's Witness, was a trainee laboratory technician. On entering employment, he came to an arrangement with his employer that he would not be required to work on Sundays,[48] although his contract did not specify fixed hours of work. A few months later, because of market pressures, the staffing policy changed such that employees on flexible contracts (including Patrick) were expected to cover the weekend shifts.[49] Patrick objected 'that he was a Jehovah's Witness and was required to attend the Kingdom Hall for the purpose of worship and other duties to the congregation every Sunday'.[50] The judgment records that his manager held extensive discussions with Patrick to see if his position could be accommodated, during which Patrick apparently became 'hostile and aggressive'.[51] He was subsequently dismissed on the basis of an unsatisfactory probation period (there was also evidence of persistent unauthorised absence and lateness).[52] He then lodged his claim for religious discrimination with the employment tribunal.

The tribunal concluded that there had been no direct discrimination. All technicians were required to start working on a Sunday and therefore Patrick had been treated no differently from anyone else. In dealing with the indirect discrimination claim, the tribunal found that Patrick was disadvantaged by being compelled to work on a Sunday but it concluded that the employer could justify its actions on the basis that it had shared out the obligation to work on Sundays equally across the workforce, irrespective of religious obligation. Without any reference to legal authorities, it observed: '[w]e do not think it would be appropriate to exempt someone who wishes to practice worship on a Sunday from the obligation to cover Sunday work provided the requirement to do so was shared out equally'.[53] This is a curious conclusion involving no apparent consideration of adverse impact – the very principle on which the law of indirect discrimination is based! It is evident that the correct application of the law requires the tribunal, having identified adverse impact, to move on to a proper consideration of proportionality. This it failed to do.

In *Cherfi* v. *G4S Security Service Ltd*,[54] the claimant, a practising Muslim and a security guard, claimed, *inter alia*, that he had been indirectly discriminated against on the grounds of religion when his employer had required

---

47   (2011) ET Case No. 3300983/2011.
48   Ibid. [9].
49   Ibid. [10].
50   Ibid. [14].
51   Ibid. [23].
52   Ibid. [24].
53   Ibid. [33].
54   (2011) UKEAT/0379/10.

him to remain on site on Friday lunchtimes from 13 October 2008. This placed him under a particular disadvantage as a Muslim who wished to attend Friday prayers in congregation. Before that, it had been his practice to attend Friday prayers at the Finsbury Park mosque, which usually required more than the standard one hour's lunch break as it was two bus rides away from his place of work.[55]

At a hearing before an employment tribunal, Cherfi was unsuccessful in his indirect discrimination claim. However, a claim for direct discrimination on the grounds of religion succeeded.[56] This was because the claimant had been singled out to be disciplined (in 2007) for taking an extended lunch break on Fridays when this was, in fact, common practice amongst the security guards[57] (although he was later given official permission to continue attending the mosque).[58]

Cherfi appealed the indirect discrimination decision before the Employment Appeals Tribunal. The Tribunal agreed with the employment tribunal that Cherfi had been placed at a disadvantage as a practising Muslim by not permitting him to attend prayers in congregation (the first stage of his indirect discrimination claim),[59] albeit that it recognised a 'desire' rather than a religious mandate to manifest Islamic religion in this way.[60] However, moving on to the second stage, the Tribunal also endorsed the earlier tribunal's findings that G4S had a 'legitimate aim' of meeting the operational requirements of a new client that security staff remained on its site for the full duration of operating hours (including paid lunch breaks).[61] It also found that the tribunal had correctly balanced the competing claims and that it was proportionate to require Cherfi to remain on site during his Friday lunch break,[62] giving weight to both the impracticability of employing a temporary replacement for Cherfi during Friday lunchtime only and to Cherfi's rejection of an offer of an alternative contract with a pattern of working Monday to Thursday with some weekend working (Cherfi was not prepared to work on a Saturday or a Sunday).[63]

In *Abdulle v. River Island Clothing Company*,[64] a manager's refusal to allow a Muslim employee time off for *Salah* prayer during a particularly busy day for the retailer where no alternative cover was available was disputed.[65] The refusal was a one-off incident and involved a temporary manager who was

55   Ibid. [10].
56   Ibid. [2].
57   Ibid. [9].
58   Ibid. [12].
59   Ibid. [43].
60   Ibid.
61   Ibid. [14].
62   Ibid. [45].
63   Ibid. [15].
64   (2011) ET Case No. 2346023/2010.
65   Ibid. [26].

unfamiliar with the particular clothing store where the claimant worked and its staff. The employee concerned made a claim for religious discrimination. Her claim was successful because the employer had not sought to justify its actions, nor did it have a formal store-wide policy for dealing with requests for religious accommodations of the kind that Abdulle sought.[66] The tribunal was particularly critical that a large employer such as River Island had not developed guidelines to assist managers in making decisions in this area. Nevertheless, the tribunal made it clear that there were, in its view, limits to an employee's realistic expectation of an accommodation by his employer and particularly that an employer may be justified in varying any arrangement at short notice in response to unexpected events such as staff sickness or extreme weather conditions.[67]

It is interesting to consider this in the light of the claimant's willingness in *Copsey* to support his employer by working on Sunday in 'emergency' situations. It may be that this emerges as a 'minimum' expectation of employees who are normally allowed time off for religious reasons. If so, employees who take a more flexible view of the timing of their religious commitments will find this less burdensome than those who believe that working at a particular time (e.g. the Sabbath) is expressly forbidden.

The final case to be examined is potentially the most significant as it progressed on appeal to the Court of Appeal – *Mba* v. *Merton Borough Council*. The claimant, Ms Celestine Mba, a Christian, was a care worker in a children's home employed under a contract that included the possibility of Sunday working. Her employer accommodated her wish not to work on Sundays for two years, which Mba later interpreted as a contractual entitlement, but then ceased to do so and required her to work Sundays on a rota basis. She refused and was given a final written warning, after which she resigned and claimed religious discrimination. The employment tribunal rejected her claim.

The Employment Appeals Tribunal acknowledged that Ms Mba held to a literal interpretation of the Fourth Commandment and believed that it was wrong in principle for her to work on Sundays. However, it refused to set aside the employment tribunal's judgment that accommodating her was, on balance, unduly costly, *inter alia*, because it was too disruptive both for staff scheduling and continuity of care for children in the home and because employing agency staff to cover her Sunday shifts was more expensive than employing them on weekdays. In coming to its decision, the Tribunal addressed a rather controversial statement by the employment tribunal that 'the belief that Sunday should be a day of rest was not a core component of the Christian religion'.[68] As the Appeals Tribunal noted,

66   Ibid. [29].
67   Ibid. [30].
68   *Mba* v. *Merton Borough Council* (2012) UKEAT/0332/12 [41].

such phrasing is capable of being construed as offensive and could certainly amount to a misdirection of law.

However, the Employment Appeals Tribunal determined that the employment tribunal could justify this assertion however 'inelegant in its phraseology' not as a learned evaluation of the content of religious doctrine but on the basis of the application of apparently more practical tests, the most important of which involves assessing how many people of that religion hold to the particular requirement.[69] Applying that test, the tribunal could legitimately claim that the belief in question was not a core belief because so many Christians did not apparently agree with it. The discriminatory impact of the employer's requirement was therefore weaker than it would be had the belief been basic to Christianity (in the sense that fewer people were affected) and, in consequence, the religious practice should be less heavily weighted when considering necessity and proportionality.

When the case reached the Court of Appeal, the Court took a different view of the controversial assertion that a belief in Sunday working could therefore be less heavily weighted when determining legitimacy and proportionality on the basis that it was non-core to Christian belief. The President, Lord Justice Kay, held that this reasoning amounted to an error of law.[70] He noted significantly that 'for some Christians, working on Sundays is unacceptable' and that Mba sincerely held to that belief.[71] This was sufficient for what he referred to elsewhere as 'Sabbatarianism' to be invested with the full status of a *bona fide* manifestation of religion or belief. He also took the view that because 'some Christians' held this view, then such a manifestation of religion or belief was sufficient to meet the plural test required under indirect discrimination – a test which should not be interpreted too strictly:

> However, the use of the disjunctive – 'religion or belief' – demonstrates that it is not necessary to pitch the comparison at a macro level. Thus it is not necessary to establish that all or most Christians, or all or most non-conformist Christians, are or would be put at a particular disadvantage. It is permissible to define a claimant's religion or belief more narrowly than that.[72]

This does appear to be a somewhat broader basis for constructing a group to identify plural disadvantage than in other cases, such as *Eweida* v. *British*

---

69   Ibid. [48] (Langstaff J).
70   *Mba* v. *Merton BC* (CA) [20].
71   Ibid. [18] (Kay LJ).
72   Ibid. [17]. Lord Justice Kay noted that, in addition, there was relevant expert witness evidence from a former Anglican bishop confirming that this belief had 'an evidential foundation' [18].

Airways,[73] and allows for an interpretation of indirect discrimination that is more aligned with Article 9 following the decision in *Eweida and Ors.*[74] One effect of this is that it should in future be easier for claimants to establish *prima facie* indirect discrimination.

Lord Justice Elias argued that, under the principles of indirect discrimination alone, the tribunal had not necessarily erred in applying a core/non-core distinction to Mba's belief whilst considering proportionality; however, if the justification defence was to be read compatibly with Article 9, as it should have been in this case, then:

> it does not matter whether the claimant is disadvantaged along with others or not, and it cannot in any way weaken her case with respect to justification that her beliefs are not more widely shared or do not constitute a core belief of any particular religion.[75]

Thus, the tribunal and Employment Appeals Tribunal had both erred. Elias referred to the decision in *Eweida and Ors* in support of his analysis. He also noted, in agreement with Lord Justice Kay, that a group test was still necessary for *prima facie* indirect discrimination to be established.

The substantive issue in the case, therefore, was how far the employer could show 'a proportionate means of a achieving a legitimate aim' in requiring Mba to act contrary to her religious beliefs. The Court of Appeal concluded that there had been no error of law on this point: Mrs Mba had failed to establish that her contract exempted her from Sunday working and the Council had established that there was a practical need for Mba to work on Sunday to run its organisation effectively.[76] Thus, her appeal failed.

This case is significant for two reasons. Firstly, as it progressed to the Court of Appeal, it has permitted that court to set out its position in relation to issues on which lower courts have reached differing judgments. Arguably it has endorsed a lower standard of justification for employers than might have been desirable. The fact that Mba's employer had been able to accommodate her desire not to work on a Sunday for two years before changing its mind did not seem to be strongly weighted in her favour (in contrast to the reasoning in *Eweida and Ors* when considering equivalent circumstances)[77] and the employer's case that cost and apparently good practice required it to force Mba to work on a Sunday was accepted perhaps a little too readily. Secondly, and more positively, the

73 [2010] EWCA Civ. 80; [2010] IRLR 322.
74 *Eweida and Ors* v. *United Kingdom* Appl Nos. 48420/10, 59842/10, 51671/10 and 36516/10 (15 January 2013).
75 *Mba* v. *Merton BC* (CA) [35] (Elias LJ). Lord Justice Vos largely concurred with this analysis [40–1].
76 Ibid. [24].
77 *Eweida and Ors* [94].

judgment has confirmed that the various different beliefs held by Christians in relation to Sunday working, including the strict Sabbatarian view, cannot be regarded as 'non-core' merely because there is disagreement amongst Christians. The key positions taken by Christians with regard to Sunday working outlined earlier both enjoy the status of *bona fide* manifestations of religion or belief and, if interfered with by an employer, qualify under the first stage of the test to determine if indirect discrimination has taken place.

Summary and discussion

The purpose of the first half of this chapter has been to examine the approach taken by courts and tribunals to issues of negative manifestation in the workplace associated with requests for time off for religious activities which take place, in large part, outside the workplace.

It was noted in Chapter 5 that the privileged position that Sunday once enjoyed in England and Wales has been largely legislated away – Sunday is in large measure a working day, particularly in the retail and hospitality sectors but also in a growing number of industrial and service settings. At the same time, it appears that courts and tribunals have been losing sight of the original imperative of the legislation which predated the liberalisation of Sunday trading – to guard the particular status of Sunday as a 'day of rest', the observance of which many Christians believe is mandatory, with certain exceptions for essential work.

Courts and tribunals have tended to be more concerned with a narrower question of how far work commitments preclude access to attendance at church services. The imposition of any restrictions on employees' freedom to attend church services is sufficient to trigger the first stage of an indirect discrimination claim. At the second stage, employers are therefore required to justify, to a greater or lesser degree, such restrictions. In terms of the ECHR conceptualisation of the importance of both 'observance' and 'worship' (in community), it would seem that the 'worship' imperative has been most significant. Observance is of course an elastic term and could be framed as referring to religious activities, such as ritual prayer, which are not quite encapsulated by the alternative word 'worship'; however, it also has a plainer meaning as respecting religious ordinances (such as the injunction not to work on the Sabbath). It is the latter aspect of observance which has been downplayed in the tribunal judgments considered in this chapter (with the exception of the reasoning in *Edge*). This found its clearest expression in the judgment of the employment tribunal in *Mba*, which referred to the belief that it is wrong to work on a Sunday as not constituting a core part of the Christian faith. Happily, the Court of Appeal in *Mba* directly repudiated this view and it is to be hoped that, as a result, tribunals will in future give fuller consideration to the different legitimate ways in which employees might wish to observe Sundays, including those deriving from traditional Sabbatarian beliefs.

In addition to Sunday services for Christians, there is a range of other examples of demands on the time of the religious employee (e.g. Friday prayers for Muslims). In such cases, it is for the employer to justify any restrictions which might be imposed on an employee's participation in such activities as a result of working time. Acceptable justification defences naturally revolve around the operational requirements of the employer. What remains slightly unclear is the extent to which employers are required actively to manage shift rotas in order to accommodate the religious employee. It may be inferred from *Copsey* (insofar as a tribunal may feel bound by relevant *obiter dicta* in that case) that an employer should, as a minimum, permit an employee to seek the cooperation of colleagues to make alternative arrangements. It is strongly arguable that the duty to accommodate (if such it be) goes further, to require that the employer is proactive in looking for ways to reorganise shifts to accommodate, where possible, the religious employee. This argument is strongest in situations where the employer has imposed a new requirement repudiating an existing arrangement with a particular employee.

Negative manifestation for reasons of conscientious objection

Having considered the first aspect of negative manifestation in the workplace, the discussion now turns to the second aspect – negative manifestation for reasons of 'conscientious objection'.[78] The concept of conscientious objection has its roots outside the workplace and is of interest to political philosophers as representing a form of non-violent resistance to the requirements of law, for reasons of principle. A number of theorists deal with conscientious objection in parallel with the concept of 'civil disobedience', implying similarities between the two,[79] whilst emphasising that there are distinctive differences.[80] Identifying those differences can help more clearly to identify the concept of conscientious objection and, for that reason, will be attempted briefly here.

'Civil disobedience' is a term originally coined by the American theorist, Henry David Thoreau, in his 1848 essay of the same name, to describe his own actions and the motivation behind them, in refusing to pay a tax to

---

78 The material in this section draws on A Hambler, 'Recognising a Right to "Conscientiously Object" for Registrars Whose Religious Beliefs are Incompatible with their Duty to Conduct Same-Sex Civil Partnerships' (2012) 7 *Religion and Human Rights* 157.

79 This is particularly true of R Dworkin in *Taking Rights Seriously* (London: Duckworth, 1977).

80 Raz devotes a separate chapter to each concept; see J Raz, *The Authority of Law* (Oxford: Clarendon Press, 1979).

fund a war in Mexico and the enforcement of a law concerning fugitive slaves.[81] The term is given useful modern definition by Raz as 'a politically motivated breach of law designed either to contribute directly to a change of law or of a public policy or to express one's protest against, and dissociation from, a law or a public policy'.[82] The resulting 'disobedience' to a particular law or laws thus represents a form of public political protest, which is often and necessarily highly visible, with the aim of gaining support from others and with the serious intention of changing a particular law (which may often be viewed as unjust and therefore morally illegitimate).[83] Civil disobedience often involves group protest, most often where that particular group interest is at stake (most famously the predominantly black civil rights protestors of the 1950s and 1960s in the USA).

Conscientious objection,[84] on the other hand, involves 'a breach of law for the reason that the agent is morally prohibited to obey it'.[85] In other words, an individual has a compelling reason to believe that he must not obey a particular law or carry out a particular legal obligation and thus chooses not to do so, whatever the legal consequences may be. Conscientious objection is thus different from civil disobedience. As Rawls notes, conscientious objectors:

> do not seek out occasions for disobedience as a way to state their cause. Rather they bide their time hoping that the necessity to disobey will not arise. They are less optimistic than those undertaking civil disobedience and they may entertain no expectation of changing laws or policies.[86]

It is perhaps fair to suggest that, unlike those engaging in civil disobedience, conscientious objectors are not radical idealists. They do not necessarily wish to engage others in their objections, nor is the intention of their refusal to effect a change in the law or public policy. Rather, they want to be left alone to quietly follow the dictates of their own consciences. Conflict with authorities only arises if a law or obligation requires them to do something which violates those consciences. Such a violation has serious consequences for the individual and, as Childress puts it, 'would result not only in such unpleasant feelings as guilt and/or shame but also in a fundamental loss of integrity, wholeness, and harmony in the self'.[87]

---

81   See H Thoreau, 'Civil Disobedience,' in H Bedau (ed.), *Civil Disobedience in Focus* (New York: Routledge, 1991).

82   J Raz, *The Authority of Law*, 263.

83   This aspect is emphasised by Dworkin, but is not, of course, a necessary precondition of civil disobedience; see Dworkin, *Taking Rights Seriously*.

84   Or 'conscientious refusal', to use Rawls' preferred term; see J Rawls, 'A Theory of Civil Disobedience', in R Dworkin (ed.), *The Philosophy of Law* (OUP 1977).

85   Raz, *The Authority of Law* (Oxford: Clarendon Press, 1979), 263.

86   Rawls, 'A Theory of Civil Disobedience', 94.

87   J Childress, 'Appeals to Conscience' (1979) 89 *Ethics* 315, 318.

This observation underlines the deep significance to an individual's personal identity of conscience and why this should be taken very seriously in a liberal state, given the weight attached by liberals to personal autonomy (and its subset, moral autonomy)[88] and dignity. For religious employees, this importance is magnified by the fact that their consciences are sharpened by the requirement of obedience to the revealed will of God, which surely brings an additional and pressing dimension to this 'intrinsic integrity, wholeness and harmony' of conscience. Childress goes on to develop the notion of conscience as a form of sanction for the individual – it is thus a heavy burden to bear (rather than a whimsy to be indulged). He concludes that the guiding principle should be that conscientious objection is accommodated at least up to the point that the state is able to *prove* that, where its interests compete, these interests are 'compelling and can be realized through no other means than a denial of the exemption'.[89]

Although Childress does not write specifically about a workplace context, his analysis provides a helpful reference point for the cases considered in this chapter that are concerned with situations where employees are faced with a dilemma when required to act in accordance with principles which offend conscience. Childress thus identifies one position which is to start with the assumption that primacy be given in the workplace to an individual's moral autonomy (unless there are pressing reasons against this). At the alternative end of the spectrum is what Litwak terms 'a dogmatic model involving absolute institutional conformity' when faced with such a moral dilemma.[90] Where this is required by an employer, individual moral autonomy is sacrificed to another imperative and the significance of conscience and its requirements is ignored.

Conscientious objection in practice

The actual term 'conscientious objector' was first used to describe opponents of compulsory vaccinations in the 1890s[91] but the label has been historically associated most often with individual objections to being conscripted for military service, a phenomenon which can be traced back to antiquity.[92] The modern notion that an individual might, because of

88   See discussion in R Dahl, *On Democracy* (New Haven, CT: Yale University Press, 1998).

89   Childress, 'Appeals to Conscience', 335.

90   E Litwak, 'Conscientious Objection in Public Service Ethics: A Proposed Procedure for Europe' (2005) 7 *European Journal of Law* 79, 85.

91   C Moskoks and J Chambers, 'The Secularisation of Conscience' in C Moskoks and J Chambers (eds), *The New Conscientious Objection* (New York: Oxford University Press, 1993), 11.

92   In Roman times, Jews were exempted from military service because of an unwillingness, for religious reasons, to swear the soldier's oath to the 'god-emperor'; the first known Christian conscientious objector was an African named Maximilian, who refused to perform a military service and was executed; see Moskoks and Chambers, 'The Secularisation of Conscience', 9.

pacifist Christian convictions, be exempted from the military activities of training, fighting and killing, without penalty, was first given formal legal effect in 1673 in Rhode Island, New England.[93] The legislation also introduced a key principle that the objector should be willing to perform an alternative form of non-combatant service (such as that of watchman or giving aid to those needing to flee from a place under military threat) to attest to the sincerity of the objection and to avoid cynical claims to escape what was (and is), after all, dangerous and unpleasant work.[94]

Conscientious objection to forced military service developed as a doctrine in the UK in the first half of the twentieth century during periods of mass-conscription during the two World Wars and the compulsory national military service in the late 1940s through to the early 1960s. When mass conscription was introduced in 1916, it became apparent that there were a range of, mostly Christian, objectors, such as Quakers, on the ground of conscience. Some of these were 'absolutists' who objected to any form of cooperation with the military, directly or indirectly (by performing non-military duties); others were 'alternativists' who were willing to perform alternative civil employment and yet others were 'non-combatant conscientious objectors', who were willing to perform non-fighting military roles.[95] As a result, the Conscription Acts of 1916, 1939 and 1948 permitted conscientious objectors to state their case before a tribunal and made provision for possible outcomes to meet each type of objection. Thus, conscientious objectors might be awarded either complete exemption from military service or conditional exemption (providing alternative civilian service was undertaken). Alternatively, they might be made available for call up to non-combatant duties or, if considered to be insincere, combatant duties.[96]

Since the era of mass-conscription in the UK has ended, conscientious objection has become a less significant issue for an all-volunteer military.[97] There has been, however, one key development: the right to conscientiously object has been extended to those who have voluntarily accepted a fixed period military service but who have subsequently developed a

93   See D Laycock, *Religious Liberty* vol. 1 (Grand Rapids, IL: William B Eerdmans, 2010), 723.
94   Ibid., 724.
95   G Harries-Jenkins, 'Britain: From Individual Conscience to Social Movement' in Moskoks and Chambers, *The New Conscientious Objection*, 70–72.
96   Ibid.
97   However, a number of European states still engage in conscription and, under the traditional interpretation of the ECHR (Art 4(3)(b)), there was no absolute right (relying for example on Art 9) to conscientiously object (see *Grandrath* v. *Germany* Appl No. 2299/64 (23 April 1965)). This was overturned in *Bayatyan* v. *Armenia* Appl. No 23459/03 (7 July 2011), a decision which set a very high standard of justification for member states not to offer a right of conscientious objection. *De facto*, the right to conscientiously object is now fully recognised under the ECHR.

conscientious objection to this service (probably for religious reasons).[98] Selective conscientious objection (e.g. in opposition to the Iraq war) whilst continuing to serve, is not permitted, however[99] (although there is an argument that international standards require that it should be).[100] Conscientious objection has thus developed as a concept in the military, originally in response to the deeply held pacifism of some, which, in turn, was often chiefly motivated by Christian convictions. There are some points to note from the military experience on which it may be useful to draw in a discussion referenced to the workplace. It is interesting to note, for instance, the process involved in dealing with conscientious objectors: a detailed inquiry by a tribunal into the nature and sincerity of the conscientious objection. Equally, it should be noted that some alternative service was required of the conscientious objector, which would also help to attest to the sincerity of convictions.[101] Nevertheless, if the nature of the conscientious objection was such that this was impossible, an absolute exemption could be granted.

'Conscientious objection', a concept most developed when applied to the military, has also been applied in modified form in other situations, some of which have arisen, as Litwak notes, as a result of the liberalisation of Western society in the 1960s and the consequent emergence of new moral controversies over which society is often polarised, such as questions related to sexual and reproductive ethics.[102] There is, however, a clear caveat required when comparing this with the military situation: the employee is rather different from the military conscript. The latter is, of course, entering into a form of working under compulsion;[103] as this is not the case for the former, the right to conscientiously object is less likely to be absolute.

Although there are various instances where employees might be required by their employers to act against conscience, some are relatively uncontroversial when it comes to public policy. There is specific provision for employees to make a public disclosure, in good faith, of information to an employer or 'other responsible person' *inter alia* if their employers require them, for example, to lie or to conceal information relating to

98 Ministry of Defence, *Guide on Religion and Belief in the MOD and Armed Forces* (London: MOD, 2011) [41], 11.

99 *Khan* v. *Royal Air Force Summary Appeal Court* [2004] EWHC 2230 (Admin).

100 United Nations Commission on Human Rights Resolution of 8 March 1995 (E/CN.4/RES/1995/83) concerning conscientious objection is ambiguous about selective conscientious objection, as the text of the resolution could be construed to include this: 'persons performing military service should not be excluded from the right to have conscientious objections to military service'.

101 See also discussion of 'sincerity' in Chapter 2.

102 Litwak, 'Conscientious Objection in Public Service Ethics', 80.

103 Albeit one that is specifically exempted from the prohibition on forced labour under Art 4(3)(b) ECHR.

criminal offences, a failure to comply with legal obligations, miscarriages of justice, dangers to individuals arising from health and safety concerns or environmental damage.[104] In such cases, provided that certain conditions are met, the individuals are protected in employment law from dismissal or other detriment by their employers.[105]

However, there are also situations where an individual might be asked by his employer to act against conscience where such a request is well within an employer's normal lawful range of discretion. In recent years, there has been particular interest in two areas of employment where conscientious objection has been common. The first area concerns those healthcare workers and scientists with a religious objection to interfering with human life either to terminate it (via abortion or the issuing of the 'morning-after pill')[106] or to in some other way manipulate it through stem cell or similar genetic research. In the UK, the right to object, at least for clinicians, in these areas of medical ethics has been enshrined in legislation and there is little case law to discuss.[107]

The second area concerns objections to the effect of legislation promoting the rights and status of homosexuals and, in particular, same-sex couples.[108] Individuals who seek to conscientiously object in this second area are likely to be slightly further removed from the source of the objection than might be the case in healthcare, in the sense that it is the indirect rather than the direct result of their actions which offends conscience. They are not, after all, being required to act as the actual agents of the perceived moral harm as might be the doctor when carrying out a termination of pregnancy. Whether this makes objectors less deserving of accommodation is further considered later in this chapter. However, it may be noted at this point that there may be inspiration to be drawn from the 'absolutist' objectors to military service who were not prepared to engage in activities which even *indirectly* assisted war preparations. Their objections were still thought worthy of respect and potential accommodation.

Questions of religiously based conscience in the workplace do not, of course, inevitably overlap only with questions relating to sexual orientation. There are other potential points of conflict; for instance, involving

---

104 Employment Rights Act 1996, s 43B(1).
105 In addition, there may also be, in certain circumstances, a 'public interest defence' for employees when breaching confidence under common law; see *Attorney General* v. *Guardian Newspapers Ltd* (No 2) [1990] 1 AC 109.
106 See, for example, Fenton and Lomasky, 'Dispensing with Liberty: Conscientious Refusal and the Morning-After-Pill' (2005) 30 *Journal of Medicine and Philosophy* 579–92.
107 With a couple of exceptions; see, generally, discussion in Chapter 5.
108 As Parkinson notes, there is now a declining public tolerance for those who do not fully accept same-sex relationships (hence the fact that conflict is likely); see P Parkinson, 'Forum: Accommodating Religious Beliefs in a Secular Age' (2011) 34 *University of New South Wales Law Journal* 281.

objections to the sale of certain products or the display of certain messages on religious grounds. Some Muslims, for example, might object to the handling of alcohol;[109] this objection has been taken sufficiently seriously by the supermarket, Sainsbury's, that it apparently allows Muslim employees to 'opt-out' of handling alcohol in the performance of their duties.[110] Equally, some Amritdhari Sikhs might object to touching meat or meat products.[111] In a further example, a Christian bus driver might object to driving a bus bearing an atheist slogan.[112]

Nevertheless, although there are fault lines for conscientious objection other than sexual orientation, the fact remains that the key cases concern this issue. There are no absolute rights in law to conscientiously object in this area (such as those applying with regard to the healthcare dilemma), nor is the label 'conscientious objection' recognised.[113] Those seeking exemptions therefore have been forced to rely on the theoretical protection for conscience (as a manifestation of religion)[114] under employment discrimination law.[115] Of the potential claims under discrimination law, indirect discrimination is the most likely to provide protections for religious expression (including the 'negative expression' of conscience), as the claimant need only identify 'a provision, criterion or practice' which disadvantages the members of a group to which he belongs (e.g. 'traditional Christians'). Thus, the claimant can show that being required to act

---

109   See, for example, J Charlton, 'Muslim Fork Lift Driver Sues Tesco After Handling Booze' *Personnel Today* (29 September 2008). Available online at www.personneltoday.com/articles/2008/09/29/47681/muslim-fork-lift-driver-sues-tesco-after-handling-booze.html (accessed 8 June 2014).

110   See D Foggo and C Thompson, 'Muslim checkout staff get an alcohol opt-out clause' Sunday Times (30 September 2007). Available online at www.thesundaytimes.co.uk/sto/news/uk_news/article72571.ece (accessed 8 June 2014).

111   See the facts of *Chatwal* v. *Wandsworth BC* (2010) ET Case No. 2340819/09. In this case the claimant was unable to show that this belief was more than an individual conviction and so failed the test for indirect discrimination.

112   'Bus Driver Refuses to Drive Atheist Bus' *BBC News* (London, 16 January 2009). Available online at http://news.bbc.co.uk/1/hi/england/hampshire/7832647.stm (accessed 8 June 2014). In a parallel case, a Christian bus driver refused to drive a bus bearing a Stonewall slogan; see N O'Doherty, 'Passengers Left Stranded on Bus After Driver Refuses to Board Because of Gay Rights Advert on the Side' *Daily Mail* (London, 16 November 2012). Available at www.dailymail.co.uk/news/article-2233849/Passengers-left-stranded-bus-driver-refuses-board-gay-rights-advert-side.html (accessed 8 June 2014).

113   It is explicitly referred to in the Abortion Act.

114   That conscientious objection (to performing a public service) constitutes a 'manifestation' of religion rather than conduct motivated by religion has been called into question in a submission in the *Ladele* case; see National Secular Society, *Submissions in the Cases of Ewedia and Chaplin v United Kingdom and Ladele and MacFarlane v United Kingdom* (14 September 2011).

115   See discussion in Chapter 5.

in a particular way represents a 'barrier' to himself and others with the same beliefs, as it forces him to act in a way which his religious beliefs forbid – this disadvantages him relative to others who do not share those beliefs. Once this provision, criterion or practice has been identified, it is then for the respondent to show that applying it to the claimant represented 'a proportionate means of achieving a legitimate aim'. In other words, the employer is required to shoulder the burden of justification.

Since 2003, there have been three particularly significant cases which generated some public debate: *McClintock*, *Ladele* and *McFarlane*. Each of these cases involved an employee or public official 'conscientiously objecting' to an aspect of their role because of its relationship to promoting same-sex relationships. These cases are examined in turn, with particular attention being given to *Ladele*. This is for three reasons. Firstly, this is the most authoritative case, having progressed to the Court of Appeal (and thence to the ECtHR). Secondly, it is the only case where there was at least one judgment in favour of the religious claimant (at first instance), thus widening the scope for analysis. Thirdly, it is arguably the most important case as the nature of the objection was clear cut and the issues raised were therefore tackled head on, without the distracting lack of clarity in terms of the claimants' intentions, which slightly muddy the waters in *McClintock* and *McFarlane*.

McClintock v. Department of Constitutional Affairs

The first case was brought by Andrew McClintock, who was a Justice of the Peace in Sheffield, South Yorkshire, and a practising Christian. He served on the Family Bench and one of his duties was to place children for adoption. When he became aware in 2004 that, as a result of the Civil Partnership Bill, he might be required to place children for adoption with gay and lesbian couples, he raised concerns by letter, requesting that he be excused from sitting in cases with a risk of needing to place a child with a same-sex couple, owing to the incompatibility, in his view, between this obligation and his obligations under the Children's Act 1989 (to act in the best interests of children).[116] At a subsequent meeting, McClintock's request was turned down; he was told that there could be no general exemption from sitting and was reminded that he was bound by his judicial oath by which he had undertaken to adjudicate on any case which came before him.[117] Following this meeting, McClintock resigned from the Family Bench and began legal proceedings. He did so, primarily, on the basis that a refusal to accommodate his request amounted to discrimination on the grounds of religion and belief.

---

116 *McClintock* v. *Department for Constitutional Affairs* (2006) ET Case No. 2800834/06 [9].
117 Ibid. [12].

The role of the tribunal and the Employment Appeals Tribunal was thus to determine whether or not McClintock had suffered direct and/or indirect discrimination on the basis of his religion or belief under the provisions of the 2003 Regulations. The initial employment tribunal concluded that there had been no direct discrimination, for two main reasons; firstly, that there had been no detriment or dismissal (which equates to 'less favourable treatment') since McClintock had resigned voluntarily and, secondly, because he had not made clear that his objection was related to his religious beliefs. It concluded also that McClintock's objection failed the test of being considered to be a philosophical belief analogous to religious, the test being articulated as follows:

> The test for determining whether views can properly be considered to fall into the category of a philosophical belief is whether they have sufficient cogency, seriousness, cohesion and importance and are worthy of respect in a democratic society'.[118]

The tribunal also rejected his indirect discrimination claim, although with limited legal reasoning, such that this became the main point of appeal. The Employment Appeals Tribunal, however, upheld the tribunal judgment, with particular emphasis on the fact that McClintock's position was not explicitly based on religious or philosophical grounds and so fell at the first hurdle for any kind of discrimination claim. Even if this were not so, the Tribunal concluded that it was a proportionate means to achieve a legitimate aim (the employer's defence in indirect discrimination claims) for the employer to insist that:

> magistrates must apply the law of the land as their oath requires, and cannot opt-out of cases on the grounds that they may have to apply or give effect to laws to which they have a moral or other principled objection.[119]

The Appeals Tribunal, applying ECtHR jurisprudence, also rejected McClintock's attempt to invoke Article 9 of the ECHR on the basis that the right to manifest religious convictions does not apply 'where a party voluntarily places himself or herself in a position where a conflict might arise between his or her religious or philosophical beliefs and the duty imposed by an employment or office'.[120]

This case anticipates, in a number of significant ways, the more weighty judgment in *Ladele* that is considered in much more detail below. This analysis is confined therefore to two key issues which arise from this case alone.

---

118 Ibid. [41].
119 *McClintock* v. *Department for Constitutional Affairs* [2007] UKEAT 0223/07/3110; [2008] IRLR 29 [62].
120 Ibid. [61].

The first key issue was whether or not McClintock could reasonably claim to have suffered religious discrimination, given that his conscientious objections to making same-sex adoption orders were based on a form of public reason[121] and he did not invoke his religious beliefs until after his resignation. His counsel creatively attempted to overcome this problem by suggesting, based on the judgment in *Williamson* v. *Secretary of State for Education and Employment* (where Lord Justice Rix opined that 'the deed does not have to express the belief in proclaiming it'),[122] that McClintock did not need to make an express link between his objection and his religious belief.[123] The Employment Appeals Tribunal thought that this was an 'absurd' argument in this context, given the burden it would generally place on the employer to second-guess the employee's true reasons for requests, especially if the employee has actively chosen to 'conceal' these.[124] From this, it can be inferred that employees need to clearly state that their conscientious objections have a religious (or philosophical) basis if they hope to pass the first stage for protection under discrimination law. This has been criticised, on the basis that there may be situations where the burden would not be too great for employers to infer that there might be an implicit religious objection,[125] particularly on an issue so sensitive that, as the Tribunal itself identified, a certain amount of confusion and even inconsistency might not be unexpected.[126]

The second key issue is how far a 'professional' oath, specifically here the judicial oath to act according to the law 'without fear or favour', trumps any possible right of conscientious objection. In McClintock's case, his employer's belief that there was an overriding public interest that he should abide by his judicial oath and deal impartially with any and every case which might come before the Family Bench, was considered sufficient justification for the refusal to countenance an opt-out.[127] McClintock had, after all, voluntarily agreed to take the oath and to apply the law in total. However, there is a caveat. As Zacharias observes, the lawyer (or indeed any public official) cannot fully foresee, when taking the oath, all the potential

---

121   See discussion in Chapter 3.
122   [2002] EWCA Civ. 1926; [2003] QB 1300 [164].
123   It is perhaps worth noting that the example given by Lord Justice Rix to support this statement was the 'passive' example of a Muslim or Jew adhering to a particular dietary law without the 'need for request or explanation'. McClintock did make a request and the employer was entitled to an explanation; see *McClintock* (EAT) [46].
124   Ibid.
125   See Hambler, 'A Private Matter? Evolving Approaches to the Freedom to Manifest Religious Convictions in the Workplace' (2008) 3 *Religion and Human Rights* 111, 120.
126   *McClintock* (EAT) [38].
127   Although this was hypothetical only as Judge Elias had already determined that there could be no religious discrimination given the non-religious nature of McClintock's arguments.

dilemmas which might arise during the course of employment.[128] In the case of the judge, he cannot anticipate exactly how the law over which he is required to preside may change and develop (how far, for example, it might move away from its original Judeo-Christian basis).

It may thus be that reliance on the judicial oath as a 'trump' is not enough. In this case, for example, inquiries might have been made into whether the Department of Constitutional Affairs had assessed exactly how the public interest would be compromised by acceding to McClintock's request. However, no such evidence was thought to be required.[129]

Ladele v. Islington Borough Council

The second case was brought by Lilian Ladele, a committed Christian who worked at the London Borough of Islington and became a Registrar of Births, Deaths and Marriages on 14 November 2002.[130] When the Civil Partnerships Act came into force in December 2005, Ladele was required by her manager, the superintendent registrar, to be formally 'designated' a civil partnerships registrar. That all registrars of marriage should also be required to register civil partnerships was a decision taken locally under the discretion given to superintendent registrars by the Registrar General. In advance of this, Ladele had let it be known to her employer that she would find it difficult to conduct civil partnerships because of her religious beliefs:

> A civil partnership is a marriage in all but name. Whether or not there are sexual relations it gives the couple who have entered into it the same rights and responsibilities as a married couple. Regardless of my feelings for the participants ... I feel unable to directly facilitate the formation of a union that I sincerely believe is contrary to God's law.[131]

Under guidance offered by the Registrar General, Ladele was offered a limited compromise whereby she would only participate in civil partnership work involving the signing of a register (as opposed to officiating at a 'ceremony'), an offer she rejected. She was then threatened, by letter, with disciplinary action; in response, she wrote that that she was 'placed in a dilemma and had either to honour her faith or the demands of the council' and asked to be treated sympathetically.[132]

---

128 F Zacharias, 'The Lawyer as Conscientious Objector' (2001–2002) 54 *Rutgers Law Review* 191.
129 *McClintock* EAT [51].
130 *Ladele* v. *Islington Borough Council* [2009] EWCA Civ. 1357 (CA); [2010] IRLR 211.
131 Ladele's witness statement: see *Ladele* v. *Islington Borough Council* (2008) ET Case No. 2203694/07 [7].
132 Ibid. [9].

Ladele did not receive a reply. However, from then on, the council turned a blind eye as she managed to avoid any civil partnerships work by changing shifts with colleagues. Nevertheless, there remained tensions, particularly involving two gay members of staff (identified by the tribunal as 'Dion' and 'Victoria'). These tensions were articulated at a team meeting on 2 November 2006. The meeting was followed by a letter, written by Dion and Victoria, in which they complained that Ladele's refusal to conduct civil partnerships was 'homophobic' and contrary to the Council's 'dignity for all' equality policy; they claimed that they themselves felt discriminated against by her actions. The Head of Democratic Services swiftly replied to this letter and subsequently engaged in informal talks with Dion and Victoria, explaining that he wished to take action against Ladele but could not do so until she became an employee of the council rather than a statutory officer (which in fact occurred on 1 December 2007).[133] This information was subsequently shared at a meeting of the lesbian, gay, bisexual and transgender forum.[134]

After some further informal (and unsuccessful) attempts to put pressure on Ladele to accept that its 'dignity for all' policy required her to undertake civil partnerships, she was subjected to disciplinary proceedings. In response, Ladele lodged a claim with an employment tribunal for direct discrimination, indirect discrimination and harassment on the grounds of religion and belief.[135]

The employment tribunal upheld all of Ladele's discrimination claims. It took a broad view of the scope of direct discrimination and compared and contrasted the different approaches that borough officials took in dealing with sexual orientation issues as opposed to religion and belief issues, drawing the conclusion that, in a number of instances, the council would not have subjected a person who was protected under the dignity for all policy because of their sexual orientation to the detriments which Ladele, protected under religion and belief, was subjected.

With regard to indirect discrimination, the tribunal identified that requiring all registrars to register civil partnerships amounted to a 'provision, criterion or practice' which put those holding 'orthodox Christian beliefs' at a disadvantage when compared with other people who did not share those beliefs. There was no dispute that Islington Borough Council had a legitimate aim in seeking to provide 'an effective civil partnership arrangement service as an employer and public authority which is wholly committed to the promotion of equal opportunities and fighting discrimination'.[136] Rather, the issue turned on whether or not it was 'proportionate'

133 Ibid. [21].
134 *Ladele* (CA) [8].
135 Ibid. [17–18].
136 *Ladele* (ET) [86].

to insist that Ladele be involved in providing that service. The tribunal noted crucially that Islington was able to provide the same 'first class' civil partnerships service without Ladele's involvement. Thus, it concluded that:

> The Respondent placed a greater value on the rights of the lesbian, gay, bisexual and transsexual community than it placed on the rights of Ms Ladele as one holding an orthodox Christian belief. The Respondent showed no respect for Ms Ladele's rights. Their action in applying the first provision, criterion or practice was not a proportionate means of achieving a legitimate aim.[137]

In relation to Ladele's harassment claim, the tribunal found that the complaints by gay members of staff that Ladele was victimising them because of her stance on civil partnerships was an act of harassment, as was the failure by management to take her view seriously, the breach of confidentiality, the disciplinary process and the failure to consider Ladele for temporary promotion.[138]

The Employment Appeals Tribunal overturned the tribunal's findings. It distinguished an overall claim of direct discrimination, arising from the decision to designate Ladele as a civil partnerships registrar, from specific detriments. With regard to the former, it concluded that Ladele had been treated no differently from how another (non-religious) employee would have been treated for refusal to conduct civil partnerships and that '[i]t cannot constitute direct discrimination to treat all employees in precisely the same way'.[139]

On the specific detriments suffered by Ladele, the Appeals Tribunal took the view that although Ladele's treatment was 'unreasonable' and thus in a sense she suffered a detriment, this detriment was not suffered for a 'prohibited' reason (i.e. her religion or belief) but rather because of her conduct in refusing to conduct civil partnerships.[140]

The Appeals Tribunal also applied the comparator principle much more narrowly than did the initial tribunal and determined that an appropriate comparator for Ladele was not the gay members of staff (because they were not objecting to performing a civil partnership) but rather a 'hypothetical' registrar who refused to conduct civil partnerships because of 'an antipathy to the concept of same-sex relationships' but where this antipathy was based on something other than religion.[141] Again, this allowed the Tribunal to conclude that, 'although management was far more sympathetic to the

---

137 Ibid. [87].
138 Ibid. [104].
139 Ibid. [53].
140 *Islington Borough Council* v. *Ladele* [2008] UKEAT 0453/08 [2009]; ICR 387 [63].
141 Ibid. [64].

concerns expressed by the two gay registrars than to the claimant's religious views', this did not constitute direct discrimination.[142]

The Tribunal then dealt briefly with the question of harassment. As the claim took the form of a series of detriments, the Tribunal applied its own logic in respect of direct discrimination and concluded that although Ladele suffered 'unwanted conduct', this was not on the grounds of religion and belief but rather on the grounds of her refusal to conduct civil partnerships.[143]

On the question of indirect discrimination, the Tribunal accepted that a requirement that all registrars should conduct civil partnerships did put Ladele at a particular disadvantage, when compared with others, on the grounds of religion and belief. The question remained as to whether or not this represented 'a proportionate means of achieving a legitimate aim'.[144] The Tribunal concluded that Islington Borough Council did indeed have a legitimate aim and this was conceptualised as 'providing the service on a non-discriminatory basis'. As the Court of Appeal later observed, this was a rather wider view of the legitimate aim of Islington Council than that assumed by the employment tribunal, which was simply the efficient provision of a service.[145] It also concluded that it was proportionate for Islington, if it so wished, to 'require all registrars to perform the full range of services' such that 'the claimant could not pick and choose what duties she would perform depending on whether they were in accordance with her religious views, at least in circumstances where her personal stance involved discrimination on the grounds of sexual orientation'.[146]

The Employment Appeals Tribunal also considered the ECHR Article 9 jurisprudence, to identify whether or not the approach it had taken was inconsistent with this Article. As in other cases, it concluded that there was no conflict – Article 9 having been construed to provide 'very narrow protection indeed for employees'.[147] It did consider that Ladele's strongest argument under the Article 9 jurisprudence was that she was not employed to carry out civil partnership duties but that these duties had later been imposed upon her and referred to Lord Rix's dissenting decision in *Copsey*.[148] However, it 'doubted' whether this argument could succeed here, as the duties of a registrar had been extended by parliament and 'the

---

142   Ibid. [67]. The Court of Appeal broadly agreed but determined that, with regard to one or two detriments, the tribunal might have identified the right comparators. It did not elaborate as it decided that nothing substantially turned on this point; see *Ladele* (CA) [39].
143   *Ladele* (EAT) [91–94].
144   Ibid. [95].
145   *Ladele* (CA) [44].
146   *Ladele* (EAT) [111].
147   Ibid. [119].
148   See discussion in this chapter (above).

claimant was being required to carry out precisely the kind of tasks those in her situation do'.[149] It went on to declare that, notwithstanding the 'doubt', Ladele's argument was 'bound to fail' for another reason and this was because she wished to be accommodated in refusing to carry out duties 'because of hostility to giving effect to the legal rights of same sex couples'.[150] The Appeals Tribunal concluded that 'it necessarily follows that the manifestation of the belief must give way when it involves discriminating on grounds which Parliament has provided to be unlawful'.[151] In reaching its conclusion, the Appeals Tribunal did not discount, however, the possibility that Islington Borough Council might have taken a 'pragmatic line' and chosen not to designate Ladele as a civil partnerships registrar and this might have been a desirable outcome.[152]

The Court of Appeal endorsed the decision of the Employment Appeals Tribunal in all substantive respects, the thrust of its reasoning clear from the following paragraph:

> Ms Ladele was employed in a public job and was working for a public authority; she was being required to perform a purely secular task, which was being treated as part of her job; Ms Ladele's refusal to perform that task involved discriminating against gay people in the course of that job; she was being asked to perform the task because of Islington's Dignity for All policy, whose laudable aim was to avoid, or at least minimise, discrimination both among Islington's employees, and as between Islington (and its employees) and those in the community they served; Ms Ladele's refusal was causing offence to at least two of her gay colleagues; Ms Ladele's objection was based on her view of marriage, which was not a core part of her religion; and Islington's requirement in no way prevented her from worshipping as she wished.[153]

The Court of Appeal went further than the Appeals Tribunal, in accepting the arguments of an intervenor, *Liberty*, which contended that not only was Islington Borough Council at liberty to require that all its appropriately designated registrars perform civil partnerships duties but it was also in fact *required* to do so by law, owing to the effect of the Sexual Orientation Regulations 2007. Liberty argued, firstly, that a refusal to carry out civil partnerships by someone who is prepared to conduct marriages amounts to discrimination under those Regulations (which expressly state that a civil

---

149 *Ladele* (EAT) [123].
150 Ibid. [124].
151 Ibid. [127].
152 Ibid. [117].
153 *Ladele* (CA) [52] (Neuberger LJ).

partnership is not materially different from a marriage).[154] Secondly, it argued that officiating at civil partnerships amounts to the provision to the public of services by a public authority exercising a function; however, under Regulation 8(2) public authorities are defined to include 'any person who has functions of a public nature' and so both Islington Borough Council and Ladele are public authorities 'exercising a function' and so to refuse to perform civil partnerships would be unlawful by either. Thirdly, it argued that under the regulations, the Borough would become liable for the unlawful act of an individual in refusing to perform civil partnerships.[155]

It is strongly arguable that this is the most significant religious discrimination employment judgment and it has generated considerable public interest, not least in the perception that it is a case where religious liberty and sexual orientation protections 'clash' and how that clash is to be resolved. There are a number of significant points to note from the judgment and the context that surrounds it, and these are set out below, according to theme.

Belief/action distinctions

At the Employment Appeals Tribunal and then (still more explicitly) at the Court of Appeal, the distinction between Ladele's religious beliefs and her actions was highlighted. The point was clearly and repeatedly made that Islington was not 'discriminating' against Ladele because of religion and belief but rather because of her conduct. It thus explicitly endorsed the notion that belief and conduct can be separated.[156] Ladele was free to believe what she wished and to be free from discrimination on that basis. Interestingly, it can be inferred from its approving comments about the registrars who objected and were not consequently disciplined that she was free to verbally express this belief (at least insofar as making her objections and their basis known to colleagues), presumably in spite of any 'offence' this might cause to colleagues. What she was not able to do was act on her belief ('expressed' or otherwise).

The Court of Appeal reframed the analysis slightly to contend that Ladele's view of marriage 'was not a core part of her religion' as it was not concerned with her personal devotions ('worshipping as she wished'). It thus cast actions, which it was universally agreed were *motivated* by religious belief, as 'non-core' as opposed to 'core' activities which take place in

---

154 Sexual Orientation Regulations 2007, Reg 3(4).
155 *Ladele* (CA) [68] (Neuberger LJ).
156 Stychin comments that this same distinction, when applied in former times to homosexuality, has resulted in injustice; see C Stychin, 'Faith in the the Future: Sexuality, Religion and the Public Sphere' (2009) 29 *Oxford Journal of Legal Studies* 729–55.

private alone or in company with others. This is, in fact, a clear application using different terminology of the *forum internum/externum* dichotomy considered in Chapter 2.

The significance of 'choice'

Both the Court of Appeal and the Employment Appeals Tribunal clearly conceptualise religious expression as a matter of individual choice – as they put it, Ladele wanted to 'pick and choose' the duties she was willing to perform.[157] Clearly, under this construction and using this language, she is the protagonist, actively choosing to indulge her whims – there is no sense that she be regarded as responding to a divine obligation to act in conformity to the will of God (or the demands of her faith) which is how she herself characterised her situation. McCrudden identifies this approach by the courts as a decision, typical of other recent judgments,[158] 'quite clearly to adopt an external viewpoint rather than a cognitively internal viewpoint',[159] and argues that judges should be encouraged to engage in efforts to understand religious issues from the internal perspective. In this case, adopting an internal perspective would involve a fuller appreciation of the demands of conscience as something beyond a simple matter of an arbitrary individual choice.

'Discrimination'

At the Employment Appeals Tribunal and Court of Appeal stages, Ladele is plainly cast less as a 'conscientious objector' than as a 'discriminator', displaying 'hostility' to same-sex relationships. Her attitude is compared at one stage by Judge Elias to that of a gay registrar who objects to performing a marriage of two evangelical Christians, for reasons of personal animosity or prejudice.[160]

It was on the basis of such a construction of Ladele as a discriminator against gay people and in the light of the initial employment tribunal's

---

157 *Ladele* (EAT) [100]. Similar sentiments were expressed by the Saskatchewan Court of Appeal in Canada when it declared unconstitutional proposed amendments to state law to permit conscience objection by registrars to performing same-sex marriages – it suggested that registrars should not be entitled to 'directly shape the office's intersection with the public so as to make it conform to their personal religious beliefs'; see *Re Marriage Commissioners Appointed Under The Marriage Act* (2011) SKCA 3 [97] (Judge Richards).

158 Such as *Eweida* v. *British Airways*; see discussion in Chapter 7.

159 McCrudden, 'Religion, Human Rights, Equality and the Public Sphere' 13 *Ecclesiastical Law Journal* 32.

160 *Ladele* (EAT) [113].

supposed endorsement of such discrimination, that Terry Sanderson, President of the National Secular Society, wrote an opinion piece in the *Guardian* in which he argued that the logic of the tribunal judgment would permit firemen to refuse to rescue homosexuals from burning buildings or doctors to refuse to treat patients with HIV.[161]

This is, however, a (deliberately mischievous?) mischaracterisation of both the tribunal decision and the nature of Ladele's objection. As has been argued, Ladele was not in fact actively seeking to 'discriminate' because of a hostility to same-sex couples *per se* but rather to the encouragement of what in her mind amounted to same-sex marriage; for her, a grave violation of God's law. Her objection was not necessarily rooted in prejudice against homosexuals, as might be a fireman's objection to rescuing a gay man from a burning building, but could equally be characterised as a measured objection to being personally involved in what she perceived to be the *promotion* of homosexual activity (a very different motivation also from that of Judge Elias's hypothetical gay registrar).

Indeed, this latter point was made by Lord Carey, the former Archbishop of Canterbury, in a witness statement before Lord Laws in support of the claimant in *McFarlane* v. *Relate Avon Ltd*:[162]

> The description of religious faith in relation to sexual ethics as '*discriminatory*' is crude; and illuminates a lack of sensitivity to religious belief. The Christian message of 'love' does not demean or disparage any individual (regardless of sexual orientation); the desire of the Christian is to limit self destructive conduct by those of any sexual orientation and ensure the eternal future of an individual with the Lord.[163]

This intervention prompted a degree of clarification on the issue by Lord Laws (presiding), who argued that 'discrimination' in the eyes of the law focuses on the effect of actions and is not linked to motive.[164] This point was recognised in *R (E)* v. *JFS Governing Body*, where, although a school was found to have discriminated in its admission policies on the grounds of race, this did not mean 'that these policies are "racist" as that word is generally understood'.[165] Nevertheless, as Hart notes, 'discrimination' is a highly loaded term and even when used 'neutrally' in the courtroom it can have

---

161 T Sanderson, 'Paying to be discriminated against' *Guardian* (London, 11 July 2008). Available online at www.guardian.co.uk/commentisfree/2008/jul/11/gayrights.religion (accessed 8 June 2014).

162 [2010] EWCA Civ. 880; [2010] IRLR 872.

163 Ibid. [17].

164 Ibid. [18].

165 [2009] UKSC 15; [2010] 2 AC 728 [9] (Lord Phillips).

clear connotations of something disreputable.[166] As noted in *JFS*, the 'choice of words is important' and it is desirable for judges to exercise care (perhaps more so than did Judge Elias in *Ladele*) in applying labels which, when used in common parlance, carry within them 'appalling accusation[s]'.[167]

Indeed, some who oppose the accommodation of conscientious objection in circumstances such as those of Ladele have sought to characterise discriminatory conduct as 'disreputable' by means of drawing an unfortunate comparison between 'discrimination' against same-sex couples and 'discrimination' against mixed-race couples. Would society allow a registrar to refuse to perform marriages due to objections based on race?[168] As the answer is plainly 'no', the implication is that neither should society tolerate objections based on sexual orientation. This contention was dealt with in the oral submissions by counsel for Ladele in *Eweida and Ors*, to the effect that objections based on sexual orientation are worthy of respect in a democratic society whereas objections based on race are not. It is thus a false comparison. This is because the majority position in the Christian Church (and indeed other faiths) is that homosexual relationships are sinful, whereas there is no such understanding in respect of mixed-race marriages. It was argued, surely correctly, that the traditional teachings of the Christian Church (particularly the established one) must, *a priori*, be worthy of respect in a liberal and democratic society.[169]

Regardless of the apparent motive of Ladele, discriminatory or otherwise, there is a more significant argument against permitting conscientious objection which focuses on a possible detrimental effect on others, primarily service users but also co-workers. With regard to the former, MacDougall argues that, if sufficient registrars (and other public servants) 'conscientiously objected' to providing services to gay and lesbian people, a situation might result in which 'gays and lesbians could become citizen pariahs, with important governmental services being made difficult for them to obtain because of the religious (or "cultural") views of others'.[170] It may be objected, however, that this is a very unlikely scenario, as it would

---

166 D Harte, 'Structures of Religious Pluralism in English Law' in N Doe and R Sandberg (eds), *Law and Religion: New Horizons* (Leuven: Peeters, 2010), 164–5; see also R Sandberg, 'Laws and religion: unravelling *McFarlane v Relate Avon Limited*' (2010) 12 *Ecclesiastical Law Journal* 366.

167 *JFS* [184] (Lord Hope).

168 See, for example, K Norrie, 'Religion and Same-Sex Unions: The Scottish Government's Consultation on Registration of Civil Partnerships and Same-Sex Marriage' (2012) 16 *Edinburgh Law Review* 95.

169 See www.echr.coe.int/Pages/home.aspx?p=hearings&w=5167110_04092012& language=lang&c=&py=2012.

170 B MacDougall, 'Refusing to Officiate at Same-Sex Civil Marriages' (2006) 69 *Saskatchewan Law Review* 351, 357.

assume a very high proportion of government officials with such strong religious convictions that they would be prepared to take the difficult path of conflict with their employer by registering an objection. Nevertheless, the point has some theoretical force, however unlikely in practice, if an absolute right to conscientious objection were afforded to registrars, irrespective of the practical implications of refusal for those seeking a civil partnership. It has rather less force, however, if a potential accommodation is highly practicable. Given the relatively small numbers of civil partnerships sought (equivalent to only 4.5 per cent of all marriages in 2008 and in decline since),[171] it is likely that accommodation will be almost invariably practicable.

MacDougall, writing from a Canadian perspective, also considers a situation where a religious 'veto' is not absolute but exercisable only in circumstances where the 'service' can be provided by someone else. In other words, the service user does not see a diminution in service. This is much closer to the claimant's arguments in *Ladele* and accepted by the initial tribunal, that the civil partnerships service could be provided irrespective of Ladele's own involvement, as other 'willing' registrars were available. However, MacDougall also rejects this:

> Imagine the position of gay and lesbian persons who are told by a civil servant that that he or she does not have to serve such people, but will 'do his or do her best' to find a replacement who has no such scruples. The civil servant will provide the service personally only if a replacement cannot be found and clearly against his or her better 'judgment' (for such a person really is *judging* the situation).[172]

The problem with this analysis, if applied to England and Wales,[173] is that it assumes an extraordinary degree of disorganisation or blatant unprofessionalism on behalf of a given public authority. In reality, there is no justifiable reason why a service user should be aware of the existence of any 'scruples' internal to an organisation; he should see only the 'external face' of that organisation and should expect to receive a professional service from a suitably qualified member of staff. It would seem that, for MacDougall, it is the mere *knowledge* that someone wishing to conscientiously object *might*

---

171 This point is helpfully made by Parkinson, using figures supplied by the Office of National Statistics, see Parkinson, 'Forum: Accommodating Religious Beliefs in a Secular Age', 281.

172 MacDougall, 'Refusing to Officiate at Same-Sex Civil Marriages', 357.

173 It is acknowledged that the situation is different in Canada where individual marriage commissioners are directly approached by couples seeking marriage solemnisation. This point appears to have weighed heavily in the outcome of *Re. Marriage Commissioners*; see [38] and [41].

be accommodated which offends.[174] Vickers argues that a workplace application of Feinberg's work, on assessing the harm caused by an offence balanced against the reasonableness of the conduct which causes the offence,[175] would lead to the conclusion that 'bare knowledge' of a practice apparently offensive to some should not be sufficient by itself to prohibit this practice.[176] Applied to *Ladele*, this would suggest that the bare knowledge offence to homosexuals of knowing (or suspecting) that a public official may not be engaging in civil partnership registrations for reasons of religious conscience would be insufficient as a basis to require that official to engage in civil partnership registrations. On balance, the demands of conscience weigh more heavily than the bare offence which might indirectly result.[177]

In *Ladele*, the only actual 'offence' (which itself might be reasonably characterised as 'bare knowledge offence') that is noted in the judgments as a result of Ladele's actions is the offence apparently given to the gay and lesbian fellow registrars (i.e. those internal to the organisation). As noted above, the Court of Appeal put some stress on this as part of its justification in rejecting Ladele's appeal. Here again, it may reasonably be argued that the right to be free from, essentially, an indirect source of offence (Ladele's objections not being directed at, in this case, the gay registrars themselves) needs to be balanced against arguably the greater rights of Ladele to be free from an anguishing dilemma.[178]

---

174 There is a contrast here with the experiences of gay couples denied a double bed in a Christian-run guest house or bed and breakfast establishment; in such situations the claimants could point to a concrete experience of *prima facie* discrimination entirely absent from *Ladele*; see, for example, the facts of *Bull and Bull* v. *Hall and Preddy* [2013] UKSC 73 and *Black* v. *Wilkinson* [2013] EWCA Civ. 820; [2013] 1 WLR 2490 (albeit that in these cases there was dispute about whether this discrimination was direct or indirect).

175 J Feinberg, *Offense to Others* (Oxford: Oxford University Press, 1985).

176 Vickers, *Religious Freedom, Religious Discrimination and the Workplace*, 64. 'Bare knowledge offence' can be likened to the concept of discrimination in the 'abstract', identified by the dissenting judges in *Eweida and Ors* (see Chapter 4).

177 See also B MacDougall, E Bonthuys, K Norrie and M Van den Brink, 'Conscientious Objection to Creating Same-Sex Unions: An International Analysis', (2012) 1 *Canadian Journal of Human Rights* 127. The authors concede, that in circumstances similar to those outlined here, that there is a strong argument that the registrar's stance is 'at most a kind of abstract, general discrimination, where there is arguably no concrete harm done' (154).

178 Laycock makes a similar point for essentially the same reasons; see D Laycock, 'Afterword' in D Laycock, A Picarello and R Wilson (ed.), *Same-Sex Marriage and Religious Liberty: Emerging Conflicts* (Lanham, MD: Rowman & Littlefield, 2008), 198–207.

The role of goods and services discrimination law

It was argued by Liberty that public officials, acting on behalf of the state, cannot 'discriminate' in ways that the state itself is not allowed to discriminate. This argument was accepted, albeit in a qualified way, by the Court of Appeal in Ladele.[179]

It may be that Liberty's interpretation of the Sexual Orientation Regulations is correct, albeit that it rests on quite a technical argument. If so, then some justification is required as to why the religious public servant should be denied any kind of protections under discrimination law, essentially at the first stage. Such an explanation may be located in terms of the actual role of the public servant, particularly regarding a matter of law thought to be entirely secular in character. In terms of officiating at civil partnerships, the religious official is simply carrying out the legal obligations of the state.[180] In theological terms, unlike the doctor performing an abortion, where individual culpability arises, the registrar is not intimately involved herself in the 'sinful' act but rather as a third party – if 'sin' results, it is the civil partners themselves who are culpable. As MacDougall et al. put it: 'civil servants do not, by officiating at same-sex marriages, become themselves parties to same-sex sexual relationships or acts, i.e. they do not engage in homosexuality; they simply engage in a function that affords status'.[181] Under this analysis, the religious official has no need personally to engage her religious conscience. In non-theological terms and as the MP Diane Abbot (who intervened in Parliament with a motion to reverse the effects of the initial tribunal judgment in *Ladele*)[182] put it: '[t]he whole point of civil partnerships is that they are legal contracts handed out by the state. They have nothing to do with religion and therefore the religious beliefs of a public servant carrying them out are irrelevant'.[183]

This argument has, in part, similarities with those arguments which seek to delineate the 'civil' character of civil partnerships from the (optional) religious character of marriages.[184] If the role of the public servant is

---

179   As Vickers notes, there remains a degree of confusion as to how far the Court of Appeal endorsed this argument, see L Vickers, 'Religious Discrimination in the Workplace: an emerging hierarchy?' (2010) 12 *Ecclesiastical Law Journal* 280.

180   See G Slapper, 'Penalties in the Penumbra of the Criminal Law' (2008) 72 *Journal of Criminal Law* 467.

181   MacDougall *et al.*, 'Conscientious Objection to Creating Same-Sex Unions', 157.

182   Parliamentary Session 2007–2008, Early Day Motion 2039, 15 July 2008.

183   H White, 'Labour MP Attempts to Remove Religious Freedom of Conscience after Christian Marriage Registrar Vic' *LifeSiteNews.com* (5 August 2008). Available online at www.lifesitenews.com/news/archive/ldn/2008/aug/08080503 (accessed 9 June 2014).

184   See, for example, Lord Faulkner of Thoroton, 'Church, State and Civil Partners' (2007) 9 *Ecclesiastical Law Journal* 5.

conceptualised entirely as performing a religiously neutral civil function then any individual objections to this are at best misplaced.[185]

There are, however, two objections to these arguments. Firstly, it is difficult to view civil partnerships merely in terms of the signing of a contract. There are also ceremonial aspects, from which, according to the compromise mooted by Islington Council, Ladele was offered an opt-out. These ceremonial aspects are clearly intended to 'celebrate' the civil partnership[186] and the registrar is fully involved in that celebration, albeit on behalf of the state.

Secondly, the distinction between acting on behalf of the state and acting in a private capacity may be far less clear to the religious public servant than it might be, for example, to an external observer such as Diane Abbott. By conducting a civil partnership, a registrar may feel just as involved personally in endorsing and promoting civil partnerships as might a doctor asked to perform a termination of pregnancy. Whether or not she is correct in this view is immaterial. As is plain from the *Ladele* judgment, as elsewhere, it is the sincere belief of the individual religious employee which matters. If the religious employee sincerely believes something she is doing offends her conscience, then this in itself should be sufficient to trigger the first stage of the available protections.

As it stands, if Liberty's position is correct and the religious official is considered to be a public authority in his own right then a significant injustice arises. This is particularly true when there is no principled justification in law for identifying an individual as synonymous with the state (in terms of performing a 'public function'). For the state, or the public authority, the requirement to carry out legal obligations in a non-discriminatory way is clear and unequivocal. The way in which it organises itself to do so, with the involvement of other staff (as in Islington) or without (as in other boroughs), is surely a very different question.[187]

185 This was also the analysis of Judge Smith (in a minority opinion) in *Re. Marriage Commissioners* 141–143.
186 Conspicuous state approval ('celebration') of gay relationships is considered essential to gay and lesbian equality by some writers and thus, by extension, an important aspect of a civil partnership ceremony; see AE Galeotti, *Toleration as Recognition* (Cambridge: Cambridge University Press, 2002).
187 S Webster, 'Misconceptions About the Nature of Religious Belief' (2010) 199 *Equal Opportunities Review* 8. One of the more positive aspects of the judgment in *Eweida and Ors* is the inference that, since signatory states have discretion not to protect the consciences of public servants in circumstances like that of Ladele (i.e. where sexual orientation rights are in some way in play), they also have discretion to positively offer protection in a way which the Liberty argument precludes [106]; see also on this point, I Leigh and A Hambler, 'Religious Symbols, Conscience and the Rights of Others' (2014) 3 *Oxford Journal of Law and Religion* 2, 22–3.

Employer sympathy and direct discrimination

At both the Employment Appeals Tribunal and the Court of Appeal it was acknowledged that Islington Borough Council had shown far more sympathy with the gay members of staff and, specifically, to the grievance they raised, than they showed to Ladele and the grievance she raised. This was clearly demonstrated by the failure to respond to Ladele's grievance and the almost instant response to the grievance by Dion and Victoria. However, the Employment Appeals Tribunal and the Court of Appeal both argued that the Council was entitled to do this without engaging in direct discrimination. Judge Elias did this ingeniously by determining that the comparison was too broadly drawn – the grievances were not concerned with the same issue and so there was no evidential value in drawing attention to the Council's differential treatment of them. Rubenstein is critical of this decision, noting 'how narrowly the comparison is drawn' (so as to suggest that a claim about discriminatory grievance handling can only be brought if the grievance is similar).[188] He attributes this to a judicial 'zeal to avoid a finding of direct discrimination' in Ladele and one of a series of judgments in discrimination cases where 'a finding that like is not being compared with like has been used by the judges to avoid a finding of direct discrimination where such a finding would conflict with the perceived merits of the case'.[189] In other words, the comparator test has been used by Judge Elias in such a way as to avoid the natural but apparently objectionable outcome of the correct application of discrimination law.

If this reading is correct, it suggests that the outcome of the direct discrimination case is particularly unfair in respect of Ladele. However, there is a wider point. It will be recalled that Elias noted that 'the tribunal was far more sympathetic to the concerns expressed by two gay registrars than to the claimant's religious views'. However, he determined that the Council was entitled to do this and indeed to treat Ladele badly (e.g. by breaching her confidentiality) because this was due to her conduct (which happened to be motivated by her religion). The judgment expressly addresses and permits a practice which many (including the initial employment tribunal) would think contrary to the spirit of discrimination law – that an employer can 'pick and choose' which protected characteristics with which to show most sympathy. It may be submitted that such a situation 'in the light of ... mainstream thinking', which the Court of Appeal thought relevant,[190] is unlikely to favour the religious claimant.

---

188 M Rubenstein, 'In the Courts' (2009) 186 *Equal Opportunities Review* 29.
189 Ibid.
190 *Ladele* (CA) [46] (Neuberger LJ).

Application of the proportionality test

The ease with which the Employment Appeals Tribunal and the Court of Appeal accepted that Islington Borough Council could demonstrate that its treatment of Ladele was a proportionate means to achieve a legitimate aim has caused some comment.[191] Vickers has helpfully compared the approach taken towards the same issue of justification in sex and race cases and found it to be more demanding of the employer, requiring it to show 'a real need' of the organisation. She notes that, although the Court of Appeal in Ladele identified the legitimacy of the aim of providing an equal service to all, it did not consider whether or not this aim reflected a 'real need' of the Council and concludes: '[i]n failing to consider the legitimacy of Islington's aim, the Court of Appeal seems to have subjected the Council to a low level of scrutiny, in comparison to the high standard usually required in discrimination cases'.[192]

Vickers' analysis leads her to conclude that a hierarchy may be developing in discrimination law, where religion and belief are less robustly protected than might be other strands such as sex, race and sexual orientation.[193] If this analysis were correct, it would allow employers to treat religion and belief as less worthy of respect than other characteristics and to be spared censure from acts which, had the protected ground been different, would have led to a successful discrimination claim.

McFarlane v. Relate Avon Limited

The third case was brought by Gary McFarlane, a Christian and former employee of Relate Avon Limited (Relate), a counselling service in the field of sexual and relationships therapy. McFarlane had been employed by Relate since August 2003, initially in the field of 'marital' and 'couples counselling'. In September 2006, McFarlane asked if he could undertake a diploma course in psychosexual therapy. Psychosexual therapy appeared to require more direct involvement in sexual issues within relationships, including advising on sexual techniques. Such work was, as the Employment Appeals Tribunal noted, 'liable to give rise to a much more intractable conflict with the Claimant's religious beliefs'.[194] At this point, McFarlane appears to have raised concerns, including a request that he should be exempted from working with same-sex couples where specifically sexual issues would be involved.

---

191 See, for example, Parkinson, 'Forum: Accommodating Religious Beliefs in a Secular Age'.
192 Vickers, 'Religious Discrimination in the Workplace: an emerging hierarchy?' 294.
193 As advocated by McColgan; see A McColgan, 'Class Wars? Religion and (In)equality in the Workplace' (2009) 38 *Industrial Law Journal* 1.
194 *MacFarlane* [5].

In December 2007, the General Manager of Relate Avon, Mr Bennett, wrote to McFarlane and refused to agree to his request, primarily on the basis that it was contrary to Relate Avon's equal opportunity policy. In his letter, Bennett also asked for written confirmation that McFarlane would continue to counsel same-sex couples in both relationships and psychosexual therapy work; failure to do this 'might' result in disciplinary action.[195] In his eventual reply, McFarlane stated that his only difficulty was in offering psychosexual therapy to same-sex couples and that his views were 'evolving'; as the issue had not yet arisen, disciplinary action was premature. On the basis of this reply, Bennett initiated the disciplinary procedure, only aborting it after the initial meeting with McFarlane in which he stated that 'if he were asked to do psychosexual therapy work with same-sex couples he would do so and that if any problems arose he would then raise them with his supervisor'.[196]

However, in a subsequent conversation with his supervisor, it appeared (to her) that McFarlane had returned to his earlier position on the issue of same-sex couples and psychosexual therapy. As a result, the disciplinary process was re-engaged and McFarlane summarily dismissed on the basis that he could no longer be trusted to carry out his role in conformity to Relate's equal opportunities policy and that this constituted gross misconduct.[197] McFarlane appealed unsuccessfully; consequently, he lodged a claim for unfair dismissal and religious discrimination with an employment tribunal.

The employment tribunal and, subsequently, the Employment Appeals Tribunal dismissed all McFarlane's claims. In the light of the *Ladele* judgment, the Appeals Tribunal in *McFarlane* did not dwell on practical considerations and instead applied the issue of principle to indirect discrimination, as it saw 'no real difference' between the two situations:

> The essence of Elias P's analysis is that in a case where a body such as the Council has such an aim it may properly insist on all employees participating in the services in question, even if to do so is in conflict with their religious beliefs, because to do otherwise would be inconsistent with the principle which it espouses. If that is the case for a local authority, we can see no material distinction in the position of a body such as Relate.[198]

A claim for harassment was found by the tribunal to be of no merit and this conclusion was not disputed before the Employment Appeals Tribunal. Permission to appeal, originally rejected by Judge Elias, was sought directly

195 Ibid. [6].
196 Ibid. [8].
197 Ibid. [10].
198 Ibid. [28] (Underhill J).

from the Court of Appeal. This application was heard by Lord Justice Laws, who rejected the application in a reserved judgment.

In terms of the substantive legal issues, *McFarlane* offers little innovation, following as it does the reasoning in *Ladele*. Unlike Ladele, McFarlane was not able to identify any specific detriments, so his only realistic claim was for indirect discrimination, a claim which failed for the same reason as *Ladele*. Once again, the claim turned on whether or not it was a proportionate to require all employees to be committed to performing all aspects of the counselling service for all 'service users' without 'discrimination'. Thus, once again, proportionality was not calibrated according to the practicability of making accommodations (although, unlike in *Ladele*, the practicability of accommodating the claimant was disputed by the employer) but rather according to this wider principle of non-discrimination by both employer and all employees alike. Human rights arguments were once again rejected for the same reasons as in *Ladele*. As McFarlane was not a public servant, arguments akin to those advanced by *Liberty* as to how far the employer was *obliged* to require all employees to act according to these principles were not advanced.

There is one key area where the facts of the case depart significantly from those of *McClintock* and *Ladele*. In *McFarlane*, the claimant was not subjected to a change in duties without his express consent; rather, it was as a result of a change in duties which he himself sought that the dilemma of conscience for him arose. In terms of the legal analysis, nothing turned on this point, yet it may be a significant issue if an alternative form of legal accommodation were mooted.

Summary and discussion

In the second part of this chapter, the ways in which employees have 'negatively manifested' their religious beliefs through 'conscientious objection' have been illustrated through an exploration of three prominent employment cases. The purpose of this concluding section is to identify the overarching themes emerging from these cases and the commentary surrounding them, in terms of how the courts are developing their approach towards conscientious objection. In the process, the situation is also considered from the perspective of the conscientious objector and what options remain to him following the precedents set by these cases.

As noted earlier, 'conscientious objection' is not a term applied by the law to refer to the examples of negative manifestation which have been considered in this chapter, nor is it so employed by judges. This is perhaps unfortunate, as the term benefits from the positive associations with a principled and longstanding tradition with its roots in opposition to military service. There are also clear parallels between the workplace conscientious objectors and traditional conscientious objectors, which makes this a useful explanatory term to apply to the former. Both categories of conscientious objector tend to manifest their resistance to requirements placed on them by others reluctantly and discreetly; they generally do not seek to make wider political statements but reference the objection to themselves alone;[199] they show integrity by taking a stand in the face of the potential hostility of others, thus placing their consciences above what is expedient and risking some sacrifice for their beliefs (for example, in the workplace, the loss of a position).

Whilst clearly not perceived in these positive terms, the negative manifestation of religion described in this chapter has been recognised by courts as having some value to the individual but, crucially, as representing a 'non-core' aspect of his religious convictions. Thus, 'conscientious objection' is regarded as a manifestation of religion or a response motivated by religion but not fundamental to the religion itself. This is in keeping with the ECHR jurisprudence but was not a necessary innovation in the interpretation of discrimination law. One result of this has been to allow the courts to perceive any detriments suffered by the conscientious objector (such as dismissal) as resulting from his actions, irrespective of any beliefs underlying those actions. This has meant that direct discrimination for workplace conscientious objectors is extremely difficult to establish. It has also illustrated the preference of courts to examine events from 'an external' (or perhaps, more correctly, the employer's) perspective only and to discount the 'internal perspective' underlying the motivation of the conscientious objector. Thus, in cases such as these involving objections to some consequences of sexual orientation rights, the conscientious objector can be construed, as noted above, as a 'discriminator' not an objector on the grounds of conscience. It is the actions (discrimination) not the motives (religious obligation) that matter to the courts, however important the religious obligation may be and however trivial the result of the discrimination (in *Ladele*, there was no negative result except some offence to other staff).

Discrimination law has, of course, two major protections (direct and indirect discrimination) and these cases show that 'conscientious objection' (although not recognised as such) is given some status for protection, *prima facie*, as a 'manifestation of religion' triggers the first stage of the test for indirect discrimination. However, at the second stage, the claims of conscientious objection are easily defeated by an employer's justification defence, which appears to receive less rigorous judicial scrutiny than is the case in race or sex discrimination claims. Whether this is a general conclusion is as yet unclear, as the high-profile cases, in

---

199 Albeit that those who fund some of the litigation in this area have been accused of so doing for political reasons; see J Wynne-Jones, 'I'll Defend Faith, Says Equality Chief: Watchdog Can Help Lift "Siege" on Religious Believers, Trevor Phillips Tells Jonathan Wynne Jones Interview' *Sunday Telegraph* (London, 19 June 2011), 12.

particular the three discussed in this chapter, all involve another protected characteristic. If the central objection does not derive from sexual orientation but from, say, an objection to handling alcohol, then it may be that the bar would be set higher for the employer in terms of the required justification defence. This is as yet unknown, as no such cases have been publicised at first instance or reached the Employment Appeals Tribunal. Interestingly, and perhaps concerningly, it may be that as a result of a 'policy' decision by the courts to lower the justification bar to prevent 'discrimination' on the grounds of sexual orientation, there may be a negative precedent set for religious conscientious objection claims on other grounds.

On a slightly more positive note, *Ladele* in particular gives grounds to assume that, although manifestation of religion may not be protected, religious identity might be. In Chapter 2, a taxonomy of religious expression was presented, using which it is possible to distinguish between religious belief in private and different degrees of expression, of which one is identity with certain beliefs. Strictly speaking, whereas Ladele is entitled, through the protection of the *forum internum*, to hold religious beliefs in private, alone or in company with others, it is less clear whether or not the *forum internum* would extend to protect her beliefs if they were articulated in some form in the workplace. Through raising objections to registering civil partnerships, Ladele was necessarily identifying herself with a religious belief that homosexuality is sinful. It is conceivable that this in itself might be grounds to trigger harassment claims by gay and lesbian staff. Indeed, the internal lawyer at Islington Borough Council considered that even the polite articulation of her position by letter to management constituted a free-standing act of gross misconduct. This case, whilst not definitive on this issue, strongly suggests that articulation of an objection in support of religious 'identity' should receive a measure of protection, particularly if the need to make clear one's religious identity has been prompted or provoked by the actions of the employer.

Conclusion

This chapter has examined the negative expression of religion in the workplace and has identified two distinct rationales for individuals to seek to 'opt-out' of work at specific times or for specific reasons. In terms of the law, the two rationales are treated quite differently, the second raising more complications than the first, although some similarities can be identified.

In Chapter 3 a range of responses towards workplace religious expression by a liberal state was set out. In this concluding section, consideration is given to how the discussion in this chapter, themed according to the two rationales considered, might relate to these models.

Time off

This particular form of manifestation is relatively inconspicuous, with the exception of situations where onsite facilities are specifically provided (of which the chief example is a prayer room for Muslim staff). In the cases considered in this chapter, the provision of prayer facilities has not been the focus of a workplace dispute and so the analysis cannot extend to consider this issue. Of the cases considered, there is no real evidence to support the contention that the state might attempt to exclude this form of negative manifestation of religion from the workplace (model I). There is some limited evidence of protection for this form of negative manifestation (model V), evidenced by those tribunal cases which have been successful, albeit that there is also evidence that tribunals will often be satisfied that an employer has justified any restrictions on such manifestation. Indeed, it may be that the successful cases form the exception rather than the rule. As both Christian as well as Muslim claimants have been successful, then there is no evidence that model VI (favouring minority religions) could be said to apply. In respect of model II (support for a preferred historical religion), there is no evidence of any special regard being paid to Sunday as a Christian day of rest.

Finally, the extent to which there is evidence in support of a *laissez-faire* approach (model III) is debatable. The employment discrimination law provisions have certainly led to a restriction on this total freedom of action by employers. However, this restriction is not necessarily as great as it could be as the case law suggests that employers are still able relatively easily to justify varying contracts to the detriment of an employee's desire to negatively manifest his religion.

Conscientious objection

In applying the six models to conscientious objection, the analysis in this chapter provides a degree of support, perhaps paradoxically, for both model I (exclusion) and model III (*laissez-faire*).

There is a repeated theme in the cases that it is for the employer to determine whether or not to accommodate the request for an 'opt-out' on the grounds of conscientious objection. The judgments, as has been seen, allow this decision to be made by the employer with less justification than might be the case under other grounds of discrimination. The tendency has been to accept the employer's proportionality defence with limited question, once a 'legitimate aim' has been established. Thus far, there is support from these cases for a *laissez-faire* approach by the courts. However, it remains to a degree unresolved as to how far, in the case of sexual orientation for example, an employer is truly free to act as it wishes in accommodating religious conscientious objection and how far the law requires it to refuse requests to conscientiously object. The compromise position proposed by the Court of Appeal in *Ladele* that, once she had been designated a civil partnerships registrar, the employer lost its discretion to accept an 'opt-out' request but not before,[200] is rather unsatisfactory and, on this point at least, there remains a degree of confusion as to the extent of employer autonomy.

In terms of the exclusion of religion from the workplace, *McFarlane*, and Lord Carey's intervention in that case, imply a growing perception that religious expression receives insufficient protection and, in fact, active hostility, in its treatment by the courts. This perception is perhaps an exaggeration. Nevertheless, it is clear from these cases that the courts, whilst expressing some vague sympathy for the religious claimant, make limited attempt to engage with the religious nature of the conscientious objection and prefer to frame the issues in terms of the actual conduct of the religious claimant in seeking not to carry out all of his or her duties. In taking an indulgent view towards employer justification, the courts have created a situation where employers who could easily accommodate the objections of religious employees are permitted to dismiss them instead. This is particularly marked in these cases as another protected right, associated with sexual orientation, is also in play. It would seem clear that when religiously motivated expression is seen in some way to undermine other rights (and consequently 'discriminate') then it is more likely to be required to give way.

The precedents set by these cases leave the religious employee with a conscientious objection in an uncomfortable place.[201] He can rely only on the hope that his employer will respond to moral persuasion or individual pressure and agree to allow him the option of conscientious objection, knowing that the law is unlikely to provide a means of enforcing this request. When faced with an employer like Islington Borough Council, which is not prepared to yield, there remains the less than enticing options of acquiescence or getting out of the role (either through resignation or dismissal). It is submitted that this is a deeply unsatisfactory state of affairs. There is a great sacrifice involved for the individual – either of conscience and self-respect or of a valued role and consequent income. There is also a negative effect on society in general, as a number public offices and roles become closed to religious people, further marginalising religious 'voices'

---

200 *Ladele* (CA) [74].

201 Following the successful passage through Parliament of the Marriage (Same Sex Couples) Act 2013, it is possible that there may be an increased number of public servants who may face such a dilemma of conscience; for example, some registrars and school teachers: see Coalition for Marriage, 'Summary of the Aidan O'Neill Legal Opinion on Gay Marriage And Liberty of Conscience'. Available online athttp://c4m.org.uk/resources (accessed 9 June 2014).

and undermining the very 'diversity' which, in *Ladele*, was afforded so much weight as an overriding policy goal.[202]

201 This final paragraph is based on the conclusion presented in Hambler, 'A No-Win Situation for Public Officials with Faith Convictions' (2010) 12 *Ecclesiastical Law Journal* 3.

7 Passive manifestation

Introduction

This chapter is concerned with 'passive manifestation' in the workplace. This term is intended to be inclusive of the various ways in which employees might seek to express their religious beliefs visually. This might involve:

i)   distinct forms of dress (including head coverings);
ii) the visible wearing of religious symbols, or symbols with religious significance to the individual;
iii) the decoration of individual workspaces with religious symbols and artefacts; or
iv) particular styles of personal grooming (such as the display of facial hair).

These forms of expression are visible in the workplace and clearly identify individuals as holding religious beliefs, even if the nature of those beliefs or the conviction with which they are held is not made clear. In this sense, the form of manifestation can be said to be 'passive'; it indicates the presence of religious convictions but does not specifically articulate them, unlike 'active manifestation', which is considered in Chapter 8. It has been suggested, based on US jurisprudence, that there is such a thing as 'symbolic speech'.[1] The use of this term at least implies congruence between speech and symbol, at least in terms of their effect on others. It is submitted that this is not necessarily an aid to the analysis of religious passive manifestation. 'Speech' and 'symbol' are different in important respects as media for conveying meaning to others – appealing to different senses and in distinctive ways. There are potentially exceptions if the form of symbolism has words attached[2] or, albeit less obviously, a graphic

---

1   See the brief discussion in H-Y Liu, 'The Meaning of Religious Symbols after the Grand Chamber ruling in *Lautsi v Italy*' (2011) 6 *Religion and Human Rights* 253, 255–6.
2   See *Boychuck* v. *Symons* [1977] IRLR 395, where an employee unsuccessfully challenged the fairness of her dismissal when she refused to take off a lapel badge displaying the slogan 'Lesbians Ignite'.

image.[3] However, it could be argued that, in such cases, the form of manifestation, because it is articulated, is better classified as 'active' or a hybrid
of 'passive' and 'active'.

The term 'passive' is employed in this chapter with reference to the religious content of the symbol, dress or grooming. It may be that an item of
religious dress interferes with an activity that is central to an individual's job.[4]
In such cases, it is difficult to describe the symbol as *functionally* passive
because of the way in which it actively interferes with work. However, for the
purposes of the analysis here, it remains passive as a form of religious expression simply because it does not explicitly verbalise religious convictions.

There are, in broad terms, four views which may be taken of passive
manifestation. The first is to view it as of relatively little importance.
Renteln argues that this flows from an Anglo-Saxon world view which gives
priority to verbal communication and thus underplays the importance of
symbols, and particularly religious symbols, to minority faiths.[5] Under this
analysis, there are two possible consequences. One is that the issue would
be relatively uncontested and religious people would be free to dress and
groom themselves as they wish. The second is that the right of someone to
dress and groom and otherwise display symbols would be seen as of lesser
significance in comparison with any conflicting rights (e.g. from an
employer's perspective, the desire to present a particular image to
customers) and would be expected to give way. In Renteln's view, the latter
is the most likely outcome. Both, though, derive from the notion that
symbolism is of relatively little significance. In terms of the models
presented in Chapter 3, this view is most likely to fit with a *laissez-faire*
approach – the issue being of little importance there is no need to seek to
constrain by law the discretion of employers through legal means.

The second view would be to recognise that, like other forms of manifestation, passive manifestation has some significance for the religious
individual, particularly members of minority religions, and thus some
efforts should be made through the courts to restrain employer discretion
in support of passive manifestation. This view would be most congruent
with the 'protection' model, particularly the protection for minority faiths
in Chapter 3. The assumption, as with the first view, is likely to be that religious symbolism is broadly neutral in its effect on others – its importance
is best understood relative to the individual concerned. Thus any
constraints would require strong justification.

---

3   In a US case, for example, an employee unsuccessfully contested the require-
    ment that she remove a lapel badge carrying an explicit image of an aborted
    fetus; see *Wilson* v. *US West Communications*, 58 F.3d 1337 (8th Cir. 1995). The
    claimant was a Roman Catholic and wore the badge to indicate her hostility,
    motivated by her religious beliefs, to abortion.
4   See, for example, *Azmi* v. *Kirklees Metropolitan Borough Council* (2007) EAT
    0009/07, discussed below.
5   Renteln, 'Visual Religious Symbols and the Law'.

A third view would be that passive manifestation should not be constrained when it reflects simply a religious belief but when it also reflects national identity (or heritage). In the UK and Western Europe, this is most likely to apply to Christian symbolism. This view is synonymous with the 'support for a preferred historic religion' model in Chapter 3.

There is, however, a fourth view, which is that religious symbolism is capable of influencing the behaviour or thinking of others and so represents a challenge to Western culture. It is thus of potentially great significance (and can only really be described as 'passive' in the sense that this term can be taken, for analytical purposes, to mean 'non-verbal'). This view is partly premised on the contention that symbolic display is, at best, 'an "ostensible" intrusion of religious identities' into the public square or, worse, 'an illegitimate act of propaganda and an aggressive act of proselytism'.[6] Proselytism, in turn, may create unhealthy pressure on some, particularly those most susceptible to pressure, to conform to a particular expression of religion. This is particularly noted in the case of the head-scarf-*hijab* where it is also argued, girls are most prone to be put under pressure by others to dress in a particular way.[7] A second and linked contention is that such pressure, particularly if exerted by men, amounts to sex discrimination as women are isolated and restricted by their seclusion within the veil and more easily controlled and subordinated as a result.[8] Thus, religious symbolism can promote discrimination. Thirdly, religious symbolism can be viewed as 'subversive' and a threat to public order. This is the contention of secular France and is summarised by Danchin (who finds it wanting):

> [Wearing] religious symbols is seen as being linked to an increased risk of threats and violence, whether because of intolerance and xenophobia directed towards an unpopular religious minority, or because of a perceived threat of the rise of religious fundamentalism directed towards the democratic values and institutions of the state.[9]

---

6   C Laborde, *Critical Republicanism: The Hijab Controversy and Political Philosophy* (Oxford: Oxford University Press, 2008), 53.

7   K Bennoune, 'Secularism and Human Rights: A Contextual Analysis of Headscarves, Religious Expression and Women's Equality Under International Law' (2007) 45 *Columbia Journal of Transnational Law* 367.

8   See discussion in A Wing and M Smith, 'Critical Race Feminism Lifts the Veil: Muslim Women, France, and the Headscarf Ban' (2005–2006) 39 *University of California Davis Law Review* 743, 768–9.

9   P Danchin, 'Suspect Symbols: Value Pluralism as a Theory of Religious Freedom in International Law' (2008) 33 *Yale Journal of International Law* 1, 6.

In this context, the Islamic headscarf, in particular, is frequently viewed as a political as much as a religious symbol;[10] one capable of inciting violence by those who oppose what it represents and also representing the deliberate rejection of the existing democratic political arrangements. Such assertions are controversial. For example, it could be argued that the state should focus on protecting individuals from a hostile reaction to the wearing of a headscarf rather than seeking to curtail the freedom to do so. Nevertheless, such arguments do provide a direct rationale for those seeking to restrict the symbolic manifestation of religion in certain public places, for example, in schools, in universities and in courtrooms.[11] This approach would correspond most clearly to model I (exclusion), presented in Chapter 3. Such restrictions will have an effect on 'workers' such as teachers and lecturers (as well as other actors such as pupils and students) and, by extension, on employees in other occupations.

As passive manifestation may affect a range of public situations beyond the workplace in a way that the other forms of manifestation thus far considered do not, there is a range of case law of direct and indirect relevance, much of it from outside the workplace. Such case law is useful as it can illuminate some of the ways in which the law grapples with the challenges of passive manifestation more generally and from a human rights perspective particularly. It has already been noted that principles from European Convention on Human Rights and Fundamental Freedoms (ECHR) jurisprudence have been applied to domestic discrimination law[12] and that domestic law must be interpreted in line with the principles of the Human Rights Act 1998. It is therefore analytically helpful to identify the evolution of ECHR principles, both at a European and a UK level, in relation to passive manifestation, with a view to subsequently assessing how far these principles have been adopted in workplace cases, chiefly under domestic discrimination law. These principles have developed largely, but not uniquely, within an educational context but, as McGoldrick notes 'can be read more widely'.[13]

In this chapter, therefore, this wider case law is examined prior to a more focused consideration of the specific workplace case law under the 2003 Regulations and the Equality Act 2010: firstly, Article 9 ECHR case law is considered and, secondly, employment cases with a relevance to passive manifestation are explored. Principles and key issues from these cases are

10   D McGoldrick, *Human Rights and Religion: The Islamic Headscarf Debate in Europe* (Cambridge: Hart Publishing, 2006), 274.
11   For a detailed assessment of the arguments for and against restrictions on the wearing of religious symbols, particularly in an education context, see E Howard, *Law and the Wearing of Religious Symbols* (Abingdon: Routledge 2012), Chapter 2.
12   For example the forum internum/externum distinction.
13   McGoldrick, *Human Rights and Religion*, 131.

then employed as part of the analysis of some recent passive manifestation employment judgments in England and Wales.

Article 9 case law

Much of the case law at a European level has been concerned with the right of Muslim women to wear the headscarf-*hijab* (or indeed other forms of Islamic dress such as the *niqab*, *jilbab* or *burka*). However, there has been a handful of cases brought by Sikhs, such as *X* v. *United Kingdom*,[14] where the European Court of Human Rights (ECtHR) found against a Sikh who had been required to wear a motorcycle helmet, despite having to take off his turban, on the grounds of the legitimate demands of UK health and safety laws.

The reason that there is a relatively extensive case law in this area is that certain states, which are signatories to the ECHR, seek, as a matter of policy, to constrain religious expression in the public square in order to promote secularism.[15] A good example of this is France, where all but discreet signs and symbols of religion have been banned in state schools since March 2004.[16] The general consensus has been that Muslim women who wish to wear the headscarf have been disproportionately affected by this; hence, the designation, '*L'Affaire du Foulard*', which has come to be associated with it.[17] It is notable, certainly, that the law does not appear to unduly affect Christians, for example, who are free to wear 'discreet' crosses. The French approach, insofar as it has been tested before the ECtHR, has been accepted as falling within a national margin of appreciation.[18]

In Muslim-majority Turkey, under its equally secular constitution, there exists a much more wide-ranging ban on the wearing of religious dress or symbols in all state institutions.[19] Other states, such as Denmark[20] and

---

14 (1978) 14 DR 234.

15 Although there are many versions of secularism; see, for a recent discussion relevant to this context, I Leigh and R Ahdar, 'Post-Secularism and the European Court of Human Rights (or How God Never Really Went Away)' (2012) 75 *Modern Law Review* 1065.

16 See, for a nuanced critique of the French approach to the headscarf, Laborde, *Critical Republicanism: The Hijab Controversy and Political Philosophy* (Oxford: Oxford University Press, 2008).

17 This term, in fact, predates the Stasi commission and was first applied following intense media interest in a school dispute in 1989 over the right of three Muslim girls to wear headscarves in class in contravention of a schoolwide ban: see N Moruzzi, 'A Problem with Headscarves: Contemporary Complexities of Political and Social Identity' (1994) 4 *Political Theory* 658.

18 See, for example, *Dogru* v. *France* Appl No. 27058/05 and *Kervanci* v. *France* Appl No. 31645/04 (4 December 2008), the facts of which predated Stasi and related to school headscarf bans during physical education lessons.

19 C Evans, *Freedom of Religion Under the European Convention on Human Rights* (Oxford: Oxford University Press, 2000).

20 Vickers, *Religious Freedom, Religious Discrimination and the Workplace* (Oxford: Hart Publishing, 2008).

France,[21] restrict the most overt visual manifestations of religious belief. As with *L'Affaire du Foulard*, the effect of such provisions has tended to be most negative for Muslim women and, for this reason, many of the challenges under the ECHR have been lodged by Muslims.

Such applications have enjoyed little success for two main reasons. First, the ECtHR allows a wide margin of appreciation in this area for member states. This position is most clearly articulated in *Leyla Sahin* v. *Turkey*, where, in a Chamber judgment, the Court rejected an Article 9 application from a medical student in Istanbul who had been denied access to lectures and an examination because she refused to remove her headscarf in contravention of a regulation forbidding the wearing of the headscarf whilst engaged in academic study at the university.[22] The Court agreed with the applicant that her Article 9(1) right to manifest her religion had been interfered with:

> The applicant said that, by wearing the headscarf, she was obeying a religious precept and thereby manifesting her desire to comply strictly with the duties imposed by the Islamic faith. Accordingly, her decision to wear the headscarf may be regarded as motivated or inspired by a religion or belief and, without deciding whether such decisions are in every case taken to fulfil a religious duty, the Court proceeds on the assumption that the regulations in issue, which placed restrictions of place and manner on the right to wear the Islamic headscarf in universities, constituted an interference with the applicant's right to manifest her religion.[23]

However, in determining whether or not this interference could be justified as 'necessary in a democratic society' (under the provisions of Article 9(2)), the Court determined that it could be justified, on the basis that, in Turkey, the headscarf could rightly be perceived as having political as well as religious significance, as well as a malign effect on those who choose not to wear it (although the judgment does not spell out the apparent nature of this effect); thus, two imperatives were in play – the protection of the 'rights and freedoms of others' and the 'maintenance of public order' – both of which justified restrictions were proportionate for the university, which had acted sensitively, to apply in this case. In the process, the Court set out clearly the principle of deference on such questions to the decisions taken by nation states:

---

21   For a critical discussion of the French legal approach, see M Hunter-Henin, 'Why the French Don't Like the *Burqa: Laïcité*, National Identity and Religious Freedom' (2012) 61 ICLQ 613.
22   *Leyla Sahin* v. *Turkey* Appl No. 44774/98 (SC) (29 June 2004).
23   Ibid. [71].

Where questions concerning the relationship between State and religions are at stake, on which opinion in a democratic society may reasonably differ widely, the role of the national decision-making body must be given special importance ... In such cases, it is necessary to have regard to the fair balance that must be struck between the various interests at stake: the rights and freedoms of others, avoiding civil unrest, the demands of public order and pluralism.[24]

It thus dismissed the application. This judgment was upheld on appeal before the Grand Chamber.[25]

Secondly, the Court (at least pre-2011) has not been particularly supportive of the right to display religious symbols, particularly the head-scarf-*hijab*. In *Dahlab* v. *Switzerland*, a primary school teacher was forbidden from wearing a headscarf-*hijab* in the classroom because it contravened the principle of religious neutrality imposed by law on the Swiss school system. The Swiss Federal Court upheld the interdiction on the basis that the wearing of the headscarf constituted 'a "powerful" religious symbol – that is to say, a sign that is immediately visible to others and provides a clear indication that the person concerned belongs to a particular religion'.[26] In consequence of her status as a primary school teacher and role model for her pupils, the wearing of this powerful symbol by Dahlab 'imposed' Islam upon them, thus potentially interfering with both their religious beliefs and those of their parents. In upholding the school's decision in this way, the Swiss Federal Court nevertheless noted the dilemma which this would create for Dahlab:

> [P]rohibiting the appellant from wearing a headscarf forces her to make a difficult choice between disregarding what she considers to be an important precept laid down by her religion and running the risk of no longer being able to teach in State schools.[27]

In dismissing Dahlab's subsequent application, the ECtHR made the following observations:

> The Court accepts that it is very difficult to assess the impact that a powerful external symbol such as the wearing of a headscarf may have on the freedom of conscience and religion of very young children. ... In those circumstances, it cannot be denied outright that the wearing of a headscarf might have some kind of proselytising effect, seeing that

24   Ibid. [100].
25   *Leyla Sahin* v. *Turkey* Appl No. 44774/98 (GC) (10 November 2005).
26   *Dahlab* v. *Switzerland* Appl No. 42393/98 (15 February 2001), 2–3.
27   Ibid., 8.

it appears to be imposed on women by a precept which is laid down in the Koran and which, as the Federal Court noted, is hard to square with the principle of gender equality. It therefore appears difficult to reconcile the wearing of an Islamic headscarf with the message of tolerance, respect for others and, above all, equality and non-discrimination that all teachers in a democratic society must convey to their pupils.[28]

The Court determined that to ban the wearing of the *hijab*-headscarf was within the margin of appreciation of Switzerland.

The effect of both of these approaches in the rulings of the ECtHR has been that:

> All the cases have accepted that restrictions may be imposed on the wearing of Islamic dress in public institutions. Though the justifications vary in detail, all generally revolve around the concept of 'protection of the rights and freedoms of others'.[29]

How far these principles might apply to Christian symbolism was, *prima facie*, explored in *Lautsi and Ors* v. *Italy*.[30] This case was lodged by Mrs S Lautsi, a parent who objected that the prominent display of a crucifix on the wall in each of her sons' classrooms. Under domestic law, the display of such crucifixes is mandatory in Italy and so the challenge had widespread ramifications.

The school governors voted to retain the crucifixes and, in 2002, Mrs Lautsi began the first of a series of legal challenges in the Italian courts on the grounds, *inter alia*, that the practice undermined the principle of secularism. Her case was unsuccessful, the courts taking the view that:

i)   the crucifix was a symbol of Christianity in general rather than of Catholicism alone, so that it served as a point of reference for other creeds;
ii) the crucifix was a historical and cultural symbol of identity for the Italian people; and
iii) the crucifix symbolised secular Western values which had originally emerged from Christianity.

Mrs Lautsi (together with her two sons) then lodged her case with the ECtHR, on the basis that the public display of the crucifix in her sons' school was contrary to her right to ensure that their education was in conformity with her religious and philosophical convictions, under Article

---

28   Ibid., 13.
29   N Addison, *Religious Discrimination and Hatred Law* (Abingdon: Routledge Cavendish, 2006), 23.
30   Appl No. 30814/06 (GC) (18 March 2011).

2 of Protocol No. 1. The presence of the crucifix also breached her free-dom of religion, as protected by Article 9 of the Convention. Furthermore, relying on Article 14, all three of them, not being Catholics, had suffered discrimination in their treatment in comparison to Roman Catholic parents and their children.

In its Chamber judgment in November 2009, the ECtHR upheld the claims.[31] Against a backdrop of public outrage in Italy,[32] the Italian government's request for a grand chamber hearing was granted and this took place in June 2010. On this occasion, the Court overturned its earlier judgment.[33] It took the view that the state could not be held to be seeking to indoctri-nate pupils in one particular religion merely through the display of a 'passive symbol'.[34] Being passive, such a symbol 'cannot be deemed to have an influence on pupils comparable to that of didactic speech or participa-tion in religious activities'.[35] Equally, there was no evidence to show that the display of the crucifixes had encouraged proselytism by teaching staff. Thus, there was no interference with the applicants' rights under the ECHR and, as there was no indoctrination, it was within Italy's margin of appreciation to continue to require the display of crucifixes in state schools.

One of the concurring opinions, in the same vein as the domestic Italian courts, stressed the importance of the crucifix as 'heritage' for the Italian people:

> A court of human rights cannot allow itself to suffer from historical Alzheimer's. It has no right to disregard the cultural continuum of a nation's flow through time, nor to ignore what, over the centuries, has served to mould and define the profile of a people. No supranational court has any business substituting its own ethical mock-ups for those qualities that history has imprinted on the national identity. ... A European court should not be called upon to bankrupt centuries of European tradition. No court, certainly not this Court, should rob the Italians of part of their cultural personality.[36]

---

31 *Lautsi* v. *Italy* Appl No. 30814/06 (SC) (3 November 2009).

32 D McGoldrick, 'Religion in the European Public Square and in European Public Life: Crucifixes in the Classroom?' (2011) 11 *Human Rights Law Review* 451.

33 *Lautsi* (GC).

34 It thus rejected the argument which had been accepted in the Chamber judg-ment that the state had, in a sense, 'personally endorsed' the symbol.

35 *Lautsi* (GC) [72].

36 Judge Bonello ([1.1] of his concurring opinion). There were, however, dissenting opinions, including that of Judge Malinverni who observed ([5] of the dissenting opinion): '[N]egative freedom of religion ... extends to symbols expressing a belief or a religion. That negative right deserves special protec-tion if it is the State which displays a religious symbol and dissenters are placed in a situation from which they cannot extract themselves'.

It should be noted in passing that this judgment is, at first blush, somewhat at variance with *Dahlab* and it is now unclear as to how far a prominent religious symbol will be regarded by the ECtHR as 'essentially passive' (as in *Lautsi*) or as having 'powerful external' force, capable of a proselytising effect (as in *Dahlab*). For some commentators, the variance is due to the limited reasoning offered by the Court in *Dahlab* as to how the symbol in question could reasonably be said to coerce others, in comparison to the more nuanced judgment of essentially similar issues in *Lautsi* which led to a different and better judgment.[37] For others, the differential treatment evident in the cases is regrettable evidence of 'double standards' depending on the nature of the religious symbol.[38] Either or both contentions may be correct but it is also instructive to note some differences between the cases that are relevant to this book. Firstly, in *Lautsi*, the presence of the crucifix was historic and prescribed by the state, thus blurring the meaning between the original religious symbolism and the role of the symbol as affirming identity or heritage (providing a clear fit with model II under the typology proposed in Chapter 3).[39] Secondly, and more significantly, the symbol was 'passive' in the sense that it was detached from the schoolteacher in *Lautsi* and thus there was not the same sense of personal endorsement seen by the conscious decision of the teacher in *Dahlab* to physically wear the headscarf, in a sense 'activating' the religious symbol.[40]

37   See, for example, Leigh and Ahdar, 'Post-Secularism and the European Court of Human Rights'.

38   See, for example, P Ronchi, 'Crucifixes, Margin of Appreciation and Consensus: The Grand Chamber Ruling in *Lautsi v Italy*' (2011) 13 *Ecclesiastical Law Journal* 287; and S Mancini and M Rosenfeld, 'Unveiling the Limits of Tolerance: Comparing the Treatment of Majority and Minority Religious Symbols In the Public Sphere' (September 2010) *Cardozo Legal Studues Research Paper* No. 309. Available online at http://papers.ssrn.com/sol3/papers.cfm?abstract_id=1684382 (accessed 9 June 2014).

39   There is a strong argument that reducing Christian symbols to examples of 'heritage' robs them of their religious value to Christians and so does them no service; see Mancini and Rosenfeld, 'Unveiling the Limits of Tolerance'. See also, on this point, Leigh and Ahdar, 'Post-Secularism and the European Court of Human Rights', 1074–5.

40   G Andreescu, and L Andreescu, 'Taking Back Lautsi: Towards a "Theory of Neutralisation"?' (2011) 6 *Religion and Human Rights* 207. McGoldrick is critical of the Grand Chamber's decision in Lautsi to compare and contrast the nature of different religious symbols; see McGoldrick, 'Religion in the European Public Square and in European Public Life', 489. As he notes, 'Islamic headscarves, worn by a minority, may be powerful external symbols that challenge neutrality. However, Christian crucifixes, a symbol of the majority religion, are somehow merely passive and do not challenge neutrality'. He argues that it would have been less contentious for the court to note the complexity of assessing the significance of religious symbols and to have left it to the national courts to make a determination within the scope of the margin of appreciation.

With these two observations in mind, *Dahlab* would appear to remain the most relevant ECtHR judgment in respect of individual symbolic manifestation, particularly with regard to the headscarf.

This would certainly appear to be the view of the domestic courts in the UK. In *R (Shabina Begum)* v. *Headteacher and Governors of Denbigh High School*,[41] for example, the approach taken in *Dahlab* was quite clearly adopted. This case involved an application under the Human Rights Act 1998 by a schoolgirl forbidden from wearing a *jilbab* during school hours. The school argued that if Begum was allowed to attend classes wearing the *jilbab*, this might put pressure on other pupils to adopt similar strict variants of Islamic dress. Begum, with her brother, successfully sought a judicial review of the school's decision, on the grounds that Begum's right to manifest her religion (Article 9 ECHR) and her right to education (Article 2(1) of the first protocol) had been violated. Although successful in the Court of Appeal, the House of Lords determined that, since there were other schools which would allow her to wear the *jilbab*, there was no interference with Begum's right to manifest her belief in practice or observance. The Lords also concluded that, had there been an interference with Begum's Article 9 rights, then it would be justified because the school in formulating its uniform policy possessed a degree of discretion comparable to 'a margin of appreciation'.[42]

To summarise, these cases are not employment cases *per se*, although they do provide some guidance in respect of some public places such as the classroom which are also workplaces. These cases suggest that Article 9 rights can be legitimately restricted at the discretion of the state, insofar as passive manifestation is concerned, if the member state is concerned about the possible pressure exerted on others through this manifestation and particularly if the form of manifestation is seen as promoting sex discrimination. It is clear that the headscarf is the manifestation which is most clearly identifiable in these terms. However, the narrowness of the context is also worthy of note – it is confined to educational institutions where the 'susceptible' young people are considered to be at risk of coercion through passive manifestation.[43] Nevertheless, within that context, a generally negative view of the headscarf is permitted, even encouraged by the ECtHR, and arguments which might be deployed to restrict its use by teachers are provided.

Also from the case law, it may be noted that states can legitimately restrict passive religious manifestation when there are practical reasons for so doing, such as those associated with health and safety obligations. Finally, the cases also provide arguments in favour of the display of

---

41   [2007] 1 AC 100; [2006] UKHL 15.
42   Ibid. [84] (Lord Hoffman).
43   See also the discussion in Chapter 8 of *Larissis and others* v. *Greece* (1999) 27 EHRR 329.

religious symbolism if this symbolism can be linked to national identity, under a heritage model (model II).

The workplace in England and Wales: pre-2003 developments

Having considered the (primarily) human rights jurisprudence on passive manifestation from outside the employment sphere, attention will now turn to the workplace, and particularly the case law preceding the 2003 Religion and Belief Regulations. This case law provides some insights into how courts have sought to balance employee freedom of expression in terms of dress and grooming with employer discretion, and how these rights are triangulated with discrimination law.

Prior to the 2003 Regulations, the extent to which employers have discretion to control the dress and personal grooming of employees 'to convey a message to their employees and customers'[44] had already been established in principle in *Schmidt* v. *Austicks Bookshops*,[45] a sex discrimination case brought by Mrs Schmidt, who had been dismissed by her employer because she refused to comply with a new dress code forbidding female members of staff who came into contact with the public from wearing trousers. The Employment Appeals Tribunal determined that she had not been discriminated against because the employer had also imposed different but equivalent restrictions on male staff.[46] It also stated as obiter 'that an employer is entitled to a large measure of discretion in controlling the image of his establishment, including the appearance of staff, and especially so when, as a result of their duties, they come into contact with the public'.[47] This suggests that a right of self-expression through dress and grooming does potentially exist but is likely to be subordinate to employer discretion, especially its discretion regarding the presentation of a particular uniform image to the public.

Other cases, pursued under the Race Relations Act 1976, involve a more explicit link to the manifestation of religious belief. Both *Singh* v. *Rowntree Mackintosh*[48] and *Panesar* v. *Nestlé*[49] involved Sikhs who were rejected at recruitment stage for work at chocolate factories on the grounds of hygiene. For religious reasons, the respective claimants refused to accept a

44   G Clayton and G Pitt, 'Dress Codes and Freedom of Expression' (1997) 1 *European Human Rights Law Review* 55.
45   [1977] IRLR 360 (EAT).
46   A decision reinforced in *Smith* v. *Safeway* [1996] IRLR 456 and later in *Department for Work and Pensions* v. *Thompson* [2004] IRLR 348, where the lawfulness of 'equal but different treatment' between the sexes in the matter of imposing dress codes was affirmed.
47   *Schmidt* [10].
48   [1979] IRLR 199 (EAT Sc).
49   [1980] ICR 60 (EAT); 64 (CA).

requirement to wear their hair short or shave off their beards. In *Singh* v. *Lyons Maid Ltd*,[50] a Sikh worker was dismissed from his job in an ice cream factory, after a personal revival of religious conviction led to him refusing any longer to adhere to a rule preventing him from wearing his hair uncut (for reasons of hygiene). In *Singh* v. *British Rail Engineering*,[51] a Sikh employee refused to put on a hard hat to meet health and safety obligations and was consequently dismissed. In each of these cases, the respective claimant lost his case, illustrating the extent to which the Employment Appeals Tribunal was prepared to accept, relatively unquestioningly, both hygiene and health and safety as justifying indirect race discrimination against Sikhs.

In *Kingston & Richmond RHA* v. *Kaur*,[52] a decision of a regional health authority to enforce the wearing of a dress as part of the uniform of female nurses was held by the Employment Appeals Tribunal not to discriminate on the grounds of race. The applicant, a Sikh, was prepared to comply on condition that she could, for religious and cultural reasons, cover her legs by the wearing of trousers in addition to the dress. Nevertheless, despite the claimant's willingness to compromise, the Tribunal held that the employer had a compelling reason to insist that she comply rigidly with the uniform so that the health authority should present a consistent image to the public.

In summary, before 2003, employment tribunals broadly followed the first of the three positions considered in the introduction in affording little importance to the right of 'passive manifestation'. Admittedly, they did accord some small weight to an individual's right to self-expression through dress and grooming.[53] However, this 'right' to self-expression, even when informed by race and culture, was easily defeated when employers provided a *prima facie* justification for restricting dress and grooming, particularly when based around the concepts of hygiene or health and safety. These are of course important considerations and fairly easy to invoke as a 'trump' but may not, in fact, withstand proper scrutiny (if attempted).[54]

---

50 [1975] IRLR 328.

51 [1986] ICR 22 (EAT).

52 [1981] IRLR 337 (EAT).

53 Whilst these cases remain the key precedents, there is some evidence from unreported cases that employment tribunals have gradually afforded more weight to passive manifestation subsequently; see 'Enforcing dress and appearance codes' (2005) 148 EOR 0–3.

54 For example, in *Sarika Watkins-Singh* v. *Aberdare Girls' High School* [2008] EWHC 1865 (Admin), health and safety justifications for a blanket ban on the wearing of the *Kara* were swiftly dismissed by Judge Silber who noted that the wearer would remove the bangle in the circumstances (in this case, PE lessons) where health and safety might be a genuine concern.

The workplace in England and Wales: post-2003 developments

Having considered the developing principles of Article 9 ECHR jurisprudence, as well as the limited employment case law, it is now possible to focus specifically on employment case law, since the implementation of the 2003 Religion and Belief Regulations, concerning the right to 'passively manifest' religious convictions in the workplace. Amongst the case law, since 2003, there have been two particularly high-profile reported cases, as well as a small number of unreported cases which nevertheless attracted media attention.

The first of the significant reported judgments is *Azmi* v. *Kirklees Metropolitan Borough Council*. In this case, a Muslim bilingual support worker in a primary school refused to remove her *niqab* full-face veil when working with children. The case thus has similarities to *Dahlab*. However, unlike *Dahlab*, the employer's rationale for imposing restrictions on the wearing of the veil was entirely unrelated to concerns about sex discrimination or the possible proselytising effect on vulnerable children. Instead, the school's objection was on the entirely practical ground that the children that Azmi was instructing would experience greater difficulty in understanding her through her veil than without it.

Azmi had indicated that she was willing to remove her veil if the school accommodated her in classes where there would be no contact with male teachers. The school rejected this potential accommodation as impractical; Azmi continued to wear the veil and, after a number of meetings and a period of stress-related sick leave, she was suspended. She subsequently lodged a complaint under all the available heads of discrimination on the grounds of religion and belief with the employment tribunal. The tribunal ruled there had been no unlawful discrimination, although procedural shortcomings in the way that her grievance was handled by the school did lead to an award of compensation for victimisation. Azmi appealed.

On the issue of direct discrimination, the Employment Appeals Tribunal agreed with the tribunal that the way the school treated Azmi should be compared with the way it would have treated a woman who (whether a Muslim or not) wears a face covering for a reason other than religious belief. It concluded that, given the importance for the children's education of non-verbal communication, anyone whose face and mouth were covered would also have been suspended. Therefore, Azmi had not been treated any less favourably than anyone else would have been in those circumstances.

On the indirect discrimination point, the tribunal accepted that the school had applied a practice that put people of Azmi's religion or belief at a disadvantage. However, it decided there was no discrimination, because the adoption of that practice was justified as a proportionate means of achieving a legitimate aim. In reaching its conclusion, considerable weight had been given by the tribunal to the 'stringent' efforts made by the employer to investigate the feasibility of alternative ways for accommodating Azmi's wishes.[55] It should be noted that, if employers do not present evidence to support their contention that there is a risk of an adverse impact on their organisations if an employee wears a headscarf, they are likely to lose tribunal cases. This appears to have been the reason why a hairdresser who wished to wear a headscarf won her case after rejection in a job interview.[56] Overall, this is suggestive of a movement away from the acceptance at a more superficial level of employers' justifications on restrictions (prior to 2003) and thus a shift from position 1 (presented in the introduction) to position 2.

Although Azmi's behaviour had been inconsistent, in that she presented herself in a headscarf but unveiled at interview and at her initial training course, this inconsistency, although noted, was not presented as evidence of insincerity and it was common ground that her desire to wear the full face veil was due to a genuine belief that this was a religious requirement. However, a key issue in the case was how far this represented a religious belief itself or a manifestation of a religious belief. This was premised on the contention that a 'manifestation' of religious belief could only be protected under indirect discrimination provisions and could not be protected under direct discrimination. The Employment Appeals Tribunal helpfully dismissed this argument and stated that a manifestation of religious belief could be protected under direct discrimination, particularly if what would otherwise be the relevant provision, criteria or practice (e.g. the requirement not to be veiled) was not 'apparently neutral' but rather it might be thought to represent a deliberate attempt to disadvantage a religious employee (in this case, a Muslim woman). In such cases, although it is a manifestation of religious belief rather than the belief itself that is in contention, it may still amount to direct discrimination. It concluded that it could therefore see 'no reason for there to be any *a priori* position that a "manifestation" of a religious belief always has to be dealt with as indirect discrimination'.[57]

It has been critically noted that some prominent government ministers, including the then Prime Minister, Tony Blair, made a number of public comments as the case was being heard, on the necessity that Muslims should better integrate into UK society and the implicit undesirability of the *niqab* in classrooms.[58] Nevertheless, it is instructive that this linking of *Azmi* to these wider concerns in public discourse (which are aligned with

---

55   *Azmi* [73].
56   *Noah* v. *Desrosiers t/a Wedge* (2008) ET Case No. 2201867/07.
57   *Azmi* [76].
58   M Ssenyonjo, 'The Islamic Veil and Freedom of Religion, the Rights to Education and Work: a Survey of Recent International and National Cases' (2007) 6 *Chinese Journal of International Law* 653.

position 4 in the introduction) was not considered by the court, which focused strictly on applying the principles of discrimination law.

The second of the two high-profile cases was *Eweida* v. *British Airways*,[59] where the right of an employee to wear Christian symbolism in the face of an employer's hostility was explored. Miss Eweida was a practising Christian who worked part-time as a member of check-in staff for British Airways. In 2004, British Airways introduced a new uniform policy for customer-facing roles, which prohibited the wearing of any visible jewellery around the neck. However, exceptions were made for religious symbols that were a mandatory requirement of a religion and could not easily be concealed beneath the uniform. On this basis, Muslim women were permitted to wear the *hijab*-headscarf, Sikh men were allowed to wear turbans and Jewish men were permitted to wear the scull-cap.

During the period 20 May to 20 September 2006, Miss Eweida attended work on at least three occasions with the cross visible. She concealed it when asked to do so.[60] However, on 20 September, she refused to conceal the cross and, having also refused an offer of alternative work involving no public contact, she was suspended without pay. On 1 February 2007, British Airways, under pressure from hostile media coverage, amended its uniform policy to allow staff to display a religious symbol with the uniform. Two days later, Eweida returned to work. She also filed a claim with the employment tribunal that she had been subjected to direct discrimination, indirect discrimination and harassment contrary to the Equality (Religion or Belief) Regulations 2003 and that British Airways had made an unlawful deduction of wages during her period of unpaid suspension.

The claim was unsuccessful at the initial tribunal and thereafter at both the Employment Appeals Tribunal and Court of Appeal. In addressing Eweida's claim, the Court of Appeal followed the Appeals Tribunal in identifying two key issues which were crucial to the case. The first of these issues concerned how far the cross could be considered to be a mandatory requirement of her religious belief. The second concerned how far the doctrine of indirect discrimination might protect a single individual, as Eweida was alone amongst BA employees in her insistence on wearing a visible cross.[61]

---

59   [2010] EWCA Civ. 80; [2010] IRLR 78.
60   It was not suggested by British Airways, nor should it be assumed, that to permit the wearing of a 'concealed' cross represented any form of recognition of the importance of the symbol to the individual concerned. Rather, when jewellery (of any kind) was worn but concealed it was of little interest to the company, and so outside the parameters of the policy, as it was the outward image of customer-facing staff which the company was seeking to regulate.
61   Pitt argues that the 'group' test should be construed to include people beyond a particular workplace – this would have aided Eweida's claim; see G Pitt, 'Keeping the Faith: Trends and Tensions in Religion or Belief Discrimination' (2011) 40 *Industrial Law Journal* 384.

It is clear from the written judgment that the Employment Appeals Tribunal recognised that Eweida's desire to wear a visible cross was 'characteristic' of her faith and thus should be accorded more value than people who might wear a cross for 'cosmetic reasons'[62] but that it was not a 'mandatory' aspect of her religious beliefs. The Court of Appeal concurred with the latter conclusion, noting that '[n]either Ms Eweida nor any witness on her behalf suggested that the visible wearing of a cross was more than a personal preference on her part. There was no suggestion that her religious belief, however profound, called for it'.[63] As the wearing of a cross is not mandatory for Christians thus, in forbidding the practice under a wider uniform policy, there was no detriment against Christians. The characterisation of the cross as non-mandatory was criticised in the aftermath of the case, for example by the Archbishop of York who argued:

> Wearing a cross carries with it not only a symbol of our hopes but also a responsibility to act and to live as Christians. This symbol does not point only upwards but also outwards, it reminds us of our duties not only to God but also to one another.[64]

The purpose of this intervention was perhaps to provide a basis in Christian theology for the wearing of a visible cross. It does not, however, provide a basis for arguing that the wearing of a cross (whether or not it is visible to others) is in any sense 'mandatory' for Christians. However, the issue was resolved in another way in *Ewedia and Ors*, when the Court rejected the necessity test as incompatible with Article 9(1).[65] On this basis, the wearing of a visible cross should now attract *prima facie* protection in the courts as a manifestation of religion, irrespective of whether or not it is mandated by Christianity.

On the second point, as the Employment Appeals Tribunal had concluded that as Eweida's preference for wearing a cross as a religious manifestation was an individual one (which was correct insofar as she was the only individual within her workforce who manifested her religion in this way), it could not be within the scope of indirect discrimination, which required evidence of 'group disadvantage'. Although it did recognise that such an individual preference was protected under the 'religion and belief' category, this protection was restricted to direct discrimination only, where there is no minimum number of adherents required to trigger the available protections.

---

62   *Eweida* v. *British Airways* [2008] UKEAT 0123/08/11; [2009] IRLR 78 [38].
63   *Eweida* (CA) [37].
64   Archbishop attacks BA cross rules' *BBC News* (London, 21 November 2006). Available online at http://news.bbc.co.uk/1/hi/england/north_yorkshire/6166746.stm (accessed 14 June 2014).
65   *Eweida and Ors* v. *United Kingdom* Appl Nos. 48420/10, 59842/10, 51671/10 and 36516/10 (15 January 2013). See discussion in Chapter 4.

The Court of Appeal was still more specific on this issue, arguing that the 'group' to be identified to demonstrate indirect discrimination must be an observable group within the particular workplace, in fact an 'identifiable section of a workforce, quite possibly a small one'.[66] This is not the only reading of the original European Commission Directive, setting out the legal formula for indirect discrimination, which uses the conditional tense ('would put persons having a [protected characteristic] at a particular disadvantage')[67] and therefore strongly implies that the group does not need to be an actual identifiable group within the workplace but could be constructed to include people from outside of the workplace.[68] In this case, an employer's injunction not to wear a visible cross *would* put Eweida at a disadvantage because other Christians, not actually in her workplace, held the same belief and would be affected therefore by the policy, should they choose to work for British Airways. In its submission in *Eweida and Ors*, the Equalities and Human Rights Commission (EqHRC) argued that this was the correct application of the relevant law. Thus, the courts should have established a hypothetical group by considering the beliefs of other people of the same religious faith but not necessarily in the same workforce.[69] Such a 'hypothetical group' would, of course, have enabled Eweida to meet the plural disadvantage threshold.

The domestic claim brought by *Eweida* was followed by a similar employment tribunal case that received considerable publicity, involving a nurse, Shirley Chaplin, who took her employer, the Royal Devon and Exeter NHS Foundation Trust, to an employment tribunal for religious discrimination having been told to remove (or conceal) a crucifix which she wore around her neck, despite having done so for 30 years as a nurse.[70] Chaplin argued that wearing a visible cross was 'an outward manifestation of her deeply held religious conviction'.[71] Her employer argued that the move was not specifically about the crucifix but about health and safety concerns. Some religious items, however, could be exempted from the rule, such as Muslim headscarves because, suitably styled, they did not pose a health and safety risk.[72]

---

66   *Eweida* (CA) [15] (Sedley LJ).

67   EC Directive 2000/34 on equal treatment [2000] OJ L303/16, Art. 2(2)(b).

68   Vickers makes this point: see L Vickers, 'Indirect Discrimination and Individual Belief: *Eweida v British Airways plc*' (2009) 11 *Ecclesiastical Law Journal* 197–203. See also N Hatzis, 'Personal Religious Beliefs in the Workplace: How Not to Define Indirect Discrimination' (2011) 74 *Modern Law Review* 287–305.

69   Equality and Human Rights Commission, *Submission in Eweida v United Kingdom* (September 2011) [27].

70   *Chaplin* v. *Royal Devon and Exeter NHS Foundation Trust* (2010) ET Case No. 1702886/09.

71   Ibid. [14].

72   Ibid. [16].

The tribunal followed *Eweida* and dismissed the case on the basis that indirect discrimination could not apply as the provision, criterion or practice in question affected the beliefs of one person rather than 'persons' as the legislation requires. This was partly a consequence of the fact that the wearing of the cross was not considered mandatory for Christians; therefore, the tribunal began from a position that it represented an individual expression of religious belief. However, in *Chaplin* this decision was somewhat more problematic and led to the dissention of one of the wing members of the tribunal. This was because a second nurse in the trust, Mrs Babcock, also wore a visible cross for religious reasons, casting doubt on how far Chaplin's belief could be said to be an individual one. However, when Mrs Babcock was asked to remove her cross and chain, she did so without objection to 'avoid confrontation'.[73] The tribunal, by majority, inferred from this that only Chaplin suffered a 'particular' disadvantage; Mrs Babcock, with her apparently weaker conviction to wear a visible cross, suffered only 'slight' disadvantage.[74] Thus the tribunal was able to exclude Mrs Babcock from the formula (of more than one person), which it conceded would invoke the first stage of an indirect discrimination claim.[75]

As in *Eweida*, it is clear that the court could have identified a hypothetical group consisting of Christians who believed that wearing a cross visibly was important to their religious convictions, and this would have enabled Mrs Chaplin to demonstrate *prima facie* indirect discrimination. It would not, of course, have aided her in the justification process where health and safety arguments, however flimsy, appear to have been accepted as trumping individual religious obligations.

Following the decision in *Eweida and Ors*, it appears that the Court of Appeal may have changed its approach to group/plural identification towards something akin to the hypothetical group approach advocated by the EqHRC. This is evident from the decision in *Mba* v. *Merton Borough Council*,[76] where there was no apparent 'identifiable section of the workforce' who believed that it was wrong to work on Sundays. Nevertheless, the empirical observation that 'some Christians' hold this belief was sufficient in this case for a group to be identified and the first stage of an indirect discrimination claim demonstrated.[77] Assuming that this approach is followed henceforward in 'passive manifestation' cases, then the fact that 'some Christians', within or without the workplace, have a belief in wearing a cross visibly to testify to their religious convictions should be sufficient to engage the plural aspects of the test for indirect discrimination and thence to progress to the next stage.

---

73 Ibid. [15].
74 Ibid. [27].
75 Ibid. [28].
76 [2013] EWCA Civ. 1562; [2013] WLR (D) 474 (CA).
77 Ibid. [18]; see discussion in Chapter 6.

To summarise, in the post-2003 case law, protections for the passive manifestation of religion are most likely to arise under the doctrine of indirect discrimination. Any protections under direct discrimination are only likely to arise if the employer is suspected of wilfully introducing a 'provision, criterion or practice' for which there is so little justification that the logical assumption can only be that the intention was to deliberately discriminate against the religious employees affected.[78]

Under the indirect discrimination protections, employers are required to provide a clear justification for restrictions on an employee's right to manifest their religion through visual/symbolic means under the formula of demonstrating that any restrictions are 'a proportionate means of achieving a legitimate aim'.[79] Prior to the judgment in *Eweida and Ors*, this justification was likely only to be required when a particular manifestation was considered to be 'mandatory' to the religious belief invoked or when there was a 'group' of current employees disadvantaged or potentially disadvantaged by the restriction. This meant that expressions of religious belief considered to be 'individual' (such as wearing a cross) were not protected. Now that situation has changed: manifestations of religion no longer need to be considered mandatory for the claimant to be afforded *prima facie* protection under Article 9 ECHR and this approach is likely to be adopted in the same way by tribunals obliged to read discrimination law, where possible, in a manner that is compatible with the Convention. Equally, there is some indication from the reasoning employed by the Court of Appeal in *Mba* v. *Merton Borough Council* that the test to determine group disadvantage for the purposes of identifying indirect discrimination will be interpreted in a more generous way in future, to accommodate a 'hypothetical group'; if so, it is likely that tribunals will more accepting of the right to wear religious dress or symbols which only a potentially small minority of adherents of a particular religion might choose (or feel obliged) to wear, irrespective of whether or not there is more than one such adherent within a particular workforce.

Conclusion

It is clear from the claims considered in this chapter, and their dogged pursuit through the court hierarchy, that some individuals have a strong

---

78   Interestingly, there has been at least one successful direct discrimination claim relating to the headscarf; however, it was pursued by a female Muslim employee who was pressurised by her Muslim manager (within a mixed workplace) to wear a headscarf; see *Khan* v. *Ghafoor t/a Go Go Real Estate* (2009) ET Case No. 1809595/09.

79   A further example of this was the respondent's success in justifying preventing an Amritdhari Sikh prison officer from wearing a *kirpan* whilst dealing with prisoners (owing to the potential risks involved in carrying something which might be stolen by prisoners and used as a weapon); see *Dhinsa* v. *SERCO* (2011) ET Case No. 1315002/09.

desire to manifest their religious beliefs in the workplace, as elsewhere, through some form of passive manifestation. Such passive manifestation may represent an external sign of allegiance to a particular religion (as for example in *Watkins-Singh*), which the individual may feel under varying degrees of obligation to express, or it may represent a personal decision to publicly testify to a religious faith (as in *Eweida*).

It is equally clear that employers often wish to regulate such passive manifestation. In the consideration of the relevant case law presented in this chapter, a number of justifications have been offered for restrictions. Some of these are *prima facie* neutral about the symbol itself; for example, restrictions based on health and safety (as in *Singh* v. *British Rail Engineering*) or hygiene concerns (as in *Panesar* v. *Nestlé*), or where the manifestation plainly interferes with a specific work role on a practical level (as in *Azmi*). Other justifications involve a judgement on the lack of congruence between particular symbols (such as jewellery in *Eweida*) and the corporate image of the organisation. Finally, some justifications may involve an unfavourable value judgement about the meaning attached to the symbol itself (as in *Dahlab*). It is also worthy of note that in some cases (e.g. *Chaplin*), there are suspicions, at least on behalf of the claimant, that a neutral explanation for a restriction masks the true reason which is related to hostility towards the symbol itself and its meaning.

The form of regulation of passive manifestation by an employer varies and it is a reasonable assumption that there will be a direct correlation between this and the justification for the regulation. For example, the restrictions in *Azmi* applied only during the process of teaching, where the wearing of the *niqab* was identified as a problem, and not at other times during the course of employment. In *Dahlab*, the restrictions applied when the teacher was visible to her pupils (i.e. all times when they might be negatively influenced by her headscarf). In *Eweida*, the restrictions applied whilst engaged in customer-facing roles (hence the offer to the claimant of alternative 'back office' work).

Recent cases shed light on how the law is developing in response to the resultant clashes when employers attempt to regulate passive manifestation. The discussion now moves on to consider this with reference to the models presented in Chapter 3. In broad terms, the courts have moved away from a *laissez-faire* approach of broadly accepting employer's justifications on restrictions with limited inquiry (as in the original claims brought under race). Exactly what they have moved towards may be less clear. ECHR jurisprudence provides a justification for the adoption of an exclusionary approach, at least in certain circumstances, based on the perceived negative implications for others of the display of certain symbols or dress, chiefly the headscarf. Thus far at least, such arguments have not been entertained in the Employment Appeals Tribunal or beyond, where the focus has been on operational or other 'business' justifications by employers for restrictions. This is particularly striking in the *Azmi* case, where arguments might have been employed (but were not) analogous to those in *Dahlab* about the proselytising effect on schoolgirls of wearing the full-face veil. Similarly, the recent decision by the ECtHR in *Lautsi* and the perceived distinction between discreet symbols and more overt symbols would provide arguments in favour of supporting the passive manifestation of Christianity as the 'preferred historic religion', either for reasons connected to national heritage and identity or because the symbolism is typically more discreet than for most other religions. However, no such arguments have been employed in the tribunals.

There does, however, appear to have been movement towards model V (protection), albeit in a qualified way, through the requirement that employers provide clear evidence that any restrictions on passive manifestation fully satisfy the test, under the doctrine of indirect discrimination, that they represent 'a proportionate means of achieving a legitimate aim'. The failure to provide such evidence is why, for example, the rejected prospective hairdresser who wished to wear a headscarf won her case. A more significant shift towards model V is also likely to result from the removal of the 'necessity test', such that protection will no longer be selective according to the perceived doctrinal requirements of a particular religion. The removal of the necessity test also represents a movement away from model VI (protection for minority religions only), which has been hitherto the practical result of this test, given that members of minority religious faiths have been often successful in demonstrating that particular dress and grooming requirements are mandatory to their religious beliefs whereas Christians have not been. This is surely a welcome development as it is clear from some of the cases considered in this chapter that displaying a visible cross as a sign of commitment to Christianity is of overriding importance to some individuals. Just because Christianity is a less prescriptive religion than other major world faiths on these matters does not mean that Christian employees should be denied the right to manifest their convictions visually without even *prima facie* legal protection.[80]

---

80   This point was sympathetically treated by Judges Bratza and Bjorgvinsson in their partially dissenting opinion in *Eweida and Ors*.

8   Active manifestation

Introduction

The term 'active manifestation' employed in this chapter is a potentially wide-ranging one that is intended to capture the different ways in which an individual might proactively articulate his religious convictions to others. The 'strength' with which these convictions are articulated has potential to vary greatly, both from individual to individual and from situation to situation. For example, a weaker form of articulation might involve an individual invoking God's blessing when serving a customer or offering to pray for a patient. Stronger forms might include speech 'in the prophetic tradition' to point out and rebuke the sin or immorality of a co-worker;[1] or making strong moral statements concerning, for example, abortion or homosexuality; or explaining religious doctrine or personal religious experience to a co-worker with a view to making a conversion of that individual (commonly known as proselytism).[2]

Active manifestation differs from negative manifestation, which is essentially reactive to the demands of an employer. An individual who finds that her religious convictions are compromised by either the timing or the nature of some of the work that she is required to do is essentially seeking an individual 'opt-out', which may have an effect on co-workers (e.g. by altering a shift rota to accommodate the objection) but such effect will be

---

1   C Evans, 'Religious Speech that Undermines Gender Equality' in I Hare and J Weinstein (eds) *Extreme Speech and Democracy* (Oxford: Oxford University Press, 2009) 366.

2   One writer specifically delineates between mild and strong forms of 'active manifestation' for analytical purposes, although he adopts the questionable terminology of 'passive harassment' and 'proselytisation'. The former is said to be 'indirect and does not occur in a targeted manner', which distinguishes it from the other form, which is presumably direct and targeted. See J Schopf, 'Religious Activity and Proselytization in the Workplace: The Murky Line Between Healthy Expression and Unlawful Harassment' (1997–1998) 31 *Columbia Journal of Law and Social Problems* 39, 45.

indirect. Active manifestation will usually be proactive,[3] with the individual directly and explicitly engaging his religious convictions vis-à-vis others. Active manifestation will often arise as a direct result of an individual's sincerely held belief that he or she is required by the doctrines of his or her faith 'to communicate religious faith to others, even if – in fact, perhaps precisely because – those truths disturb and unsettle those who hear them'.[4] For example, many Christians believe that Jesus' final words before the Ascension contain a continuing mandate for all Christians to witness to, and to attempt to convert, non-Christians:

> Go therefore and make disciples of all the nations, baptizing them in the name of the Father and of the Son and of the Holy Spirit, teaching them to observe all things that I have commanded you; and lo, I am with you always, even to the end of the age.[5]

Active manifestation also differs from passive manifestation in that the display of religious convictions in visual form certainly has the potential to make an impact on others. However, this impact is essentially generalised in character, the symbols or grooming bearing a witness to groups of people in general (such as colleagues and clients) – particular individuals are not specifically addressed[6] as they would tend to be when religious convictions are articulated verbally; equally, the impact of the symbol may be muted by its continued presence, whereas verbal articulation will tend to be briefer, more occasional and therefore of more immediate impact on others. As noted in the discussion in Chapter 5, active manifestation has the potential to be considered a form of harassment of those other actors in the workplace (such as co-workers), for whom being exposed to prose-lytism and other forms of active manifestation may create (or be claimed to create) a hostile environment. That said, if active manifestation is to be considered a form of harassment then it is helpful to apply a distinction between *animus* and *non-animus* harassment.[7] As the religious employee

---

3   Although, if the individual has been questioned about his beliefs by a colleague and responds, this could be reasonably characterised as, at least initially, reactive.

4   TC Berg, 'Religious speech in the workplace: harassment or protected speech?' (1998–1999) 22 *Harvard Journal of Law and Public Policy* 959, 964.

5   Matthew 28: 19–20. It should be noted that Muslims are confronted by a simi-lar scriptural injunction to preach and debate with non-Muslims to make converts (*Quran* 16: 125).

6   Although certain 'groups' may be disproportionately affected, e.g. Muslim schoolgirls when a school teacher wears a headscarf (see discussion in Chapter 7).

7   See DN Kaminer, 'When Religious Expression Creates a Hostile Work Environment: The Challenge of Balancing Competing Fundamental Rights' (2000) 4 *New York University Journal of Legislation and Public Policy* 139.

might be most fairly characterised as acting in the perceived best interests of others (rather than out of malign intent), then active manifestation conforms to the non-animus category. Although a benign (or 'non-animus') motivation does not mean that employees are necessarily protected from the disciplinary consequences of harassment, it is clearly a factor which weighs in the judicial process in the United States and has resulted in some judgments in favour of religious employees.[8] This is surely right, as there are two interests to consider – the freedom for some to avoid apparent 'harassment' on religious grounds but also the freedom for others to follow the dictates of their conscience. As a result, as Berg observes, '[a]lthough these proselytizing activities may offend others in the workplace, bans on such activities impose a serious burden on religious freedom and should be subject to exacting legal standards'.[9]

The purpose of this chapter is to explore active manifestation in the workplace and how the courts approach it, using the reference points, firstly, of the European Court of Human Rights jurisprudence and, secondly, workplace cases under religion and belief discrimination law (some of which have been settled out of court). The workplace cases are divided into three categories: (i) proselytism; (ii) religious speech short of proselytism (e.g. an offer to pray for others); and (iii) religious statements that are condemnatory of the actions or lifestyles of others (e.g. homosexuality). This is not to suggest that other examples of active manifestation might be added but the key cases (or publicised *cause-célèbres*) relate to these issues.

Article 9 case law

The European Court of Human Rights (ECtHR) has considered the legality of religious proselytism *per se*. A very significant case was *Kokkinakis* v. *Greece*,[10] which involved a challenge to a Greek law that prevented proselytism in most circumstances, particularly in relation to the vulnerable or where 'inducements' were offered. The case was brought by Mr Kokkinakis, who, alongside his wife, was a Jehovah's Witness. They had both visited the home of an orthodox Christian and Mr Kokkinakis had persauded her to allow them in. During the course of a subsequent discussion, he had tried to convert her. Mr and Mrs Kokkinakis were duly convicted of proselytism (Mrs Kokkinakis being acquitted on appeal). Mr Kokkinakis claimed before the ECtHR, *inter alia*, that his Article 9 freedoms had been violated by Greece.

Although the Greek law in question did not outlaw all forms of proselytism, the ECtHR helpfully addressed the question of whether or not

8   Ibid.
9   Berg, 'Religious speech in the workplace', 964.
10   (1993) 17 EHRR 397.

proselytism itself could be considered to be legitimate and determined that it could:

> First of all, a distinction has to be made between bearing Christian witness and improper proselytism. The former corresponds to true evangelism, which a report drawn up in 1956 under the auspices of the World Council of Churches describes as an essential mission and a responsibility of every Christian and every Church.[11]

This is an important statement, as it upholds the legitimacy of 'bearing witness' to others as an essential Christian duty at both a corporate and an individual level. The Court also explicitly concluded that 'bearing witness' can be considered a manifestation of religion and therefore falls under the protections of Article 9.[12] In so doing, it also argued that the act of witnessing to others was also justifiable on the basis that persuasion might be a necessary catalyst for an individual to exercise his freedom to change his religious beliefs (another fundamental freedom under Article 9 ECHR):

> According to Article 9 (art. 9), freedom to manifest one's religion is not only exercisable in community with others, 'in public' and within the circle of those whose faith one shares, but can also be asserted 'alone' and 'in private'; furthermore, it includes in principle the right to try to convince one's neighbour, for example through 'teaching', failing which, moreover, 'freedom to change [one's] religion or belief', enshrined in Article 9 (art. 9), would be likely to remain a dead letter.[13]

Thus, according to the Court's reasoning, the right to 'bear witness' (or engage in 'true evangelism') is both a manifestation of an individual believer's religion and also necessary to non-believers and other-believers because, without it, the Article 9 rights of the latter groups (allowing the opportunity to change religion) would not be fully exercisable.

The actual aim of the disputed Greek law was, however, upheld. Seeking to restrain 'improper proselytism' to 'protect the rights and freedoms of others' was considered by the ECtHR to be an appropriate purpose for national governments.[14] In this case, however, the Greek courts had failed to specify in what way Mr Kokkinakis had behaved 'improperly' and neither did the facts support that finding.

The ECtHR has therefore categorised proselytism in two ways – 'proper' and 'improper', respectively, and only the first category enjoys full

---

11   Ibid. [48].
12   Ibid. [31].
13   Ibid. [31].
14   Ibid. [44].

protection as a manifestation of religion.[15] The Court did give some guidance on what might constitute improper proselytism:

> The latter represents a corruption or deformation of it. It may, according to the same report, take the form of activities offering material or social advantages with a view to gaining new members for a Church or exerting improper pressure on people in distress or in need; it may even entail the use of violence or brainwashing; more generally, it is not compatible with respect for the freedom of thought, conscience and religion of others.[16]

This guidance is useful to a certain extent – it suggests that proselytism will be improper when it involves bribing or pressurising people in vulnerable situations. However, as it is couched in generalised terms, it can rightly be criticised as leaving 'too much room for a repressive interpretation' and more precise and specific definition by the Court would have been helpful.[17] However, this is no easy task.[18]

Another and subsequent case, again involving a challenge to the same Greek law, *Larissis and others* v. *Greece*, directly relates to employment, albeit to the very specific employment context of the military. In this case a group of airforce officers who were Pentecostal Christians were convicted of seeking to convert to the Christian faith some amongst the junior ranks who were under their command, by repeatedly inviting them to church and by initiating discussions on religious matters. They applied to the Court on the basis of an interference with Article 9.

The Court agreed with the applicants that their convictions for proselytism amounted to interferences with the exercise of their rights to manifest their religion but it found that such interference was justified. Although there was no 'evidence that the applicants used threats or inducements',[19] the Court nevertheless considered that the activities of the officers involved improper proselytism. In so determining, it focused on the imbalance of power between the officers and the airmen in the context of 'military life':

15 A Hambler, 'A Private Matter? Evolving Approaches to the Freedom to Manifest Religious Convictions in the Workplace' (2008) 3 *Religion and Human Rights* 127.
16 *Kokkinakis* v. *Greece* [48].
17 Ibid. (partially dissenting opinion of Judge Pettiti).
18 For an attempt to provide more specific guidelines see T Stahnke, 'Proselytism and the Freedom to Change Religion in International Human Rights Law' (1999) 251 *Brigham Young University Law Review* 252–353. The author argues that 'whether an act of proselytism is improperly coercive will depend upon the characteristic of the source, the characteristics of the target, the place where the act takes place and the nature of the target itself.' (343).
19 *Larissis and others* v. *Greece* (1999) 27 EHRR 329 [52].

In this respect, the Court notes that the hierarchical structures which are a feature of life in the armed forces may colour every aspect of the relations between military personnel, making it difficult for a subordinate to rebuff the approaches of an individual of superior rank or to withdraw from a conversation initiated by him. Thus, what would in the civilian world be seen as an innocuous exchange of ideas which the recipient is free to accept or reject, may, within the confines of military life, be viewed as a form of harassment or the application of undue pressure in abuse of power.[20]

As Evans put it: '[s]uch cases raise complex issues of competing rights, where it is not clear why one set of rights should take precedence over another'.[21] In this case, the sense of obligation to promote Christian beliefs felt by the Pentecostal officers, irrespective of the military environment, was clearly subordinated by a national government to the rights of non-religious (or other-religious) airmen to be free of proselytism. It could also be argued that other rights of the airmen had been infringed as, by the Court's own reasoning in *Kokkinakis*, an absence of proselytism may have a negative impact on the right to change religion.

The decision in this case is clearly intended to have an application to the military environment only, with its 'hierarchical structures' and given the nature of the power differentials between officers and other ranks. However, it is difficult to accept the implication that the civilian world is entirely different. In most employment contexts, for example, hierarchy and power differentials exist and may affect relationships between employees of different levels of seniority, albeit not necessarily to the same degree as in military organisations. It might, for example, be 'difficult', in the words of the Court, for a junior employee 'to rebuff the approaches' of a manager 'or withdraw from a conversation initiated by him'. Indeed, the significance of organisational hierarchy in claims for religious harassment (because of unwelcome proselytism) has been recognised in the civilian workplace in the United States. For example, in *Chalmers* v. *Tulon Co*,[22] a court stated that an employee's supervisory position heightened the possibility that her religious speech could create a hostile work environment for more junior employees. There remains, therefore, a question as to how far the reasoning in *Kokkinakis* might, in fact, be applicable beyond the military employment context into a civilian employment context as this has yet to be tested.

20   Ibid. [51].
21   C Evans, *Freedom of Religion under the European Convention on Human Rights* (Oxford: Oxford University Press, 2000), 164.
22   101 F.3d 1012, 1021 (4th Cir. 1996).

Employment discrimination cases

Proselytism

Case law in the UK concerning this form of manifestation is at an early stage. There is only one relevant case which has gone beyond the initial tribunal level: *Chondol v. Liverpool City Council*.[23] In this case, a social worker contested the decision of his employer to dismiss him on the basis, *inter alia*, that he inappropriately promoted his religious beliefs to 'service users'. This charge related to two instances: in the first, Chondol apparently gave a Bible to a service user; in the second, he appeared to have engaged in a conversation with a different service user in which, according to a subsequent complaint, 'he was talking about God and church and crap like that'.[24] These incidents took place in 2006.

Chondol was dismissed, following a disciplinary investigation, on 24 May 2007.[25] He subsequently brought proceedings before an employment tribunal for unfair dismissal and religious discrimination. The tribunal rejected his claims and the Employment Appeals Tribunal upheld that finding.

The Appeals Tribunal found that Chondol was 'aware that the Council prohibited the overt promotion by social workers in the course of their work of any religious beliefs that they might hold'.[26] It also appeared to be common ground between the parties that this restriction amounted to a reasonable management instruction. Thus, Chondol did not dispute that his employer was entitled to discipline him for sharing his religious views with clients. Chondol's defence, in respect of the first incident, was that he had provided a Bible in response to a specific request and that, regarding the second incident, he had simply asked the question as to whether or not the service-user believed in God or went to church.[27] The employment tribunal (endorsed by the Employment Appeals Tribunal) clearly found this explanation insufficient and determined that he was fairly dismissed for 'improperly foisting [his beliefs] on service users' rather than for holding those beliefs himself.[28]

The rationale for the prohibition on 'promoting' religious belief is found in Chondol's dismissal letter:

> [W]hile undoubtedly religious beliefs can potentially be an important factor in an individual's life, this is not the case for everyone. A social worker acting in a professional capacity should not be placing an emphasis on religious beliefs that is out of proportion to a consideration of the

---

23   (2009) EAT/0298/08.
24   Ibid. [9].
25   Ibid. [1].
26   Ibid. [8].
27   Ibid. [10].
28   Ibid. [23].

many other factors that impinge on an individual's wellbeing. An over emphasis on religion could cause distress to service users who are already in a fragile mental state.[29]

No internal policy document was presented as an exhibit in support of this stance; neither was any reference made to the social workers' professional code of practice.[30] This latter document, in its current form, does not, in fact, offer any specific guidance on religious expression and provides rather generalised guidelines only to the effect that a social worker 'must protect the rights and promote the interests of service users and carers', which, *inter alia*, involves '[r]especting diversity and different cultures and values'.[31]

It is interesting that the position adopted in the dismissal letter was never challenged. Not only would the letter itself appear to be an example of policy making on the hoof (and thus procedurally unfair, particularly in a situation involving a conduct dismissal), the content of the letter may be considered objectionable as it requires that social workers suppress any sense of obligation to share their faith with those they meet, even by apparently 'light touch' means (such as offering to give someone a Bible). It is seemingly taken as a given in this case that sharing religious beliefs, even in tactful and sensitive ways, is liable to cause 'distress' to others and impinge on their rights to avoid religious discourse.[32]

Another case, which was not subject to an appeal hearing, concerned an ex-employee of the Young Men's Christian Association, Monaghan, who had been dismissed from his job as a temporary manager for proselytism, having ignored an instruction from his manager 'that he should not try to convert people to the Christian faith' as he 'did not want the people who the respondent served being subjected to attempts to convert them'. He claimed, *inter alia*, direct discrimination on the grounds of religion and belief.[33] As this was a direct discrimination claim, the tribunal considered the issue of a comparator and found that the manager's attitude would have been the same regardless of an employee's religious beliefs. As a result, Monaghan had not been discriminated against because he was a Christian *per se*, as his manager would have taken the same action had he

29   Ibid. [16].
30   For the current version of the code, see General Social Care Council, *Codes of Practice for Social Care Workers* (2010). Available online at www.fassit.co.uk/pdf/ CodesofPracticeforSocialCareWorkers.pdf (accessed 9 June 2014).
31   Ibid., 6.
32   In a case with parallels to *Chondol*, a nursery manager unsuccessfully appealed her dismissal for 'harassment' of staff by discussing her religious beliefs in the context of an unofficial training session; see *Grace* v. *Places for Children* (2013) UKEAT/0217/13.
33   *Monaghan* v. *Leicester Young Men's Christian Association* (2004) ET Case No. 1901830/04

attempted to convert people to other religions. As the tribunal put it: '[t]he grounds were not the religion or belief of the claimant, but the fact that he was trying to convert people which was against the principles of the respondent'.[34] Monaghan therefore lost his direct discrimination claim.

Monaghan and *Chondol* involved claims for direct religious discrimination and these were given short shrift for the reasons noted. With hindsight, it is surprising that the claimants did not also bring claims for indirect discrimination, which would have required the employer to demonstrate the proportionality of imposing a requirement which had an adverse impact on Christians.

Both direct and indirect discrimination claims were, however, brought in similar circumstances in *Amachree* v. *Wandsworth Borough Council*. In this case, a homelessness housing officer, Duke Amachree, brought a complaint of discrimination and unfair dismissal following the termination of his job at Wandsworth Borough Council. A disciplinary investigation leading to his eventual dismissal followed from a complaint by a 'service user' in January 2009, who was seeking housing advice and was interviewed by Amachree. The tribunal referred to her as 'Ms X'.[35] During the course of the interview, Ms X revealed that she had a chronic illness and needed to live near a hospital as a result. According to the complaint by Ms X, Amachree then 'proceeded to give [her] a half-hour lecture on the fact that there was no such thing as incurable illness, doctors should never be trusted, that [her] problem was that [she] did not have God or faith in [her] life and so was ill as a result'.[36] This left her feeling 'shocked' and 'upset'.[37] Amachree's own account was softer in tone but not materially different in substance, except that his recollection was of a much shorter conversation.[38]

The Council took the view that this alleged conversation was a serious offence under the relevant disciplinary code such that Amachree might be summarily dismissed and suspended him pending investigation.[39] It was, however, later pointed out before the employment tribunal that there was no actual written policy or guidance about raising religious (or any other) issues with service users[40] and, indeed, no guidance of this kind was produced in evidence by the respondent. This is arguably an important point which was worthy of greater consideration by the tribunal than it received. As Berg points out, where employers have no clear overarching 'content-neutral' policy concerning employee speech, then 'a danger exists

34   Ibid. [28].
35   *Amachree* v. *Wandsworth Borough Council* (2009) ET Case No. 2328606/2009 [12].
36   Ibid. [13].
37   Ibid.
38   Ibid. [14].
39   Ibid. [15].
40   Ibid. [31(1)].

than the employer's restriction of speech will be selective' (i.e. more likely to be punitive in the case of religious speech than other forms of speech).[41] This argument might have been put (and considered) more strongly than was the case. Equally, it could be argued that the absence of clear employee guidelines should substantially increase the burden on the employer to show that gross misconduct was a reasonable finding on investigation, as the employee was patently not engaging in activity that was expressly forbidden.

Amachree was supported by the Christian Legal Centre,[42] which provided a solicitor to accompany him to his internal disciplinary hearings. During the course of one of these hearings, the solicitor asked two pertinent questions designed to probe the extent of the application of the apparent policy: firstly, would there be a problem manifesting a belief 'physically' (giving the example of a turban)?; and, secondly, would it be acceptable to say 'God bless' as a valedictory greeting? No response to the first question is recorded in the judgment but the response to the second was that it would not be appropriate.[43]

Following this meeting, and with Amachree's consent, the Christian Legal Centre issued a somewhat inflammatory press release, headed: 'London Homelessness Prevention Officer told "say God bless" and we'll sack you'.[44] The press release itself contained information about Ms X, including the fact she was homeless and had a chronic health condition. Further newspaper articles, for which Amachree was thought to have been a key source, provided more information about the woman's age, health condition and occupation, to the point where she could be identified by at least one person who knew her father.[45] What this meant for Amachree, still at this stage an employee, was that the employer had a much more powerful case for his dismissal, this time on the grounds of breach of the confidentiality which a service user was entitled to expect.[46]

---

41   Berg, 'Religious speech in the workplace', 982.
42   *Case Summaries*, Christian Legal Centre (Spring 2012), 19. Available online at www.christianconcern.com/sites/default/files/docs/ChristianLegalCentre-Case-Summaries.pdf (accessed 9 June 2014).
43   *Amachree* [18].
44   Ibid. [19]. The press release is found in full at Christian Concern, 'London Homelessness Prevention Officer Told Say God Bless and We'll Sack You' (29 March 2009). Available online at www.christianconcern.com/press-release/clc-case-say-god-bless-and-well-sack-you (accessed 9 June 2014).
45   Ibid. [19]. The judgment records that officials at the council were also quoted anonymously in newspaper articles and gave comments which could be construed as biased against Amachree; see, for example, E Andrews, 'Council Worker Suspended for Talking to Terminally Ill Client About God', *Daily Mail* (London, 30 March 2009). Available online at www.dailymail.co.uk/news/article-1165633/Council-worker-suspended-talking-terminally-ill-client-God.html (accessed 9 June 2014).
46   *Amachree* [24].

At length, Amachree was dismissed on two counts of gross misconduct: the original incident itself and the subsequent breach of Ms X's confidentiality.[47] At the employment tribunal, Amachree claimed direct and indirect discrimination and unfair dismissal. The direct discrimination claim was unsuccessful on the familiar grounds that the employer had not penalised Amachree because of his religious beliefs but because of his actions. This was, of course, predictable in the light of preceding cases, particularly *Chondol.* The claim for indirect discrimination was, however, made imaginatively, including the submission that for the Council to instigate a policy prohibiting religious discussion amounted to a provision, criterion or practice which had an adverse impact on Christians, putting them at a particular disadvantage compared to people of other religious faiths, agnostics or atheists. The rationale for this contention was that Christians are uniquely required, by virtue of their faith, to 'live out' their religious beliefs 'in both word and deed'.[48]

This argument was dismissed by the tribunal on the basis that other religions required a similar commitment by followers live their lives in conformity to religious teachings. This is, of course, a reasonable conclusion and, with hindsight, it is perhaps regrettable that the claimant's case that he was obliged to 'live out' his faith was constructed so widely, rather than focusing on a more specific Christian obligation to 'bear witness' verbally to others. It should be noted, however, that the tribunal did consider this possibility, although not asked to do so, and opined that a narrower rule preventing proselytism would also adversely affect other religions in the same way.[49] This point is, of course, contentious but the relevant arguments were not raised. This is a pity because there is an argument that Christians, for whom there are no mandatory religious dress or grooming requirements, receive little benefit from religious accommodations by employers which relate to dress and grooming only.[50] Instead, they may feel mandated to articulate their beliefs to others verbally. Although the rules were not expressly set out in policy terms in this case, it is apparent from the responses to questions by the Christian Legal Centre's solicitor that Wandsworth Borough Council's emergent policy prevented verbal rather than visual expression. This suggests that the policy could indeed be construed as having a differential adverse impact on Christians vis-à-vis people of other faiths, contrary to the reasoning of the tribunal. However, this would only meet the first part of the test for indirect discrimination. The

---

47 Ibid. [30].
48 Ibid. [47].
49 Ibid. [168].
50 This point was made in oral argument in *Eweida and Ors.* Some Christians, of course, do feel convicted to wear religious symbols (see discussion in Chapter 7) but as there is no convincing religious mandate to do so it is likely that such Christians represent a small proportion of the total.

second is, of course, the employer's justification. In this case, the tribunal argued that Wandsworth would in any event be able to justify its position as a proportionate means of achieving a legitimate aim. As it stated:

> Further, if there were any evidence of disparate impact, it was the tribunal's assessment that ... a practice of not allowing the discussion of irrelevant matters at interviews was legitimate – namely to ensure that a professional, focused, efficient and cost-effective service was delivered to members of the public – and that this was achieved by the proportionate means of preventing staff from straying off the relevant subject matter.[51]

The claim for unfair dismissal also failed but this was chiefly a result of the breach of confidentiality, the tribunal expressing doubts as to whether or not to dismiss Amachree on the sole basis of his remarks to Ms X would meet the test of reasonableness.[52] This is a highly significant point, suggesting that, if discrimination law cannot provide protection to individuals dismissed for verbally articulating their religious convictions, there remains the possibility that the unfair dismissal protections of the Employment Rights Act might.[53] If this were to be adopted as a standard by a higher court, it would also suggest that employers may be limited in how far they can go in reacting to verbal religious expression, even in situations involving clients. It may be, for example, that a warning is considered to be more proportionate than a summary dismissal.[54] It is also rather salutatory to note that Amachree and his advisers were, with hindsight, unwise in the decision to put the case in the media spotlight, at least in the way that this was done, presumably with the intention of putting pressure on Wandsworth Borough Council to drop their disciplinary proceedings – a tactic which backfired to the extent of providing a basis for his dismissal which the tribunal considered to be well within the employer's band of reasonable responses.[55]

---

51   *Amachree* [168].
52   *Amachree* [136].
53   Although, as it will be recalled from *Copsey* v. *Devon Clays Limited* [2005] EWCA Civ. 932, Article 9 ECHR is still not engaged in the event of a dismissal; thus, any protection derives from the Employment Rights Act 1996 (Part X) alone (see Chapter 5).
54   This point was also made by a bank nurse who felt that his employer had overreacted by ending his contract, rather than merely offering him corrective advice, as a result of a brief training simulation where he advised 'patients' to pray; see A Alderson, 'Nurse Loses Job After Urging Patients to Find God During a Training Course', *Daily Telegraph* (London, 23 May 2009). Available online at www.telegraph.co.uk/news/religion/5373122/Nurse-loses-job-after-urging-patients-to-find-God-during-a-training-course.html (accessed 9 June 2014).
55   Per the test established in *BHS Stores* v. *Burchell* [1980] ICR 303.

As noted in Chapter 5, professional employment is governed by regulation as well as employment law and the case of Dr Richard Scott involved the alleged contravention of the latter, established by the General Medical Council (GMC).[56] Scott was one of six Christian partners in Bethesda Medical Centre, a general medical practice in Kent. The Christian character of the practice and its bearing on the service patients are likely to receive is clear from its stated aims, publicised on its website:

> The six partners are all practising Christians from a variety of churches and their faith guides the way in which they view their work and responsibilities to the patients and employees. The Partners feel that the offer of talking to you on spiritual matters is of great benefit.[57]

Further text advises that patients can 'opt-out' of such discussions about faith issues and explains how this can be done.

In 2011, a complaint to the GMC that he was 'pushing religion' was brought against Dr Scott by the mother of a 24-year-old patient (but on his behalf). Dr Scott had reportedly told the patient that '[he] had something to offer [the patient] which would cure him for good and that this was his one and only hope in recovery' and that 'his own religion could not offer him any protection and that no other religion in the world could offer [the patient] what Jesus could offer him'.[58] Following an investigatory hearing, Dr Scott was given a formal warning for failing to meet the standards expected of a doctor, having 'sought to impose [his] own beliefs on [his] patient [and] thereby caused the patient distress through insensitive expression of [ ] religious beliefs'.[59]

The case is interesting in two ways. The first is the conclusion reached by the GMC, that Dr Scott was in breach of professional guidelines by discussing his religious beliefs with his patient. The relevant section in the GMC's binding guidance on good practice (which was then in force) relating to a doctor's religion and belief stated that: 'You must not express to your patients your personal beliefs, including political, religious or moral beliefs, in ways that exploit their vulnerability or that are likely to cause them distress'.[60] Supplementary guidance offered slightly more detail:

---

56 The GMC is empowered to issue guidance on 'conduct, performance and ethics' and to investigate complaints of non-compliance under the Medical Act 1983, s 35.

57 Bethesda Medical Centre, 'Our Ethos'. Available online at www.bethesdamc.co.uk/about_us.html (accessed 9 June 2014).

58 General Medical Council, Dr Richard Scott Investigation Committee Decision (14 June 2012). Available online at www.gmc-uk.org/news/13333.asp (accessed 9 June 2014). The precise phrasing was a matter of dispute.

59 Ibid.

60 General Medical Council, *Good Medical Practice: Maintaining Trust in the Profession* (13 November 2006) [33].

> You should not normally discuss your personal beliefs with patients unless those beliefs are directly relevant to the patient's care. You must not impose your beliefs on patients, or cause distress by the inappropriate or insensitive expression of religious, political or other beliefs or views. Equally, you must not put pressure on patients to discuss or justify their beliefs (or the absence of them).[61]

The problem in this case is one of interpretation. The guidelines are clearly not rigid; if they were, there would be an explicit prohibition on discussions involving a medical practitioner's religious beliefs. Instead, the guidelines appear to allow scope for such discussions. Indeed, the guidelines were broadly welcomed by the Christian Medical Fellowship, at the time of drafting, on the basis that there was an implicit recognition in the guidelines that expressing religious beliefs can be considered legitimate:

> We support the view ... that doctors should not 'impose' their beliefs, and likewise that there should not be 'inappropriate ... expression' of them. But the use of the word 'inappropriate' means that there must be possible [sic] an expression of beliefs which is 'appropriate'. We are glad the GMC recognises this.[62]

Whilst the restrictions on doctors expressing their beliefs are not definitive, they clearly revolve around concepts such as the apparent vulnerability of patients, the sensitivity with which a doctor expresses her beliefs and the relevance of these beliefs to patient care. The latter is particularly problematic, as a Christian doctor might see what she believes to be Christian truths as highly relevant to an individual patient's health and wellbeing (perhaps particularly mental health) in a way that others might not. This would appear, *prima facie*, to leave a large degree of discretion to individual practitioners. Dr Scott's interpretation of his actions was that they were within the margins afforded to him by the guidance and he would appear to have a reasonable basis for this belief; the GMC apparently differed.[63]

---

61   General Medical Council, *Personal Beliefs and Medical Practice* (March 2008) [19].

62   Christian Medical Fellowship, 'An Online Submission from the Christian Medical Fellowship to Personal Beliefs and Medical Practice – GMC Consultation' (25 September 2007). Available online at www.cmf.org.uk/ publicpolicy/submissions/?id=47 (accessed 9 June 2014).

63   Some of this ambiguity was (arguably) removed (but in a manner further restrictive of a doctor's freedom of religious expression) by the publication by the GMC of amended guidance in 2013, which states: 'You may talk about your own personal beliefs only if a patient asks you directly about them, or indicates they would welcome such a discussion'; see General Medical Council, *Personal Beliefs and Medical Practice* (25 March 2013) [31]. Available online at www.gmc-uk.org/ guidance/ethical_guidance/21171.asp (accessed 9 June 2014).

The second issue follows from the first. The interpretation of the relevant guidance by the GMC in Dr Scott's case was certainly a restrictive one, to the point where it seems difficult to envisage how the Bethesda Medical Centre would be able to continue to act upon its aim of talking to patients about spiritual matters (unless the patients choose to 'opt-out' of this). Among the religious liberty issues at stake here is the notional right of individuals to group together into islands of exclusivity – here, for Christian doctors to work together to provide what they regard as a Christian medical service to the community. This right, in its fullest form, is significantly curtailed if they are prevented from articulating their Christian beliefs, and the value of these, to patients.

Religious speech short of proselytism

The Scott case relates to a form of proselytism, a proactive sharing of religious convictions with patients. As discussed in the introduction, there are other forms of active manifestation in the workplace. Employees may, for example, wish to invoke God's blessing when dealing with others,[64] or they may wish to pray for others. How far making an offer to pray for someone during the course of employment leads to the risk of disciplinary action was illustrated in the case of a Christian nurse, Caroline Petrie, who was suspended from her work as a community bank nurse at North Somerset Primary Care Trust following complaints that she had offered to pray for an elderly patient after visiting her home. She was suspended pending investigation for misconduct by the Trust on the basis that she had failed to meet her obligations in respect of equality and diversity under the Nursing and Midwifery Council (NMC) code.[65] This was apparently the second incident in which Petrie had been accused of transgressing the code – a year earlier she had been reprimanded for handing a prayer card to a patient.[66] The NMC code is much briefer than the GMC equivalent. There are two relevant sections. The first states that the nurse 'must demonstrate a personal and professional commitment to equality and diversity'.[67] Quite what is meant by 'equality and diversity' is left unexplained. Perhaps more problematically still, whatever it means, nurses are apparently required to demonstrate both a 'personal' and a 'professional' commitment to it. Whilst the latter might be unsurprising, representing the public attitude of the nurse, the former is

64   For example, in a US case, two employees sued their employer following their dismissals for saying 'Praise the Lord' and 'God bless you' to customers; see *Banks* v. *Service America Corp.*, 952 F. Supp. 703 (D. Kan. 1996).

65   Alderson, 'Nurse is suspended for offering to pray for a patient', 5.

66   Ibid.

67   Nursing and Midwifery Council, *The Code: Standards of Conduct, Performance and Ethics for Nurses and Midwives* (1 May 2008), s 48. Available online at www.nmc-uk.org/Publications/Standards/The-code/Introduction (accessed 9 June 2014).

more troubling as it appears to transgress into the *forum internum* – the private and personal beliefs and convictions of an individual. It is submitted that this is likely to contravene the European Convention on Human Rights and Fundamental Freedoms (ECHR).[68] The second relevant section states that the nurse must not use his or her 'professional status to promote causes that are not related to health'.[69] In its plain meaning, this certainly may be interpreted as preventing straightforward 'proselytism' (i.e. seeking to convert others to a religious belief). Such a prohibition seems in keeping also with the spirit of rather poorly written guidelines intended to have general effect amongst National Health Service (NHS) employees (albeit that they confusingly conflate together proselytism, religious discussions and religiously motivated comments about sexual orientation):

> Members of some religions, including Mormons, Jehovah's Witnesses, evangelical Christians and Muslims, are expected to preach and to try to convert other people. In a workplace environment this can cause many problems, as non-religious people and those from other religions or beliefs could feel harassed and intimidated by this behaviour. This is especially the case when particular views on matters such as sexual orientation, gender and single parents are aired in a workplace environment, potentially causing great offence to other workers or indeed patients or visitors who are within hearing. To avoid misunderstandings and complaints on this issue, it should be made clear to everyone from the first day of training and/or employment, and regularly restated, that such behaviour, notwithstanding religious beliefs, could be construed as harassment under the disciplinary and grievance procedures.[70]

However, it is difficult to see how Petrie's offer of prayer, by comparison to proselytism a relatively unobtrusive expression of religious belief, can be said to fall within the definitions of either 'promotion' of her beliefs (under the NMC guidelines) or of proselytism (under the wider NHS guidelines), except by a very broad and creative construction by her managers.

Petrie's case was taken up by the Christian Legal Centre and given widespread publicity.[71] At length, Petrie was reinstated by the Trust, which

---

68   See discussion in Chapter 4.
69   Nursing and Midwifery Council, *The Code: Standards of Conduct, Performance and Ethics for Nurses and Midwives* [59].
70   Department of Health, Equality and Human Rights Group, *Religion or Belief: A Practical Guide for the NHS* (Department of Health, January 2009), 22. Available online at www.clatterbridgecc.nhs.uk/document_uploads/Equalityand Diversity/ReligionorbeliefApracticalguidefortheNHS.pdf (accessed 9 June 2014).
71   See Christian Concern, 'Caroline Petrie'. Available online at www.christianconcern.com/cases/caroline-petrie (accessed 9 June 2014). On this occasion personal details about the patient who complained were not made public.

issued a statement that it now recognised that '[i]t is acceptable to offer spiritual support as part of care when the patient asks for it'.[72] This represented some movement away from absolute hostility to verbal religious expression but was still too restrictive for Petrie and, by extension, others with similar beliefs. As Petrie reportedly said, 'I cannot divide my faith from my nursing care'.[73]

Although Petrie herself was unwilling to separate her work from her religious convictions, however, some recent research into the 'identities' of student nursing staff with religious convictions suggests that many others, perhaps particularly those being inducted into the NHS culture, have felt forced into implementing just such a divide between their professional and private selves. The authors of the research concluded:

> In the hospital, they put on a front which was professionally acceptable by concealing the religious beliefs that they perceived as a possible cause of conflicts between values ... the students were able to return to their 'true' identity as religious people when they joined fellow believers in their Sunday congregations.[74]

It may be that a combination of specific policy, and also the 'chilling effect' of cases like that involving Caroline Petrie, have resulted in a reluctance by some religious employees to make their faith convictions known in workplaces like the NHS.

There is some further evidence that 'verbal' religious expression even in its mildest form is unwelcome in some parts of the NHS. This is illustrated by the outcome of *Drew* v. *Walsall NHS Healthcare Trust*.[75] Although this was a complex case of unfair dismissal involving a range of issues beyond unwelcome religious expression, the claimant, a consultant paediatrician, was in fact finally dismissed after refusing to accept that part of an independent report into various grievances and counter-grievances in which he was involved, that he should 'refrain from using religious references in his professional communication, verbal or written'.[76]

However, the examples of such 'religious references' are somewhat mild. For example, the Employment Appeals Tribunal judgment records a quotation from an email written by Dr Drew: "I know you have looked at DM

---

72   C Gammell, 'Nurse Caroline Petrie: I will continue praying for patients' *Daily Telegraph* (London, 7 February 2009). Available online at www.telegraph.co.uk/news/religion/4537452/Nurse-Caroline-Petrie-I-will-continue-praying-for-patients.html (accessed 9 June 2014).

73   Ibid.

74   S Timmons and A Narayanasamy, 'How do Religious People Navigate a Secular Organisation? Religious Nursing Students in the British National Health Service' (2011) 26 *Journal of Contemporary Religion* 451, 462.

75   (2013) UKEAT/0378/12.

76   Ibid. [16].

before and interviewed him. *"mene mene telel uparsin"* [sic] (Daniel Chapter V as I remember it)'.[77] Similarly, the judgment records that Dr Drew circulated a prayer by Ignatius Loyola to colleagues, describing it as a source of 'personal inspiration' in his efforts to serve his patients.[78] These examples appear to be fairly typical of the supposed religious language of Dr Drew and it does seem difficult not to agree with Dr Drew's own assessment of his conduct: 'I am not a fanatic. I am not a proselytiser. My purpose is purely expressive and not religious at all'.[79]

Despite the contextual factor of the troubled employment relationship, it is rather concerning, from the perspective of religious freedom of expression, that an individual's refusal to refrain from using moderate religious language (without conscious intention of proselytism) should be the final cause of his dismissal. Nevertheless, the Employment Appeals Tribunal declined to set aside the decision of the tribunal that there was no direct discrimination on the basis that a hypothetical claimant from a different religious background (or non-religious background) would have been treated in the same way in comparable circumstances. As in both *Monaghan* and *Chondol*, it is perhaps unfortunate that Dr Drew did not claim indirect discrimination, which would have required rather more sophisticated reasoning by both the employment tribunal and the Employment Appeals Tribunal in their respective disposals of the claim.

Active expression and sexual orientation

As noted in the NHS guidelines, it is recognised that some employees may 'actively manifest' their religious beliefs by expressing a critical view of aspects of some people's lifestyles or conduct. This may be directed specifically to other actors in the workplace (for example, by sending letters to fellow employees pointing out particular sins they were thought to be committing).[80] Alternatively, it may be generalised but might offend particular groups of people (such as supporters of termination of pregnancy).[81] Most interest in public discourse has been where religious views are expressed which are critical of homosexuality. Such views are almost

---

77 Ibid. [23].
78 Ibid. [8].
79 Ibid. [18].
80 Per the facts of the US case, *Chalmers* v. *Tulon Company*, 101 F.3d 1012, 1021 (4th Cir. 1996).
81 For example, a Roman Catholic health worker was reportedly suspended from Central North West London Mental Health Trust for handing out a booklet critical of abortion to colleagues; see T Ross, 'Defiant Christian health worker refuses to stop handing out anti-abortion book' *Daily Telegraph* (London, 22 December 2010). Available online at www.telegraph.co.uk/news/uknews/8220299/Defiant-Christian-health-worker-refuses-to-stop-handing-out-anti-abortion-book.html (accessed 9 June 2014).

invariably labelled 'homophobic' and, outside the workplace sphere, even mildly critical views have triggered police investigations in response to complaints of 'homophobic hate speech'.[82] Within the workplace itself, workers are protected from harassment under the protected characteristic of sexual orientation.[83] However, the right to be critical of homosexual behaviour is also an aspect of religious expression and, as such, is likely to fall within the notional protections for the protected characteristic of religion and belief. In consequence, there are competing rights at play.[84] It would appear from the cases which follow in this section that a likely outcome is that sexual orientation rights are generally to be preferred over religious expression and thus 'homophobic speech' is likely to be forbidden in most workplaces (e.g. the NHS), certainly those with discrimination or harassment policies in place. Quite how 'homophobic speech' is defined and with what enthusiasm it is punished are, of course, different questions.

In an early case under the 2003 Religion and Belief Regulations, Apelogun Gabriels, who had worked for the London Borough of Lambeth,[85] claimed that his dismissal for distributing 'homophobic material' to co-workers was unfair.[86] He also claimed, *inter alia*, direct and indirect religious discrimination. Gabriels was a lay preacher and he also organised prayer meetings for Christian staff, which were held (by permission) on council premises. During one such prayer meeting, Gabriels presented a handout to participants which contained verses which he had selected from the Bible that were critical of homosexual activity. The handouts were also shared with a small number of co-workers who were not members of the prayer group and were seen by some other staff members who, finding them offensive on the grounds of sexual orientation, made an official complaint. Following this complaint, Gabriels was subject to the disciplinary process and was, at length, dismissed for reasons of gross misconduct.

It is unsurprising that Gabriels was disciplined, given that he allowed material which was offensive on the grounds of sexual orientation to be promulgated, quite unnecessarily, outside of the prayer group forum. Nevertheless, the decision to dismiss him may have been unduly harsh. The

---

82 For example, the writer Lynette Burrows was questioned by police (investigating a reported 'homophobic incident') after she said on a radio programme that gay men might not be suitable to adopt children; see S Pook, 'Police warn author over gay comments' *Daily Telegraph* (London, 10 December 2005), 2. Available online at www.telegraph.co.uk/news/uknews/1505143/Police-warn-author-over-gay-comments.html (accessed 9 June 2014).

83 As discussed in Chapter 5.

84 See I Leigh, 'Homophobic Speech, Equality Denial, and Religious Expression' in Ivan Hare and James Weinstein (eds), *Extreme Speech and Democracy* (Oxford: Oxford University Press, 2009), 375–99.

85 *Apelogun Gabriels* v. *London Borough of Lambeth* (2006) ET Case No. 2301976/05.

86 Ibid. [3].

material he circulated was not targeted against particular co-workers and, although apparently rather careless, it was not suggested that he deliberately handed the material to people who he expected to be offended by it.

Whilst both the employer and, subsequently, the tribunal took seriously the right of gay and lesbian staff to be free from harassment, both appeared to take the competing claim – the right of a Christian employee to quote Bible verses – rather less seriously, to the extent that this right barely weighed at all in the decision-making process. Indeed, the tribunal appeared to have difficulty with the Bible itself, commenting, 'the Tribunal considered the wording of the selected extracts from the Bible involved to be uncompromising and strongly condemnatory of homosexual conduct'.[87] As it is not easy to find references to homosexuality within the plain meaning of the Bible that are not in some way 'uncompromising and strongly condemnatory', it is difficult quite to see what the tribunal was driving at here, except unwisely to do what in effect the Court of Appeal in *Amicus* v. *Secretary of State for Trade and Industry* refused to do and to seek to exclude 'homophobic verses' of the Bible from acceptable discourse.[88]

It may be that tribunals should more sensitive to Lord Walker's guidance that 'in matters of human rights, the court should not show liberal tolerance only to tolerant liberals'[89] and appreciate that religious views (for example, about homosexuality), which many people consider to be beyond the pale, find a basis in a legitimate understanding of sacred texts. This is not to suggest that religious employees should have *carte blanche* to air these views whenever they wish in the workplace. However, the mere fact that these views are expressed should not tilt the outcome of a disciplinary investigation or a tribunal hearing before other factors are taken into consideration.[90] There is a strong hint of this in the *Apelogun Gabriels* decision.[91]

---

87   Ibid. [9].

88   *R (Amicus MSF Section)* v. *Secretary of State for Trade and Industry* [2004] EWHC 860 (Admin); [2004] IRLR 430. The tribunal did not go as far as some courts have gone in condemning the quotation of biblical texts that are condemnatory of homosexuality; see, for example, Judge Barclay's observation that 'the Biblical passage which suggest that if a man lies with a man they must be put to death exposes homosexuals to hatred' in the Canadian case, *Owens* v. *Saskatchewan Human Rights Commission* (2002) SKQB 506 (CanLII) [21].

89   *Williamson* v. *Secretary of State for Education and Employment* [2002] EWCA Civ. 1926; [2003] QB 1300 [60].

90   See also Hambler, 'A Private Matter'.

91   Arguably, this was also the case in *Haye* v. *Lewisham BC* (2010) ET Case No. 2301852/09, where the claimant had been dismissed for emailing, from a work computer, the Revd Sharon Ferguson, Chief Executive of the Lesbian and Gay Christian Movement, to accuse the recipient of being enslaved to an evil sexual spirit and urged her to repent or go to Hell [6]. There were some ambiguities around the conduct of the claimant, particularly the extent to which she believed that her email, sent through an anonymous 'gateway' could be traced back to her employer. Nevertheless, the employer chose to dismiss her for gross misconduct rather than impose a lesser sanction.

Whereas in *Apelogun Gabriels* it was clear that the 'active manifestation' took place within the workplace and in work time, the boundaries between work time and an employee's 'own time' may not always be immediately evident. For example, a shift worker in a care home, David Booker, was reportedly suspended in 2009 after a co-worker complained about his Christian views on homosexual clergy and same-sex marriages, which had come to light during a 'wide-ranging conversation' between the two workers during a night shift.[92] How far such a conversation can be said to have been a work conversation and how far a private one is not entirely clear cut, taking place as it did in a work environment but voluntarily between two people during a period well outside of normal working hours and where the work itself clearly did not require concentrated attention.[93] As a result, suspension (with the possibility of dismissal) might be considered a somewhat heavy-handed response by the employer.

A further example illustrative of the apparent grey area between private and public conduct is the High Court action brought by Adrian Smith, a housing manager and committed Christian, worked for Trafford Housing Trust and who was demoted with a 40 per cent reduction in pay as a disciplinary sanction.[94] This was because he had made comments on his Facebook site mildly critical of the prospect that same-sex marriages might be conducted in church. His employer argued, *inter alia*, that posting such comments on Facebook had the potential to prejudice the reputation of the Trust and breached the staff code of conduct (by promoting religious views to colleagues and customers),[95] and that this amounted to gross misconduct.[96]

Significantly, Judge Briggs, who found that Mr Smith had been wrongfully dismissed, determined that, although on his Facebook page Mr Smith had listed his occupation as a manager at the Trafford Housing Trust, no reasonable reader would thereby conclude that his postings were made on

---

92   A Alderson, 'Charity worker suspended over "religious debate" with work colleague', *Daily Telegraph* (London, 11 April 2009). Available online at www.telegraph.co.uk/news/religion/5140133/Charity-worker-suspended-over-religious-debate-with-work-colleague.html (accessed 9 June 2014).

93   For further discussion of the private/public divide in the workplace, see V Mantouvalou, 'Human Rights and Unfair Dismissal: Private Acts in Public Spaces' (2008) 71 *Modern Law Review* 912–39; see also discussion in Chapter 2.

94   *Smith* v. *Trafford Housing Trust* [2012] EWHC 3221 (Ch).

95   Ibid. [38].

96   Ibid. [41]. For a critical account of employers' surveillance of employee social networking spaces and the consequent violation of privacy that this may entail, see L Clark and S Roberts, 'Employer's Use of Social Networking Sites: A Socially Irresponsible Practice' (2010) 95 *Journal of Business Ethics* 507–25. The legal issues are considered in A Broughton *et al.*, *Workplaces and Social Networking: The Implications for Employment Relations* (ACAS Research Paper 11/11, 2010).

the trust's behalf.[97] He also considered that there was no realistic damage to the reputation of the trust by association with the comments, given that they were made by an employee in a private capacity, outside working hours and in a moderate way.[98]

Judge Briggs also dealt with the issue of to what extent the trust could legitimately claim that its code of conduct applied beyond the workplace to govern the opinions expressed on Smith's own Facebook page and accessible to colleagues, concluding that it did not:

> it was his colleagues' choice, rather than his, to become his friends, and that it was the mere happenstance of their having become aware of him at work that led them to do so. [Smith] was in principle free to express his religious and political views on his Facebook, provided he acted lawfully, and it was for the recipients to choose whether or not to receive them.[99]

He also opined that an employer's prohibition on the promotion of religious views could only apply within the workplace because of the clear 'potential to interfere with the employee's rights of freedom of expression and belief' if the employer attempted to apply it to an employee's non-work activities.[100] He did acknowledge some (presumably rare) exceptions to this rule, such as the sending of an email from home targeted at work colleagues.[101]

Although the facts of this case arguably made the decision clear cut, the judgment is nonetheless welcome for making it clear that an employer cannot normally fetter an employee's religious expression outside the workplace, with a particular emphasis on the private use of social media. Whether or not an employer would be acting reasonably if it attempted to fetter 'moderate' religious expression (like that of Smith) *within* the workplace remains however an issue to be properly tested in a court or tribunal in the future (although the analysis in the *Smith* judgment gives a hint that perhaps it would not be).

Conclusion

In this chapter, a range of examples of 'active manifestation' have been considered and how both employers and tribunals have responded. In this section, some general, and tentative, observations will be made on the basis of these examples.

97 *Smith* [57].
98 Ibid. [63].
99 Ibid. [78] (Briggs J).
100 Ibid. [72] (Briggs J).
101 Ibid. [73].

The first point to note is the apparently hostile reaction by some employers to active manifestation. In one sense this is not surprising, given the legal framework in place. As Berg notes with reference to the United States (but with equal applicability to the UK):

> Remember that religious speech is, at least potentially, singled out for special limitation in the workplace by the very existence of anti-harassment rules. ... Without the duty to accommodate weighing in the balance, the law arguably creates incentives for employers to restrict religious speech.[102]

As there is no specific duty to accommodate (except that very weak version which can be inferred from the first stage of the test for indirect discrimination),[103] it is perhaps unsurprising that many employers have taken a hostile stance which is in this sense the easiest option. However, such a policy may be shortsighted for other reasons, as it entails a failure to recognise the malign effects on employee morale of using workplace regulation to outlaw religious speech in total.[104]

The second point to note from evidence considered in this chapter is that some employers appear not only to be hostile to active religious expression but seem to overreact when faced with examples of it. This is particularly evident in the various decisions to dismiss staff often for a one-off incident. Although tribunals have been reluctant to find dismissals in such circumstances unfair, it is noteworthy that in *Amachree* the tribunal strongly implied that dismissal for the 'incident' of proselytism itself would not be reasonable. Such an overreaction creates injustice for the religious employees concerned and may intimidate other staff to hide their religious beliefs in the workplace for fear of possible consequences.

The third point to note is that, in the (admittedly limited) evidence considered in this chapter, employers may not always seek to draw distinctions between different forms of active manifestation, particularly in the interpretation of their policies. Thus, in the NHS, an offer to pray for a patient may be seen in a similar light as an attempt to convert that patient. This suggests, *inter alia*, that the ECHR concepts of 'proper' and 'improper' proselytism have not percolated downwards to inform policy making and interpretation. Not employing this dichotomy has potential advantages and disadvantages. In this instance, it is the disadvantages that are in play, as a failure to distinguish between milder forms of religious expression, such as

102 Berg, 'Religious speech in the workplace', 982.
103 See discussion in Chapter 5.
104 D Epstein, 'Free Speech at Work: Verbal Harassment as Gender-Based Discriminatory (Mis)Treatment' (1997) 85 *Georgetown Law Journal* 649, 664. The author does not specifically refer to religious speech but her analysis is clearly applicable to religion.

an offer to pray (to which it might be argued no reasonable person could legitimately take offence) and stronger forms (where there might be legitimate objection), merely results in the suppression by employers of both.

However, to rely without further discrimination on a straightforward dichotomy between proselytism (forbidden) and expression short of proselytism (permitted) could also lead to injustice. A proposed way forward for employers when engaging in policy making and for tribunal investigations would be to use the 'proper/improper' filter (although adopting more useful terminology) as a first-stage test, such that 'mild' expression is always permitted; 'stronger' expression is not forbidden *per se* but may be subject to further restrictions (which may depend on the nature of the work or the job role or the organisational environment). In policy formation, the onus should always be on the employer to offer genuine and credible reasons for restrictions on stronger forms of religious expression. As Berg suggests:

> [R]equiring the employer to show some disruption or other significant cost before it restricts the speech can ensure that the employer acts from more than just disagreement with or hostility to the employee's message. The high status of religious speech justifies efforts to root out such hostility.[105]

The fourth point to note is the implications of active manifestation beyond the workplace. Amongst the cases considered in this chapter, there have been some instances where employers have penalised employees for active manifestation within a grey area between the work and non-work spheres. This 'grey area' is perhaps in part a consequence of the fact that the domains of work and 'non-work' cannot always be neatly compartmentalised.

In Chapter 3, various models of potential state responses to workplace religious expression were set out. The discussion now turns to a consideration of the application of these models to active manifestation. Conclusions concerning how courts approach this issue remain tentative because of the very limited authoritative case law. However, what can be ascertained so far is that tribunals certainly have not acted to 'protect' religious expression (model V). Where Article 9 arguments have been advanced (usually indirectly), the specific situation rule has been applied to deny the right to active manifestation. Equally, indirect discrimination claims have been rejected at both the first and the second stages. Instead of protecting active religious expression, tribunals rather allow employers the leeway to exclude religious expression (model I). This is particularly evident in the discrimination decisions. When it comes to unfair dismissal, the evidence appears to be that tribunals adopt a more *laissez-faire* approach (model III). The

---

105 Berg, 'Religious speech in the workplace', 982.

emerging evidence here is not necessarily one of uncritical endorsement of decisions to dismiss because of active manifestation but nevertheless a reluctance to substitute a finding of unfair dismissal – hence, in *Amachree*, there is a clear suggestion that the employer had overreacted by dismissing Amachree but the dismissal was allowed to stand (ostensibly for different reasons).

The reasons for the tribunals' stance may well be due, in part, to a general suspicion of 'individuals whose religious beliefs and practices are an integral part of their daily lives'[106] (a suspicion shared by employers). However, it may also be due, in another part, to tribunals' awareness of laws concerning harassment and their double effect on religious expression. Consideration of the possible effects of 'offence' to others forms part of the analysis, implicitly or explicitly (for example, in *Apelogun Gabriels* and *Monaghan*).

As well as providing some indications of the development of judicial approaches (largely at first instance), these cases and examples also provide some evidence of the approaches taken by the state in its capacity as employer. Here, the 'exclusion' model is even more evident. For example, NHS policy, buttressed for many staff by legally recognised professional regulations, appears to outlaw proselytism and other forms of religious speech without any serious attempt to find any accommodations for those employees for whom religious speech is of primary importance to their identities. Religious employees are therefore forced to 'privatise' their faith, as their employer subordinates their right of active religious expression to the rights of others not to encounter religious expression, whether or not they would find it objectionable.

106 Kaminer, 'When religious expression creates a hostile work environment', 112.

9 Conclusion

Introduction

In this concluding chapter, the extent to which the various models of legal approaches towards religious expression in the workplace are reflected in the law of England and Wales is finally assessed, with reference to the different forms of manifestation. It will be noted that the two most influential models are 'exclusion' and 'protection' – a seemingly contradictory position and one which reflects a degree of confusion over the role and value of religious expression in the lives of individual employees. It is argued that this confusion results from three competing accounts (referred to here as 'dichotomies') of the nature of different aspects of religious manifestation:

i)   whether individual religious expression is a private matter only or, alternatively, both private and public;
ii) whether the need to manifest religion is 'core' or 'non-core' to religious identity; and
iii) whether religious people are under an obligation to manifest their religion or whether to do so is a matter of choice.

These dichotomies are analysed and it is mooted that the perspectives that offer more weight to religious expression are to be preferred, not least because they more accurately reflect the internal perspective of the religious individual. To ignore this perspective risks compromising the dignity and autonomy of religious individuals; dignity and autonomy being values which a liberal society such as the United Kingdom claims to hold in high regard.

For this reason, it is argued that the law and public policy should move further towards the protection model. Some options of how to achieve this are considered. A key conclusion is that amendments to two of the current definitions of 'prohibited conduct' in discrimination law would be potentially transformative.[1]

1   This chapter draws in part on material first published in A Hambler, 'Recognising a right to "conscientiously object" for Registrars Whose Religious Beliefs are Incompatible with their Duty to Conduct Same-Sex Civil Partnerships' (2012) 7 *Religion and Human Rights* 157.

The models revisited

The purpose of Chapter 2 of this book was to attempt to conceptualise and categorise religious expression. To help to achieve this, a 'taxonomy' of religious expression was presented, ranging from belief and identity to more contentious forms of expression, using the headings passive, negative and active manifestation. The purpose of the discussion was therefore, in large part, to identify which aspects of religious expression might have an effect on others, with an aim of understanding both the nature of such expression and the motivation underlying it. The second chapter dealt with how the law might react to religious expression and set out various models, each of which represented a particular imperative:

(I)   the exclusion model with the aim of suppressing religious expression;
(II) support for a preferred historic ('majority') religion only;
(III) *laissez-faire* (to allow the employer to respond);
(IV) protection but only within 'islands of exclusivity' (religious organisations);
(V)   protection; and
(VI) protection for minority religions only.

These models have been used as reference points in the analysis presented in this book and are revisited in the first part of this concluding chapter.

There are three immediate and perhaps unsurprising conclusions which may be drawn from the application of the models. The first is that modern law in England and Wales does not offer any enduring 'special' support for the expression of the 'majority' historic religion of Christianity in the workplace. There are some very limited exceptions: for example, the existence of an 'opt-out' from Sunday working for some retail workers[2] and the remnants of restrictions on Sunday trading[3] but, it has been argued, these were concessions during a rapid process of the erosion of state sponsorship of an official rest day.[4] Administratively, many government activities cease on Sunday (and often Saturday also), thus providing a day off for staff, but it may be argued that this is entirely due to the cultural legacy of the timing of a rest day (rather than to any enduring deference to Christianity), which a majority of writers agree would be problematic to dismantle, given the difficulties of reaching a consensus on an alternative.

The second exception is that the principle of forming 'islands of exclusivity'[5] for religious workers to retreat to has been largely rejected. Exemptions from discrimination law are, with the theoretical exception of

2   Employment Rights Act 1996, Part IV; see discussion in Chapter 5.
3   Sunday Trading Act 1994.
4   See discussion in Chapter 5.
5   A Esau, '"Islands of Exclusivity": Religious Organizations and Employment Discrimination' (1999) 33 *University of British Columbia Law Review* 720.

denominational schools,[6] narrowly drawn for religious ethos organisations making it difficult for them to maintain robustly 'religious' staffing policies,[7] particularly given the subordination of these exemptions to other rights in cases where they might involve discrimination on other grounds such as sexual orientation.[8] Looked at more positively, the assumption is therefore that religious people will remain in 'mainstream' employment rather than being marginalised into religious 'ghettos'. The third is that employers' freedom of action has been reduced over time, particularly since 2003, by the passage of laws to regulate religious discrimination, although a degree of discretion still remains.

It is also apparent that the model, protection for minority religions, is influential but not in its fullest form. The argument that religion should be protected because of its cultural value has not been embodied into law or its interpretation and remains a theoretical possibility only, albeit one that enjoys a degree of academic support.[9] Nevertheless, the model has some practical influence, not least in the focus on minority religions in some of the guidance material (e.g. the ACAS guide)[10] and, more significantly, in the more positive impact on minority religions, as opposed to Christianity (a religion more characterised by personal convictions), of the development of the 'necessity test' for recognising *bona fide* religious manifestations, albeit that this is now defunct.

Where conclusions are more difficult to draw is in respect of the reach of the remaining models: exclusion and protection. The Equality Act 2010, for example, contains elements of both. In making unlawful direct and indirect discrimination because of the protected characteristic of religion, the legislation appears to be congruent with the protection model. Yet, in applying the definition of harassment to religion and belief in the same way as the other relevant protected characteristics,[11] such that workplace religious speech might be considered to create an offensive environment for others and giving employers a clear incentive to suppress it, the legislation appears to be congruent with the exclusion model.

The tension between the models is also evident at a judicial level. In one respect, judges acknowledge the value of religious expression to individual claimants yet, at another, they arguably fail to give religious rights sufficient

6   Under the School Standards and Framework Act 1998 (s 58); see discussion in Chapter 5.
7   Equality Act 2010, Sch 9, s 3.
8   See *Reaney* v. *Hereford Diocesan Board of Finance* (2007) ET Case No. 1602844/06.
9   See, for example, McColgan, 'Class wars? Religion and (In)equality in the Workplace' (2009) 38 *Industrial Law Journal* 1–29.
10   ACAS, *Religion or Belief in the Workplace: A Guide for Employers and Employees* (March 2014). Available online at www.acas.org.uk/media/pdf/f/l/religion_1.pdf (accessed 9 June 2014).
11   Equality Act 2010, s 26(1).

weight when balancing them against other interests. For example, in *Ladele*, the domestic courts rejected the concrete 'right' of the claimant to conscientiously object on religious grounds to participation in civil partnerships in favour of the abstract 'right' of gay people not to be offended by this objection.[12]

What this overall tension between these two (opposite) imperatives points towards is perhaps a more general confusion in respect of religious expression and how far it is deserving of protection. This confusion finds its expression in part in a linked series of dichotomies which appear to have an effect on law making and judicial interpretation in the United Kingdom: the apparently public or private nature of religion; core and non-core expressions of religion; and the respective roles of choice and obligation in religion.

Public/private dichotomy

In Chapter 2, the notion of a public/private divide was considered in the context of religious expression; in applying such a division, it is possible to view religion and its outworking as essentially private in nature and not therefore something which should be brought into the workplace.[13] Under this perspective, the workplace is considered to be in some way a part of the 'public' forum and, by contrast, activities which take place in the non-work sphere are (usually) 'private' in nature. Historically, this view has powerfully influenced the approach taken by the European Court of Human Rights (ECtHR), in particular, the specific situation rule which, during the years in which it was applied, was underpinned by the assumption that an individual's religious convictions could be taken off at the entrance of the workplace and put on again at the exit.[14] Such a view might also lead to greater sympathy for that form of negative manifestation of religion in the workplace where employees request time off for pursuing what are, essentially, private devotions. Although these activities may be carried out in community with others, they are nevertheless separate from the workplace (unless the employer has agreed to provide facilities such as a prayer room). The partial success of some of the early employment tribunal claims, where time off for religious activities outside the workplace was denied, supports this contention.

There is, however, a problem with this view. It is a highly questionable assumption 'that human beings should worship God on Sundays or some other chosen day and go about their business without reference to God the

---

12 *Ladele v. Islington Borough Council* [2009] EWCA Civ. 1357 (CA); [2010] IRLR 211.
13 This view is also, to some extent, aligned with the notion of 'public reason', discussed in Chapter 3.
14 See discussion in Chapter 4.

rest of the time'.[15] Religious employees do not necessarily accept that their most cherished beliefs should be kept discreetly hidden in public; rather, they may 'seek to integrate their lives and integrate their activities'.[16] Indeed, they may feel under an obligation to do so. The public/private (or, alternatively, work/non-work) division denies religious employees the opportunity to express their beliefs in the workplace; it also risks trivialising religious practices as being at the same level as a sport or leisure activity which an individual pursues in her spare time, with little implication for the rest of her life, including her working life. The removal of the specific situation rule as a filter in *Eweida and Ors* suggests that the public/private dichotomy will be, in future, much less influential in informing judicial reasoning (although it will still be a factor to consider when conducting a proportionality balancing exercise) and this is to be welcomed.[17]

Core/non-core dichotomy

A second dichotomy is that which can be identified between 'core' and 'non-core' religion; applying this means that it is possible to distinguish between elements of religious belief and practice that are seen as giving rise to an absolute right as opposed to those elements that are seen as somehow less significant and with the potential to have restrictions applied. Article 9 of the European Convention on Human Rights and Fundamental Freedoms (ECHR) encapsulates this aspect of the dichotomy by identifying the right to freedom of religion as somehow separate from freedom to 'manifest' religion. Freedom to manifest religion is clearly a qualified rather than an absolute right, as it is this which can be subjected to restrictions. Essentially, the same dichotomy was applied by Lord Justice Neuberger (in *Ladele*), who described Ladele's conscientious objection (a manifestation of her religion) as 'not a core part of her religion';[18] he then gave what can only be taken to be an example of what would constitute a core part of her religion: 'worshiping as she wished'.[19]

As has been seen, in ECHR jurisprudence, a distinction (which shares similarities with the core/non-core dichotomy) is applied between the *forum internum* and the *forum externum*.[20] The precise boundary between these two terms may not always be easy to draw (and theoretically the *forum internum* could be construed very narrowly indeed). However, it would seem that in

15   *EEOC* v. *Townley Engineering and Manufacturing Co* 859 F.2d 610,625 (9th Cir. 1998) (Noonan J, dissenting).
16   Ibid.
17   *Eweida and Ors* v. *United Kingdom* Appl Nos. 48420/10, 59842/10, 51671/10 and 36516/10 (15 January 2013).
18   *Ladele* (CA) [52].
19   Ibid. See also the use of this terminology in *Mba* v. *Merton Borough Council* [2013] EWCA Civ. 1562; [2013] WLR (D) 474 (CA), discussed in Chapter 6.
20   *C* v. *United Kingdom* (1983) 37 DR 142; see discussion in Chapter 2.

broad terms, and to use the typology of religious expression presented at Chapter 2, religious belief and identity and the right to worship with others are seen by courts to belong to the *forum internum* and so could also be seen as 'core'; whereas the forms of expression discussed in Chapters 6 to 8 are considered part of the *forum externum* and so potentially 'non-core'.

A very similar distinction has been read into religious discrimination law, such that detrimental treatment due to religious belief receives full protection under the doctrine of direct discrimination where justification defences are not permissible; whereas religious expression tends to find more qualified protection under the doctrine of indirect discrimination, where justification can be offered as a defence.[21] 'Non-core' religious expression does therefore receive some legal recognition; there is *prima facie* protection but there are various bases for restricting such expression, including in consideration of the rights of others,[22] or if the employer is able to show that the restriction represents 'a proportionate means of achieving a legitimate aim'.[23]

The problem with the core/non-core dichotomy is that not all religious adherents conceptualise their faith in this way. For many Christians, for example, a desire not to displease God by doing something at work which might offend him may be just as important, possibly more so, than being free to worship alongside others in a church building. Identifying some aspects of a religious belief system as 'core' and some as 'non-core', unless based on genuine and thoughtful theological inquiry, will inevitably involve making value judgements which come from an external not an internal perspective. These judgements are unlikely to reflect the way in which religious people perceive their own belief systems and the reach of the obligations which these systems impose. In that sense they may be regarded as arbitrary and understandably resented.

Obligation/choice dichotomy

A third dichotomy is reflected in the very different attitudes towards the role of choice and its alternative, obligation, as the primary motivation underlying religious expression. One view is that religion is a matter of obligation – an individual responds to the call of God which he could not resist even if he wanted to.[24] Another view is that religion is essentially a matter of choice. An individual chooses his religion and so chooses to take on the beliefs and obligations associated with that religion. As Lord Justice Sedley put it in *Eweida*:

21 See discussion in Chapter 5.
22 Art 9 (2) ECHR.
23 Equality Act 2010, s 19(2)(d).
24 Alternatively, particularly in the case of minority religions, there may be an additional obligation which is owed to a wider group of religious adherents, to follow its 'cultural' practices.

[T]he same definition is used for all the listed forms of indirect discrimination, relating to age, disability, gender reassignment, marriage and civil partnership, race, religion or belief, sex and sexual orientation. One cannot help observing that all of these apart from religion or belief are objective characteristics of individuals; religion and belief alone are matters of choice.[25]

But choice is a questionable concept to apply without qualification to religion and belief. If actions motivated by or manifesting religion and belief represent a deliberate choice, then that choice can be denied. The value placed on individual autonomy gives some value to those choices but allows them to be subordinated to other imperatives (such as those arising from the other apparently immutable protected characteristics) with some ease.[26] Moreover, when seen through the prism of 'choice', the decisions an individual may make can allow him to be characterised negatively. Thus, a person convinced because of his religious beliefs that he should 'conscientiously object' to an aspect of his job, can be described (depending on the nature of the objection) as a 'discriminator' and the conscientious objection denied.[27] Such a view plays into a lurking suspicion of religious expression, in its 'stronger' forms, as something potentially malign and destabilising and likely to intrude on the rights of others.

Thus far, an analysis has been presented which suggests that protections for religious expression are in practice weak, not least due to the influence of perspectives which are at best sceptical, at worst hostile. Some of these perspectives find expression in legal approaches which remove protection entirely from some forms of religious expression. Many other imperatives may 'trump' the right to religious expression, particularly any rights connected to other protected characteristics, even where indirectly engaged (such as in cases of conscientious objection to activities promoting same-sex relationships). It is submitted that this treatment of religious expression derives from a series of contested beliefs about the essentially private nature of religion, the optionality of various forms of manifestation and the primacy of choice, rather than obligation, in forming religious convictions. The problem with this approach is that it sees religious expression through an external prism and fails to engage with the experience and values of the religious employee.

An alternative approach is to view religion, subject to a test of sincerity,[28] as a highly significant, if not the most significant, aspect of an individual's

---

25   *Eweida* v. *British Airways* [2010] EWCA Civ. 80; [2010] IRLR 322 [40] (Sedley LJ).
26   This analysis gives some advantage to those members of minority religious groups who are also recognised as protected on the basis of their ethnic or racial grouping.
27   As in *Ladele;* see discussion in Chapter 6.
28   See discussion in Chapter 2.

life and the personal autonomy which allows her to pursue that life.[29] Indeed, many religious people build their lives around their religious convictions and are not prepared to compromise these convictions, as they feel that their obligations to God outweigh their obligations to human authorities.[30] If this alternative approach is to be preferred, then it follows that the right to express and manifest religious beliefs should be accorded a high status in law – higher than is currently the case – such that 'protection for religious expression' should be the dominant legal model. How this might be achieved is the subject of the next section.

Moving further towards the protection model – an assessment of the options

Thus far it has been argued that, whereas there is some protection for workplace religious expression, there is a competing imperative, exclusion, which manifests itself in various ways. The result is that religious expression enjoys only partial protection and tends to be relegated to second place when other rights are in play. For religious employees, such protection is therefore inadequate. It is submitted that, given the arguments considered on the subject of dignity, equality and personal autonomy,[31] not to mention the paramount significance for religious adherents of religious obligation, this situation should be addressed and the law reconsidered to give greater priority to, and indeed to buttress, the 'protection' imperative. To this end, in the following section, the options for improving legal protection for workplace religious expression are considered and assessed and, where appropriate, recommendations made. The analysis is structured according to possible alternative approaches, either at a legislative or judicial level, which might move the operating legal imperative further towards protection and away from exclusion. This is followed by a brief discussion of some practical ways in which public policy might also move, in tandem, in the same direction.

Option 1: increased use of statutory exemptions

The first option is to amend existing legislation to incorporate more statutory exemptions or 'conscience clauses'. Whereas these are most likely to act as a mechanism to accommodate people who wish to 'opt-out' of certain aspects of a job role for reasons of religious-based conscientious objection (a form of negative manifestation), conscience clauses can also

29   See discussion in Chapter 3.
30   See R Ahdar and I Leigh, *Religious Freedom in the Liberal State*, 2nd ed. (Oxford: Oxford University Press, 2013); and also discussion in Chapter 3.
31   See discussion in Chapter 3.

be used more widely in support of other aspects of religious manifestation.[32] Writing such clauses into new legislation, where a conflict might arise for people with religious convictions, should also be enshrined as an ongoing principle at a legislative level.

It will be recalled from Chapter 6 that a proposed amendment to the Equality Bill 2006 to incorporate a specific statutory exemption for registrars and social workers with a conscientious objection to the outworking of the Civil Partnerships Act 2004 for their respective roles was set out in full.[33] It is a useful example of a 'conscience clause' or a specific 'opt-out'. There are at least four interesting points to note from the way in which it is drafted. First, it sets out three situations in which employees (in this case, public servants) might wish to invoke a conscientious objection – objections arising from situations not covered by this amendment are thus ineligible for protection. Second, the situations in which conscientious objection might arise are widely drawn (in contrast to section 4(1) of the Abortion Act). Third, the right to conscientiously object is specifically referenced to an underlying religion and belief giving rise to the objection. Fourth, the right to object, following in the tradition of the Abortion Act, is absolute.

Lady O'Cathain's amendment sets out one formula for identifying and accepting conscientious objection. There are, however, other possible formulae, most of which would involve a degree of flexibility around one or more of the four points outlined in the preceding paragraph: i.e. the right could apply to more situations; it could be more narrowly drawn; the link to religion could be omitted; and the right could be conditional. If the right to conscientiously object is to be conditional, then this conditionality is likely to relate to the availability of other employees willing and able to perform the relevant duties. In a US context, Wilson proposes a free-standing conditional constitutional right for conscientious objection to participation in same-sex marriage on religious grounds for individuals but this right does not apply if 'another government employee or official is not promptly available and willing to provide the requested government service without inconvenience or delay'.[34] What is meant by 'prompt', 'inconvenience' or 'delay' is not of course specified.

This indeed illustrates the problem with specific conscience clauses. The way they are drafted and interpreted is crucial. As noted from *Janaway*, the abortion conscience clauses are very narrowly understood and potentially

32   There are a few current examples in law; for example, to allow some shop and betting workers to opt out of Sunday working or to allow Sikh construction workers to wear a turban instead of an otherwise mandatory hard hat.

33   Equality Bill 2005, Amendment No. 191A.

34   R Wilson, 'Insubstantial Burdens: The Case for Government Employee Exemptions to Same-Sex Marriage Laws' 5 (2010) *Northwestern Journal of Law and Social Policy* 368. Such a right, in theory, could be adopted as a statutory right in the UK.

strongly held objections to indirect involvement in abortion are not recognised or protected.[35] Thus, although the O'Cathain amendment appears to be carefully drawn to be inclusive of direct and indirect participation in civil partnerships, it is quite conceivable that an alternative (compromise?) formulation might make a distinction for registrars, for example between officiating at a ceremony and the simple signing of a register.[36] In this example, the conscience clause could be narrowly drafted to apply to participation in ceremonies but exclude the formal registration of the civil partnership union. Such a conscience clause would not have availed some registrars (such as Ladele) whose conscientious objection embraced both activities.

Conscience clauses (at least when applied to negative manifestation) are also open to criticism on the basis that they are potentially inflexible to the needs or rights of others, because if too many people availed themselves of a conscience clause then others might be deprived of a service or experience delays in obtaining that service. Whilst it is difficult to cite realistic examples of this scenario in practice, to accommodate the theoretical objection there is the additional permutation of a right to conscientiously object being conditional on the practicability of accommodating the objection. In principle, this has potential to create uncertainty for the would-be conscientious objector, as the conscientious objection, having first been accepted, may be at any time later denied if the conditions for permitting it no longer apply (to continue the example of the registrar, demand for civil partnerships comes to outstrip the supply of non-objecting registrars). It is submitted that it would provide a greater degree of certainty to the dissenting employee if the objection were to be accepted for a given period, based on an assessment of capacity at the time the request was made. At the end of this period the situation could be reviewed to identify if either the supply of similarly qualified employees or the demand for particular services had changed and whether this assessment could justify the withdrawal of the acceptance of the conscientious objection. The alternative, a continuing case-by-case conditionality, would create, for the conscientious objector, too great a burden of uncertainty and consequent employment insecurity to be a realistic or fair approach to adopt.

In summary, 'opt-out' clauses are not a panacea for improving protection for negative manifestation by reason of conscientious objection. Much depends on the way they are drafted and the extant examples (in the medical field) are generally narrow in nature and thus offer quite limited protection. In situations where it is difficult to make the case for absolute, as opposed to conditional, conscientious objection there are difficulties in identifying the exact scope of the relevant opt-out. Thus, opt-out clauses on

---

35 *R v. Salford AHA ex parte Janaway* [1988] 3 All ER 1079.
36 The compromise offered to, and rejected by, Ladele; see *Ladele* (CA) [10].

their own are unlikely to provide comprehensive protection for religious manifestations, particularly conscience-based ones. This analysis is not intended to imply that such clauses should be dispensed with. Indeed existing conscience clauses should be retained and where possible more should be sought (e.g. if assisted euthanasia were to be legalised). However, other legal mechanisms, with more general application, are also likely to be needed.

Option 2: introduce a 'duty of reasonable accommodation'

Another means of offering greater protection to religious claimants (for all forms of manifestation) would be to amend the Equality Act to create a statutory duty on employers to 'reasonably accommodate' the needs of religious employees.[37] This would require employers to proactively identify and alter workplace rules and practices in order to accommodate workers' religious beliefs where it is 'reasonable' to do so, not unlike the current obligations they have to make 'reasonable adjustments' for disabled employees.[38]

There are, however, some potential problems with a duty of reasonable accommodation. Firstly, there is no guarantee that case law arising from the application of a duty of reasonable accommodation would apply in the same way to religion and belief as has a requirement to make reasonable adjustments in the case of disability. Reasonable accommodation might develop as a much reduced right, not least since religion and belief appears to be lower down the hierarchy of protected characteristics than is the case in respect of disability.[39] In the USA, for example, the duty of reasonable accommodation is circumscribed at the point that it creates 'undue hardship on the conduct of the employer's business'.[40] The US courts have interpreted this in favour of employers such that undue hardship is suffered if the costs of accommodation are more than 'de minimis'.[41] This is quite different from the corresponding duty in UK disability discrimination law which can require employers to go to considerable lengths and some cost to accommodate disability.[42] If a such a 'de minimis' rule were adopted in the UK and applied to a request by an employee for the reasonable accommodation of conscience, this could conceivably lead to a

---

37   See B Hepple and T Choudhury, *Tackling Religious Discrimination: Practical Implications for Policy-Makers and Legislators*, Home Office Research Study 221 (London: Home Office Research, Development and Statistics Directorate, 2001) and also discussion in Chapter 5.

38   Equality Act 2010, s 20.

39   L Vickers, 'Religious Discrimination in the Workplace: an emerging hierarchy: An Emerging Hierarchy?' (2010) 12 *Ecclesiastical Law Journal* 280.

40   Title VII Civil Rights Act 1964, s 701(j).

41   *Trans World Airlines* v. *Hardison* 432 U.S. 63 (1976).

42   See, for example, Lady Hale's judgment in *Archibald* v. *Fife Council* [2004] UKHL 32; [2004] IRLR 651 HL.

realistic request being 'legitimately' turned down, depending on the circumstances, in particular how the associated 'costs' of accommodation are interpreted and subsequently calculated.[43]

A more fundamental problem is that the introduction of a requirement for reasonable accommodation would privilege religion and belief (alongside disability) ahead of the other protected characteristics in the sense of conspicuously endowing the characteristic with an additional (apparent) legal protection not available to the other characteristics. Of course, the need for accommodation for other characteristics (except for maternity, where separate provisions exist) may not be obvious. Nevertheless, bolstering the protection for religion and belief or, more particularly, being seen to do so is likely to prove contentious (as a form of special pleading) particularly in view of the hostility towards religious expression in the workplace from groups such as the National Secular Society. Given the negative reaction which the adoption of a duty of reasonable accommodation might create, it is particularly important that such a duty, if enacted, should truly provide the protections, for example for religious conscience, which are required to buttress the protection model in the way suggested here. Since there appears to be no guarantee that this would be the result, adopting reasonable accommodation would be costly (politically) without necessarily bringing the needed benefits.[44]

To summarise, therefore, as far as reasonable accommodation is concerned, the exact value for individual religious expression of adopting the approach is not entirely clear and, unless this is known, it may be that focusing on the shortcomings of the existing mechanisms for protecting religious expression, in particular the concept of indirect discrimination, would be a surer route to enhancing legal protections. There is a particular attraction in considering this area because of the possibility of amending the formula by which employers are able to justify *prima facie* indirect discrimination – something which would apply equally to all the

---

43 It should be noted, however, that Trotter provides a more positive account of the benefits of 'reasonable accommodation' for conscientious objectors based on his analysis of Canadian law; see G Trotter, 'The Right to Decline Performance of Same-Sex Civil Marriages: The Duty to Accommodate Public Servants – A Response to Professor Bruce MacDougall' (2007) 70 *Saskatchewan Law Review* 365.

44 Even when hypothetically applying the more robust Canadian criteria for reasonable accommodation to conscience situations such as those in *Eweida and Ors*, Gibson concludes that *McFarlane* would still have no case and, whilst more positive about *Ladele*, he does not definitively show that even this claimant could have been successful, given that, as he concedes, the employer might be able to argue 'undue hardship' at the level of public relations or policy; see M Gibson, 'The God "Dilution"? Religion, Discrimination and the Case for Reasonable Accommodation' (2013) 72 *Cambridge Law Journal* 578–616.

protected characteristics (and consequently there would be no 'special pleading'). This discussion is the subject of the next section.

Option 3: amend discrimination law

The third option for increasing protection for religious claimants would be to amend discrimination law, in particular the Equality Act 2010. As discussed in Chapter 5, discrimination law in England and Wales penalises employers who engage in 'prohibited conduct' towards workers because of a 'protected characteristic', one of which is religion and belief.[45] Prohibited conduct is defined in various ways but arguably the three most significant definitions are: direct discrimination, indirect discrimination and harassment. Direct discrimination refers to the unlawful application of 'less favourable treatment'.[46] Indirect discrimination refers to the unlawful application of 'a provision, criterion or practice' which puts those who share a protected characteristic at a disadvantage compared to others, and which the employer cannot justify as 'a proportionate means of achieving a legitimate aim'.[47] Harassment is defined as 'unwanted conduct' related to a protected characteristic which has the effect of 'violating' someone else's 'dignity' or 'creating an intimidating, hostile, degrading, humiliating or offensive environment' for that person.[48]

It is suggested here that alterations to the legal formulations for 'indirect discrimination' and 'harassment', in relation to religion and belief, are most likely to extend protection for religious claimants.

Indirect discrimination

Indirect discrimination is currently the most obvious mechanism for employees to use in seeking redress when they are denied the right to manifest their religious beliefs.[49] It has been repeatedly argued in this book that the approach which tribunals and courts adopt to claims of indirect discrimination has been wanting. This has been particularly evident in two ways. The first concerns the requirement to show plural disadvantage before indirect discrimination is *prima facie* triggered. This has been extremely difficult to show for those employees who wish to manifest their religious faith in apparently individual ways but, nevertheless, sincerely. However, it would appear that, following *Eweida and Ors*, the courts in England and Wales have altered their approach to be more accommodating of individual

---

45   Equality Act 2010, s 10.
46   Ibid. s 13.
47   Ibid. s 19.
48   Ibid. 26(1).
49   See the legal reasoning in *Azmi* v. *Kirklees Metropolitan Borough Council* (2007) EAT 0009/07, discussed in Chapter 7.

disadvantage.[50] Thus, the first of the two issues with indirect discrimination may have been, to some extent, resolved. The second problem is more pressing, however, and has yet to be satisfactorily addressed. This concerns that part of the legal formula for indirect discrimination which allows the employer a justification defence if the apparently discriminatory 'provision, criterion or practice' which it is employing can be said to fulfil a 'legitimate aim' and that it is 'proportionate' to apply that legitimate aim to the workers who are adversely affected.

At regular intervals in the analysis presented in this book, it has been argued that the courts have failed to apply the justification defence properly to manifestations of religion in the workplace, to the detriment of the claimant. This problem is most starkly illustrated in relation to conscience-based claims, for example, in the analysis of *Ladele* v. *Islington Borough Council*. The judgments in this case were analysed in some detail in Chapter 6 and it was concluded that the reasoning in the Employment Appeals Tribunal and Court of Appeal judgments were substantially flawed, not least in allowing an employer to trump an employee's right to 'conscientiously object' based on abstract principles rather than on the basis of a necessary operational justification (which the employer in *Ladele* was unable to show).

This is unsatisfactory. However, the question arises, could existing discrimination law be recalibrated in some way to provide a greater degree of recognition of the right to manifest religious belief? McCrudden argues that judges should be given training to enable them to better understand the position of the religious claimant (the 'internal viewpoint').[51] Judges in England and Wales receive both induction and continuation training in 'substantive law, evidence and procedure and, where appropriate, *subject expertise*' and in 'the social context in which judging occurs'.[52] Training of the kind recommended by McCrudden appears to be in keeping therefore with the current objectives of judicial training and should be welcomed by open-minded judges. The outcome of such training might be to contribute to the rebalancing of the 'proportionality equation' to give more weight to religious claims.

Equally, and perhaps more importantly, the definition of indirect discrimination could be redrafted in an amendment to the Equality Act such that the word 'proportionate' is replaced by the term 'necessary' or an analogous term. This would make it more difficult to justify *prima facie* religious discrimination as it would require an employer to identify a

---

50   See *Mba* v. *Merton BC* (CA).
51   C McCrudden, 'Religion, Human Rights, Equality and the Public Sphere. (2011) 13 *Ecclesiastical Law Journal* 26–38.
52   See Courts and Tribunals Judiciary, 'Training'. Available online at www.judiciary.gov.uk/training-support/judicial-college/training (accessed 9 June 2014) (my emphasis).

concrete and definite need or requirement for applying any provision, criterion or practice which has an adverse impact on religious employees. This formula thus puts the employer under a greater burden of justification to show that it has no reasonable alternative but to indirectly discriminate. In fact, such a change would more accurately reflect the text of Council Directive 2000/78/EC, establishing a general framework for equal treatment in employment and occupation, which requires that indirect discrimination is 'objectively justified by a legitimate aim and the means of achieving that aim are appropriate and *necessary*'.[53]

Harassment

In the first part of this chapter, it was noted that there is evidence of hostility towards active manifestation (or workplace religious speech). In Chapter 8, it was posited that a likely justification for such hostility is grounded in an awareness of the harassment provisions of the Equality Act 2010, which serve to create an incentive for employers, considered under discrimination law to be vicariously liable for the actions of their employees,[54] to ban religious speech, with no corresponding incentive to support it.

A large part of the problem then is the way in which harassment is defined under the Equality Act, with its recognition of a perceived offensive environment as sufficient to trigger claims. It is submitted that a one-size-fits-all approach to harassment, across the protected characteristics to which it applies,[55] is failing to protect legitimate religious speech. To remedy this, the bar needs to be raised for religious speech so that greater consideration is given to the religious claim. There is possibly more than one legal mechanism to achieve this but the most obvious would be an amendment to the Equality Act to include a separate definition of harassment of others (on both religious and other grounds) as a result of religious speech. This definition of harassment would need to be carefully considered. What it should not do is allow religious employees free rein to intimidate others or create a genuinely hostile environment. However, it may be that there are occasions when it is unavoidable that a co-worker is 'offended' by religious speech, because in that instance the religious right outweighs the offence caused. It may be that the word 'offensive', which serves to set the bar for harassment very low, is the major problem and should be omitted or cast differently in respect of harassment related to religious speech. This would still allow employers to identify and prohibit stronger forms of harassment, for example those which are animus-related or which can be genuinely said to amount to 'improper' proselytism (e.g.

---

53   Art 1(2)(b)(i) (my emphasis).
54   Equality Act s 109; see discussion of the concept in Chapter 5.
55   Marriage/civil partnerships and pregnancy/maternity are not protected from this form of prohibited conduct.

where a vulnerable member of staff is repeatedly subjected to unwanted and 'strong' forms of religious speech personally directed at him).[56]

Public policy

Whereas movement towards protection is most likely to be achieved through legal changes, there are also implications for public policy arising from the analysis presented in this book.

The Equalities and Human Rights Commission (EqHRC) is the key body established by statute to promote equality, involving, *inter alia*, a duty to 'work towards enabling members of groups to participate in society'[57] in the United Kingdom. It will be recalled from the discussion in Chapter 5 that the EqHRC has not been wholly supportive of all forms of religious mani-festation. There were signs of a slight shift in approach as a result of its intervention in *Eweida and Ors* in which it supported the claimants Eweida and Chaplin and argued that the English courts had decided those cases wrongly. However, it did not extend its support to the other 'conscience-based' claimants, apparently confirming its preference for sexual orientation rights (albeit, in this case, abstract ones) over religious rights (which has also found expression in its choice of which party to support in provision of goods and services discrimination cases such as *Bull and Bull* v. *Hall and Preddy*).[58] It is strongly arguable that this stance will need to change if the EqHRC is to fully fulfil its statutory duty to promote rights connected to all the protected characteristics. To adopt the language of the EqHRC, it could be argued that religion-based conscientious objectors are a 'marginalised group', vulnerable to unfair treatment by their employers and at risk of being excluded from participation in certain job roles – indeed, precisely the sorts of people which it might be imagined the EqHRC has a duty to champion.

It will be recalled that government funding has been given to organisa-tions not known for their sympathy with religious expression to produce apparently official 'neutral' guidance for organisations on how to approach religion in the workplace, such as the British Humanist Association and Stonewall. However, with an exception specific to expressions of Islam in the workplace, it has not provided any support for religious organisations to provide similar semi-official guidance to employers. This would be worthwhile, both for the symbolic value of offering government support for religion-based guidance to employers (having offered it to other interested parties) but also for the fact that religious organisations are surely the best

56 See discussion of the usefulness of a distinction between 'strong' and 'mild' forms of proselytism (at Chapter 8).
57 Equality Act 2006, s 10(1)(d). 'Religion or belief' is one of the foundations for 'group' status (s. 10(2)(f)).
58 [2013] UKSC 73.

placed to understand the needs of religious employees – their advice to employers would be therefore valuable if the employer is truly seeking to manifest 'good practice' by accommodating religious expression. Such advice can of course be offered without government support or endorsement, but such endorsement gives credibility and thus affords greater weight to the advice when employers are formulating or reviewing organisational policy.

Conclusion

Legal approaches to the manifestation and wider expression of religion are currently inconsistent, drawing heavily on two fundamentally opposing imperatives – protection and exclusion. Such inconsistencies are manifest in a number of areas but, most particularly, in the treatment of religious speech and conscientious objection.

The manifestation of religion in the workplace has been brought to the fore of public debate as a result of the groundbreaking hearing before the ECHR in *Eweida and Ors*. Although only one of the four applications was successful, the Court made it clear that a signatory state has the discretion to choose to accommodate claimants in a similar position to the other three applicants in the case should it wish to do so. Given the favourable aspects of the ruling and the public debate which has taken place since the judgment was handed down in January 2013, it is surely an opportune time to take a longer and deeper look at laws in England and Wales designed to protect religious expression in the workplace *per se* and, it would be hoped, to remove inconsistencies in approach in a manner compatible with the protection model. Some options of how this could be achieved have been considered in this chapter, alongside some policy recommendations. To do otherwise would perpetuate a situation where the significance of religious expression continues, in large measure, to be devalued and the deep sense of obligation which can underpin it underplayed. As has been argued, this approach is out of step with core liberal values (of equality, dignity and personal autonomy) and, for this reason, there is a pressing case for fundamental revision.

Select bibliography

Addison, Neil, *Religious Discrimination and Hatred Law*. Abingdon: Routledge Cavendish, 2006.

Ahdar, Rex, 'The Right to Protection of Religious Feelings' (2009) 11 *Otago Law Review* 629–56.

Ahdar, Rex, and Ian Leigh, *Religious Freedom in the Liberal State*, 2nd ed. Oxford: Oxford University Press, 2013.

Alexander, Larry, *Is There a Right of Freedom of Expression?* Cambridge: Cambridge University Press, 2005.

Allen, R. and G. Moon, 'Substantive Rights and Equal Treatment in Respect of Religion and Belief: Towards a Better Understanding of the Rights and their Implications' (2000) *European Human Rights Law Review* 580–602.

Alston, William, P., *Philosophy of Language*. Englewood Cliffs, NJ: Prentice-Hall, 1964.

Andreescu, Gabriel, and Liviu Andreescu, 'Taking Back Lautsi: Towards a "Theory of Neutralisation"?' (2011) 6 *Religion and Human Rights* 207–12.

Audi, Robert, 'Liberal Democracy and the Place of Religion in Politics' in Robert Audi and Nicholas Wolterstorff, *Religion in the Public Square: The Place of Religious Convictions in Political Debate*. Lanham MD: Rowman and Littlefield, 1997.

Audi, Robert, *Religious Commitment and Secular Reason*. Cambridge: Cambridge University Press, 2000.

Baker, Aaron, 'Proportionality and Employment Discrimination in the UK' (2008) 37 *Industrial Law Journal* 305–28.

Bandsuch, Mark R., and Gerald F. Cavanagh, 'Integrating Spirituality into the Workplace: Theory and Practice' (2005) 2 *Journal of Management, Spirituality and Religion* 221–54.

Banton, Michael (ed.), *Anthropological Approaches to the Study of Religion*. London: Tavistock, 1966.

Barrett, Justin L., *Why Would Anyone Believe in God?* Walnut Creek CA: AltaMira Press, 2004.

Barry, Brian, *Culture and Equality: An Egalitarian Critique of Multiculturalism*. Cambridge: Polity, 2001.

Beauchamp, Tom, *Philosophical Ethics: An Introduction to Moral Philosophy*, 2nd ed. London: McGraw Hill, 1991.

Becker, Gary, *The Economics of Discrimination*. Chicago, IL: Chicago University Press, 1957.

Bedi, Sonu, 'Debate: What is so Special About Religion? The Dilemma of the Religious Exemption', (2007) 15 *Journal of Political Philosophy* 235–49.

Benedictus, Roger, 'Closed Shop Exemptions and their Wording' (1979) 8 *Industrial Law Journal* 160–71.

Benhabib, Seyla, *The Claims of Culture: Equality and Diversity in the Global Era.* Princeton NJ: Princeton University Press, 2002.

Bennoune, Karima, 'Secularism and Human Rights: A Contextual Analysis of Headscarves, Religious Expression and Women's Equality Under International Law' (2007) 45 *Columbia Journal of Transnational Law* 367–426.

Benson, Ian, 'Notes Towards a (Re)Definition of the "Secular"' (2000) 33 *University of British Columbia Law Review* 519–49.

Berg, Thomas C., 'Religious speech in the workplace: harassment or protected speech?' (1998–1999) 22 *Harvard Journal of Law and Public Policy* 959–1008.

Boice, James M., *Foundations of the Christian Faith.* Downers Grove IL: InterVarsity Press, 1986.

Bradney, Anthony, *Law and Faith in a Sceptical Age.* Abingdon: Routledge Cavendish, 2009.

Bradney, Anthony, *Religions, Rights and Laws.* Leicester: Leicester University Press, 1993.

Bratton John and Jeffrey Gold, *Human Resource Management Theory and Practice*, 3rd ed. London: Palgrave-Macmillan, 2003.

Campell, Iain D., *On the First Day of the Week: God, the Christian and the Sabbath.* Leominster: Day One Publications, 2005.

Campos, Paul, 'Secular Fundamentalism' (1994) 94 *Columbia Law Review* 1814–27.

Carter, Stephen L., *The Culture of Disbelief: How American Law and Politics Trivialize Religious Devotion.* New York: Basic Books, 1993.

Carter, Stephen L., 'The Religiously Devout Judge' (1989) 64 *Notre Dame Law Review* 932–44.

Chaplin, Jonathan, 'Law, Religion and Public Reasoning' (2012) 1 *Oxford Journal of Law and Religion* 319–37.

Childress, James, 'Appeals to Conscience' (1979) 89 *Ethics* 315–35.

Clark, Leigh and Sherry Roberts, 'Employer's Use of Social Networking Sites: A Socially Irresponsible Practice' (2010) 95 *Journal of Business Ethics* 507–25.

Clarke, Peter B. and Peter Byrne, *Religion Defined and Explained.* London: Macmillan, 1993.

Cookson, Catharine, *Regulating Religion: The Courts and the Free Exercise Clause.* New York: Oxford University Press, 2001.

Coyle, Joanne, 'Spirituality and Health: Towards a Framework for Exploring the Relationship Between Spirituality and Health' (2002) 37 *Journal of Advanced Nursing* 589–97.

Cumper, Peter, 'The Public Manifestation of Religion' in O'Adair, Richard, and Andrew Lewis (eds), *Law and Religion.* Oxford: Oxford University Press, 2001.

Cumper, Peter and Peter Edge, 'First Among Equals: The English State and the Anglican Church in the 21st Century' (2005–2006) 83 *University of Detroit Mercy Law Review* 601–23.

Dahl, Robert A., *On Democracy.* New Haven, CT: Yale University Press, 1998.

Daintith, Terence, 'The Techniques of Government' in Jowell, Jeffrey and Dawn Oliver (eds), *The Changing Constitution*, 3rd ed. Oxford: Oxford University Press, 1994.

Danchin, Peter G., 'Suspect Symbols: Value Pluralism as a Theory of Religious Freedom in International Law' (2008) 33 *Yale Journal of International Law* 1–66.

Davie, Grace, 'From Obligation to Consumption: A Framework for Reflection in Northern Europe' (2005) 6 *Political Theology* 281–301.

Davie, Grace, *Religion in Britain Since 1945: Believing Without Belonging*. Oxford: Blackwell, 1994.

Davies, Anne C. L., *Perspectives on Labour Law*, 2nd ed. Cambridge: Cambridge University Press, 2004.

Deakin, Simon, 'Equality, Non-discrimination, and the Labour Market: a Commentary on Richard Epstein's Critique of Anti-discrimination Laws' (41–56) in Richard A. Epstein, *Equal Opportunity or More Opportunity? The Good Thing About Discrimination*. London: Civitas, 2002.

Dickens, B. and Rebecca Cook, 'The Scope and Limits of Conscientious Objection' (2000) 71 *International Journal of Gynecology and Obstetrics* 71–7.

Donald, Alice, Karen Bennett and Philip Leach, *Religion or Belief, Equality and Human Rights in England and Wales*, Equality and Human Rights Commission Research Report 84. Manchester: EHRC, 2012.

Dunn, Marylin, *The Emergence of Monasticism: From the Desert Fathers to the Early Middle Ages*. Oxford: Blackwell 2003.

Durkheim, Emile, *The Elementary Forms of the Religious Life*, trans. J Ward Swain. London: Allen and Unwin, 1976.

Dworkin, Ronald, *Is Democracy Possible Here?* Princeton, NJ: Princeton University Press, 2006.

Dworkin, Ronald, *Taking Rights Seriously* (London: Duckworth, 1977).

Eberle, Christopher J., *Religious Convictions in Liberal Politics*. Cambridge: Cambridge University Press, 2002.

Edge, Peter, 'Determining Religion in English Courts' (2012) 1 *Oxford Journal of Law and Religion* 402–23.

Edge, Peter, 'Religious Rights and Choice under the European Convention on Human Rights' (2000) 3 *Web Journal of Current Legal Issues*.

Elias, P., 'Religious and related discrimination' (2008) 175 *Equal Opportunities Review* 16.

Epstein, Debbie, 'Free Speech at Work: Verbal Harassment as Gender-Based Discriminatory (Mis)Treatment' (1997) 85 *Georgetown Law Journal* 649–66.

Epstein, Richard A., *Equal Opportunity or More Opportunity? The Good Thing about Discrimination*. London: Civitas, 2002.

Epstein, Richard A., *Forbidden Grounds: The Case Against Employment Discrimination Laws*. Cambridge, MA: Harvard University Press, 1992.

Esau, Alvin, '"Islands of Exclusivity": Religious Organizations and Employment Discrimination' (1999) 33 *University of British Columbia Law Review* 719–827.

Estep, William R., *The Anabaptist Story: An Introduction to Sixteenth Century Anabaptism*, 3rd ed. Grand Rapids, IL: William B Eerdmans, 1996.

Evans, Carolyn, *Freedom of Religion Under the European Convention on Human Rights*. Oxford: Oxford University Press, 2000.

Evans, Carolyn, 'Religious Speech that Undermines Gender Equality' (357–74) in Ivan Hare and James Weinstein (eds), *Extreme Speech and Democracy*. Oxford: Oxford University Press, 2009.

Evans, Gillian R., *A Brief History of Heresy*. Oxford: Blackwell, 2003.

Evans, Malcolm, *Religious Liberty and International Law in Europe*. Cambridge: Cambridge University Press 1997.

Evans, Malcolm, 'The Freedom of Religion or Belief and the Freedom of

Expression' (2009) 4 *Religion and Human Rights* 197–235.

Faulkner, Charles, 'Church, State and Civil Partners' (2007) 9 *Ecclesiastical Law Journal* 5–9.

Feinberg, Joel, *Offense to Others*. Oxford: Oxford University Press, 1985.

Feldman, David, 'Human Dignity as a Legal Value: Part 1' (1999) Winter *Public Law* 682–702.

Fenton, Elizabeth, and Loren Lomasky, 'Dispensing with Liberty: Conscientious Refusal and the Morning-After-Pill' (2005) 30 *Journal of Medicine and Philosophy* 579–92.

Fredman, Sandra, *Discrimination Law*, 2nd ed. Oxford: Oxford University Press, 2011.

Galeotti, Anna Elisabetta, *Toleration as Recognition*. Cambridge: Cambridge University Press, 2002.

Galston, William, *Liberal Purposes: Goods, Virtues, and Diversity in the Liberal State*. Cambridge: Cambridge University Press, 1991.

Gavison, Ruth and Nahshon Perez, 'Days of Rest in Multicultural Societies: Private, Public Separate' in Cane, Peter, Caroline Evans and Zoe Robinson (eds), *Law and Religion in Theoretical and Historical Context*. Cambridge: Cambridge University Press, 2008.

Gennard, John and Graham Judge, *Managing Employment Relations*, 5th ed. London: Chartered Institute of Personnel and Development, 2010.

Gibson, Matthew, 'The God "Dilution"? Religion, Discrimination and the Case for Reasonable Accommodation' (2013) 72 *Cambridge Law Journal* 578–616.

Goodwin, Robert E., and Philip Pettit (eds), *Contemporary Political Philosophy, An Anthology*, 2nd ed. Oxford: Blackwell, 2006.

Green, Yosef, 'When Does The Day Begin?' (2008) 36 *Jewish Bible Quarterly* 81–7.

Greenawalt, R. Kent, *Private Consciences and Public Reasons*. New York: Oxford University Press, 1995.

Greenawalt, R. Kent, 'Religion as a Concept in Constitutional Law' (1984) 72 *California Law Review* 753–816.

Greenawalt, R, Kent, 'The Significance of Conscience' (2010) 47 *San Diego Law Review* 901–18.

Habermas, Jurgen, 'Religion in the Public Sphere' (2006) 14 *European Journal of Philosophy* 1–25.

Hambler, Andrew, 'A No-Win Situation for Public Officials with Faith Convictions' (2010) 12 *Ecclesiastical Law Journal* 3–16.

Hambler, Andrew, 'A Private Matter? Evolving Approaches to the Freedom to Manifest Religious Convictions in the Workplace' (2008) 3 *Religion and Human Rights* 111–33.

Hambler, Andrew, 'Establishing Sincerity in Religion and Belief Claims: A Question of Consistency' (2011) 13 *Ecclesiastical Law Journal* 146–56.

Hambler, Andrew, 'Recognising a Right to "Conscientiously Object" for Registrars Whose Religious Beliefs are Incompatible with their Duty to Conduct Same-Sex Civil Partnerships' (2012) 7 *Religion and Human Rights* 157–81.

Hardy, Lee, *The Fabric of This World*. Grand Rapids, IL: William B Eeardmans, 1990.

Harries-Jenkins, Gwyn, 'Britain: From Individual Conscience to Social Movement' (67–79) in Moskos, Charles and John Chambers (eds), *The New Conscientious Objection*. New York: Oxford University Press, 1993.

Harte, David, 'Structures of Religious Pluralism in English Law' (159–90) in N. Doe and R. Sandberg (eds), *Law and Religion: New Horizons*. Leuven: Peeters, 2010.

Hatziz, Nicholas, 'Personal Religious Beliefs in the Workplace: How Not to Define Indirect Discrimination' (2011) 74 *Modern Law Review* 287–305.

Hepple, Bob, *Equality: The New Legal Framework*. Oxford: Hart, 2011.

Hepple, Bob, and Tufyal Choudhury, *Tackling Religious Discrimination: Practical Implications for Policy-Makers and Legislators*, Home Office Research Study 221. London: Home Office Research, Development and Statistics Directorate, 2001.

Hepple, Bob A., Mary Coussey and Tufyal Choudhury, *Equality: A New Framework. Report of the Independent Review of the Enforcement of UK Anti-Discrimination Legislation*. Oxford: Hart 2000.

Hicks, Douglas, *Religion and the Workplace: Pluralism, Spirituality, Leadership*. Cambridge: Cambridge University Press, 2003.

Hill, Daniel J., 'Abortion and Conscientious Objection' (2010) 16 *Journal of Evaluation in Clinical Practice* 344–50.

Hill, Mark, 'Religious Symbolism and Conscientious Objection in the Workplace' (2013) 15 *Ecclesiastical Law Journal* 191–203.

Hill, Mark, and Russell Sandberg, 'Is Nothing Sacred? Clashing Symbols in a Secular World' (2007) *Public Law* 488–506.

Hill, Mark, Russell Sandberg and Norman Doe, *Religion and Law in the United Kingdom*. The Hague: Wolters-Kluwer, 2011.

Holden, Andrew, *Jehovah's Witnesses: Portrait of a Contemporary Religious Movement*. London: Routledge, 2002.

Holloway, David, *Church and State in the New Millenium*. London: Harper Collins, 2000.

Horton, John, 'Liberalism, Multiculturalism, and Toleration' in Horton, John (ed.), *Liberalism, Multiculturalism, and Toleration*. Basingstoke: Palgrave Macmillan, 1993.

Howard, Erica, *Law and the Wearing of Religious Symbols*. Abingdon: Routledge 2012.

Hunt, Ruth, *Religion and Sexual Orientation: How to Manage Relations in the Workplace*. London: Stonewall, 2009.

Hunter-Henin, Myriam, 'Why the French Don't Like the Burqa: Laïcité, National Identity and Religious Freedom' (2012) 61 *International Comparative Law Quarterly* 613–39.

Jackson, Jennifer, *Ethics in Medicine*. Cambridge: Polity, 2006.

Jensen, David, *Responsive Labor: A Theology of Work*. Louiseville, KY: Westminster John Knox Press, 2006.

Jones, Mark, *Religious Liberty in the Workplace: A Guide for Christian Employees*. Newcastle upon Tyne: Christian Institute, 2008.

Jones, Peter, 'Bearing the Consequences of Belief' in Goodwin, Robert E. and Philip Pettit, *Contemporary Political Philosophy, An Anthology*, 2nd ed., Oxford: Blackwell, 2006.

Kaminer, Debbie N., 'When Religious Expression Creates a Hostile Work Environment: The Challenge of Balancing Competing Fundamental Rights' (2000) 4 *New York University Journal of Legislation and Public Policy* 81–142.

Knights, Samantha, *Freedom of Religion, Minorities and the Law*. Oxford: Oxford University Press, 2007.

Laborde, Cecile, *Critical Republicanism: The Hijab Controversy and Political Philosophy*. Oxford: Oxford University Press, 2008.

Lamore, Charles, *Patterns of Moral Complexity*, Cambridge: Cambridge University Press, 1987.

Langlaude, Sylvie, 'Indoctrination, secularism, religious liberty and the ECHR' (2006) 55 *International and Comparative Law Quarterly* 929–44.

Laycock, Douglas, *Religious Liberty* vol. 1. Grand Rapids IL: William B Eerdmans, 2010.

Laycock, Douglas, A. Picarello and R. Wilson (eds), *Same-Sex Marriage and Religious Liberty: Emerging Conflicts*. Lanham, MD: Rowman & Littlefield, 2008.

Leader, Sheldon, 'Freedom and Futures: Personal Priorities, Institutional Demands and Freedom of religion' (2007) 70 *Modern Law Review* 713–30.

Leigh, Ian, 'Balancing Religious Autonomy and Other Human Rights under the European Convention' (2012) 1 *Oxford Journal of Law and Religion* 109–25.

Leigh, Ian, 'Hatred, Sexual Orientation, Free Speech and Religious Liberty' (2009) 10 *Ecclesiastical Law Journal* 337–44.

Leigh, Ian, 'Homophobic Speech, Equality Denial, and Religious Expression' (375–99) in Ivan Hare and James Weinstein (eds), *Extreme Speech and Democracy*. Oxford: Oxford University Press, 2009.

Leigh, Ian, and Andrew Hambler, 'Religious Symbols, Conscience and the Rights of Others' (2014) 3 *Oxford Journal of Law and Religion*, 2–24.

Leigh, Ian, and Rex Ahdar, 'Post-Secularism and the European Court of Human Rights (or How God Never Really Went Away)' (2012) 75 *Modern Law Review* 1065–98.

Leigh, Ian, and Roger Masterman, *Making Rights Real: The Human Rights Act in its First Decade*. Oxford: Hart, 2008.

Lester, Antony and Paola Uccellari, 'Extending the Equality Duty to Religion, Conscience and Belief: Proceed With Caution' (Issue 5, 2008) *European Human Rights Law Review* 567–73.

Litwak, Erik, 'Conscientious Objection in Public Service Ethics: A Proposed Procedure for Europe' (2005) 7 *European Journal of Law* 79–87.

Liu, Hin-Yan, 'The Meaning of Religious Symbols after the Grand Chamber ruling in *Lautsi v Italy*' (2011) 6 *Religion and Human Rights* 253–7.

Locke, John, 'A Letter Concerning Toleration', *The Works of John Locke*, vol. 6. Aalen: Scienta Verlag Aalen, 1963.

Lustgarten, Laurence, and Ian Leigh, *In From the Cold: National Security and Parliamentary Democracy*. Oxford: Clarendon Press, 1994.

MacDougall, Bruce, 'Refusing to Officiate at Same-Sex Civil Marriages' (2006) 69 *Saskatchewan Law Review* 351–73.

MacDougall, Bruce, Elsje Bonthuys, Kenneth Norrie and Marjolein Van den Brink, 'Conscientious Objection to Creating Same-Sex Unions: An International Analysis', (2012) 1 *Canadian Journal of Human Rights* 127–64.

Mancini, Susanna and Michel Rosenfeld, *Unveiling the Limits of Tolerance: Comparing the Treatment of Majority and Minority Religious Symbols In the Public Sphere*. Cardozo Legal Studies Research Paper, No. 309. New York: Benjamin N. Cardozo School of Law, Yeshiva University, September 2010.

Mantouvalou, Virginia, 'Human Rights and Unfair Dismissal: Private Acts in Public Spaces' (2008) 71 *Modern Law Review* 912–39.

McColgan, Aileen, 'Class wars? Religion and (In)equality in the Workplace' (2009) 38 *Industrial Law Journal* 1–29.

McConnell, Michael W., 'Why is Religious Liberty the "First Freedom"?' (2000) 21 *Cardozo Law Review* 1243–2119.

McCrudden, Christopher, *Buying Social Justice*. Oxford: Oxford University Press, 2007.

McCrudden, Christopher, 'Human Dignity and Judicial Interpretation of Human

Rights' (2008) 19 *European Journal of International Law* 655–742.

McCrudden, Christopher, 'Religion, Human Rights, Equality and the Public Sphere' (2011) 13 *Ecclesiastical Law Journal* 26–38.

McGoldrick, Dominic, *Human Rights and Religion: The Islamic Headscarf Debate in Europe.* Cambridge: Hart Publishing, 2006.

McGoldrick, Dominic, 'Religion in the European Public Square and in European Public Life: Crucifixes in the Classroom?' (2011) 11 *Human Rights Law Review* 451–502.

Meyerson, Denise, *Rights Limited.* Cape Town: Rustica Press, 1997.

Meyerson, Denise, 'Why Religion Belongs in the Private Sphere not the Public Square' (44–71) in Cane Peter, Carolyn Evans and Zoë Robinson (eds), *Law and Religion in Theoretical and Historical Context.* Cambridge: Cambridge University Press, 2008.

Moens, Gabriel, 'The Action-Belief dichotomy and freedom of religion' (1989) 12 *Sydney Law Review* 195–217.

Montgomery, Jack G., 'A Most Delicate Matter: Religious Issues and Conflict in the US Library Workplace' (2003) 23 *Library Management* 422–34.

Morris, Gillian, 'Fundamental Rights: Exclusion by Agreement?' (2001) 30 *Industrial Law Journal* 49–71.

Moruzzi, Norma C., 'A Problem with Headscarves: Contemporary Complexities of Political and Social Identity' (1994) 4 *Political Theory* 653–72.

Moskoks, Charles and John Chambers, 'The Secularisation of Conscience' (3–20) in Charles Moskos and John Chambers (eds), *The New Conscientious Objection.* New York: Oxford University Press, 1993.

Mulleur, F. Max, *Introduction to the Science of Religion.* London: Longman, 1893.

Nagel, Thomas, *Equality and Partiality.* New York: Oxford University Press, 1991.

Noonan Jr., John T., 'How Sincere Do You Have to Be to Be Religious?' (1988) *University of Illinois Law Review* 713.

Norrie, Kenneth, 'Religion and Same-Sex Unions: The Scottish Government's Consultation on Registration of Civil Partnerships and Same-Sex Marriage' (2012) 16 *Edinburgh Law Review* 95–9.

O'Adair, Richard, and Lewis, Andrew (eds), *Law and Religion: Current Legal Issues,* vol. 4. Oxford: Oxford University Press, 2001.

Ogilvy, Margaret H., 'And Then There Was One: Freedom of Religion in Canada – the Incredible Shrinking Concept' (2008) 10 *Ecclesiastical Law Journal* 197–204.

Oh, Irene, *The Rights of God: Islam, Human Rights, and Comparative Ethics.* Washington DC: Georgetown University Press, 2007.

Okin, Susan M., *Is Multiculturalism Bad for Women?* edited by Joshua Cohen and Matthew Howard. Princeton NJ: Princeton University Press 1999.

Parekh, Bhikhu, *Rethinking Multiculturalism: Cultural Diversity and Political Theory,* 2nd ed. London: Macmillan, 2000.

Parkinson, Patrick, 'Forum: Accommodating Religious Beliefs in a Secular Age' (2011) 34 *University of New South Wales Law Journal* 281–99.

Pava, Moses L., 'Religious Business Ethics and Political Liberalism: An Integrative Approach' (1998) 17 *Journal of Business Ethics* 1633–52.

Pitt, Gwyneth, 'Dress Codes and Freedom of Expression' (1997) 1 *European Human Rights Law Review* 52.

Pitt, Gwyneth, 'Keeping the Faith: Trends and Tensions in Religion or Belief Discrimination' (2011) 40 *Industrial Law Journal* 384–404.

Pitt, Gwyneth, 'Religion or Belief: Aiming at the Right Target?' (202–30) in H. Meenan (ed.), *Equality Law in an Enlarged European Union*. Cambridge: Cambridge University Press, 2007.

Posner, Richard A., *Economic Analysis of Law*, 8th ed. New York: Aspen Publishers, 2011.

Rawls, John, 'A Theory of Civil Disobedience' (89–111) in Dworkin, Ronald (ed.), *The Philosophy of Law*. New York: Oxford University Press, 1977.

Rawls, John, *Political Liberalism*. New York: Columbia University Press, 1993.

Rawls, John, 'The Idea of Public Reason Revisited' (1997) 64 *University of Chicago Law Review* 765–807.

Raz, Joseph, *The Authority of Law*. Oxford: Clarendon Press, 1979.

Reaume, Denise G., 'Discrimination and Dignity' (2002–2003) 63 *Louisiana Law Review* 645.

Renteln, Alison D., 'Visual Religious Symbols and the Law' (2004) 47 *American Behavioral Scientist* 1573–96.

Robinson, George, *Essential Judaism*. New York: Pocket Books, 2000.

Ronchi, Paolo, 'Crucifixes, Margin of Appreciation and Consensus: The Grand Chamber Ruling in Lautsi v Italy' (2011) 13 *Ecclesiastical Law Journal* 287–97.

Rorty, Richard, 'Religion in the Public Square: A Reconsideration' (2003) 31 *Journal of Religious Ethics* 141–49.

Rousseau, Denise, *Psychological Contract in Organizations: Understanding Written and Unwritten Agreements*. Newbury Park, CA: Sage, 1996.

Sadurski, Wojciech, *Moral Pluralism and Legal Neutrality* (The Hague: Kluwer, 1990)

Sandberg, Russell, 'Laws and Religion: Unravelling *McFarlane v Relate Avon Limited*' 12 *Ecclesiastical Law Journal* (2010) 361–70.

Sandberg, Russell, and Norman Doe, 'Religious Exemptions in Discrimination Law' (2007) 66 *Cambridge Law Journal* 302–12.

Savulescu, Julian, 'Conscientious objection in medicine' (2006) 332 *BMJ* 294.

Schauer, Frederick, 'Fear, Risk and the First Amendment: Unravelling the "Chilling Effect"' (1978) 58 *Boston University Law Review* 685–732.

Schopf, Josh, 'Religious Activity and Proselytization in the Workplace: The Murky Line Between Healthy Expression and Unlawful Harassment' (1997–1998) 31 *Columbia Journal of Law and Social Problems* 39–59.

Shadid, W. A. R. and P. S. van Koningsveld, *Religious Freedom and the Position of Islam in Western Europe: Opportunities and Obstacles in the Acquisition of Equal Rights*. Kampen: Kok Pharos 1995.

Singh, Pashaura, and N. Gerald Barrier (eds), *Sikh Identity: Continuity and Change*. New Delhi: Manohar, 1999.

Slapper, Gary, 'Penalties in the Penumbra of the Criminal Law' (2008) 72 *Journal of Criminal Law* 467–9.

Smith, Adam, *An Inquiry into the Nature and Causes of the Wealth of Nations*, Book II. London: Nelson 1886).

Ssenyonjo, Manisuli, 'The Islamic Veil and Freedom of Religion, the Rights to Education and Work: a Survey of Recent International and National Cases' (2007) 6 *Chinese Journal of International Law* 653–710.

Stahnke, Tad, 'Proselytism and the Freedom to Change Religion in International Human Rights Law' (1999) *Brigham Young University Law Review* 252–353.

Stychin, Carl, 'Faith in the Future: Sexuality, Religion and the Public Sphere' (2009) 29 *Oxford Journal of Legal Studies* 729–55.

Tayeb, Monir, 'Islamic Revival in Asia and Human Resource Management' (1997) 19 *Employee Relations* 352–64.

Thoreau, Henry, 'Civil Disobedience' (28–48) in Bedau, Hugo (ed.), *Civil Disobedience in Focus*. Abingdon: Routledge, 1991.

Tillich, Paul, *The Dynamics of Faith*. New York: Harper and Row, 1957.

Timmons, Stephen and Aru Narayanasamy, 'How do Religious People Navigate a Secular Organisation? Religious Nursing Students in the British National Health Service' (2011) 26 *Journal of Contemporary Religion* 451–65.

Trigg, Roger, *Equality, Freedom and Religion*. Oxford: Oxford University Press, 2012.

Trigg, Roger, *Religion in Public Life: Must Faith Be Privatised?* Oxford: Oxford University Press, 2007.

Trotter, Geoffrey, 'The Right to Decline Performance of Same-Sex Civil Marriages: The Duty to Accommodate Public Servants – A Response to Professor Bruce MacDougall' (2007) 70 *Saskatchewan Law Review* 365–92.

Van Der Schyff, Gerhard, 'The Legal Definition of Religion and Its Application' (2002) 119 *South African Law Journal* 228–94.

Vickers, Lucy, *Freedom of Expression and Employment*. Oxford: Oxford University Press, 2002.

Vickers, Lucy, 'Freedom of Religion and the Workplace: The Draft Employment Equality (Religion or Belief) Regulations 2003' (2003) 32 *Industrial Law Journal* 23–36.

Vickers, Lucy, 'Indirect Discrimination and Individual Belief: *Eweida v British Airways plc*' (2009) 11 *Ecclesiastical Law Journal* 197–203.

Vickers, Lucy, 'Is All Harassment Equal? The Case of Religious Harassment' (2006) 65 *Cambridge Law Journal* 579–605.

Vickers, Lucy, 'Religion and Belief Discrimination and the Employment of Teachers in Faith Schools' (2009) 4 *Religion and Human Rights* 137–56.

Vickers, Lucy, 'Religious Discrimination in the Workplace: An Emerging Hierarchy?' (2010) 12 *Ecclesiastical Law Journal* 280–303.

Vickers, Lucy, *Religious Freedom, Religious Discrimination and the Workplace*. Oxford: Hart Publishing, 2008.

Waldron, Jeremy, *God, Locke and Equality: The Christian Foundations in Locke's Political Thought*. Cambridge: Cambridge University Press, 2002.

Webster, Sam, 'Misconceptions About the Nature of Religious Belief' (2010) 199 *Equal Opportunities Review* 8.

Weller, Paul, *Religious Discrimination in Britain: A Review of Research Evidence, 2000–10*. EHRC Research Report 73. Manchester: Equality and Human Rights Commission, 2011.

Wicclair, Mark, 'Conscientious Objection in Medicine' (2000) 14 *Bioethics* 205–27.

Wilson, Robert F., 'Insubstantial Burdens: The Case for Government Employee Exemptions to Same-Sex Marriage Laws' 5 (2010) *Northwestern Journal of Law and Social Policy* 318–68.

Wing, Adrien, and Monica Smith, 'Critical Race Feminism Lifts the Veil: Muslim Women, France, and the Headscarf Ban' (2005-2006) 39 *University of California Davis Law Review* 743–90.

Wittgenstein, Ludwig J., *Philosophical Investigations*. Oxford: Blackwell, 1953.

Wolgast, Elizabeth, 'The Demands of Public Reason' (1994) 94 *Columbia Law Review* 1936–49.

Wolterstorff, Nicholas, *Justice: Rights and Wrongs*. Princeton NJ: Princeton University Press, 2008.

Wolterstorff, Nicholas, 'The Role of Religion in Decision and Discussion of Political Issues' (67–9) in Robert Audi and Nicholas Wolterstorff, *Religion in the Public Square: The Place of Religious Convictions in Political Debate*. Lanham MD: Rowman and Littlefield, 1997.

Wolterstorff, Nicholas, 'Why We Should Reject What Liberalism Tells Us' (162–81) in Weithman, Paul J. (ed.), *Religion and Contemporary Liberalism*. Notre Dame, IN: University of Notre Dame Press, 1997.

Yinger, J. Milton, *The Scientific Study of Religion*. New York: Macmillan, 1970.

Zagorin, Perez, *How the Idea of Religious Toleration Came to the West*. Princeton, NJ: Princeton University Press, 2003.

Zaheer, Bilal, 'Accommodating Minority Religions Under Title VII: How Muslims make the case for a new interpretation of section 701(J)' (2007) *University of Illinois Law Review* 497–531.

Index